SANITY

LOST & FOUND

A TRUE STORY
OF BRAINWASHING AND RECOVERY

TARRA JUDSON

STARIELL

LMFT, CBT

Ranch House Press

PO Box 241

Escondido, CA 92033

FIRST EDITION

Cover and interior design by Gwyn Snider, GKS Creative, Nashville, TN.

Library of Congress Cataloging-in-Publication Data has been applied for.

ISBN 978-0-9992955-0-2

ISBN 978-0-9992955-1-9 (ePub)

ISBN 978-0-9992955-2-6 (mobi)

Printed in the United States of America

DEDICATION

Life brings us both vicissitudes and gifts, and among the most precious gifts are the people who positively impact us. This book is dedicated to my Mother and Father who gave me life and my first taste of love; my Brother who supported that life; my Grandmother who saved it with her unconditional love; my cousin Donna who taught me the power of forgiveness; and to all the people who supported me in my recovery and subsequent growth.

CONTENTS

PROLOGUE

Y ou know you need to complete your mission. You cannot turn your back on God . . ."

The truck door opened, and a massive arm shoved aside the curtain separating cab from camper shell. Solar reached back and dropped a clear, pyramid-shaped amethyst crystal onto the mattress where I lived 24/7.

"Here. We'll call this 'Athena'. Smash it and make more combos with it. Now get to work, we have lots to do."

He withdrew, and a moment later the pickup began to move forward.

The amethyst crystal was at least six inches in diameter at its base and covered the palm of my hand. Little piles of trinkets, pennies, and a roll of scotch tape—the raw materials of our "combos"—were tucked into crevices. Dark-brown curtains shielded me from the outside world; I would need to work quickly in the waning light.

I picked up the small silver hammer I had used previously to smash "Baby," a massive clear crystal—but then I hesitated, admiring the beauty of this ancient creation of nature. I wondered where Solar had gotten it.

His shout came from the cab: "I don't hear you working. Get busy. We don't have that much time!"

I slammed the hammer onto Athena, then opened my eyes to see the crystal intact, only a small divot marking the wound I had inflicted. I swallowed the sickness welling up my throat and, with more pounding, soon broke off enough pieces to bundle together with the trinkets, creating several combos.

Solar and I would use these on the next stop of our journey as "vortex plumbers," as we seeded crystals throughout the country to facilitate the cleansing of areas in history where humans have preyed upon each other.

I wonder where we are now? God, please help me complete my mission. How can I warn people that life as we know it will change dramatically if humans don't stop living the way we are? I wish I hadn't been given that message. But Solar's right. I can't stop until this quest is complete; I can't turn my back on God.

The truck stopped, interrupting my thoughts. Looking down at the pile of combos, I breathed a sigh of relief with how many I counted.

"Come on, get out!" Solar ordered. "I need a witness to this. Don't look around, do you understand? Give me all the combos you made before you get out."

I piled them into his open hands and then slid onto the front seat, pushing bare feet into my flip-flops waiting on the passenger side. Scooting over to the open door, I staggered on legs that had not stood upright the entire day. As I hurried after Solar, snow crunched under my steps. My bent head proved that my gaze was glued to the ground.

"Come on, hurry up before anyone comes around!"

Dwarfed by his six-foot, 300-pound body, I meekly gazed into the depths of the Grand Canyon as shadows settled onto the peaks below. *Cold! My clothes are still wet from our last cleaning ritual. I'm freezing.*

Solar raised his voice to the great chasm. "One Heart, One Mind, One Spirit. We leave these combos to help cleanse and purify this vortex and release it of all negative energies and vibrations. Let any trapped spirits be freed now to return home, out of this illusion. One Heart, One Mind, One Spirit, and so it is."

He repeated this prayer for each of the four directions. As he pivoted in place his hands started at the center of his chest, moved up past his forehead and outward each time, before finally flinging the combos far into the canyon.

"Did you see them?" he demanded. "Did you watch them fall into the Canyon?"

"Yes, I saw them go into the Canyon."

"Don't look around, but make sure we didn't drop anything."

"I don't see anything."

"Are you sure?"

"Yes, there's nothing here."

"Look again."

"There's nothing."

"Okay, fine. Let's get going. Sit in the front because it's almost dark and I'm going to take you somewhere to pee. Make sure we didn't drop anything."

As he backed the truck out, I peered through the windshield.

"I'm watching where we were, and there's nothing."

"Look again."

"Okay, free to go, there is nothing on the ground."

"Are you sure? Look again."

"Nothing."

"Okay, let's go. One Heart, One Mind, One Spirit, please release all our energies and vibrations from where we just were and don't let any negative entities use them against us. One Heart, One Mind, One Spirit, and so it is. Close your eyes and don't look around."

"Okay," I emptily replied.

A minute later the truck stopped. "Get out here. Go quickly, do you understand?"

"Yes, thank you." I held my pants around my thighs as I squatted to urinate. It had been twelve hours, and I was bursting.

"Stop! There's someone coming. Stop right now! Put your pants back on!"

"I'm hurrying!" I could not stop my urgency and continued to relieve myself.

"I said stop. Come here now!"

By then I had forced my bladder to empty and was walking back towards him.

"Get in! You're in big trouble! See that car, they could have seen you!"

I scurried back into the cab but did not dare look in the direction he indicated. Instead, I held my hands aloft to be sprayed with cleaner. I rubbed the disinfectant and sea salt solution on them.

And then my head exploded as he slugged the side of it.

"That's for not obeying me when I said stop! You should have stopped immediately!"

"Yes," I whispered.

How much longer, God? How much longer do I have to do this?

PART I: THE RANCH

People are like stained glass windows: they sparkle and shine when the sun is out, but when the darkness sets in their true beauty is revealed only if there is a light within.

—Elizabeth Kubler-Ross, psychiatrist and author (1926-2004)

ONE

Conceived on Christmas Eve in 1948, I was a surprise pregnancy to young lovers attending college. Named Sandra Linn Judson, I lived the first week of my life in a hospital incubator.

Two months before I came into this world, my maternal grandmother died, and five months later my maternal grandfather died as well. My twenty-year old mother, an only child, had cared for both her parents as they succumbed to cancer.

Death continued to haunt my depressed mother who miscarried two babies, one right after another. My father attended veterinary school at the University of California, Davis, caring for me while he studied until I was three, when we abruptly moved to Southern California. His father had suffered a heart attack and needed his son back on the ranch, located in a rural section of Northern San Diego County.

Before I was four years old I was hospitalized twice with life-threatening gastroenteritis. On the second occasion, I watched from the ceiling as medical staff rushed around my body lying on a gurney below me.

"We've done everything we can; the rest is up to God," the doctor said to my mother.

I awakened strapped to the hospital bed with tubes in my arms. "Mommy, where am I?"

"You're in the hospital. You were very, very sick, and now you're going to get better and go home soon."

I went home with a heart murmur.

Soon after that my brother Bruce was born with the aid of forceps, but otherwise a healthy baby. Our mother delivered a stillborn baby after him. No one ever discussed the children who did not come home from the hospital, and my parents distanced themselves from their grief by moving further away from each other, my brother, and me.

Like members of previous generations, my father had been born and raised on the family farm. He had left it twice—first during World War II, when his desire to become a fighter pilot ended along with the war, and later when he went to college. That dream also ended in disappointment with his return to the life of a dairyman. Not able to be his own man, he began withdrawing from life and, most notably, his family. The close relationship I had enjoyed with him until that time evaporated.

My parents were an attractive couple. In his day, my father was quite handsome, with thick, dark hair framing his clear blue eyes set in the softness of his kind face. With her glamorous beauty and many talents, my platinum blond mother was out of place on the ranch. A protégé at four years old, she had been groomed to be a concert pianist.

They both soured with unhappiness when we moved to the farm.

My brother and I grew up surrounded by extended family on land that had been homesteaded in 1872 by my paternal great-great-grandfather. My father's parents lived in a farmhouse at the center of the dairy, surrounded by an extensive yard, acres of orchards, pastures, and field crops. Large pens held dairy cows and those soon to calve. Our grandfather managed his ranches, the workers, and their families with the care and control of a benevolent monarch watching over his kingdom. He was extremely hardworking and a strict disciplinarian. Although his heart was soft for his grandchildren, his son did not fare as well.

Trees studded the ranch I roamed as a child. I was forbidden to enter the dairy by myself due to the constant movement of tractors, heavy machinery, and the bulls. Instead, I found my own amusement since neither parent seemed to have enough time for me. Squishing bare feet into fresh cow patties, I shoved dry ones into the air, watching them fly like pancakes through dust clouds of dirt and powdered manure.

Sitting very still in the heifer pasture gained me entry into their herd. Slowly circling around, they nuzzled and licked me with curiosity. I welcomed their contact; although wet and gooey, it was better than nothing.

My mother hid her frustrations behind housework, chores, and anger. Given to frequent outbursts, she often frightened me. One day I was in our small house when she came rushing inside, yelling and crying. Their bedroom door slammed shut behind her.

"Mommy, Mommy, are you okay?" I cried, leaning against the door.

"*Goddamn it! Leave me alone!*" she shrieked, and I jumped back when she abruptly opened the door, her tear-streaked eyes blazing red with anger and hurt. Afraid and not knowing what was wrong, I felt helpless and empty. Later I was told that she had accidentally run over the family dog.

Death was a common occurrence on the ranch, and from an early age I worried about what happened afterwards. Sometimes in my wanderings I saw stillborn calves lying in the pasture, or those that had died in their pens. Snowy, a calf I had befriended, disappeared one day with no explanation from my caretakers. Non-producing cows were butchered while we ranch kids watched with curiosity. But when a sick cow was dragged outside the coral and left to struggle toward her demise, I felt sickened and had even more unanswered questions about death. No one offered explanations; it was simply a part of life. My questions without answers bothered me at night, and my unease deepened.

What happens when we die? Where did we come from? If we came from God, what is God? Where did God come from? Why can't anybody tell me answers?

My spiraling angst ended only after fear gripped me so painfully I would plead to God aloud—and then feel calmed until the next time. These questions usually haunted me in a four-to-five-month cycle. I even slept on the floor once, thinking that if I gave Jesus my bed, the sacrifice would gain me enough worth to receive answers to the questions that plagued me. Even though I was cold, I didn't climb back into bed until I felt my sacrifice sufficient to merit Jesus's love.

TWO

We lived in one of the tiny ranch houses my grandfather had built for the farmhands after he and our grandmother had stopped boarding workmen. Ours was in the corner, nestled up against a eucalyptus grove.

"Help! Help me! Help, he's going to kill me!" I ran around the perimeter of our house, desperate and scared.

"I'm going to chop you up!" Danny, a neighborhood boy, was swinging a hatchet behind me. He trained his eyebrows to look like the devil's, and delighted in torturing the neighborhood cats as well as me until his family was asked to leave.

I had trouble with another neighborhood boy who kept taking my bike. Skewing up my courage one day, I challenged him.

"Quit taking my bike without asking! You left it out and I got in trouble."

"Oh yeah, you going to make me?"

A short time later he walked home, humbled and out-wrestled.

With no fences separating our yards, we led fishbowl lives. One day, the family station wagon saved my mother as she gardened. The steel frame of our 1951 Plymouth stopped the rifle bullet our neighbor shot at his wife. They were also asked to leave, as was the family whose son beat up my brother.

At five, I gave up dance lessons for a surgery to cure my squinty eye, which eventually would have gone blind. Children's Hospital in San Diego had the only surgeon capable of performing the operation.

After I was wheeled into a large, brightly lit room, a cloth-covered face leaned over me and asked, "Do you want one of these masks too?"

"Yes."

A rubber device reeking with a disgusting smell was instantly slapped on and held tightly against my face.

"No! No! No!" I kicked and fought to rip off the mask with its foul odor, but my arms were held down. I awoke with my left eye patched, the muscle stretched to correct the problem. It was common practice to trick children or mislead them about surgery. From then on, I was terribly frightened of doctors, and cried whenever I encountered them or needed a medical procedure.

Our lives changed for the better when the Smith family, with four boys and one girl, moved in. For the first time that I could remember, my mother and father were happy, and became close friends with our playmates' parents. Life was good as our families enjoyed time together.

The Smiths' lawn wrapped around their entire house. Joe, the father, delighted in swinging us kids until we got dizzy and tumbled against one another. Aerial acrobatics were also a favorite; Joe launching us into the air for a soft landing on the lawn. Our father never engaged in such playful activities.

For a while, the Bakery Truck made weekly visits to our farmhouses clustered tightly together. Barefoot, shirtless, and scruffy, we huddled around his converted vehicle.

"Now stand back and give me some room," the deliveryman chortled as we crowded in. With a push or tug of his hand, each drawer silently glided open and closed, teasing us as we breathed in the sweet aroma of freshly baked doughnuts and bread.

"Oh, I want that one!"

"Me too. I want one too!"

If we were lucky we had money to buy something. Otherwise, we had to settle for dreams of sinking our teeth into sweet fantasies.

I was a frequent visitor at my grandparents' home on the ranch. Always welcomed, I often tagged along behind my grandmother as she labored inside or worked in their yard.

"Here are the eggs, Gramma." The chicken pen was extensive. Hens that stopped laying eggs were served for dinner.

Standing on a bench pushed against the cupboards on the other side of the sink, I watched my grandmother scowl and wrinkle her brow as her hand tugged at something inside the chicken cavity.

"Gramma, are you mad at me?"

She looked over her glasses, fogged with perspiration. "Why no, I'm not, you poor dear. I'm just disgusted with this chicken I'm trying to clean."

I sighed gratefully as she continued gutting the chicken for dinner. I was accustomed to anger, but my grandmother never directed hers at me.

As a six-year-old, I would soon be joining five other children in first grade.

"When is school going to start?"

"Not yet, but it's getting closer."

"I want to learn how to read better."

"Um hum. Now go outside and play."

The yellow school bus slowed, and I stepped into my first day of school. We were first to be picked up since the river crossing was flooded. There were only two main rooms in the school with bathrooms outside. It was the same building my father had attended many years before, with one teacher managing four grades at a time. There were fewer than fifty students in all, and kindergarten and preschool were unknown entities then.

Miss Kennedy's slender form glided through our room, stopping to answer questions or offer encouraging words. Jet-black hair bounced against her pale skin as she approached me.

"Why don't you go show Mrs. Trussell how well you're reading? If you'd like, you can read to her from your book."

I followed her across the hallway and proudly demonstrated my newly acquired ability.

"That's great, Sandy." My aunt grinned down at me. She taught grades five through eight in the "upper room."

Reading opened my world. Miss Kennedy was a wonderful teacher who was helped on the days the Book Mobile and Shop Truck visited our rural school.

Every Thursday, Mr. Barnes parked his white utility truck behind the school building. Dressed in his tan uniform and black utility boots, he slipped an apron over his head before his beaming smile and deep voice beckoned us to stand back while he opened his treasure trove of tools. The groundskeeper's son, Chris, was a lanky teenager who helped his father and us children on Shop Days.

"Chris, will you help me move the tables out now?" Mr. Barnes asked.

We stood back while the two of them situated wooden tables in between the truck and Quonset hut where our projects would take form.

"Sandy, would you like some help with that?" Chris offered.

"Sure, thank you," I said as he held the thick cutting board in the shape of a pig I was smoothing off with sand paper.

"You're doing a good job there."

"Thank you." I loved making things, and Shop Day was pure fun. School was remarkably different from the raw life I had witnessed on the ranch, with birth and death occurring on a regular basis.

Even so, I was not prepared for the shock I soon encountered.

In days past, housing was provided for the teacher of rural communities. Straddling the boundary between our school yard and farmland, a small house called the "teacherage" sat about five hundred yards away from the building housing our classrooms. Now it was home for the groundskeeper and Chris, who lived there with his parents.

One day as we sat quietly working in class, Miss Kennedy opened our door after hearing a knock. She spoke briefly with Chris and then stepped back, turning to face us.

"He wants to know if anyone knows where the shop class left his screw-driver after using it."

I raised my hand to speak. "I know where it is."

Miss Kennedy nodded for me to show him, and I got up from my desk and walked towards the open door.

"I thought you'd know." Chris smiled. "You're so helpful and I've seen you keep good track of the tools on shop day."

I warmed with his compliment as we walked into the Quonset hut; Chris was behind me.

"It's up there; see it?" I pointed to a shelf and turned to face him.

He grabbed me, trapping my arms in his as he sat down hard and forced me onto his lap. I struggled to free myself but he tightened his grip and I froze. Reaching up my dress, he shoved my panties aside and forced his finger deep inside me. I drifted away until a strange and confusingly pleasant sensation brought me back. Thrashing at him, I broke free.

Bursting out of the Quonset, I ran back and stood in front of the classroom door, immobilized, shaking with terror. *I mustn't tell anyone or they will get angry with me and Miss Kennedy will get in trouble; it will all be my fault. They wouldn't believe me anyway; and would only get mad at me for making up stories.*

Smoothing my dress, I stiffened by body to stop the shaking so I could knock and be let in. Gritting my teeth, I silenced any thoughts of telling someone as I walked back to my seat.

Not long after this, my world crashed again when the Smith family moved away from the ranch. Without our friends, my brother Bruce and I roamed the hills, using the ranch as our refuge.

THREE

As a timid eight-year-old, I rode bareback on one of the numerous mustangs brought from the cattle ranch in Nevada. Neva was an exquisitely trained cutting horse and very capable of outsmarting me.

"If you can't handle her, just take off the bridle and let her go," was my father's sole lesson on horsemanship. "She'll find her way home."

Down the road and far from the ranch, Neva started rearing and carrying on. Scared, I got off and slipped off her bridle. Away she ran. Twenty minutes later I walked up the driveway to find Neva patiently waiting for me.

"Maybe she's too much horse for you to ride," my father offered. I was humiliated and noticed my grandfather smirking behind him. My mother and father were excellent riders, as were both grandparents. My grandfather had won several awards with his prized horse Cedro, and until my grandmother was eight months pregnant with my aunt, she rode to help round up their cattle.

Stubbornly, I bridled Neva again, climbed onto her back and rode through her next attempt to buffalo me.

I rode her every chance I had. Daily jaunts on horseback in the unspoiled terrain was my means of survival. Family gatherings, my grandparents, nature, and animals—both domestic and the wild ones Bruce and I rescued and raised—were lifelines in my turbulent youth.

I was a misfit in grammar school. "Here comes Little Miss Know It All" was a favored greeting from the other girls. Soon I discovered that dropping my panties behind the bus barn for some of the older boys got me the positive attention I craved. Ignoring the yucky feelings this gave me, I was easy prey, as the attention made me feel special.

An older boy from school invited me to meet him at a local barn. His bike was on the ground when I pedaled up, but he was nowhere to be seen. I took a few steps inside the hay barn and stopped—it was dark and felt dangerous. I turned around, jumped on my bike and rode away as fast as I could. This was another escapade I did not share with my mother, fearing she would lash out at me in anger. She did that so frequently, I didn't want any more.

My father remained an elusive swatch of blue with his standard work shirt tucked into 501 Levis, a red bandana hanging from a hip pocket. A yellow straw hat completed his wardrobe on the ranch.

Unlike my father, who was stocky, our grandfather was tall and lanky. His work shirts were tan; pockets bulging with little notebooks meticulously filled with data on each of the cows, when they were bred, how many calves they had and how much milk they were producing. Stetsons covered his head, one for the ranch and his "town hat" for good occasions. In charge of everyone, he monitored us grandkids by threatening a "tin ear" if we broke his rules.

"Ow!" Bruce and a cousin howled each time they faltered in keeping up with Grandpa's long stride. His grip tightly held the top of each ear closest to him. They had been chasing chickens inside the pen when he caught them.

Usually, our grandfather was very loving and entertaining. He produced malted eggs from the knots in the wooden ceiling or delighted us with stories about his old dog Roscoe. Enraptured, we stayed to the inevitable end, enjoying being tickled as he demonstrated how Roscoe "grabbed and shook and shook and shook those rascally crows eating the corn."

In 1960, our grandfather fulfilled his promise to my folks and built them a home perched on the hill overlooking the dairy. It had been their dream to live in an adobe house.

Barely a year later, our parents gathered Bruce and me together one morning. As we sat on my bed, they stood before us and announced: "Grandpa died in his sleep last night."

I was crushed. Despite his garbled speech from a recent stroke, I had enjoyed conversing and sharing time with my grandfather. I admired his strength in managing his disabilities. His right arm was paralyzed and hanging uselessly in a sling. Needing a cane to walk, he had a brace wrapped around his right leg that he could only drag. I could feel his frustration—no longer able to work, being helpless and dependent.

We visited him before the funeral. As I gazed at his body lying in the casket, grief welled up inside me and escaped in loud sobs. My father wore dark glasses to hide his eyes, and from then on, he grew increasingly more detached as he fell into a deep depression, using food and alcohol to numb his pain.

With my grandfather gone, I felt the rejection from my parents even more acutely. I was not at ease and would spend time trying to figure things out for myself while gazing at the hillsides across from us. They framed a long, cascading rock waterfall. Stories that the Indians had used it for ceremonies fascinated me. Several times, my eyes deceived me as the landscape shifted and I saw the same mountains in different versions of themselves, like watching a slide show of progressive changes. Puzzled by these images, I shrugged them off as I could not make sense of what I was experiencing.

To ease my restlessness, I started doing yard work for my grandmother. Not long after that, at the age of twelve, I decided instead to work on both family-owned ranches along with a trusted employee.

For several years, we planted and irrigated countless fields of crops, bucked hay, fed cows, and trimmed the horses' feet. He taught me how to drive a stick-shift truck, bulldozer, and all the tractors on the farm. I enjoyed his mentoring until he touched me in the crotch with a corn root one day. We were resting in the middle of a cornfield, and there was a small rip in my pants, revealing my upper thigh when I sat down. Frozen, I watched him inch the long, spindly root up through the hole in my Levis.

"Can you feel that?" he asked.

Waking from my stupor, I stood up and bolted through several rows of corn to get away. I finished my jobs that day but never returned to work on the ranch again. I did not offer my father an explanation for suddenly quitting and, sadly, no one ever asked.

Although my parents had repeatedly reminded me that I would have to pay for my college education if I wanted one, I was never paid for my ranch work. It now occurred to me I needed to start stockpiling money. My grandmother's brother, Uncle Franklin, lived down the road with his wife (my teacher) on part of what used to be their father's large dairy farm. He could grow anything. Well ahead of his time, he raised organic fruits and vegetables to sell. He was a kind man with a generous heart, so I approached him for a job, and enjoyed working for him and absorbing his wisdom.

My father was mostly absent from our lives, but woke us for school every morning.

"Good morning, sunshine."

"Okay, Dad. I'm getting up," I mumbled before drifting back to sleep.

"Time to get up." My snooze alarm had returned. Up at five, he was cheerful in the morning but came home exhausted at the end of his day. Caring for the cows, farm equipment, ranch hands, and the problems each presented left him grumpy and elusive, with little energy for us. Some nights, even his sleep was interrupted with an emergency call from the ranch.

"Where's Dad going?"

"The wind blew down a power pole, and he has to start the generator," my mother explained. We knew that without electricity, thousands of gallons of milk in the storage tank would spoil before the truck arrived to transport it.

FOUR

Our parents seemed to be numbly passing through the motions of life. I never saw them show affection and rarely witnessed them speaking with one another. My father's sole activities outside the ranch were serving as school board president and his membership in the local Dairymen's Council & Association. Although he and I rarely spoke, I was always searching for ways to engage him. "Hello, kid" felt great when we passed each other on the ranch. "Hey, bubble butt" didn't, but it seemed better than nothing at all.

Most of my contact with him revolved around our nightly entertainment. I memorized the television schedule for each day and would recite it upon request. Besides no onscreen TV schedules, there were also no remote controls or all the services available today. Getting up to change the channels and being a walking TV catalog earned me interaction with my father.

For several years, our mother took Bruce and me to church, where she played the piano for services and eventually applied to become a member. Several primly-dressed older ladies came to visit our house and were ushered into the living room. After they left, our mother angrily announced: "We're never going back to that church again! They told me we couldn't become members because your father won't accompany us to church, even though I've been playing the piano for them all these years."

Although a Thirty-Three Degree Mason, my father was inactive with his lodge and had flatly refused to attend church with us. Deeply hurt and humiliated by the church ladies' harshness, my mother started to search fervently for answers, needing to discover how a "loving God" justified the church's cruel treatment of her. Mark Twain's *Letters from Earth* became a favorite reference she quoted often.

Instead, I enjoyed attending Mass with a friend and frequented Seventh-Day Adventist services and Vacation Bible School with cousins. Attending church offered temporary respite from my insecurities, but as I grew, the insecurities did too.

Reading was another form of escape for me as I tried to find answers to my questions about death and God in the encyclopedias we had. "Go look it up!" was my mother's ready answer to the questions I brought her. Spanning the bottom shelves of the large bookcase in the living room, the Encyclopedia Britannica volumes were my access to an unknown world. Decades before the Internet, they were our source of information.

Dinnertime was a tense family event. With the nightly news blasting on TV, conversation was limited to terse criticisms of us, political figures or world events. Cleaning up afterwards was even worse as I anticipated the inevitable criticism.

"I've got to go to the bathroom," I would announce, racing down the hall.

"There she goes again, with 'dish-a-rhea' when it's time to clean up and wash the dishes." My father chided me for my nervous reaction. "Too gull-ible" for him, I struggled to do things right.

"Don't use hot water when first washing out the milk bucket. Rinse it in cold water first! How many times do I have to tell you that?"

"I did."

"Well, do it again. I didn't see you!"

Growing up with a steady diet of angry criticism, I generally felt guilty, ashamed, or afraid of doing something wrong. "Don't put dish soap on the salad bowl, just rinse it out. You don't want to ruin it, do you?"

No, I want to do everything perfectly, but it's never good enough for you or Dad. I guess I'm just a failure.

I frequently asked, "Mommy, do you still love me?"

Her curt reply was, "Of course I do."

One time, while I was staying at the beach with relatives, a cousin overheard me pleading for reassurance. "Mommy? Do you still love me?" he mocked. Shamed and exposed, I never asked the question again. All I ever wanted was a hug, a soft look, or some indication I was loved and lovable, despite all the mistakes I made.

FIVE

My mother played classical compositions exquisitely on the piano. I loved listening to her play, and was soothed by the music. It was a way for us to connect, and with her encouragement I took piano lessons for several years. I grew in competence, and even though nervous during recitals, with perspiring hands slipping along the keys, I enjoyed having my parents and brother in the audience.

Since my piano teacher was just as controlling as my mother, I eventually pushed back at her—because I could. Entering high school was the end of my piano-playing days and the beginning of freedom from being so closely monitored at home.

All seven students in my class transitioned from eighth grade in our tiny rural school to a high school in town, where there were forty-five times the number of students. With my heart yearning for connection, I embraced this next step in my life and eventually found wonderful friends. Even so, it was a constant challenge to emancipate myself from my home life—that imploding vortex of sadness and oppression.

"You must limit your after-school activities because we cannot keep driving into town to pick you up."

"What about my clubs and team sports? We have practice and games after school. Can't I please do this?" I pleaded.

"Well, if you can find someone to bring you home, I suppose you can."

I was desperate, afraid my lifeline was going to be cut. After-school activities kept me away longer from the brewing cauldron of tension at home. "No one wants to drive so far out here to bring me home."

"Well then, offer to fill their gas tank if they do."

"You mean I can give them gas from the ranch?"

"Yes, I suppose so. If that's what it takes. Just mark it down."

Fortunately, I had an older friend with a car and the willingness to drive me home. With bribes of gasoline, my social life remained nurtured.

My father could be very rational and benevolent at times, but his attention was sparse. When I was old enough for a learner's permit, he drove with me only twice, but was immensely helpful. "You might not want to do that again," his steadfast voice calmly advised from the passenger seat.

On the other hand, my mother would shriek or try to grab the wheel. Maneuvering tractors along the cow-manger roads was never as complex as negotiating city streets, and my fear escalated with hers as I blundered along.

I abruptly gained more emancipation when my mother began leaving for San Diego every Saturday morning before I awakened and not returning home until late Sunday night. She was caring for our Aunt Dora, who had become very ill—but continued this routine even after Aunt Dora passed away.

"Why do you always go away now?"

"I'm renovating Aunt Dora's home and taking care of the tenants."

"Does it take all weekend?"

"Yes, it does. Aunt Dora was so sick she was not able to keep up with the repairs the house needed."

"Well, Dad is not approachable until his third martini, and even then, he vents his anger at me when you're gone. He told me I'm the only person he knows that can burn boiled water." Without instruction about what to cook or how, I was learning the hard way.

"I'm only staying with him for the sake of you kids," was her answer.

As my parents' marriage deteriorated, our family fragmented further. The adobe home we lived in was never welcoming. Even though it had beautiful wood paneling throughout and open-beamed ceilings, it was hot and stuffy in the summer and very cold in the winter. The roof was not made according to a typical adobe home design with material or insulation between ceiling and roof. Lacking protection from the elements, the temperature inside our home reflected the outside. A floor heater in the kitchen/family room and one in the living room were insufficient. Constantly cold, Bruce hovered over the one in the family room or retreated to his room, where he dribbled his basketball against a bedroom wall, with his door closed and wall heater cranked up.

I sequestered myself in the "office," sitting at my father's college desk, pushed up against the wall where no one bothered me.

My parents barely tolerated each other. Alcohol was my father's escape, and my mother was never home on weekends. High school friends and activities soothed me, but towards the end of my senior year I felt powerless to ameliorate the situation. Helpless sadness weighed on my heart and I searched for ways to ease my discomfort.

"What are you smoking?" My father opened the office door and pushed his face inside late one night.

Jerking my feet off the desk and jolting upright, I meekly answered, "A cigar."

"Crazy kid," he muttered through a smile as he closed the door. I could hear him struggling through an asthma attack as he sat in the kitchen. Two packs of cigarettes a day sometimes forced him up in the middle of the night to soothe his coughing fits.

He never told my mother about his discovery, or I would have been in trouble. As weekends continued without her, I begged my father to talk to her, take her out—do something other than get inebriated every night. I also spent hours trying to convince a school counselor I needed help because my parents' marriage was disintegrating. "Everything will work out" was her only response.

I didn't share her faith, and felt insignificant. *I wonder if anybody would notice or care if I died. Would my counselor come to my funeral? Would my parents stop fighting?* As my family's fragmentation continued, I entertained those dark fantasies more frequently.

As my impending graduation drew me closer to an unknown future, I began smoking cigarettes behind the gymnasium during pep rallies. Traditionally, our high school bused the senior class to Disneyland for a night of celebration. I asked my mother to take me shopping for the trip, and while looking for a dress, I began to feel increasingly uncomfortable. As we walked through a courtyard in the mall, I gasped, "I can't breathe!"

"What's wrong?" Her voice tightened. "Here, sit down," and she led me to a chair. I struggled into it. "Are you feeling any better?" Worry filled her face.

I shook my head as I labored to breathe. Minutes later, we were headed to the emergency room.

The doctors thought I had pneumonia, but tests and X-rays proved otherwise. Bed rest was diagnosed until they could discover what was wrong. After attending a seminar in San Diego on Valley Fever, my mother consulted with the doctors, and further testing showed I had contracted this disease. The family cemetery had been a Native American site, and Valley Fever, or coccidioidomycosis, is endemic to those areas. Cleaning our ancestors' burial plots on Memorial Day was a family tradition. I never knew if my clandestine smoking activities had left me vulnerable to the spores I inhaled that day.

The penicillin I had been taking for my heart murmur had apparently fed the fever, making it worse. When I stopped taking the antibiotics, I improved enough to return for the last day of school and to march in our graduation.

SIX

After working one last summer for my uncle, the organic farmer, I attended community college in the fall. A local pharmacy hired me, but I was offered a month's vacation my first summer there because the owner had employed too much help. I seized the opportunity to take a friend up on his offer to accompany him and others on a road trip into the interior of Mexico.

The goal was Cozumel for its pristine waters, good for snorkeling and diving. Our first major stop was in Mazatlán, a small village at the time. After enjoying a communal *paella* at our trailer park, we headed to Guadalajara and dropped down to see Tula, outside of Mexico City. The magnificent statues atop their stone structures planted seeds of wonder inside me, kindling questions about this ancient and vanished culture.

In Mexico City, as we were leaving our hotel to visit the Pyramids of the Sun and the Moon, I noticed people huddled around a small black and white television in the lobby. I stopped to watch a sketchy image of the Apollo astronauts landing on the moon.

The juxtaposition of witnessing our budding space technology before going out to scale those ancient stone wonders sparked more questions within me. *What happened to these people? Where did they come from and where did they go? What's next for us after the Moon?*

Upon my return to the States, previously suppressed emotions began escaping through a door that had been opened by my curiosity. Remembering my love of clay during a summer high school art class, I took ceramics as an elective at my community college. Mentored by a dream professor who encouraged my self-expression, I hungrily explored this pleasure, spending hours and hours throwing pots.

By now, my parents were divorcing, and my father had moved out. My mother, brother, and I remained in our home, joined by a friend from college whose family life was even more chaotic than mine. She and I paid my mother rent, and supported one another like sisters while we worked full-time and attended college.

Soon I was introduced to marijuana, and left my art for this stronger relief from the negative emotions growing inside me. I was furious with my parents for their behaviors and for not trying to work things out. I also hated the thought of leaving our beloved ranch, and yet that seemed imminent.

Quite accidentally, I crossed paths with a friend who worked at the Peace Corps training camp at Deer Park. She invited my roommate and me to a barbecue hosted by the volunteers in the agriculture program. Soon after we arrived, we became separated and I started looking for her. While walking across the patio, I heard a voice speak from the corner.

"Hello."

I turned to see who owned this deep voice. As my gaze settled, I felt mesmerized by a handsome, bearded stranger with soft brown eyes.

"My name is Graham."

"I'm Sandy. Are you one of the volunteers?"

"Yes, I am. I'm heading to Colombia, South America, to work in their Agricultural Program."

"Wow, that sounds interesting." *Why would he do that?*

"Actually, it's a way to avoid being drafted. I have a low draft number and don't care to fight in Viet Nam."

"I don't blame you. I've been in protests against that war."

"Killing someone is not something I would like to do. In fact, at one time,

I was studying to be a doctor—to save lives."

I took a step closer. "Where did you attend school?"

"Wake Forest. It's in North Carolina. I have family there. I took some time off from school to go home to Argentina—but then I was sent my draft number."

"Oh. You're from Argentina? I never would have guessed; your English is perfect."

"I was educated and grew up in both countries."

"How come they want to draft you if you're from Argentina?"

"I have dual citizenship. My father worked for the CIA during the war and my mother is from there. We travelled back and forth between both countries while I was growing up."

"Cool. That sounds interesting."

I lingered with Graham to swap details from our lives; discovering a shared love for horses, the country life, and a desire to help the oppressed in the world. We had a deep connection with one another, even though his life had been privileged, living in Buenos Aires and escaping to a family-owned ranch in the country.

Graham wanted experience on a dairy farm, and my father agreed to let him work there; free labor was rarely turned down. While he worked on the ranch, Graham lived with us. He and I fell in love as our relationship blossomed.

Even though my father had moved out of our home, I tried to connect whenever I saw him. Each time, my attempts were rebuffed.

"I don't have time to talk with you right now."

"Well, you can at least tell me how you are doing."

"Your mother and I are separated, and it looks like we're getting a divorce. How do you think I'm doing?"

"Don't you think you should try and work things out with her?"

"No, and I don't want to talk about it. She was unfaithful to me and that's all there is to it."

"Well Dad, like I said the day you left the house. You drink a lot and maybe that has something to do with her actions."

"You've already added your two cents, and like I told you the first time, I don't want to talk about it. You had no right to say what you did, and I don't forgive you."

"All that just because I mentioned that your drinking might have something to do with your marital problems?"

He grunted.

"Well, even though you and mom are getting divorced, I want you to know that I love you."

"Well, I don't love you, and I'll never forgive you. That's all I have to say." He turned his back and walked away.

You were drunk that day you found out about mom's infidelity. Why can't you see that your drinking was part of the problem and the two of you needed to discuss things instead of blowing up the marriage?

Shortly after that, my mother announced that she was moving to town. "You're welcome to join me."

Although Graham was headed to Colombia for his two-year Peace Corps assignment, he helped my mother, brother, roommate, and me move from the ranch into suburbia to begin a different chapter in our lives.

I then lost two important men in my life. My father had stopped speaking to me, and my beloved Graham left for South America.

I transferred to San Diego State University and enrolled in ecology and oceanography classes to supplement my educational track to become a teacher. I started with a minor in physical education and played college sports, but my Valley Fever returned, requiring more rest. It was a good excuse, as some of the women on our teams intimidated me with their masculine mannerisms. I was glad to leave behind something that was uncomfortably pulling on me.

Instead, I found refuge in the countercultural movement against the unchecked exploitation and destruction of the environment and the escalating Viet Nam war. My sentiments were contrary to what our society had embraced, and I greedily plunged into exploring alternative mores.

With the development of oral contraceptives, the "pill" was all the rage, liberating sexuality for women at a time when STDs were not an issue. We rocked out to Janis Joplin, Jimi Hendrix, and Jim Morrison; our own drug use unphased by the fact that these icons had all fatally overdosed. Women, along with people of color and culture, still faced discrimination. Budding concerns about ecology had birthed the first Earth Day, and I found far too many causes to rally around. Mescaline and LSD became my favorite psychedelics, and I used marijuana frequently. The "peace and freedom" movement of the sixties and seventies spawned experimentation with music, sex, and drugs, and I was right there with it all. I worked a full-time job by day, attended university at night, and escaped through sex and drugs on the weekends.

When Graham finished his Peace Corps assignment in Colombia, he proposed to me, and in-spite of being phobic about marriage, I accepted. Although I was working on a teaching credential, the prospects of securing a position were slim. Stories were abundant of recent graduates camping out on school lawns to be first in line for the few job openings available.

Disillusioned with the States, Graham accepted a staff position with Peace Corps Colombia. "If we're going to have any kind of a life, we need to move away from your mother. I plan on returning to Medellin."

I gladly dropped out of school and packed up my life to follow him.

PART II—PILLARS OF LIGHT

The best and most beautiful things in the world cannot be seen or even touched. They must be felt with the heart.

—Helen Keller

SEVEN

I had visited Columbia once before, in 1971, while Graham was serving out his Peace Corps assignment. On that occasion, I landed in Bogotá, over eight thousand feet in elevation—a cold city darkened by cloud cover. As we walked hand in hand down the street, a rat crawled out of the sewer and died right in front of me. People bumped us for space on the crowded sidewalks, and the poverty and countless beggars on the street were overwhelming.

"Why are those children begging? Don't they have homes?"

"No, the *gamines* live on the street. They've been abandoned by their parents to fend for themselves."

"Is there this kind of poverty in the city where you live?"

"No, Medellin is very different. It's warm and has far fewer people. I think you'll like it."

He was right. I had enjoyed my visit and now, over a year later, I was eager to return to Medellin, the "City of Eternal Spring." Orchids grew wild in the countryside surrounding the city, and it was similar in climate and vegetation to Hawaii but much older with its stately, colonial architecture. Graham and I made our home there.

I did not resemble the Colombians, and my clothes were a dead giveaway that I was an outsider. Being different was isolating and uncomfortable, as I could not speak their language or communicate about the simplest of things. On the city streets, I was harassed, groped, and subjected to other indignities before I recognized the need to change my appearance to fit in. Copying the Colombian women, I tied up my long hair, traded my miniskirts and braless wardrobe for something more native, and focused on learning Spanish.

Graham loved his job with Peace Corps and could not relate to my struggles to fit in. Instead, he encouraged me to find work at a language center and I began teaching English to students, learning a little Spanish in the process. Shortly thereafter, I was gifted some private students by another instructor who was returning to the States.

Both resisting and absorbing this new life, I was christened into Colombian culture by two of my private students—nuns covered from head to toe in white habits. Female babies in Colombia have their ears pierced shortly after birth, and the nuns decided mine needed to be done. I supplied the earrings, and they brought rubbing alcohol and a sewing needle to class, where the deed was performed.

My other private student was a psychiatrist—an ambitious, innovative and powerful woman. She was an anomaly in her country, where women had just earned the right to wear pants in public. She owned the foundation she had created for mentally challenged children and invited me to visit her school. I was surprised that my limited Spanish did not inhibit my communication with these children. What profound lessons they taught me, for I too was floundering, attempting to make sense of my reality. I had left a society I did not support, but felt incompetent in my efforts to fit into this new culture I did not know. My rigid, myopic attitudes and cultural perspective were slowly being shattered as I witnessed how difficult life was for too many in this world.

Initially I was not able to purchase food, available only in the open market, but eventually I learned enough Spanish to function. On my first solo trip, I even found my way home in the middle of a political demonstration, as elections were near and many were dissatisfied with their corrupt government. Hurled rocks, roving tanks, and soldiers perched on street corners with fixed bayonets pervaded the streets of Medellin, which entertained countless political rallies. It would be several more years before the drug cartels took over.

"It scares me when the military shows up on the streets," I told Graham. "Is it always going to be like this with all the political upheaval? I don't want to get hijacked by a mob, or hurt in the fracas. What if I get lost?"

"You don't need to worry. It's going to stop once the elections are over. It was always like this growing up in Argentina. You get used to it."

Graham was immersed in supervising the volunteers in his program. They taught and organized recreation programs and team sports in the undeveloped communities surrounding the city. He had an office at the agency managing the contract with Peace Corps. At agency functions, I sat next to him, surrounded by Colombian dignitaries benefiting from the work provided by the volunteers Graham supervised. Well-dressed, immaculately coiffured ladies gleamed next to their spouses. Clueless as I listened to their conversation, my laughter and smiles were fake.

Cultural schisms seemed to widen the gulf between Graham and me, diminishing our empathy and connection with one another. We drifted further apart as I tumbled into depression, struggling to find purpose and a sense of belonging.

Sometimes I accompanied him on site visits. On one occasion, the village mayor greeted us, excitedly explaining that guerrillas had just passed through. He warned us to leave immediately, and we only stayed long enough for Graham to finish his business before exiting unharmed.

I was always looking for ways to embrace this different culture, and found purpose in giving haircuts and immunity shots to those volunteers who asked, saving them a trip to the pharmacy. Our rambling apartment became a safe-haven for two women in the Nutrition Program when they returned from their remote assignments in the jungle.

In hopes of bringing different skills to the children in the special needs school, I decided to venture on my own to an outlying town famous for its woodworkers. I rode a bus to this pueblo and arrived in time to eat lunch at one of its two restaurants. While waiting for the town to reopen after siesta time, I purchased a newspaper to practice my Spanish. Sitting in the plaza, I heard the roar of a bus engine and watched the dust trailing behind as it raced down the road. With my broken Spanish, I learned to my horror it was the last bus for the day headed to Medellin.

There were no taxis or phones in this small village, and I had no way of letting my fiancé know I was stranded. Credit cards were nonexistent for me, and I had not brought enough money to pay for a room for the night. *I guess walking is my best option. I hope to reach the main road and hitch a ride home. If not, spending the night in the woods seems much safer than taking my chances in the village.*

I found a large stick for self-defense and carried it as I walked along the dirt road. Each time a car passed, I placed the stick at my feet while I waved for a ride. When a truck went by, fearing it could be trouble, I kept walking with stick in hand. Several trucks and only a few cars had passed by the time night fell.

I was walking in the dark when headlights approached me. *Definitely not a truck.* Dropping my stick, I reached out an arm, but my heart sank when the car drove past. I watched as it slowed and stopped about twenty feet away. Abandoning my stick, I ran to the passenger side and through the partially cracked window, a female voice asked in Spanish, "What are you doing out in the *campo* at this hour?"

I explained my predicament and faintly heard the driver say something.

"We will take you back to the city. Get in," the feminine voice at the window announced as the passenger door popped open from the inside. I slid into the backseat and expressed my gratitude for their kindness.

I learned the driver was a doctor who, along with his nurse in front, visited the village once a week to offer medical services. As he maneuvered around the ruts and holes, inching our way to the main road, I listened to their lecture.

"You are lucky we came along. It is especially dangerous for North Americans out here. There is always the threat of being mugged, raped, tortured, and/or taken prisoner by the guerrillas."

EIGHT

While I struggled to fit in, my relationship with Graham had become quite strained. He was so passionate about his work that I felt more and more left out as I competed for his time with an increasing need for purpose and validation.

"I know you're not happy here. You're not the same person; you seem depressed all the time."

"Well, I'm trying to find my place, and think that maybe I should join Peace Corps. It would solve my visa problem, so we don't have to leave the country every three months to get it renewed. I know you resent the time away from your work."

"I don't like being around you because you're not happy. I didn't bring you here to be depressed."

"I know you didn't, but it's hard when I don't speak the language very well or know their customs. I like my work with the *Doctora's* school, but I don't get paid for it."

"Well, if you joined Peace Corps, you could work in my Sports and Recreation Program and get paid to work in her school. Although it might be kind of weird, me supervising you."

My application process proceeded, but tension between Graham and me continued.

"You still seem unhappy."

"What if Peace Corps doesn't accept me? It's stressful not knowing when my visa has expired. What will happen if I don't get accepted and then Peace Corps won't issue me a new passport? I don't like being here illegally. Couldn't you be a little more understanding of how difficult it has been for me?"

"We've had this discussion before, and I'm tired of it."

He left for work, and although he didn't come home until late, I waited up for him.

I caught him frowning at breakfast the next morning. "What's bothering you?"

"I can't believe it takes such an emotional low to get us back together."

"What do you mean? What about last night when we made love? I thought that we ended with a better understanding."

"It shouldn't be like that. I don't see how we can go on like this any longer. I'm going to move in with Justin. I'll see you tomorrow after work and we'll discuss this further."

I sat at our table, dumbfounded and crushed. The pain grew worse as I tried to figure out how we had gotten to this point. By nightfall, I counted out twenty pills in front of me—tranquilizers I had brought from the States for work-related stress. I was numbly sitting there when I heard the door unlock. Melania, a college professor from Poland who rented one of the numerous rooms in our apartment, walked in.

"Sandra, what are you doing?"

"Graham said he's moving out because he's tired of our relationship and doesn't see how we can continue."

"But what is this? What are you planning on doing with all these pills?"

She stayed up late that night talking me through my helplessness about the emotional distance between Graham and me.

"I came to Colombia after I was given a terminal diagnosis," she said. "I wanted to travel before my health failed me completely. Life is precious, Sandra. You don't know what is in store for you, but please do not do something rash."

"You're right. I'm so sorry. I had no idea. Why didn't you ever speak of this before?"

"I could tell you weren't getting along very well, and didn't want to add to your problems. Please promise me you won't do anything stupid."

"I promise." Exhausted, she excused herself and I put away my pills after taking a couple to help me sleep.

I picked up my mail late the next day and opened a notification from Peace Corps: I had been accepted. Not sure what to do next, I stopped by the apartment of some friends.

"That's great, congratulations!"

"Do you know where Graham is? I'd like to share this with him; maybe he'll change his mind. He said he was going to move in with you."

Justin glanced at his girlfriend, and then back to me. "You don't know, do you?"

"Know what?"

"Graham has been seeing Frederica again."

"Frederica? The one he dated while he was in Peace Corps?"

"Yes, she's the one. Did you know about her?"

"Graham and I had decided to date others while he was in Peace Corps, but when he returned to the States, we committed to each other. He asked me to marry him!"

"Oh. Well, he's been seeing her for a couple of months now. He told us not to say anything because he said he was going to tell you."

"What a liar. He's never said a word about her. I've got to go."

Furious, I walked to Graham's office to confront him. "I just got accepted into Peace Corps, and Justin told me you're involved with Frederica. What's that about?"

"I'm sorry I didn't tell you. I went to talk to her when things got rough between the two of us, and we resumed our relationship."

"I can't believe you. We're committed to each other. What were you thinking?"

"I couldn't take any more of your unhappiness. I think you need to return home, take some time to sort this out. You can come back with the next group headed to Colombia."

"I just don't get you. I thought we'd gotten through the worst of our problems."

"We can't do this here at my work. Why don't you come with me for a drive and let's talk this over?"

I got in his work truck and we drove in silence until he pulled over. Turning to me, Graham repeated: "I think we need to have time to sort things out. I think you should return to the States."

Slamming the door behind me, I took off running, and when I got back to our apartment, started preparing to return home.

After nine months of struggling, I had finally embraced the culture and was looking forward to serving with Peace Corps. With a broken heart and yet some hope that Graham's promise to "sort things through" would come true, I left with plans to return with the Peace Corps.

A few months later, my group convened in Bogotá for "immersion language training." We studied Spanish with an instructor and used workbooks and listened to tapes all day. Living with Colombian families helped with our enculturation until we were released to our work assignments. My destination was Pasto, where Quechua-speaking Incan ancestors still lived in the mountains surrounding the southern end of Colombia.

It was Peace Corp's policy to send its volunteers to their work sites for introductions with our Colombian colleagues before being permanently assigned there. A religious holiday coincided with my arrival, so I cashed in one portion of my flight and bought a bus ticket for a twenty-four-hour ride to San Augustin. I had learned about the unusual stone carvings there. Wrapped in my wool *ruana*, I slept upright in the bus, impervious to the chickens and goats surrounding me.

When we rolled into San Augustin, it was pitch dark. There was no phone service, and the Internet had not been invented. I had figured on finding lodging when I arrived, but little did I know how undeveloped this place was.

"Do you know of any *pensiónes* here?" I asked the bus driver in Spanish as he slowed into the plaza.

"No, miss," he replied, his raised eyebrows reflected in the rearview mirror.

"I know of a place," offered a young man leaving the bus. "I will help you find a room; I'm sure they have plenty."

I followed him through the first set of doors into a large colonial building. He placed a key inside the second door and then whirled around and pulled me to him. "Oh, *senorita*, come to me. I will please you tonight."

"What? What do you think you're doing?" I yelled, shoving him off me. He fell into the corner as I bolted through the outside doors.

I ran to where the bus had left us. *Nobody. Not even the bus is here. Oh, man, what have I done? It's so cold and dark. Keep walking to stay warm.* As I rounded the corner, a single light bulb cast a small triangle of light into the blackness. I headed toward it, and heard voices and the sound of an engine. A Russian jeep with the right hood lifted was in the middle of the road. As a man leaned over the engine, I could hear him shout, "Accelerate!"

"More?" a feminine voice returned.

Cautiously I approached, raising my voice above the engine's roar. "Excuse me, *senor*? May I please ask you if either of you knows of a rooming house in this town where I could stay tonight?"

"Eh?" said the man as he straightened and sized me up. "What are you doing here? Are you CIA, huh?"

"Oh, no sir. I'm a Peace Corps volunteer, headed to Pasto. I came to San Augustin to see the ruins. The bus just arrived. I am looking for lodging, but nothing seems to be open. Please? Do you know of a place where I might stay tonight?"

"You sure you're not CIA?"

"Oh, *Dios mio*, no. I promise you I am not. I'm just afraid I'll freeze to death if I don't find a place to stay this evening."

"Huh. Follow me. Turn off the motor and wait here," he said to the woman, and I followed as he strode up the hill. Stopping at a large door, he turned to me. "I know this woman and she's like family to me. I hope you're telling me the truth."

"I promise you, I am."

He pounded on the door until a small square opened above us.

"Hello, Don Raul. What are you doing at this hour?"

"Hello. This *gringa* needs a place to stay for the night, and wants to see the ruins."

"Oh, but it's so late, Don Raul."

"She has no place to go. Please put her up for the night, Doña."

The door creaked open, as we stepped through a cutout portion of the massive outer door. We followed the Doña through another door and stairs her strong legs briskly ascended. As we entered a large room with a table and chairs, her dress revealed a woman of humble means. Eyeing me, I smiled back and exchanged greetings. Her face softened, realizing I spoke her language.

"Please bring some *aguardiente* for my new friend; it's very cold tonight. Here, sit down, please."

I dropped into the chair and obediently took the shot glass offered me.

"We need to drink together, and then I will leave you with the Doña. She will prepare a bed for you, and her son will be your guide tomorrow. Yes, *senora*?"

"It will be our pleasure."

"Thank you, thank you both. Please let me know how much the room is."

"You can pay her after I leave. Now, we drink. To Peace Corps!"

"To Peace Corps." I downed the shot, its warmth flushing me. My half-frozen bones welcomed this Colombian tradition called "firewater."

Raul poured another shot, downed his and announced, "Well, I must be going. It has been a pleasure. May you enjoy our quaint little town and your visit to our ruins. I bid you a good evening."

"Thank you again. I cannot tell you thank you enough."

"This is what we Colombians do."

As promised, the next day the quiet *senora's* son led me along the path through the overgrowth next to the carved stone statues.

"Where did the stone carvers come from?" I asked my guide, who only shrugged and replied in Spanish, "No one knows."

"What does this one have in his hands?"

"Who knows?"

Stone figures towered above, while others faced me or were simply carved heads without bodies or answers. I clicked away, preserving their enigma on film. *Look at this one—like he has a helmet or something on his head. Strange; I wonder if they have any relationship to the carvings I saw in Mexico. That's odd, this one is incomplete, like it was abandoned. Where did the carvers go; what happened?*

Full of unanswered questions and excitement about the vanished and mysterious culture I had just witnessed, I left on a bus headed for Pasto.

My assignment responsibilities loomed as I arrived in what was then the small town of Pasto. After asking for directions, I easily found my rooming house; the *residencia* where the Peace Corps volunteers lived was well-known.

After securing a room, I left my bag and visited the school where I was to work. Bound by tradition, the school authorities balked at the idea of a woman teaching sports and recreation. I was told that my services were not wanted. For good measure, they added, "You will be arriving during summer break. We do not hold classes or have the school open then."

The sense of purpose I sought eluded me as I walked back to the *pensión*, but I was determined to pierce through their rigidity when I was permanently assigned here after reporting back to Bogotá. I walked upstairs to the room where the owner told me the former volunteers lived. Knocking on their door, I almost whispered in English, "Hello, anybody home?"

The door opened, revealing a tall, slender woman with dark hair and chiseled features.

"*Hola*, I'm Gwyn." She gestured me in. I took one step inside, hesitated, and then cautiously entered. There were twenty-plus people seemingly standing on the wall behind her, all life-sized and so colorful I thought they were alive. Another North American, even taller than Gwyn and with bright red hair braided in long pigtails, was sitting at a table and stood up.

"*Que tal*? I'm Carlota," she said, extending her hand as she greeted me.

Another woman with soft, earthy features waved me to a chair. "Hi, I'm Leann. Are you with the new group of volunteers?"

"Yeah, you guys all live here?" They nodded. "Who painted that incredible mural? I thought those people were alive."

"I did!" said Gwyn. "The wall represents actual people who stayed here at the *pensión* while passing through."

"They look so real. Where were all those people going after they left here, do you know?"

"Most were headed down through Ecuador to Machu Picchu in Peru. There are some incredible ruins there."

"Yeah, I've heard. I'd love to go there some day. I just came from San Augustin. Have you been there?"

"I haven't, but I've heard about it," chimed in Leann.

"It was amazing. There were all kinds of stone statues—some of them were even incomplete, like half-carved. They're all along a jungle-like path. Some of them were about my height and then others were just a head—those were some of the incomplete ones. The kid who took me through the ruins said they don't know where those stone carvers came from or went to. He said some people in his village believe the carvings were connected to aliens."

"Wow, that's pretty crazy," mused Carlota.

"Yeah, I thought so too."

"The people in La Florida where I worked talk about UFOs all the time. People lined up around someone's house whenever they saw a *guacha* (spirit light)," Gwyn explained.

"What do you mean?" I asked.

"It's a spirit that shows up somewhere. It can appear in a glass of water or look like a dancing light in a room. They figure it is an angelic spirit bringing miracles and healing powers. They wait so they can ask for a miracle. The locals have all kinds of ghost stories."

"Yeah, here in Pasto they talk about UFOs too," Leann chimed in. "I found out in Machu Picchu that the people there believe in UFOs. Haven't you ever seen one?"

"No, I haven't. Do you think it's because they smoke so much marijuana?" Gwyn laughed. "Just because the *campesinos* (farmers) grow marijuana in their corn and smoke it doesn't make them crazy! Do you think that?"

"No, just wondering."

"Are you the only volunteer that's coming to Pasto from your group?" asked Leann, saving me from my discomfort.

"There are three of us, but I'm the only one located in the city."

"Oh, too bad. The *campo* is beautiful here. Want some?" A frying pan with peanuts was offered. I cupped my hands to receive the warm treats. Wafting through my nostrils was a hazy mix of roasting nuts and marijuana. *I think I'll stay here when I return to begin my assignment.*

"Do you think Don Jose would let me rent a room by the month?" I asked.

"Sure, just ask him. We've always had this room, using it when we came in from the *campo*. We've finished our assignments and will be here until we're done traveling."

As we huddled around their kerosene heater, they swapped more tales of their adventures. I inhaled the smokes and foreign experiences they narrated.

The next day I visited the school I had been assigned to, and was frustrated again with the patriarchal response to my gender working in sports and recreation. I still wanted to work here and hoped that Peace Corps could influence their attitude toward me. I had enjoyed my new friends and looked forward to my return.

As I headed back to Bogotá to accept my assignment, thoughts distracted me. *Those volunteers had some amazing stories to tell. If I stay there, I wonder what mine will be?*

I returned to Bogotá with my viewpoint a bit stretched. I was eager to live in Pasto with its mysteries, but was still in love with Graham. He had written so many letters promising another chance for us, I thought there was still hope we could make a life together.

Excruciatingly, when he came to visit, our conversation looped around and round. "I still love you," he said, "and yet I love her too."

With no chairs in the room, I leaned upright against a doorjamb while he sat on his bed. "You told me I was to return to the States so we could think things over and start again. And you found a relationship? That's not fair."

"I'm sorry. I am still in love with you, and I'm in love with her too."

"But you can't love two people at the same time. What about all those letters you wrote me? Just recently you wrote me about how much you love me and want to reconcile."

"I'm sorry. I can't live with you anymore. I love her and we're planning on returning to the States together."

"You came here to tell me that? After all this? You're unbelievable!" I crumpled to the floor, choking on my tears and pain. I had bronchitis, and all my pleading, crying, and carrying on wasn't helping. Crushed with defeat and feeling sicker, I left his hotel room and returned to my Colombian family's home. After several days in bed, I visited the street market and consulted an herbalist, who gave me something for my congestion.

My heart was not so easily healed.

NINE

When the time to leave for our work sites arrived, I felt eager to live in mysterious Pasto even if I did have to fight their prejudice against women.

This time I took the direct route there by air, and sat in wonder as our "prop job" skirted along the mountaintops and then circled to approach a paved plateau sandwiched in between towering Andes Mountains. We had to make a second pass, since the pilot had not dropped down enough to make a safe landing on our perch. With brakes screeching, we stopped just before reaching the deep chasm at the end of the runway. As the plane taxied toward the small terminal, I noticed all the passengers crossing themselves, giving thanks for our safety.

I secured a room on the bottom floor of the rooming house where Carlota, Leann, and Gwyn shared their quarters, along with everyone on their wall. Over another religious holiday, Carlota invited me to accompany her to Barbacoas. Curious and excited to see the jungle, I said yes. Even with her tall stature and red hair, she related well to the Colombians and was a great traveling companion. Carlota wrote about our excursion in her diary:

> August 25, 1973
> Barbacoas was just terrific. It's way out, 150 kilometers from Pasto

in the jungle and very isolated. A few buses and trucks serve as transportation to the outside world. But of course, the people from the area use canoes made from hollowed-out logs, and the rivers are their main means of travel. There was a gringo mining company in Barbacoas for about twenty years, and they just left two months ago because the gold vein is too deep. But the campesinos pan gold to sell to the jewelers who fashion it into beautiful earrings, rings, and chains (like what we saw in Bogotá). The main river upon which Barbacoas is set is very clean even though the majority of the people there wash in it. Sandy (a new volunteer with whom I went) and I couldn't resist swimming in the river even though we forgot our bathing suits. So, we went in nude. There was nobody around, no one. Just thick jungle rising high above the riverbank throwing vines from tree to tree and the green, cool river. The people there are so tranquillo. If a boat occasionally went by, the boatman would discreetly look the other way. Well, anyway, we had a terrific time.

Charlotte L. Pinsky

Carlota and I arrived back in Pasto at one in the morning after a full three days away. The gentleness of the Barbacoans had deeply impressed me. I had also been moved by the extraordinary beauty of the pristine foliage we saw thriving in that area. I had never witnessed such dense jungle growth with its spectacular palette of colors; it was even more beautiful than what I had seen in Mexico.

Upon our return, Carlota departed with Leann for Quito, Ecuador, leaving Gwyn to finish her mural. I continued my attempts to convince the school authorities to include me when school opened again. Whenever I could find a school official, I pestered him to let me organize some activities at the school grounds during their vacation, but I was roundly dismissed each time. I remained in the rooming house for another month, when my stomach broke out with red spots.

"What do you think is wrong?" I asked Gwyn, showing her the marks.

"Those look like bites from bed bugs."

"You're kidding. Bed bugs?"

"Yeah, I've seen them before. In the *campo,* sometimes straw mattresses would get infested with them. They've probably hatched and decided you're lunch."

"Well, I'm going to tell Don Jose." I left to give notice to the owner, and then visited my work site.

Gwyn was there when I returned. "Don Jose told me he feels terrible about your bed bugs. He has a small house near the airport he's willing to rent to us if you're interested. Leann and Carlota are heading back to the States soon but I'm not ready to go back, even though I've finished my mural. Are you interested in renting that house together?"

We loaded our paltry possessions into a taxi, which soon left us off at the dirt path leading to our new home. The air was pure and thin in our furnished mountain cottage, clustered in a tiny settlement along the Pan American Highway. In the 1970s the highway was an incomplete road that ended at the airport. The houses were perched on the side of a somewhat dormant volcano called "Galeras" for its resemblance to a Spanish galleon. (About ten years later Galeras erupted in a tragic display of its strength.)

I continued my efforts to break through the cultural mores so I could work within the school system, but each time I was sent home, rejected. I used marijuana to ease the pain, and listened to Gwyn's stories shrouded in mystery.

Every Friday we indulged ourselves by dining at the best tourist hotel in town. Pasto was Colombia's last stop along the dirt road ascending the Andes into ancient Incan territory and the hotel's cuisine catered to the steady stream of tourists passing through to Ecuador.

After one such meal, Gwyn and I stepped outside and carefully walked around the blanket a "gravedigger" had spread next to the door. I impassively admired his loot, dug from some nearby ancient burial site. It was not unusual to see such a vendor, but I was more focused on finding a ride home. Climbing the hill to where the taxis parked, I stumbled as if something had pulled at my feet. Instinctively I turned around, surprised to find my gaze settling on the gravedigger's blanket. An urn with a man's head on the body of a frog seemed to be staring at me. I shrugged the feeling off and continued walking, but once again something pulled at me, stopping me in my tracks. I turned around, walked back and inquired, "How much for the urn?"

"Five hundred pesos."

What am I doing bargaining for something dug up from a grave? Besides, it probably had somebody's ashes in it at one time.

"Take it for two hundred," I heard him offer through my mental chatter.

What? It must be an archaeological relic; I can't pass this up. Who knows how old it is? Maybe a thousand years or more.

I counted out the money to the vendor and cradled my treasure in both hands as I walked back to join Gwyn for the ride home.

Juan Carlos was a favorite driver since he often traveled our route; his taxi was a luxury American car—an archetype from my childhood. With his lilting accent, he caught us up on family news, speaking in the singsong cadence of the local dialect influenced by the *Quechua* tongue of the regional Indians. Like birds chirping and singing to one another, we chatted back and forth until he dropped us off on the road leading to our cottage. Steam escaping from the bowels of the volcano created a surreal atmosphere this time of day by surrounding us with clouds. When the night air blew them clear, the towering structure of Galeras was revealed above.

With just enough light to see by, I entered my room and searched for the piece of wood I had carved and polished while others roasted peanuts to pass the time. I placed the urn on its pedestal and put both on the small table to the left of my straw bed. My bedroom was lavishly furnished with a table, a bed, and a window.

Before going to sleep, my ritual was to blow out my candle and survey the rolling hills through the window to my right before gazing up at the multitude of stars. This night, after snuffing out my candle, I turned toward my window and my heart stopped. Staring back at me was a white, glowing face. Petrified, I grabbed the covers and threw them over my head as my back thudded against the mattress. I didn't breathe and my frozen silence was interrupted by a scraping sound from the direction of my nightstand.

What was that? It's in my room. My heart pounded even louder. *Don't make a noise,* I cautioned myself. *Huh...I don't hear anything now. Maybe it's gone.*

I waited and then peeked out from the covers. *Nothing. It's so dark, I'll light a match.* The flame startled me, and I jumped again when candlelight exposed the urn staring directly at me. *I know I placed it looking toward the doorway. Its beady eyes are staring right at me. How did it move?*

I reached over and turned it back and forth on the wooden pedestal. *That's the sound I heard from under the covers. How can that be?* I moved it again and I heard the same sound as I twisted it back and forth.

Hoping she could explain what had happened, I called for my roommate. "Spook! Spook! Please come here. I think I just saw a ghost."

Gwyn had been given the nickname of "Spook" because, like the locals, she embraced the supernatural.

Another time, while on a trip she and I took from Pasto to a remote, undeveloped region nearby, we stopped to have a cigarette. Standing on a small hill overlooking a narrow dirt road, we watched a *campesino* walking along it. Dressed in the typical white clothing they wore, he approached us and walked up to me.

"Soon you will find what you are looking for," he said in Spanish.

"Thank you," I replied. He took a few steps and stopped in front of Gwyn. I could not make out what he said to her, but watched him turn around and start walking back the way he had come. After about ten steps, he vanished.

"What? He just disappeared!"

"He's probably an angel," Gwyn said, shrugging.

"That's totally impossible," I gasped and ran down the road looking for him. *He HAS to be here somewhere; nobody can simply vanish in thin air.*

Desperate to find him, I ran back to Gwyn, still standing where I had left her.

"Did you see him? Did he come back?"

"No," she calmly reported.

"That's not possible!" I ran back down the road much farther this time until I found a small path leading away from the road. *I'll bet he went this way.* There was a lone hut at its end with a woman sitting on the ground weaving. "Did you see a man walking by here?" I pleaded with her.

"No," she said, shaking her head. "There has been no one." She gave me a strange look.

"Excuse me," I backed away, realizing I had invaded her privacy in my frantic searching. Returning to the road, I continued to run away from where Gwyn stood. *I'm sure to catch up with him because I know my eyes are deceiving me. Where is he? I've searched everywhere. Even if he were far away, we would have seen him, just like when he approached us. What happened?*

Without success, I returned to where Gwyn was still on the knoll. "I could not find him."

"Like I said, he was probably an angel," she nonchalantly replied.

TEN

Religious holidays were always occurring, which meant no work or school. Over one such holiday break, Gwyn and I decided to drop some LSD. She wanted to use my body as a canvas, and I agreed to the painting as I basked in the Andean sun in my bathing suit. Each brushstroke leaving paint on my body felt more erotic than the last, and we ended up making love. It was the first romance with another woman for both of us. Our unplanned, continuing relationship was unwelcomed by one ex-pat living in the area who criticized and harshly judged us when she found out.

In our two-bedroom cottage with no electricity, we cooked with natural gas and boiled our water for drinking. We had been there for a couple of months when I got very ill.

"You look like you have hepatitis," Gwyn offered. "Your skin is yellow."

After a few days of bed rest, I felt strong enough for a taxi ride and rode to town for help.

"You have hepatitis," the pharmacist confirmed. (With a lack of doctors, pharmacists often assumed that role.)

"What should I do?"

"Take this vitamin B-12 until you can get to a doctor." I purchased it and the requisite needles, climbed back into the waiting taxi and stumbled back to bed.

Jabbing myself in the leg every day to administer the B-12 was almost as painful as being sick, but it assisted me in reclaiming enough strength to contact Peace Corps about my health.

I was ordered to evacuate immediately. The two guys in my group stationed in Pasto had also gotten extremely ill. One had typhoid fever and had already been ordered to leave. The other's problem was so serious he was being returned to the States.

I caught a bus to Popayan and stayed with friends until I was well enough to fly to Bogotá. Gwyn remained in Pasto and we lost track of one another. Our relationship was forced to an abrupt end, since I had no way to write her and telephone communication was not available.

While in Bogotá, I stayed in another *residencia*, a hotel with meals included, and then lived with friends stationed in the capitol city while I healed. Without an official assignment, I decided to pass my time with the street children, called *gamines*. Orphaned or forced out of the house by overwhelmed parents, these young children lived in the streets and survived by stealing, begging, and prostituting themselves. They exist today and number in the thousands.

Eventually I was given medical clearance to resume working, and was contacted by the Colombian official in charge of an agency we worked with. A charming and handsome man, he invited me and another female volunteer from my group on a site visit outside Bogotá. She had also been prevented from working with the school system due to their patriarchal beliefs at the time.

The agency chief directed me to sit in the backseat with him, and the other volunteer sat in front with the driver. We were headed to an outlying neighborhood where he wanted us to work. As we passed through the lesser-known districts of Bogotá, I was fascinated with the scenery until the agency chief started to grope me. "Look at that," he offered as his hand slipped inside my blouse.

I grabbed his hand and pushed it back, exclaiming in Spanish, "Excuse me, director, please stop. You are a married man, and I am not interested in breaking your marriage vows!"

"That is of no importance!" he offered, attempting to brush my arms aside.

It would not be good for a Peace Corps volunteer to offend this powerful man in charge of the Colombian schools and agencies interfacing with our sports and recreation programs. Attempting to avoid any political backlash, I politely continued to block his advances even as he protested and resisted my attempts to restrain his wandering hands. He was relentless until the driver stopped the car at our destination.

I kept my distance, and when the tour was over I rushed to the front seat, ignoring his pleadings. *I feel sorry for the woman he's sitting with now, but I don't hear her protesting. Maybe he's not bothering her. I know I'm not safe if I work here.*

Back at Peace Corps headquarters, I politely declined the invitation to work there and was finally given my next assignment.

While I was waiting in the Peace Corps office for my plane tickets and contact names, Graham walked in. I started shaking, mystified that he still affected me so.

He was surprised to see me. "Are you stationed in Bogotá now?"

"No. I've been reassigned to the coast. What brings you here?"

"We're heading back to the States to live there permanently. We leave tomorrow."

"Well, goodbye and good luck to you."

The boarding area was vacant as I stood watching his plane taxi down the runway and lift off.

My flight soon left for my new home at the northern end of Colombia on the Caribbean coast. Pasto anchors the southernmost part in the country, and I was headed for Cartagena—a polar shift in dialect, culture, and geography.

When the Conquistadores were sacking gold and treasures from the Indians of Pasto and areas farther south to Peru, Cartagena became the departure point for untold quantities of gold bullion to Spain. To protect their loot from pirates, the Spaniards brought slaves from Africa to construct a fortress and walls to surround the city.

Many of the citizens of Cartagena were descendants of these slaves, and were still treated as second-class people. They lived in neighborhoods of shanty structures that lined the shore, using inlets of water only large enough for a dugout canoe to access the ocean. Fish was their main source of food and provided a livelihood. These ghettos were among the worst in South America, and their inhabitants were being forcibly relocated. I would be working in their newly formed neighborhoods.

Although some of these people retained their native language, Spanish was spoken here with a staccato cadence. The endings of many words were dropped, and my singsong dialect was the brunt of much laughter until I adapted to the regional differences. The locals made fun of the inhabitants of Pasto and ridiculed their mannerisms, most of which had become automatic for me.

Before leaving for Cartagena, I had stopped using psychedelics, and in Bogotá I gave away the remaining cocaine I had brought from Pasto. However, I continued smoking marijuana, using it to mask the dark and unwanted emotions that kept bubbling up and overwhelming me. I rented a room in a beach house full of Canadians who were all marijuana smokers. One day while riding the bus home, a young boy sat beside me and started laughing hysterically like a hyena. As we got closer to my stop, I could hear people behind me murmuring "*burros.*"

In Cartagena, North Americans were called "gringos," and the gringos who smoked marijuana were called "*burros.*" *Burros* means "jackasses" in Spanish. The name was fitting, for both consume grass and behave badly.

The boy would not stop laughing, and as I exited the bus, I heard their criticism of the house of *burros.* Feeling ashamed and guilty, my face turned bright red. When I related these events, my roommates told me I was making a big deal of nothing. Not long afterwards, I ran into a couple I had known in Pasto, and they invited me to dinner. She and her husband were staying in a hotel in Boca Grande, where all the fancy tourist hotels were. They invited me to share some smokes in their room after dinner, and I left feeling high and very uneasy. I was unfamiliar with Boca Grande but managed to catch a bus I knew passed by my house.

Slowly ambling along, the bus was driving deeper into the poor section of Boca Grande where the service staff for the hotels lived. People kept getting off, but no one had boarded the bus except me. With just a few passengers left, I asked the driver if he was returning to the central part of town.

"This is the end of the line," he said, glancing at the woman sitting in front, close to him. "I'm going home after I park the bus."

"Ohhhh. Please let me off here."

I was disoriented in an unknown neighborhood and needed to find the main road. I walked and walked as I searched for familiar street names or something I could use to navigate a way to finding transportation home, many miles away. There were no taxis in this poor section, and as I stumbled along, my fear grew each time I checked my watch. *I left the bus over twenty minutes ago and I'm lost. What are they doing milling around those streetlights? Oh, man, I passed by here earlier; I've been walking in circles.*

I stopped with this realization, and instinctively snapped my hand, a local gesture done when faced with something of emotional or physical impact. The usual expression accompanying such a hand gesture tumbled out of me without warning. "*Mieeerrrcoles!*" (This is the word for "Wednesday," used instead of *mierda* just like "shoot" is used in English instead of saying "shit.")

I had prided myself on fitting into the culture and not being ostentatious like most North Americans were. Even though the gesture and expression were commonly used in that region, my loud and very public display shocked me. *Why did I have to shout like an idiot, drawing such attention to myself? As if it isn't bad enough that I'm lost. How many times have I passed by those people huddled under that streetlight? I hate myself; I wish I could just disappear. I need to get out of here and find my way home!*

When I finally made it to the house, my roommates were still up and getting high. Shaken by my behavior, I pulled out a thirty-gallon garbage sack I had filled with marijuana. Saving a very small portion for my personal use, I gave them my stash. A few days later when one of them accidentally destroyed my guitar, I realized it was time to move.

There were other Peace Corps volunteers in the city, even some from my group who had been assigned here originally when I was sent to Pasto. Their house was full, with two couples and another single volunteer, but they agreed to let me rent their maid's quarters, a little hut in the back-yard of their house. Thinking I was undetected, I continued to smoke marijuana, but soon was asked to find another place to live. I found a small duplex next to a *tienda* (store) far away from the middle-class neighborhoods where I had first settled. The floors were bare cement, and the ceilings open, with exposed rafters. There were no screens or glass on the barred windows, only shutters. Since the cockroaches entered at will and scurried across my floor at night, I learned to walk with a scooting motion to avoid stepping on them. I could tell how long it had rained, by how high my walls had wicked up the water.

My new place looked and felt like our hay barn at the ranch. The kitchen was bare, except for a brick charcoal stove and a small sink hanging on the wall. I paid a local to construct shelves for dishes and a countertop to surround the sink for my hot plate. He also made a table for the chairs I purchased.

I slept in a hammock with mosquito netting draped over a rope suspended above. Relentlessly, I continued smoking marijuana, this time with the butt end inside my mouth to mask the smell—imitating how the native women smoked their cigarettes while washing clothes by hand.

One night, my guilty conscience grew so loud I flushed the remaining drugs I had down the toilet. *I am accepted here and I love my work. I'm a fool to risk all this. I don't feel depressed and worthless anymore with this new job. Why am I still smoking this?*

The brief time I had spent with the *gamines* had been rewarding but frus-trating, since I had been helpless to make a difference in their circumstances. Sobriety was not a difficult choice with the validation I was feeling through my work. Mobilized in a positive direction, I felt for the first time in my life that I was doing something worthwhile. Once I disposed of my drug cache, my sense of wellbeing and worthiness increased even more.

The agency Peace Corps had contracted with was *El Instituto de Bienestar Familiar* (The Institute for Family Wellness, aka "Bienstar"), a nationally organized provider of social services. They managed several community day-care facilities, some constructed for the shoreline inhabitants forced to relocate from their ghettos. I worked in two of these neighborhood centers whose schools were located on the grounds of an order of nuns called *La Asuncion* (the ascension of the Virgin Mary into heaven).

Supported by aid from the U.S. and other countries, Bienestar offered nutritional, educational, and recreational programs to impoverished and malnourished children and their families. I started as a recreation specialist, teaching games and activities in the daycare facilities to the children and their caretakers. Soon, however, my job expanded to being a social worker when I assumed the responsibilities of another volunteer. She and her husband had taken a different assignment and were moving to another country with the Peace Corps.

Immersing myself completely into my duties as I worked with this population, I discovered incredible gratification. As a social worker, I became the liaison between a people and the government that had bulldozed their homes. The community centers were a combined effort to address the multiplicity of problems festering in these neighborhoods.

Never before, had I felt so driven or loved and fulfilled in my work. My heart opened more in love and appreciation for these people who were teaching me so much. As I witnessed the suffering of the *tugurio* (shanty town) residents—a struggle for survival that seemed without end—I searched in vain for answers to justify the inequality and unfairness happening to these good people of faith. I began to question everything; it made no sense to me why innocent children were birthed into abject poverty, starvation, and disease. Question upon question plagued me as I grappled with the lack of rational explanations for the inequities confronting me daily. *Why do they face a destiny of limited opportunities and inequality because of their race or social status? What did they do to deserve such limited chances for life? It seems like most of them will fail to find a way out of this endless cycle of oppression. Why? How is this coming from a loving God?*

"How is this acceptable to anyone?" I asked one of the social workers from my agency. "I don't see how they are treated is considered fair or even justified." "Oh, you don't know any better because you're a foreigner," my native coworker explained. Beautiful, with dark ebony skin, Magdalena was educated but not expected to treat others sharing her skin color with egalitarianism. I was being asked to accept this—to conform without questioning the fairness of it all, even though their deprivation and overwhelming need assaulted us daily.

Walking through the tropical mud and sludge from the afternoon's downpour, I headed for a house at the end of one row of square cement boxes—all the same. For centuries, the natives had lived along the waterways surrounding Cartagena, the walled city we called home. Their wooden huts and swampy ghettos used to line the route from the airport to resort hotels. But this embarrassing reality had so threatened the burgeoning tourist industry that the tugurio inhabitants were forced to Las Lomas (The Hills), which overlooked the city. Isolated on these clay-covered hills, they no longer had access to the ocean—their cultural matrix and source of livelihood.

I went to the opening—there was no door—and called for the woman who lived there. Greeting the abuela (grandmother), I asked how they were doing. Older than her years, with bones and body straining under the weight of a hard life, her toothless smile welcomed me as she struggled to rise, offering me the only seat in the room. Waving away this invitation, I walked toward her to exchange abrasos (hugs).

She was the sole caretaker for her three grandchildren, whose parents had abandoned them. The youngest was sickly and weak—so gravely malnourished he badly needed hospitalization. I carried instructions he had to wait, for there were not enough beds to accommodate the starving children in this neighborhood.

My eyes adjusted to the haze as I stood upon the hard-packed floor and inhaled the cool smell of damp earth—a welcome relief from the arid sun. She and the children were doing fine, she told me, and, "God willing," they would live to see another day. She was happy to be alive, a peaceful soul, struggling only with the strands of cloth she was mending, a rag more than tattered shirt. They would "get by," she said. And I knew they would, because she said so.

I choked back tears welling up in my chest; her unremitting faith deeply touching me. Exhaling a noiseless sigh, I stayed longer to converse with my mentor, absorbing every smell, every word, every second with this magnificent human being, who threw my perspective an awesome curve.

ELEVEN

Since I was an anomaly, neighbors sometimes dropped by on the weekends to meet the "gringa." I become good friends with some of them, and one day was shown a picture of Jesus with water stains running down from his eyes. My Colombian friend told me she had seen the picture shedding real tears. I lacked an explanation for her experience; having been taught that paranormal and psychic phenomena were psychological delusions, trickery, or just plain evil. Those belief systems were continually challenged with stories of people being thrown out of their beds during the night and how the deceased were left to lie in state for a week while the bereaved said their goodbyes and paid their respects to avoid being haunted by the newly departed. I listened with rapt attention to these tales of the supernatural; the storytellers were convinced they were absolutely real.

Work replaced my obsession with drugs as my job consumed my life; I often returned home from work late. I lived next door to the only store in the neighborhood but its doors were always shuttered early and so I was forced to skip my usual dinner of bread with cheese. Lacking refrigeration, breakfast was on the street corner from my favorite vendor lady. Standing in front of a rectangular cart framing her mobile kitchen, the opening allowed her access to a small Bunsen burner in the middle. Deft hands moved from side to side as she patted the ball of corn dough until it grew into a round-disk. We chatted and caught up with each other's news as she worked her magic. I watched her push a thumb into the ball, opening a hole that she fashioned into a pocket. Cracking an egg with one hand, its partner held the mouth open and then sealed the egg dropped inside. My treat sizzled and rolled in the tin of spitting oil until she plucked and blanketed it with a square of brown paper. I gladly exchanged brightly colored money for my morning delicacy.

Lunch was at the Instituto de Bienestar when I was there. This was not very often, as I mostly worked in the community centers. Since I was gone when the charcoal vendor came to my neighborhood and had no refrigeration, cooking for myself was not an option. Not long into this routine, I developed anemia—and shortly thereafter my little home was broken into.

I had brought the frog/man urn from Pasto and a few other artifacts with me to Cartagena, but found the frog/man shattered on the floor when I came home one evening. I distinctly remembered tucking the urn safely into the corner of my shelf on the wall of my bedroom. Gone were my camera with extra lenses and my tape recorder, but my duffle bag with extra clothes, passport and emergency dollars remained untouched on the floor. As I surveyed the damage, I had a vision of the urn jumping off the shelf, but dismissed it. I was grateful for whatever it was that had scared off the robbers.

As I stood with my landlord in my backyard, he explained how the robbers had helped themselves to my possessions. "They pried this board loose and crawled in." Spying my clothes hanging on the line, he added: "You should not be washing your own clothes; that is what maids do. If you hire one, the neighborhood guard will protect your home. She will also cook and clean for you."

I had prided myself on being self-sufficient, but had unknowingly paid for it. After I learned their customs the hard way, my home was never robbed again and I enjoyed a delicious cooked meal upon arriving home from work every day.

To deepen my understanding of the people, I began attending Mass in the neighborhoods where I worked. A visiting Mother Superior to the convent-run school where I had my office offered to tutor me in Catholicism, and I attended a few classes until she left.

Months passed, and the passion and satisfaction I felt for my work and life had grown so much I decided to remain in Colombia after my assignment ended. Even so, I continued to ponder the inequalities I witnessed daily and deepened my commitment to make a difference; to somehow impact the unfairness and oppression that perpetuated their suffering.

"Ma'am," my maid told me one day, "I am pregnant and we cannot afford to have another child. I need a few weeks off. I'm going to take some remedies to terminate the pregnancy." Her dialect reflected the staccato of the locals but was slower than usual—sounding burdened and faltering with the pain of her situation.

"Yes, of course, I am so sorry. Is there anything I can do for you?"

"No, thank you. I will be back in two weeks."

"Your job will be waiting for you upon your return. Please take care." Seeing the fear in her eyes, I embraced her. "May God be with you."

When two weeks passed and she did not return, I visited her home. Meeting me at her door, she was very ill and barely able to stand. Abortions were illegal and she had been victimized through medical quackery and her desperate situation. After giving her some money, I said goodbye to my loyal friend.

Recognizing that I would not be safe from robbers without the services of a maid, and would face food challenges again, I decided to move. Through my Colombian friends, I found a room to rent from a family whose maid cooked for me and washed my clothes.

Except for occasional meetings with my volunteer coordinator, my interface with Peace Corps was minimal. That year, our program conference was being held in Medellin. It had been almost two years since I had joined the Corps. *It's strange being back here; seems like another life. All the volunteers from then are gone. I wonder if Juanita is still here?*

Juanita was a university professor and formerly a volunteer from the early years of Peace Corps. She had helped me get my documents cleared when Graham and I had split up. My visa had lapsed and I was in the country illegally, which would have been very problematic if I had tried to leave. She had met me at the *Departamento Administrativo de Seguridad*, (DAS) office, where these issues were handled. I anxiously waited outside for an hour before a smiling Juanita emerged.

"I've spoken with the immigration authorities and they have stamped your visa with permission to leave. You need to leave the country immediately and they will give you no trouble."

I wanted to find and thank her again for helping me. After my conference, I called her number.

"*Hola*, Sandra! So good to hear from you! How did you get back here?"

I responded to her questions, and she invited me to her apartment that evening, stating that she was eager to share about her recent visit to Machu Picchu. Pressing on her mind was a book she had found called *I Visited Ganymede*, written in Spanish by a Peruvian named Yosip Ibrahim.

"This book is so fascinating. It tells of this guy's contact with outer space beings and the information they gave him. He told his friend Pepe everything the space beings shared with him, and then left with them."

"Oh really?" My skepticism was difficult to hide.

"Yes. Yosip told Pepe that the space beings claimed the Earth was going to undergo major changes and end in the year 2000. The beings told all of this to Yosip and much more when they took him on a spaceship to the planet Ganymede. They all live there under the surface of the planet and are much more advanced than us."

"They would have to be, to fly back and forth in space ships," I quipped.

"I'm going back to the States to spread the book's message. But I need to translate it into English first," an enraptured Juanita explained. "You should also think about returning home to share this information with everyone."

I laughed. "I'm not leaving for a very long time. I've searched my entire life for the fulfillment I have now. I plan on staying here several more years, and then I'm going to travel. I have so many places I want to visit."

When the last of my words escaped me, an eerie silence filled the room. I felt uneasy as I noticed an inexplicable electric bluish-white energy forming to my left. *What is that?*

In shock, I watched what seemed like two pillars of light take shape near the table where I sat. A rushing sensation started flowing through me, and I heard a voice speak in my head: "You need to return home and share with your family and others that life as you know it on Planet Earth will end if humans do not change the way they are living."

I hadn't moved, and was still trying to figure out what was happening to me, when the voice returned: "Humans are creating the devastation we speak of that threatens your planet." The voice stopped, but my head was flooded with more information, and then the lights disappeared.

Stunned, I stared blankly at where the lights had been. *What just happened? Was that real? Did I just hear that I'm supposed to return to the States because humans are destroying the planet?*

I dropped my head onto my arms and started to cry. "No, no, no!" Lifting my head, I asked Juanita. "Did you hear that?"

"I didn't hear anything. What's wrong?" She looked quizzically at me.

"Someone just told me that I need to return to the States and spread the word that the world as we know it will end if humans do not change their ways."

"Oh. Well, the manuscript says that the world is going to end in the year 2000. What are you going to do?" Juanita asked.

"I don't know. I've heard before the world is ending from numerous religions. But I was just told that humans are going to destroy the planet if we don't change the way we live. I don't get any of this, and have no explanation for it. I am confused, though, because what just happened felt real and true. But I don't want to leave here!"

"That's what I felt, too, but I've decided that it's time to listen to the book and return to the States. The space beings from Ganymede claim that the world is ending in the year 2000."

"But this voice didn't say that. This doesn't seem like the same thing. Even though it was in my head; it felt *real*."

"What are you going to do?"

"I don't know. I have an early-morning flight back to Cartagena; I need to go. I'll write you and let you know what I decide. I don't like this one bit!"

In my hotel room that night, I cried deeply as I wrestled to understand the disturbing message.

This can't be. It's not fair. Why tell me? I didn't ask for this and I don't want to leave Colombia. I'm happy for the first time in my life.

I was glad to be back in Cartagena, but noticed how tense I felt on the bus ride from the airport. The shocking events from the night before haunted me. *Am I losing my mind? I want to remain here and continue my work. At last, everything is falling into place for me. What has happened to me? I feel so different. Why now? This just isn't fair!*

That night while lying in my bed, I prayed for guidance. Without warning, my skull filled with an intense white light. Beyond my control, my head vibrated and shook from side to side for several minutes.

What's happening? Please, make it stop! God, please help me! I just want to stay here and do my work. Please . . .

After a few minutes, the shaking stopped and the light inside my skull went out. But I was still scared; I could not explain that I felt as if a light bulb had been turned on and off inside me while my head rocked back and forth beyond my control.

The next day, although I was still reeling from the events of both nights, I went to work as usual.

That night, despite my prayers, the light returned. This time I felt illuminated from head to toe, and the shaking occurred throughout my body. I again prayed fervently for it to stop, and felt terrified while it was happening. Strangely, though, as soon as the light faded I noticed a calming sensation permeating me.

I wondered if I was losing my mind.

This sequence of light and vibrations continued for several nights, and during the day an increasing frequency of coincidences started happening. When I was not working in the barrio I usually spent time on the weekends with the youths in my neighborhood. We played guitars and conversed about our different cultures. But following the light experiences, I started hearing a buzzing sound in my ears several minutes before one of the neighbors would knock on my door. There had never been a set time for our visits, but the buzzing accurately informed me each time of someone's imminent arrival.

Even though many Colombians readily embraced miracles, local folklore and paranormal events, I wrestled between accepting these experiences and fearing that I was losing my mind. I had not taken psychedelics or smoked marijuana in over a year, and even with this sustained abstinence, these inexplicable events were distressing to me and added to my overall distrust of myself; for I lacked rational explanations for all of them.

In an effort to find peace, I shared with Juanita my fears and internal battles around the experiences with the lights. She responded with a desire to visit me in Cartagena, and wanted to come in a month.

Face to face, I asked her whether she thought the space beings connected with her book might have anything to do with the light treatments I had been given at night.

"I don't know. Let me meditate and pray on it."

"You can use my hammock in the patio if you wish."

I was reading when I noticed that over an hour had passed since Juanita went outside, and I had not heard from her. When I walked out, I froze. *Where is that beam of light coming from? It's so small.* I silently took a step closer and noticed that the beam was hitting Juanita in the middle of her forehead. *What is this? Who and what is doing this?*

Just then she woke, although I had said nothing to disturb her. "I guess I must have dozed off. Why do you look so strange?"

"You just had a beam of light boring into your forehead. It looked like what I described was happening to me. How do you feel?"

"No different."

"This is just too weird."

"I don't feel these are negative things that are happening to us. I sense that we're being helped to get our doubts and considerations out of the way."

"It's not helping me in that regard, because I still feel very upset with all of this."

"All I know is that I'm returning to the States, and feel very strongly that's what I'm supposed to do."

"And then what?"'

"I guess I'll wait for guidance."

After Juanita left, and despite my resistance, I noticed an awareness stirring deeply within me: the certainty that none of these experiences were imaginary or the fabrications of a crazed mind. Somehow, now, seeing a *guacha* or the appearance and disappearance of an angel seemed insignificant compared to the implications of being told that the "world will cease to be as we know it if humans do not change the way they live." Feeling that somehow I had to spread that message, I felt burdened and desperate to understand its implications. *Was that message from God? If it was, then how can I ignore it? But I have felt so much love for these people, and them for me. How can that be bad?*

I need to know if that message was from God. Why would God ask me to choose between the work I'm doing and returning to warn my family and the rest of humanity? Who's going to listen? Who am I to tell people what to do? I really need some answers.

TWELVE

After assuming the other volunteer's job, I had combined both jobs, spending most of my time in the community of Las Lomas and at the school the nuns ran to serve that neighborhood. I worked out of the office the nuns provided, next to their personal living quarters. A simple curtain covered the entrance to a hallway leading to their cloistered rooms, and one of the nuns who worked with me in the children's groups, Sister Ana Maria, had become a mentor. Desperate to resolve my conflict and hoping she would lend some insight, I shared with her the experiences with the lights and the message I had been given in Medellin.

She related similar stories of supernatural events. "It has happened at our spiritual retreats, that some of the nuns have witnessed angelic lights and astral traveling. We believe these are sent from God." Her disclosures eased my torment about going crazy, but I still sought some sort of guidance to resolve the growing rift within me.

At home, I obsessively consulted the *I Ching*, and with Ana Maria's encouragement, spent time before and after work praying in the nuns' chapel. I recited the prayers she had given me, and asked for guidance and the strength to overcome the conflict I felt between obeying this new direction and my desire to remain with these people whom I loved so much.

I hoped my intense commitment to prayer would gain me insight, but I filled my prayers mostly with begging and pleading with God. *How can all this be happening to me? Was that a message from you? Why don't you give me answers?*

I did not want to return home. My relationship with my mother and father was disjointed and broken, and I could not see myself finding meaningful work like I was doing here. And yet the longer I resisted winding down my job and making plans to leave, the more my anxiety grew.

Shortly thereafter, my agency accepted two more Peace Corps volunteers to work in different programs. I hosted them during their site visit; speaking English was strange—I was so accustomed to Spanish. I shared my plans to leave before my termination date because I thought I'd been asked to warn my fellow-human beings that we were going to destroy the earth if we didn't stop living the way we were.

"How do you know leaving is the right thing to do, Sandra?" one of the volunteers asked.

"I believe that I've been asked by God to spread this warning."

"But how do you know it's coming from God?"

"I don't know. I really, don't know anything anymore, but I do know that the more time I spend here, the more anxious I feel. I have never felt so at home, so loved and so accepted as I do here—and yet I feel pulled to return to the States, to serve in a different capacity by warning people that we need to change our ways, or face major changes on our planet."

Eager to begin their Peace Corps adventure, they were not impressed with the urgency I felt. In fact, not until after I returned home would I learn how much I had disturbed them.

Later that month I was still struggling to coalesce these two paths colliding within me. To provide a smooth transition after I left, I wrote out pages and pages of curricula, games and activities, and gave them to the Institute's secretary for typing and distribution. She lost them—my only copy—and I grew more frantic with the fear I was leaving my programs incomplete and in turmoil. This added to my guilt over leaving.

While rushing to complete enrollment of the neighborhood women into nutrition and food programs that I hoped would continue in my absence, I was asked by several mothers to be a godmother for their newborn babies. I had no way of keeping in touch with these families after I left since most could not read or write.

"Don't go, ma'am."

"I'm sorry. I wish I didn't have to." Choking back tears, I watched her open the small box I offered. Her calloused and stained fingers, worn rough from years of washing clothes by hand, held up a tiny gold medal reflecting the tropical sun. Tears glistened cheeks weathered and creased with struggle as her face deepened with gratitude.

"Because I cannot be here," I whispered as we embraced. "May God and Saint Christopher protect and take good care of him, you, and your family."

"You will come back to visit us, won't you?"

"My home is very far away, but, yes, I will come back to visit you." We exchanged hugs again, then I kissed her baby and walked to my next destination. Repeating the ritual, I grew heavier with grief each time.

My heart broke when Sister Ana Maria hugged and blessed me. "*Vaya con Dios* (Go with God)," she commanded as we parted. Behind me, I heard a familiar voice through my sobbing.

"Sandra, you must leave now," Fortune urged. The new volunteers had come to the barrio looking for me.

"I know. I haven't finished packing yet, as I'm giving away as many of my belongings as possible."

"We'll help you finish."

We waited for the bus out of the neighborhood but it arrived later than usual, pressing us for time. With instructions for the belongings I was gifting, they were cramming the rest into my duffle bags when the power went out. Searching for my flashlight, I bumped the board I used as a bookshelf and blindly pawed through the spilled contents.

"I found it!" Holding the light aloft, they frenziedly packed my remaining belongs. The lights came back on and someone exclaimed.

"Look at the time!"

We rushed outside, hailed a taxi and had crammed ourselves into the back seat when I blurted out. "I can't find my ticket."

"We have to leave right now!" Fortune was emphatic.

"But I don't have my ticket!"

"It doesn't matter! Driver, take us to the airport!" Dana demanded.

As we started down the road I shouted at the driver: "Stop! I know where my ticket is. I'm going to get it!" The car had stopped and I started to get out when Dana ordered: "No, keep going." I bolted just as he started moving again.

I ran back into my room and found it behind the shelf where it had fallen while searching for my flashlight. By the time we reached the airport, my plane had already taken off.

The next day, I finally arrived in Bogotá and signed the papers to terminate before my official ending date. It was December 1974; I would be home before Christmas.

PART III—A NEW QUEST

No army can withstand the strength of an idea
whose time has come.

—*Victor Hugo*

THIRTEEN

Back in the States, the first time I walked into a grocery store with shelves stacked high with brightly packaged food, I ran out with tears streaming down my cheeks. So much food, so many choices; it was overwhelming. The starvation, poverty, and market smells I had left behind haunted me, making it extremely difficult to embrace the abundance all around me. Opening a refrigerator bulging with food filled me with nausea. I had become desensitized to the canals of sewage and rotten produce edging their way through the open market with rows of raw, unrefrigerated meat and piles of dirt-encrusted vegetables and freshly picked fruits.

I celebrated Christmas at my mother's home. After opening our presents, I overheard my brother's girlfriend say, "Sandy's really different now. What happened to her?"

I did not hear my brother's response.

Not long afterwards, I attempted to share some of my experiences with my mother, in whose house I was staying.

I still felt alienated from her. Before I'd left for the Peace Corps, I had confronted her once again about her infidelity. Instead of calling her "Mom," I had used her first name to show my disdain for her behavior.

Now I hoped to gain some favor with her by relating my pillars of light experience and sharing about the book Juanita had read. "I loved my work in Columbia; I only left because I believe I've been called to serve in a much more important capacity. I believe the future of our planet is at stake."

"You sound like a crackpot. Where did you get such crazy ideas? Is this what your time in Peace Corps taught you?"

"I'm talking about the destruction of our planet if we don't change our habits; the way we're living."

"I think you've lost touch with reality. That's what I think."

"You don't understand. I left the most rewarding work I've ever done to bring this message back to you and the rest of my family. I was *instructed* to come back."

"Oh, so you didn't want to come back here to live where you belong? Isn't your family important to you?"

"Yes! That's precisely why I came back."

"Maybe we don't appreciate the information you feel so compelled to share. It's obvious that you've changed. I'm not so sure that I like who you've become. Why don't you eat meat anymore?"

"I'm a vegetarian now. I stopped eating meat after a breakout of blackleg contaminated the meat supply in Pasto."

"So, what exactly *do* you eat? You have some very different mannerisms now. Your friends are concerned about all your strange behavior, and some people who used to work with you said you were acting crazily in Cartagena."

"What do you mean?"

"I'm just saying that they were concerned about you."

Since all my coworkers had been Colombians and did not speak English, I suspected she was talking about the two volunteers who had visited me shortly before I left.

My suspicions were confirmed when I found a letter they sent her. Part of it follows:

We doubt that Sandra ever had the paranormal experiences she talked about and question the information she shared with us. She claimed the world was coming to an end and acted so strangely. She even jumped out of the car as we were driving to the airport and purposely hid her ticket so she would not have to leave.

I was furious and hurt that they would betray me like that, for I had gone out of my way to help them—I thought we were friends. I had no idea what my mother had written in reply, but this correspondence kindled so much anger that I moved back to the ranch to live with my grandmother until I could find a place of my own.

The fact that my mother did not accept my new paradigm wounded me deeply. Her failure to take the warnings seriously felt like more personal rejection of me. I had struggled to feel loved by my parents all my life, and erroneously thought my experiences would soften our relationship. I also desperately sought reconciliation with my father and had hoped his heart would open to me again if I shared myself. But he refused to hear of my experiences in Colombia and the message that brought me home to save the world.

"I don't want to hear about the bandwagon you're on now. I don't want to talk to you, I don't love you and never will again."

"Dad, can't you forgive me for what I said? That was ten years ago."

"I'm not interested in discussing anything further with you."

Much to his credit, my brother listened to my experiences and concern for our future on the planet. But for the most part his life was focused on work, his girlfriend, and the things he enjoyed, like the dune buggy he was constructing. The topic of the world ending did not much appeal to him.

No matter how hard I tried to share my information, my family members reminded me that my truth was not theirs. They had not been given information by light pillars, nor struggled daily to end rampant suffering and starvation. Their experiences and mine remained worlds apart.

The unbridled grandiosity of the notion that I could spread the message I'd been given never occurred to me. The revelations haunted me, but my failure to be credible about them brought back old feelings of low self-esteem.

In those days, the idea of vanishing planetary resources was an awareness entertained by only a select few. Recycling was in its infancy; only glass and aluminum cans were collected for reuse at a single facility for all of San Diego County. Earth Day was still fairly ignored, as national attention was focused elsewhere. The Khmer Rouge were slaughtering millions of Cambodians, and the Viet Cong were successfully marching toward Saigon. In the final days of the Vietnam War, the United States scrambled to evacuate its armed forces, along with ninety thousand Vietnamese citizens. The big news was that thirty thousand U.S. supporters were left behind to face systematic extermination or tortured incarceration. Rwanda, where at least two hundred thousand lost their lives, simmered with violence.

With so much human tragedy and suffering going on, saving the Earth itself was not breaking news. Furthermore, exposure to paranormal phenomena was still limited to marginal groups considered controversial. Instead, people turned to entertainment for distraction, struggling to guess words and phrases when Vanna White turned over a vowel for the newly minted "Wheel of Fortune."

I continued living with my grandmother, found work, and grew a garden in her old chicken pen. My cousin Donna lived nearby, and became a close confident and mentor. We shared many hours gardening together at her place down the road in the original homestead of my father's family, built in the late 1800's. Once, Donna invited me to spend the night and join her family for dinner and evening worship. I slept upstairs in one of the numerous rooms in their three-story wooden frame English-style farmhouse.

That night, startled awake by the stomping of heavy steps up the stairs, I lay in bed frozen and unable to move or speak as something choked me.

Finally able to wrestle free, I jumped out of bed and sped downstairs to wake my cousin. After I explained what had occurred, she brought her *Bible* upstairs and the two of us prayed together until I felt calmed and safe enough to go back to sleep.

The next morning, she related a story about someone who had heard noises inside the house long ago. There was no one there, but they saw a black shadow moving outside one of the windows upstairs.

"What do you think happened to me last night?" I asked.

"I think that when you delve into mysticism, you invite dark spirits from the Devil to bother you."

"What is the remedy for such an occurrence?"

"Praying to Jesus. He can stop anything negative from the Devil. Don't forget that, Sandy."

My grandmother was willing to let me stay with her, but I wanted to move out and get settled on my own. She played bridge on a regular basis and returned from one such engagement with some news.

"Sandy, Alice Guyer said that her neighbor who owns the avocado grove next to her has a place for rent. She's a widow and lives above the grove but rents her cottage out. Would you be interested in seeing it?"

My new residence was ideal, with a yard, three bedrooms and a sun room— surrounded by avocado trees and much closer to my work. After moving, I visited my grandmother on a regular basis, but remained estranged from my father and emotionally distant from my mother.

With their rejection fresh in my heart, my search became a quest to find a method or modality through which I could reach them and the world. I worked at a local middle school, teaching English as a Second Language until I discovered how incompatible I was with my co-worker, who brought a switchblade to class to impress the students. When the principal disregarded this, along with my discovery upon a home visit that another student had stopped coming to class because one of her classmates had assaulted her, I decided that earning a teaching credential was no longer my goal.

I left at the end of the year and took a job teaching preschoolers. The younger children at the Parks and Recreation Department were more enjoyable to work with and not so chaotic. I needed stability as I grappled with the ever-present thought that the Earth was about to be rendered terminally ill by its inhabitants.

As I searched for answers to the unusual and disorienting experiences in my life, I began consuming literature on UFOs and paranormal activities. The Philosophical Library offered programs and speakers, and I became a regular. I met others who shared my curiosity, and together we travelled to Landers, California in the Mojave Desert to meet George Van Tassel. He was a retired aeronautical engineer and follower of Nikola Tesla's research. Published, and a self-proclaimed authority on UFOs, Van Tassel had since the mid-1950's hosted an annual UFO convention at his Giant Rock airport. I hoped he could shed light on my paranormal experiences in Colombia.

He graciously received us, but was not interested in hearing about my experiences or what had led me to him. Instead, we heard about his Integratron Project, built close to his home and airport. Although the exterior dome was finished, he was unwilling to let us go inside, stating it was still incomplete. He claimed the structure was initially to be a rejuvenation machine whose inspiration came from his contact experiences with extraterrestrial beings. Van Tassel likened it to Moses' Tabernacle, explaining that it was meant to be an anti-gravity device. I left his home believing that extraterrestrials were visiting and bringing advanced technology to Earth, and resolved to return for his next UFO convention to learn what I could.

In my searching, I studied Native American teachings, Christianity, Edgar Cayce, Tibetan Buddhism, and the Kabbalah. I practiced yoga, rebirthing, and Sufi dancing, and attended various workshops and a Zen Enlightenment Intensive. But nothing seemed to touch that place within me that needed answers and validation for the experiences I sought to proselytize.

In 1975, I discovered Werner Erhard's Erhard Seminars Training (*est*), and eventually took most of the *est* workshops and seminars, as well as the Six-Day Training Course. Hoping to find a place of common experience, I shared the *est* training with my mother, and she also took it.

Shortly thereafter, Juanita, the former Peace Corps volunteer with the book from Machu Picchu, showed up at my doorstep.

"How did you find me?" I asked.

"It wasn't easy. I was guided to return to the States, and then to find you. I've translated *Yo Visité Ganimedes* (*I Visited Ganymede*) into English and call it The Manuscript. I brought a copy with me and thought you'd want to help me spread the word, since you followed the instructions you were given and came back."

"Aren't you going back home?"

"It's not really my home any longer. I moved out long ago and lived in Colombia for years after finishing up with Peace Corps. I wondered if I could rent one of your rooms here."

"I guess you could do that. What do you plan on doing out here? Do you have any work lined up?"

"No, I thought first I'd find out if I could stay here and then would go look. I taught at the University for years, I'm sure I can find a job. I thought we could work together on sharing The Manuscript."

My focus had been on the information given me during the pillars of light experience. When I read her English translation that stated the world was soon to end, I did not question its validity, and committed to helping her share The Manuscript.

After Juanita moved in, she also took the *est* training and our lives became centered around *est,* and sharing the translated copy of *I Visited Ganymede.* (It has since been officially translated and printed in English.) We gave a couple of presentations at the Philosophical Library. Dr. Bronner, the soap maker, often attended these lectures, and during one of ours, he sat in the audience quietly chanting, "One God, we are all one." His message felt validating to my attempts to align people in caring about each other and the planet.

Although I enjoyed working with the preschoolers, I also felt pressured to share the information that I'd been given. I decided that teaching people to love plants and nature could be a way to spread the message I felt entrusted to share.

Toward that end, I formed my own landscaping and maintenance business, incorporating years of working in my grandmother's yard, on the farm, and with my uncle. I enjoyed being outside, and the work felt very natural to me. Werner Erhard had iconic space in my mind then, and he often used the expression "it works" to describe functionality. I borrowed that concept for my business, figuring that every time someone uttered my company's name, The Earth Works, they would be affirming that the Earth was transforming rather than continuing to be a place of negativity, self-destruction, and suffering. I hoped that teaching awareness about nature and its life force and the affirmation that my company's name represented would help prevent the paranormal warnings I had received.

Women in the 1970s were not usually seen doing physical work commercially; especially not outside. For my atypical job, I was featured in a local newspaper. I renamed myself San Li Son, and went by San Li (Saan Lee). I thought the name sounded more artistic. It had come to me in a meditation but was basically aspects of my birth name put together and pronounced differently.

Meanwhile I feverishly shared "The Manuscript," putting the message I had personally been given on the back burner. It was not long into our working collaboration that Juanita and I became romantically involved. However, with so much energy directed towards saving the world, Juanita's and my finances suffered. After about a year together, our relationship was waning when I received a letter from Gwyn. Before the Internet, it was quite a feat to be found after all those years. She had returned to the States and wanted to visit, and so Juanita and I agreed it was time for her to move out.

When Gwyn arrived, we resumed our relationship and I introduced her to *est* as well. A community of like-minded lesbians formed around us, sharing common bonds through The Manuscript and *est*. Our beliefs, coupled with being lesbians, made us outcasts. Spirituality was not well-regarded, and those who embraced the paranormal were considered kooks. Reception of gays and lesbians was quite chilly then. Even twenty plus years later, when Ellen DeGeneres announced she was a lesbian, she faced dropped sponsors and network rejection.

I came out to my parents, and although my mother was accepting, my father behaved quite differently. "Oh no, not that too," he muttered as he turned his back and walked away.

Rejected by him again, I took my need for support to a post-graduation *est* seminar called "About Sex." After sharing my experience, a few men from the seminar offered to help "reform" me back to heterosexuality. I accepted an invitation from a guy I knew, and even though the experience was pleasurable, sleeping with him did not "cure" me of my attraction to women. Sadly, I was unaware my sexual orientation was beyond my control or of my choosing.

Not long afterwards, I drove out to the ranch to visit my grandmother. All the pastures were empty and an eerie silence had settled upon the ranch. She was not home, and I ran into my father instead.

"Dad, where are all the cows? What happened?"

"I sold them! I got tired of dealing with the City," he said, referring to San Diego. "They wanted a percentage of my profits and were telling me how to run my business. They told me I had to ship my milk up north and couldn't sell it to distributors down here."

"But couldn't you have found a different way to deal with them instead of shutting down the dairy? I mean, doesn't the fact that the family has been here since the 1800's mean something to you?"

"We had no control over how the City forced us to sell our land. I'm not discussing this with you. I've made my decision and it's final."

Grieving the end of the ranch added to my emotional turmoil. To mask these emotions, I retreated deeper into my work and *est*. Devoting copious amounts of time and energy in service of this "greater cause," I became an "est hole." Being part of the elite who supported the trainings, I was honored to chauffeur around a trainer or rub her back when requested to do so—donating countless hours to *est* after work and in my free time. I often found myself dozing off behind the wheel as I drove home every night after working and volunteering afterwards to *est*. I ran onto the shoulder one night and scared myself, but did not stop this obsessive routine.

Although I had plenty of jobs, I was not a savvy businesswoman and allowed *est* to compete with my work. I was angry with both parents and determined not to ask anything from either one, assuming they would reject or criticize me. Festering in self-pity and loathing, my frustrations and fears escalated. In fact, they drove my impractical approach to most things. Instead of bidding jobs by factoring the costs of materials and labor, I decided prices off the top of my head. Understandably, I often ended up owing more money than I earned.

During this difficult time, more paranormal experiences plagued me. Lying in bed one night, I heard my front door open and footsteps walk across the carpeted floor. *I know I locked that door.* I lay there frozen as the floorboards squeaked under the weight of the steps coming into the living room. From my bedroom, I could see the redwood picnic table in the dining room, and watched as a ghastly-looking figure sat down on the bench closest to me. *Creak.* The familiar sound of the wood giving into the weight of someone sitting on it. Immobilized, it took me a while until I found my voice. "Go away!"

The figure vanished.

"I think that has something to with the urn you brought back from Colombia," Gwyn offered. "You're under psychic attack."

"I've never heard of such a thing."

Later that day, I became nauseous and felt as if I were spinning in space.

"The spinning sensations and your sickness could be from whatever came into the house," Gwyn said. "I think we need to bury the urn facing the full moon and see if it helps you. That's what the Colombians did when they were visited by unwanted guests from the supernatural. They recited prayers to Jesus for protection. We can also demand the spirit return to where it belongs. Didn't you say that you can't find your watch?"

"Yes."

"Well, if the spirit took your watch, we can demand that it be returned before it leaves. I think we have a poltergeist that's trying to get your attention."

"If that's what this is, it succeeded."

We buried the urn with our prayers, beseeching "Jesus the Christ" to help us in demanding the spirit return to where it belonged, to leave me alone and give me back my watch.

The next day, I awoke feeling much better, and went outside to rest in the sun.

As I opened a folding lawn chair, my watch was tucked inside one of the layers.

"Hey, look at this. I found my watch," I reported to Gwyn.

"Where was it?"

"You're not going to believe this, but it was outside in the lounge chair."

"Did you take it outside and leave it there?"

"Are you kidding? That's my good watch. I only wear it for dressy occasions."

"Then the only explanation is that the spirit couldn't come inside because we demanded it return your watch, but prohibited it from coming back inside the house." Gwyn stated this as a matter of fact.

"Hmm. . . "

Struggling to comprehend these unusual experiences was confounding. Adding to my emotional stress were mounting financial issues. Gwyn was working at a local horse ranch, but paying our bills each month was challenging. I started drifting away from our relationship, and soon we decided to split up. Gwyn moved in with friends and I resolved to work on getting myself more financially solvent.

I felt lonely and distant from what I had originally intended to accomplish. The separation within me was growing to extreme proportions even as I continued to share The Manuscript with as many as were interested.

Adele was one of them. An educated and working single mother, she attended the UFO convention in Yucca Valley with me. It would be the last ever hosted by Van Tassel.

Finding refuge in someone who shared my interest in The Manuscript and making the world a better place to live, I visited her in my free time. Not long after the convention, I was there when her demeanor changed abruptly. Grabbing her *Bible*, she lifted it in the air, and words poured out of her: "The world has too much evil in it. We are to do something to help with its transformation! I'm channeling that we need to go north to meet with the space brothers. We are to wear no shoes, take no purses, or any form of identification with us. You are to drive us, San Li."

We piled into her car and, without question I drove as she directed.

"You are not to stop at any intersection. Go through them as a sign of your faith and you will be protected," Adele ordered from the back seat.

"What?"

"You heard me!"

I dutifully ran through each stop sign as we headed to the freeway onramp. Our journey continued uneventfully until we neared Orange County, when I heard a commotion in the backseat. Suddenly, Adele pulled me from the driver's seat as she climbed up front and took the wheel. "Let me drive, you're not going fast enough!"

She succeeded in wrestling the steering wheel away from me as I retreated to the back seat. "We need to gain enough speed so that when we pass through the back end of that car in front of us we'll be transported up by the space brothers."

It was all happening so fast, I sat paralyzed as I watched the speedometer climb past ninety miles an hour and the trunk of the car in front loom closer. *CRASH!*

I came to with my face against the gearshift knob in the center console. Outside, voices were shouting. "Here, get out of the car. Be careful. Step out now."

I staggered and grabbed the hands of the Good Samaritans assisting us. As I sat on the side of the road, my head cleared a little. The car was crumpled against a bridge stanchion and Adele was sitting about four feet away from me.

She turned her head. "San Li, YOU'RE the cause of this. YOU'RE EVIL! YOU'RE THE REASON WHY THE SPACE BROTHERS DID NOT PICK US UP!"

Dazed, I sat there until emergency responders arrived and ushered us into ambulances.

After we were released from the hospital, Adele's significant other drove us back to her home. He did not ask questions, and not a word was spoken as we exited his car. I climbed into my van and sat for a while, searching for reality. "Now what?" I asked the distorted image looking back at me from my rear-view mirror.

My badly bruised body ached and my mind reeled as I drove away. I did not want to go home, and instead drove to Valley Center, where I knew Dr. Elizabeth Kübler-Ross had a retreat center. I had been there before, to see Dr. Bernard Jensen for an iridology reading when he owned the property.

It was dark when I walked into the office. "Hello, my name is San Li, and I'd like to speak with Dr. Kübler-Ross, please."

The receptionist looked shocked, reminding me of how frightful my face was. Bruised and bloated, I was also now missing a tooth.

"May I please speak to Dr. Ross?" I pleaded again. "I've just been involved in a car accident and I need to speak with Dr. Ross about demon possession."

"Well, um, she's not here right now. Just a moment and let me make a call." She spoke so softly I could not hear the conversation, but eventually she nodded her head and handed me the phone. "Here."

Dr. Kübler-Ross listened to my story and desperate pleas to know if I had just encountered the devil.

"I'm sorry you have experienced so much pain. However, I do not believe in such things as demon possession—they are not real in my experience.

Perhaps you would benefit from going home and getting some rest after such an ordeal. I'm sure the rest will do you some good. Do you have any other questions?"

"No, thank you so much. You have been very kind, and I feel comforted by your words. Thank you again." I handed the phone back. "Thank you for calling her," I said to the receptionist as I turned to leave.

Climbing back into my van, I processed what Dr. Kübler-Ross had told me as I drove home. *Yes, I do need to rest.*

The next day, I could barely move out of bed. I called my mother and grandmother, and although I didn't offer much of an explanation about what had happened, my mother brought food and a boyfriend with her. My grandmother sat down and looked concerned. "What happened to you, dear?"

"I was involved in an accident, Gramma. I'll be okay."

She left with a worried look, and I lay in bed for several days struggling to figure out what I had gotten myself into. I visited a dentist and my old family doctor, and tried to resume my work and life.

Living near Juanita and Gwyn, with our common bonds of Colombia and the other lesbians in our small community who shared The Manuscript, and *est,* had been comforting. But my life had drifted away from them, and now I was not feeling as committed to The Manuscript as I was to the message originally given to me. I also wanted to avoid reminders of Adele's and my behavior leading to the car accident.

I had failed in my attempts to relate to family, my country, and myself, and had even lost touch with high school and college friends. They had all moved on, making lives for themselves while I was in Colombia.

Grasping for what had soothed me previously, I started reciting prayers in Spanish every morning; ones that Sister Ana Maria had given me in Cartagena. I asked God to "make me as clay in your hands that I would be shelter for many," much like a passage from the Book of Psalms in the *Bible*. While I thrashed about trying to find a grounded reality, these prayers comforted me as I begged God to show me my next step.

Frustrated, I moved to San Diego to live with friends I knew through *est*. As I searched for transformation for self, family, and the world, I terminated my landscape business and drifted from job to job. Despite my unceasing quest, I was floundering; unhappy, in debt from my landscaping business and reaching bottom fast.

Perhaps I was already there. I felt emotionally shattered and still had not been able to reorient beyond the culture shock and weight of the irrational events I wrestled to embrace. Even though I had rallied and plunged into each new endeavor with the conviction that *it* would give me the answers I sought, I had yet to find an ascetic life or philosophy that offered what I so desperately needed. Still searching, I attended a different kind of workshop called "Feldenkrais"—a modality touted as creating "awareness through movement." I liked it so well, I worked as a recruiter to fill their workshops.

Witnessing how the *est* training program had made a profound difference in so many lives, I still believed their philosophy could lead to world transformation, and continued volunteering copious amounts of my time and energy to spreading this transformative movement. *Est* became an obsession as my life continued to spiral out of control.

Needing full-time work led me to a job as a statistician and real estate appraiser. When that contract ended, I began managing a vegetarian restaurant, signing on to buttress the owner through his investigation by the IRS. Thinking my sacrifices would correct and transform his ailing business, I spent nights sleeping at my desk. He continued drinking and sabotaging my efforts and eventually framed me, accusing me of throwing a deposit bag onto the roof. I never knew how it was found or how blaming me for the deed was justified, but I was fired from that position and moved on to selling life insurance by day. To supplement my income, I waitressed during the graveyard shift at a local watering hole; two o'clock began my busiest hours.

Since having taken the training, I had spent four years as a constant volunteer in varying capacities with *est*. When I failed to keep a deadline to pick up Christmas presents for distribution to hospitalized Veterans, I was confronted by the team leader above me.

"San Li, what happened? Why did we have to remind you of your agreement? This is not okay. You agreed to fulfill your responsibilities. What do you have to say for yourself?"

"I'm sorry, Seth. I didn't realize that I had forgotten to do that."

"Yeah, but you almost sabotaged the entire program. What if I hadn't caught your mistake? What were the volunteers to do without presents to distribute?"

"I know, I'm sorry."

"What's up with you?

"I'm so sorry," and began to cry.

"I don't understand you. You were doing so well, and now you've dropped out your responsibility for something important. Please explain yourself."

As my crying deepened, I collapsed on the floor.

"San Li? Why?"

"Because I'm evil. I'm just evil."

Seth reached down and picked me up. "You need to go clean up your mistake. Let me know when you're finished."

The presents were delivered, as should have happened before I was confronted, but shortly thereafter the staff in the San Diego *est* office encouraged me to take time out from my involvement.

"San Li, we think you need to get your life in order and manage it in a more productive manner. We're relieving you of your volunteering duties."

Indeed, I was overwhelmed—but was also clueless how I might accomplish their suggestion. I had learned much, but the *est* paradigm and my paranormal experiences were at odds with each other.

The friends I had made in *est* had become another family. I had left my lesbian community, was still estranged and feeling rejected by my parents and now felt even more unlovable and unworthy. I had started out strong, but with each year of failing to inform the world of the paranormal message, I became convinced I was evil to my core: that something must be wrong with me for all my failures. I did not understand my life experiences, and since I was no longer using drugs to deaden overwhelming emotions, sex and obsessions like *est* had become my outlets. However, as I moved through relationships with both men and women, I felt tremendous shame about my behaviors and ambivalent sexual orientation.

FOURTEEN

I moved again, this time renting a room in a two-bedroom condo in Point Loma, California, from another friend I had met through *est*. Bernie was a cabinetmaker selling advertising space. Like me, he was searching for his next step. Considering ourselves "liberated," we played our guitars together in the nude. This was 1979, when a gallon of gas cost eighty-six cents and the average annual income was around $17,500. *Close Encounters of the Third Kind* was a year old, and *The Amityville Horror* and the first *Alien* movies were captivating American cinematic audiences. *Little House on the Prairie* was still playing regularly on television and had competition from the likes of *The Waltons*, *Mork and Mindy*, and *Dallas*. Iran had taken Americans hostage, and I was removed from it all, struggling to overcome my own battles grinding away at me.

My relationship with Bernie was platonic, but our mutual dissatisfaction with our lives bonded us. He did not like his job, and one day announced he was consulting a psychic who had helped him previously. "I'm going to get a reading from Solar to find out what I should be doing."

The day after Bernie's reading, I was home alone when the phone rang. As answering machines were nonexistent then, I answered it.

"Hello, is Bernie there?" a deep, soft voice asked.

"No, this is San Li, his roommate. Bernie is working and won't be back until later today. Shall I give him a message?"

"Yes, please let him know that Solar called. Do you know about me?"

"Bernie said that you gave him a great reading and were very helpful to him."

"I'm glad to hear that. I also know Marta and Edward. I'd like to meet you; Bernie spoke highly of you. Are you free this evening? I could give you a reading at no charge."

"I'm not working today. So, yes, that would be nice. Thank you."

Later that evening I answered a knock on our door and stepped back as an imposing figure of a man—six-feet tall—stood before me. His hair streamed down his back, and a full, untrimmed beard framed his face. He wore a long-sleeved, embroidered white shirt that hung loosely over Levis, covering a large belly and stocky build. His flip-flops crossed my threshold as he walked into the condo with an air of familiarity and confidence. As he gazed into my eyes, the room filled with his energy.

"Solar?"

"Yes, that's me."

Swept up in his rapt attention, I sat with him on the couch.

"So, tell me about yourself."

Dismissing the cautionary alarms ringing inside, I gushed forth the time-line of my life, from Graham and the Peace Corps to the pillars of light experience and the resulting message and mission I had been given. I also described how I had tried to share the information from the Manuscript, hoping it would lend credibility to my efforts to awaken people to changing.

"I've had paranormal experiences, too," Solar said. "I've been directed to drive into the backcountry to spot UFO's. Go ahead, tell me more."

"Well, I've never seen a UFO, but this woman and I were involved in an auto accident because we thought the Space Brothers were going to rendezvous with us to teach us how we could facilitate a shift in humanity's consciousness."

"That's interesting. What happened?"

"Well . . ." I hesitated. "It's embarrassing. She wrestled the steering wheel away from me and drove us into a bridge stanchion and . . ." My voice trailed off as I started crying.

"It's okay, you can tell me everything. I understand." His muscular arms encompassed me, muffling what was becoming convulsive sobbing. "I understand; you can tell me. Talk to me; I believe what you've experienced. I've also been to South America. One night I floated up to the ceiling and passed right through it into a space ship above."

More details tumbled out of me as I described my quest for answers since returning from South America.

"I was at that UFO convention and met Van Tassel too," Solar interjected.

The knots into which my bizarre experiences had twisted me loosened as he listened to me and validated all that I said. With his encouragement, I purged myself-telling him about the paranormal experiences I'd had and all my frustrations with being unsuccessful in sharing my message.

I also related the shame I felt: shame for my past drug use, my extensive and varied sexual history, financial failures and indebtedness. But worst of all was my belief that I had botched the necessity of enlightening and warning others of the impending end of the world. I loathed myself for not being able to translate my experiences into something viable, even for family and friends.

Solar thoughtfully listened to it all, and then suggested, "Let's drive up to Mount Laguna. Maybe we'll be lucky and see some UFO's."

Feeling much lighter after being heard without being rejected or shamed, I agreed. He drove us to the mountains, where we stopped at a deserted campground. The crisp air framed our breath. "Brrr," I said, "it's really cold here!"

"Yeah. I like coming up in the winter because hardly anyone camps here then. Look up. Have you ever seen so many stars?"

Jamming half-frozen hands into my pockets I gazed at the multitude of stars, unspoiled by city lights. *Growing up in the valley I used to spend hours looking up at the stars wondering about it all.* "It is amazing how many stars there are. I really don't see how we could be the only conscious life in the universe."

"Oh, I know we aren't. My readings have told me that."

"What do you mean?"

"There's inhabited life on other planets, just not in the form that we humans have. I, myself have come from a very far-away place to fulfill my mission here on Earth. Would you like to know who I am?"

"What do you mean?"

"I mean from past lifetimes. Aren't you curious why we've met? I think you've been searching for me your entire life. I can help you fulfill your mission, Sandy. Why don't you meditate on who I am?"

The moon shone around his silhouette as I closed my eyes. "Hmm. I'm hearing Zeus, Jupiter . . ." and I stopped short of saying *Satan,* the name that came to me next. Since Dr. Kübler-Ross had told me "the devil is not real," I failed to recognize my mind's metaphorical warning—the names of negative beings who had abused their power in mythology.

"You know," Solar said, "we have many things in common. I can help you attain enlightenment. You said you want to get closer to God and accomplish your mission, didn't you?"

"Yes. I need to share with the world what I was told in South America about humans destroying the Earth if we don't stop living the way we are."

"I can help you do that. I can also help you attain enlightenment—I've helped many. I worked on the Crow Indian Reservation as their medicine man, and have helped many people in their spiritual growth and development. I have a system I call 'The Program.'"

PART IV—THE PROGRAM

If words are to enter men's minds and bear fruit, they must be the right words shaped cunningly to pass men's defenses and explode silently and effectually within their minds.

—*J.B. Phillips*

FIFTEEN

I felt rescued from my downward spiral of self-doubt that I was failing to spread the message, and feeling ashamed of myself for the inexplicable things about my life. Solar was offering me something I had lost: hope.

"The Program," he said, "is the way I will instruct you on becoming enlightened so you can accomplish your mission."

My prayers seemed to have been answered at last, yet I hesitated to commit to this Program. Less than a month before I had caved in to a supervisor's unabated pressure to sleep with him. I had desperately needed that job, and sexual harassment in the workplace was all too common for young and naïve women like me who lacked clear boundaries. I had resisted until I feared losing my job, but after having sex with him, I had even more reasons to hate myself.

This time, I wanted to take more time before I jumped into something I might later regret.

Solar seemed undaunted; he started visiting our condo on a regular basis.

"Are you ready to join The Program and get on with your mission?"

"No, not yet. I have too many debts to pay off before doing that."

"Let's at least go out to the backcountry again. Don't you enjoy our talks?"

"Yes, yes I do." And I did.

Every chance he had, Solar parked himself in our condo and we deepened our discussions of our paranormal experiences and hopes and aspirations in life. One night, as we were walking back from eating dinner together, he reached out and took my hand. "I like you, and would like to have a relationship with you."

I pulled away. "Thank you, but I'm not ready for a relationship just yet."

"Bernie said that Janet is house-sitting for your mother in Escondido. Isn't Janet one of your lesbian friends you knew before meeting me?"

"Yeah. So?"

"Isn't she also involved in *est*? Maybe she'd want a reading."

"She's still in *est*, but I don't know if she wants a reading."

"Bernie said he wanted to go visit her. Let's all go together."

I ended up driving the three of us there. Janet was happy to see us, and invited us into the living room. Solar sat right next to me and grabbed my hand. He kept squeezing it and then moving his eyes towards the back of the house where the bedrooms were.

Excusing myself, I motioned for Solar to join me in the family room.

"What's up?" I said.

"Don't you want to have sex? I really like you."

Thinking I could prove something with the opportunity, I consented. When it was over I marched into the room and declared to our friends: "I'm happy to announce that we just had sex, and I'm no longer afraid I'm a lesbian." Although recognized for thousands of years in some parts of the world, bisexuality was not accepted in my culture or within my own awareness.

"You don't have to tell them, do you?" Solar's red cheeks betrayed embarrassment.

Driving back that night, I indulged my curiosity about this man I had just shared myself with. "How did your arms and legs get so muscular?"

"I used to lift weights because I played football, and was training to compete in the Olympics throwing the javelin."

"Did you make it to them?"

"No. I threw my knee out and had to stop training. I used to run up and down Mt. Helix every day."

"Oh, that's impressive. I'm sorry about your knee."

"Yeah, me too. When I couldn't run, my stomach started growing."

"Hmm." *Maybe it could also have something to do with all the fast food you eat.*

"Now that we're in a relationship, are you ready to join The Program?" Solar said abruptly.

"What? No, I'm not ready and we're not in a relationship. I'm still working two jobs, trying to pay off my debts."

His voice was slow and gentle. "There are other ways, you know; you don't need to let that hold you back. How are you ever going to accomplish your mission? You remember how depressed you were when I met you? Well, maybe it's because you're not doing what you should be doing in your life."

I had no intention of forming a relationship with Solar, but the comfort his validation offered nurtured my blighted self-esteem. And he was right: I was desperately focused on finding a way to fulfill the mission I had been assigned in South America. That desperation blinded me to his stalking as he circled in closer and closer, waiting for the seeds he had planted to take root in the fertile soil of my guilt and shame.

Other than providing psychic readings, Solar did no work, and was in our condo often. When I received an invitation to my family's annual summer gathering, I asked him if he wanted to go.

At summer's end, extended family on my father's side customarily spent an evening together celebrating with a bonfire and picnic on the beach. In 1979, the family decided to gather at the restaurant Tony's Jacal instead, and I took Solar as my dinner guest. We arrived late and were unable to sit next to each other. Solar was positioned between my cousins at one end of the table. As I visited with relatives at the other, I noticed Solar was frowning. *That's weird, why is he making that face at me?*

I never asked him why he'd skewed his face, and his conversation with my cousins remained unknown to me until many, many years later.

"I'm going to join the family soon," Solar had announced to my cousins as he sat down.

"Not if we have anything to do with it," my cousin Ed, a sheriff at the time, said to Gary, another cousin on the other side of Solar. Conservative and clean-cut, they both chided Solar for his long hair, strange dress, and mannerisms.

In reality, I was not interested in marrying anyone, especially Solar. I had only known him a couple of months, and my attraction to him was to the spiritual growth and development he had offered.

Perhaps being spurned by my family goaded him, because thereafter he pursued me doggedly—calling, showing up at my job, and above all, pressuring me to enter his Program.

His proposal was not that unusual. At that time, spiritual communities were sprouting up throughout the country as some from my generation sought a better way of life through higher consciousness and awareness. People I had known from *est* joined Rajneesh in Oregon, and airport terminals and street corners were usually filled with groups of yellow-robed Hare Krishnas who sold flowers, chanted, and sang their entreaties as they recruited new members. Someone I knew from the Peace Corps had disappeared into a cult in South America called "Children of God." And there was Rev. Sun Myung Moon, who professed to be the reincarnation of Jesus Christ, and was world-renowned for seeking converts ("Moonies") into his organization. His group had started by preying on the college students who were rampantly protesting the Vietnam War. Promising inner peace and a way to transform the world, the Moonies eventually gained thousands of converts in the United States as well as globally. Silva Mind Control Method, another self-help movement using brain-training, was also big at the time. L. Ron Hubbard's *Dianetics* had become a best seller, and his Church of Scientology had sprung from its aftermath, trolling for converts among those searching.

Perhaps my saturation in *est* techniques had served to further desensitize me. As an undergraduate, I had been exposed to the technique called the Synanon Game. My English professor used our class to create an encounter group rather than having us write essays or papers as in a traditional class.

We sat in a circle confronting one another's beliefs and behaviors along the Synanon format. My bizarre experiences and frantic searching had opened the door for me to walk into Solar's Program.

SIXTEEN

I had read numerous books on Tibetan Monks who sequestered themselves in caves for purification and spiritual awareness, as well as accounts of others in monasteries, searching for the Divine and the meaning of life. Accordingly, Solar's prescription for spiritual growth did not seem odd to me.

"Your first step will be to get rid of the material possessions associated with your past. This will free you of the negative emotions and encumbrances that cause your depression. To renew yourself, you need to start withdrawing from the world and all associations with your failures and pain. I've rented a house with another woman who's interested in The Program. You can live there, and for a time separate from your past—your family and everything you've known. This will give you a fresh start so you can free yourself of your negative emotions, grow in spiritual awareness, and be closer to God."

It sounded like a golden opportunity. Temporarily retreating from the world for total immersion in meditative thought without outside distractions—like the monks in their caves—it seemed ideal.

Believing this was my path to salvation, I quit my jobs and started preparing for this new life. My grandmother agreed to purchase back the property she had given me—where I had planned to develop a spiritual healing center of my own.

That will need to wait. Besides, Solar told me we're going to build one together. Now I have a way to pay back the money Gramma loaned me, and to pay off my business debts. I can start fresh—I'm ready to join Solar's Program.

As directed, I managed to sell or give away most of my personal property—keeping only my most prized possessions: gifts given me by family members, books, artwork, and poetry. Solar had warned that my Colombian treasures, although beloved to me, would also have to go. Thinking that my grandmother would like some of them, and my cousins would want to buy the others, I took them to her home.

"I'm going into retreat to find myself and a deeper connection with God, Gramma. I've been searching for a way to spread the message and experiences I came back from South America with, and this seems to be a way to do all of that."

"I hope you're doing the right thing by giving your land back to me and pursuing this. Please be careful," she cautioned with a worried look.

"I will be."

To finalize my readiness for The Program, I wanted to personally pay off my landscaping debts. Solar insisted on going with me. Parking at my first destination, a vendor I had used for landscaping materials, I started to get out of the car. "Why don't you let me do this for you?" Solar suggested.

"Because I want to thank them for their support. Many of them were really helpful in teaching me aspects of landscaping."

After paying a couple of them, I drove to the office of my accountant. Solar followed me inside.

"What exactly are you going to do?" my accountant asked.

"I'm going into a spiritual retreat called the Program."

"I worked with the Crow Indians, serving as their medicine man. I have helped many awaken spiritually," Solar chimed in.

My accountant thought for a moment, and the dismay on her face softened.

"Well, I wish you well."

As we walked back to my car, Solar said, "You should just let me do this; you don't want to be out in the public any more than you have to. You're delaying the benefits of your spiritual retreat. Why don't you let me handle the rest of these payments? We can even use my checkbook so you don't have to wait for your checks to clear before closing your checking account."

"I guess that makes sense," I agreed, and gave him the balance of the money destined for my bills. I watched Solar write out each check and stuff them into envelopes I had stamped and addressed.

"I'll mail them tomorrow," he said. "We need to get you moved first. Let's go pick up the rest of your things from the condo."

On August 4, 1979, we climbed the stairs to my condo. It was a typical warm summer day, with a cool breeze brushing over us. My condo was a few miles away from Ocean Beach, in San Diego. A jet screamed overhead as I led the way into my room. Empty boxes lay on the floor, waiting for the rest of my possessions. "Don't do it all, I want to help you," he had insisted.

I was packing my clothes when Solar walked over to my watercolor paintings and yanked one off the wall, sending the pins holding it flying everywhere. I watched in horror as he shredded the paper.

"Hey, I painted that! I don't want those destroyed; they're mine," I protested.

"They're part of your past—what has dragged you down. Either you want to stay stuck, or you want to grow spiritually—and you need to let go of all of this to grow." He ripped another one from the wall, its brightly colored remnants littering the floor.

I stood frozen and confused as Solar walked over to my books. Picking up one, he ripped it apart, tossing mangled pages onto the pile.

"Those are my books! I don't want them destroyed! I planned on taking them with me!"

"You need to be free of these old influences so you can grow spiritually. It's a small sacrifice for what I'm offering you."

In shock, I watched him walk to another shelf.

"Those are my poetry journals," I said. "I wrote that stuff. Please don't destroy those things; I want to save them. They're special to me; some I even brought back from Colombia."

In one furious movement, he grabbed and tore them up. "Anything from your past, especially Colombia, has to go!" His huge hands mulched everything he could find, tossing it all onto the growing mound on the floor.

"I can't believe you're doing this. I wish you'd stop and listen to me. Those are all important to me."

"Either you enter The Program and fulfill your mission, or you're going to fail in that, too. You need to trust that I know what I'm doing."

I sighed and dropped my head. *He's right. I have failed. This is my last chance. I just wish it didn't hurt so much.*

After surveying the carnage, he asked, "Do you have anything else stored anyplace? What about your father's home? Didn't you say you had some stuff there?"

"Just some books, and my yearbooks from high school."

"All that has to go too. Let's go there now so we can complete this phase."

I drove toward the ranch, ignoring the growing dissonance within me. *Remember that book you read about the woman who did a walkabout in Australia. The aboriginals burned her possessions, including the clothes she was wearing. . .*

As we inched up the hill to my father's house, I attempted to rationalize Solar's behavior, but the pain of my losses left a vacuous space inside me. Solar softly voiced assurances. "Remember, you wanted to get closer to God. In order to grow and attain spiritual awakening, you need to let go of your past—all the old stuff that has held you back. This is your fresh start!"

I watched without protesting as Solar dumped the remaining artifacts of my life into the trash bin, but my gut gnawed at me.

Solar looked in my direction. "You'll be able to recreate yourself when you're free of the patterns that led you to the frustration and hopelessness you were struggling with when I met you. Your rebirth will come with my

Program. I'll instruct and guide you to enlightenment. You need to trust me; I know what I'm doing."

He insisted on driving us back to San Diego. "The sooner you begin The Program, the sooner you'll accomplish all that you've wanted to do. Letting me drive will allow you to start slowly withdrawing from society so you can complete your mission."

I relinquished my car to him, and he drove us to a neighborhood in La Mesa, just outside San Diego. Creeping along Mohawk Street, he pulled into a gravel driveway and stopped in front of a stucco home, humbly like all the rest in that neighborhood. I would learn that Solar had chosen a location familiar to his history and family: we were not far from where his mother—whom I had yet to meet—lived.

He unlocked the front door and led the way into a modest living room with a kitchen looking out on the back yard. "This is where we're going to live for now. Leave your things in the car and I'll bring them in later." He walked to another door. "You'll be doing your spiritual retreat in this room."

I walked into the master bedroom. My sanctuary was smaller than my room in the condo, with a petite bathroom off to the side. There was a closet beyond a simple desk and chair to my left. The only window in the room had filtered light coming from the street outside. I breathed out a sigh of resignation as I sized up my new domain, so different from the sweeping panoramic view of trees and green walkways I had given up.

SEVENTEEN

The transition from the condo to the house on Mohawk Street was swift and total.

"To do this correctly, you must not linger with goodbyes or let your friends or family know where you are, or why you're doing this. You don't want people from your past contacting you. You must trust me. I know what I'm doing."

My process of contemplation and purification had begun.

The second day into my retreat, after Solar left me alone to transcribe his readings, I remembered the custom-made leather jacket I had left in the entryway closet at the condo. Intending to give it to a friend, I was glad it had been forgotten, or Solar would have destroyed it when he was trashing everything else. I had a near-photographic memory then, and remembered my friend's telephone number. *I'll just go find a phone booth and call* her.

"Hi, Marta, this is San Li. I'm in a 'non-interaction' program with Solar and forgot to give you my leather jacket. It's hanging in the hall closet at the condo. I wanted you to have it. Bye." I walked the short distance back to the house and returned to the bedroom.

Later, Solar walked in. "What kind of a day did you have? Did you speak to anyone or leave the room?"

I thought his questions rather odd, but explained my phone call. He blanched.

"You will never reach a higher level of spiritual awareness if you continue to fraternize with the people you used to know. You're not supposed to leave the house or talk to anyone, remember? The length of your isolation will determine how quickly you advance."

Surprised, I meekly replied, "Oh. I didn't know that I wasn't supposed to leave. I just wanted to make sure Marta got my jacket was all."

Solar lowered his voice. "Connecting to people you've known in your past will prolong the process. Your purification is only possible if you refrain from contacting your family as well as all your friends. You are to discipline your mind by not allowing it to drift into thinking about people and places before this time, right now. This is all there is. You are not to think of or remember anyone from before you met me. That is all now your past, and you are not to think of it. This will help you develop your mind to become more spiritual."

"Okay," I said, "but it seems difficult. All I do is sit here transcribing your tapes all day. I'm hungry, and it's hard not to think of the people I've known and loved all my life."

"Are you saying this is too hard? Are you going to give up so easily? Will this be another failure to add to your list of failures? What about your mission?"

"I'm not saying it's too hard; I'm just saying it's not easy. I'll try harder."

"You'd better, because it doesn't look like you've done very well so far."

A few days after this conversation, Solar lectured me as we drove toward what would prove to be my last visit with my family for quite a while.

"You need to tell them you won't be seeing them for a long time. As part of your purification, I want you to look down at the floor and avoid eye contact with them. Tell them your mouth is sore from dental work so they won't engage you in conversation."

When we showed up at my grandmother's house, my aunt Louise was visiting. I announced: "I'm withdrawing from the public and the world for a while to enter a spiritual retreat. I'm on a quest to fulfill my mission."

"How long will this take?" my aunt asked.

"As long, as it takes," Solar interrupted.

"Yes," I said. "I want to develop my relationship with God."

Since I wasn't supposed to look at anyone, I quickly became quite an authority on what the floors looked like as I struggled to distract myself from the pain of not being able to look at my beloved grandmother and dear aunt.

The same scenario was repeated at my mother's home. Holding my hand, Solar steered me wherever we went.

My non-interaction program had begun in earnest.

A steady stream of people paraded through the house on Mohawk Street to visit Solar or have a psychic reading. Crow Indians came one time, and Solar allowed me to meet them. They were from Montana, where Solar had been the reservation's medicine man. As we sat together, one started to speak, then broke into silent tears as he bowed his head and shared how troubled he had felt with information Solar had given him while serving in that capacity. The others joined in with their concerns, and during a lull in their conversation, Solar ushered me back into our bedroom. He never discussed this interaction or elaborated on what the Crow Indians were so upset about.

Solar insisted that I no longer leave the room as part of my purification. I ate breakfast and lunch in the room, and used the bathroom there. The window curtains were to remain closed, and I was not to open the door under any circumstances except for an emergency. Solar was gone all day, and when he returned in the evening, he always asked for a report on my daily activities.

"Did you leave the room today or look out the windows?"

"No."

"How many times did you think of someone from your past today?"

With unwavering honesty, I confessed my mind's weaknesses. "I had fleeting memories of the ranch."

"Did you think of anyone in particular?"

"I thought about my grandmother today, and loved ones I used to see on the ranch."

"What do you think you're doing here? You're supposed to be gaining mastery over your thoughts. I've asked you to do a simple task of not remembering anyone in your past, and you can't do that. There are some very dark things you've done in your past, and I suggest that you stop remembering all that evilness."

Within a month I had become Solar's maid and concubine as he added servicing his ever-present sexual needs to my responsibilities. My own sexual compulsivity paled in comparison to his libido. His appetites were as large as his girth, leaving no room for my choices, needs, or desires. He judged masturbation harshly, and preferred to be effortlessly satisfied.

Since these behaviors were incorporated into his Program for spiritual enlightenment, I believed they were all necessary for my spiritual growth and serving God. The readings I had transcribed were account after account of people travelling back through their lifetimes, ending at the center of a spinning disk where their sense of self disappeared into a bliss-filled peace, transcending all space, time and fears. At the center of this experience they had followed Solar's prompt that he was *The Source* or their "Creator." "God's God" was how Solar described himself.

I believed it all, thinking he must have special powers to facilitate readings where people went back to their "point of creation."

In my trance, I failed to recognize other things, such as the fact that he lacked a sense of humor, and could not acknowledge vulnerability or laugh at his own imperfections. The last time I attempted a display of humor was when I carefully placed his pajamas as a silhouette in the position where he always lay on the bed with his feet over the edge. It made him angry.

He often derided me for my pleasures and preferences: my dietary choices, my wardrobe, my speech. He took control over all those aspects, down to the kind of toothbrush I used, insisting I use a hard-bristled brush. When I made the bed in the morning or cleaned up after him, I was criticized. To avoid his berating, I stopped doing these chores even though he was quite messy.

Every evening, I was interrogated about my thoughts. Each time I trespassed the boundary of "my past," I confessed, and he berated and shamed me for my admissions of guilt for a wandering mind.

After sharing with Solar that I wanted to lose the extra pounds I had gained, I received one granola bar for breakfast and another for lunch. Although I felt weak from lack of nutrition, I was determined to master his Program and leave it spiritually expanded and closer to God.

I was supposed to be developing a stronger connection with God during my alone time in the room; Solar informed me that this would help me in spreading the message I had been given. However, after I finished transcribing his readings, he asked me to help him compile the books he was writing. Happy for the distraction, I organized the pages he gave me, some of them obviously torn out of other books.

"But that's someone else's information."

"Don't question me; I know what I'm doing."

I can't imagine how that's going to be okay.

I'm so hungry.

I wish I could go outside.

I want something nutritious to eat.

Look at how much weight I've lost, my clothes are hanging on me now.

Everything changed in the Mohawk Street house. Before joining his Program, I had told him "I haven't eaten meat for years, and prefer to not even cook it in my pots and pans."

"We'll see about that," he had responded. He only purchased the food he liked, and our tastes could not have been more opposite. His favorite food was from McDonald's or Jack in the Box. One night, instead of rushing me as I scurried around the kitchen to prepare dinner, he brought me a plain cheeseburger.

"Here, eat this."

I glanced at the limp sandwich, oil stains on its wrapper. "No, thanks. I don't eat those."

"Suit yourself. Don't say that I didn't offer you food," he managed to say while gulping down his appreciably larger Big Mac.

After inhaling the burger, he grabbed mine and wasted no time in devouring it as well. "You need to kiss your vegetarian ways goodbye. It doesn't matter what you eat; what's important is that you learn how to master your body. This is teaching you mind over matter."

"What about you?" I dared to ask. "Aren't you also supposed to be learning how to master your body?"

"Ha! I don't answer to anyone. I was sent here to help light workers like you to get their acts together so they can escape this illusion. You're going to learn that it's *all* an illusion, and it doesn't matter what you put into your body; it's all in your mind. I've already mastered mind over body."

"But I'm always hungry, and have lost so much weight my clothes are hanging on me."

"You said you wanted to lose weight, didn't you? Besides, the body doesn't matter; it's what's in your mind that counts."

That night my belly hurt and growled, and since hunger was my constant companion, I started eating what was given me. Solar had a point, after all. The concept of "mastering my bodily needs" was not new to me, since I had read books by Lobsang Rampa and others on how Buddhist monks in Tibet prepared for spiritual retreats by reducing their meals to once a day to diminish worldly distractions so they could focus on their meditations and spiritual growth. *I can handle this, because it will help me develop a disciplined mind and become more spiritually aware. With a better connection to God, I'll be guided as to how to deliver my message to the world.*

Every day brought a new challenge. "Today I want you to send a letter to your mother. To facilitate your withdrawal from the world, write what I say:

Dear Mom,

Thanks for the card and note. I really had a beautiful birthday.

I want you to know that I'm fine and am working with Larry [Solar] on his second book. I want you to quit worrying about me because I'm all right and will continue to be.

I have depended on you for too many years, mostly for your approval of what I was doing in my life. I can no longer live my life seeking the approval of others. I need to release this self-destructive habit and am doing so. I am releasing the need to have your approval for what I'm doing.

I now ask you to release me as I do you, to live your life as you wish, to release me to myself to live my life how I see fit. In other words, I'm releasing any worry or concern about you. I'm releasing you to you. Please do the same with me.

I won't be in touch with you as often as I used to be but know that I am all right and okay.

Love,

Sandy

Hmm, that's okay. Mom and I weren't getting along anyway.

The memory of a recent and painful event tore through my mind: how shocked I had been to meet my mother's new boyfriend on a recent visit with her. When he excused himself to use the bathroom, I had accosted her.

"How *old* is he?"

"Thirty. Why?"

"You must be kidding! He's my age!"

"I can do whatever I choose to in my life."

"Yeah, that's right, Alice! I forgot. Bye!" and I had stomped out, feeling furious and ashamed. *He was so young—nervously picking his fingers as we met.*

Blinking away the flashback, I handed the letter to Solar.

"What's the address?"

I gave it to him, and with letter in hand he left, saying, "Don't think about her anymore. Leave all this to me, and stop thinking of your family and the people you knew before meeting me. Remember, they're part of your past and need to be released before you can reinvent yourself."

Solar had commandeered my car, and loved to take us deep into the backcountry where he could watch for UFO's without interference from city lights. The first time he tossed our trash out the window instead of getting out and throwing it away properly, I protested.

"I can do anything I want to," he said, "and you have no right to criticize me. That's why they have help, to clean up the parking lot."

"Huh? That's littering; it's against the law."

"I'm above the law. I came here to this illusion to help you with your mission and these rules do not apply to me. You want to get closer to God and have help in spreading your message, don't you?"

"Yes."

"Then don't question me or what I do. I've been sent here to help you and the others who have been called. I know what I'm doing, so don't question me. Okay?"

"Okay," I answered, trying to understand his logic.

Everything in my life became subject to his judgment.

"Did you do anything you weren't supposed to do?" he asked during my nightly interrogation.

"I thought of my family briefly."

"Are you so stupid and evil you cannot control your mind and not think of them? How hard is it to leave them where they belong? They're in your past. Stop thinking of them! Why is it so difficult for you to leave your past alone? Maybe you're not ready to leave your evil past behind."

"I'll try harder tomorrow. I'm sorry I failed again."

The next day represented another failure. "I cannot believe you're so stupid that you can't accomplish this simple task. Did anything happen today?"

"Well, I heard squeals of laughter and the sounds of a small child running about the house."

"Squeals of laughter?"

"You know, I heard a child having fun and running around."

"Were you purposely listening?"

"No. It was so loud; it was hard to miss."

"That's Peggy, who lives in the other part of the house. You are not to pay attention to any sounds you hear. She's interested in The Program, but isn't ready to start it just yet."

I had not been introduced to them, but once had caught a glimpse of a little girl with wavy blond hair as she ran around the corner.

"Okay," Solar said, "now get to the kitchen. I'm hungry. I need you to prepare our dinner, but be quick about it. You don't want anyone to see you, or to run into Peggy. How long will it take for you to fix dinner?"

"Everything takes some time."

"I bought some fish sticks. You can heat them in the oven and make sandwiches with them."

"Fish sticks?"

"You don't know what they are?"

"No, I can't say that I do. I've never had them."

"You've got to be kidding. Everybody eats fish sticks."

"Well, I haven't."

"Too bad. That's all we have, so get going. I'll have two sandwiches, and make yourself one. Put melted cheese on mine, and you can have cheese on yours if you want. Hurry up! You don't want to interrupt The Program by getting caught in the kitchen if anyone comes over. Make it quick!"

Lucky Peggy, she gets to do what she wants. I'll be there soon enough. Got to stop thinking of my family. Don't think about them, don't picture them—stop thinking. I don't even know what day of the week it is. Solar said my isolation and deprivation are necessary to master what controlled me before and led me to such despair. Well, it will be worth it—at least I can share my mission then.

The intensity with which Solar queried me about my daily transgressions grew more oppressive every day, as did the criticism for my failures and his insistence that I defer always to his needs over mine.

"My non-interaction program represents confinement only long enough to help you let go of your ego—the negative choices you have made," he explained.

But it's not fair that I don't get to voice my preferences; I don't like being confined and having you tell me what to do all the time.

"Are you listening to me? You need to let go of your negative past. Do you understand that this is what you asked for, what you wanted in order to get to know God better and accomplish your mission?"

"Yes."

"Then I don't want to ever hear you complain—do you understand? I know what I'm doing."

Slowing my progress in the Program was my constant struggle to disconnect with familiar people, especially my grandmother. She had always been a healing presence in the chaos of my life, and still lived on the ranch I loved so much. However, each time my mind meandered into memories of life experiences or people I had known, I encountered Solar's emotional outbursts.

One night after I admitted I had thought about my grandmother, Solar exploded.

"Can't you do the one thing I ask for? Nothing existed before you met me. I am the only person you've ever known. Do you understand?"

"I'm sorry, I'm such a failure. I'm trying really, hard. Even though I'm doing it less and less, people, facts, and events continue to seep into my consciousness. God, please give me a blank mind," I pleaded out loud, and started banging my head against the wall.

"STOP!"

The stage was set for me to separate totally from reality. Yelling and insulting me had become Solar's way of communicating with me; physical abuse would be next.

One night about three months into my retreat, Solar announced: "We're going into the backcountry to look for UFOs again."

Several times in the past we had witnessed erratic lights swirling about at rapid speeds and moving in directions beyond the capabilities of modern aircraft. More often, however, he would spot a light and claim it was a UFO when I suspected it was from a plane or satellite. That was how it was on this night. Frustrated, Solar started the car. "Let's go, we're obviously not going to see anything tonight."

Back home in the driveway, I let my eyes drift away from the ground as I got out of the car. Solar ushered me into the bedroom, and once the door was closed he wheeled on me.

"I saw you looking around! You aren't supposed to look at anyone or anything. You're breaking The Program! I thought you wanted to succeed, but you can't do that if you keep breaking The Program! Don't you dare refute me! I saw you!"

In bed that night, he pulled my hand onto his belly—his signal I was to "rub his stomach." This was how he had instructed me to arouse him before giving him fellatio.

I pulled my hand away. *You wrongly accused me. I'm not going to rub your—*

SLAP! His hand hit the side of my face.

I had never been struck as an adult. Anger flared in me as a flashback raced through my mind: me sitting in the back seat with a friend as my mother turned around and slapped me. "That's for sassing me."

Humiliated and angry; I had said nothing. And I said nothing now.

Days faded into one another as I rushed to prepare Solar's meals, got steered wherever we went, and remained isolated in the bedroom, struggling not to think of anything familiar.

"How many times did you think of your past?" he still asked every night upon returning home.

I would not lie. "I thought of the ranch and my grandmother. I wondered how she's doing."

"You're not supposed to have those thoughts! When are you going to learn to let that all go?"

"I'm trying."

"Well, it's not good enough. You need to STOP THINKING! STOP THINKING OF YOUR PAST! DO YOU UNDERSTAND?"

Tirade over, he plopped onto the end of the waterbed and fell asleep with his feet dangling over the edge. I sat softly weeping in my chair.

"What's the matter?" a soft and distinctly different voice asked. Solar was snoring, and I blinked as I peered over at him, then looked around the room. The corners were dimly lit, but visible enough to reveal their emptiness.

"I asked, what's the matter?" the voice said again.

"Who are you?" I whispered.

"I am the Flame," was the gentle response. "Try to understand, he is only human."

"What?"

At that moment Solar snorted and woke up. I never mentioned the conversation to him, not certain whether he was faking the voice, or if it genuinely was a different entity speaking through him. There were so many unanswered questions in my mind; this new one just collided with them as I tried to accommodate yet another enigma.

The next day, as I sat in solitude once again, my thoughts drifted to the woman living in the house with us. *I envy you, Peggy, whoever you are, with your freedom to come and go as you please. Oh, that must be her daughter I hear. I wonder what they're like. Where did Peggy come from? Does she work? She's gone all day; I wonder what she does to support herself. As a matter of fact, how does Solar support us? I'm going to ask him when he comes home.*

After his usual interrogation and shaming of me, I risked the question. "How are you supporting us? You said you haven't had many readings lately. Aren't you worried about money?"

He stiffened. "LEAVE ALL THE THINKING TO ME! Let ME worry about the money; let ME worry about the outside world. YOUR job is to STOP THINKING of YOUR PAST and the outside world. None of that exists for you right now! JUST TRUST ME!"

"Okay. . ." Relieved that someone else was in control of and worrying about money, I did not ask again.

After I'd been in the Program for about four months, Solar opened the door and nudged a pregnant woman into the room.

"This is Peggy. She's joining you in The Program. Don't speak to one another unless it's an emergency. You don't want to slow down your progress. You are to help Peggy and take care of her if she needs anything. She's carrying my child."

"Okay." My initial elation at the thought of having company soured when Solar announced we could not communicate. He closed the door behind him, and Peggy found the chair he had brought in for her. I stole a glance in her direction, observing in that visual flash a fair-complexioned blonde with long hair. She was about my height but more slightly built. Her pleasant face was gentle but passive-looking.

I wonder where her little girl is. I hope nothing happened to her; she seemed so cute and happy.

As with most information, it would take years to learn that Solar had convinced Peggy to surrender her daughter to be raised by relatives. He had argued that Peggy needed to be free to enter his Program so she could become enlightened and spiritually aware. Besides, she was carrying *his* child.

For several days after Peggy joined The Program, Solar busied himself in the house outside our bedroom. I could hear the all-too-familiar sounds of destruction, and figured Peggy's possessions were going the same way mine had months earlier. I had resigned myself to the sacrifice I felt necessary for my enlightenment, but spent much of my early time in The Program mourning the loss of my belongings. Even though I was not supposed to remember what they were, I could feel the pain from losing them.

Shortly after all the noise stopped, Solar opened the door and said, "We're moving to Sedona, Arizona, where I'm going to build the Mother Light Center you wanted to create. It will be a place where light workers from all over the world can come for refuge and spiritual awareness. Peggy, you said that's what you wanted, right?"

"Yes," she softly responded.

"Sandy, what about you? This is the opportunity you've been waiting for to accomplish your mission!"

"Yes," I eagerly agreed. *Finally, it's going to be worth it, a ray of sunshine through all this dark routine.*

EIGHTEEN

In January of 1980 we packed up my car for the move to Sedona. "Sandy, you and Peggy are not to look around while we're outside. Do you understand?"

"Yes," was our simultaneous reply.

"We're going to spend some time at Giant Rock before heading to Arizona. Any objections to that?"

"No," in unison again.

"There's a hotel there, and I need to use that energy for building the Light Center. It's near the location of the UFO convention. Sandy, you and I were at the last one— even though you didn't know I was there. Now, don't go thinking of that just because I mentioned it. Do you understand?"

"Yes, I won't."

"Don't think of anything and don't listen to the radio or say anything until we get there."

"Okay."

Several hours later, we pulled to a stop and Solar ordered us out.

"Follow me. This is Giant Rock; it's a power vortex. Van Tassel built his airport here for the UFO conventions because of its energy."

Solar had driven us to a location just west of Joshua Tree in California's extensive desert. The air in Yucca Valley was fresh and crisp as our footsteps crunched in the sand. Solar's right hand gripped a massive shepherd's staff, which he thrust forward as he walked. Leading the way onto a well-trodden path, he descended flagstone steps into a space underneath this massive boulder called "Giant Rock." It was deep enough to accommodate us standing upright. I could see how there was enough room for someone to live there, but all that was left was a hollowed-out shell burrowed underneath the rock. (It has since been filled in.)

Solar tapped his chest-high staff three times onto the stone floor. "I proclaim, as Solar, that I will build a Mother Light Center in Sedona, Arizona. I am the reincarnation of Moses and call upon all the forces in the universe to support me. And so, it is!"

Stomp, stomp, stomp. He thumped his staff on the floor again.

He had paid for a week's stay at the hotel, and once our encampment had begun, he shoved a piece of notebook paper in my face.

"Write what I tell you."

> Dear Mom,
>
> We've been doing a lot of traveling since leaving San Diego. I am really happy and am enjoying myself.
>
> All of us are working on the fourth book—soon to be finished.
>
> I hope all is well with you and that you are taking care of yourself.
>
> Thanks again for sending my birth certificate. Here is the original as I mentioned I would return.
>
> Take care of yourself.
>
> Love,
>
> Sandy and Larry

The three of us stayed at the Giant Rock Motel in Landers, California— deep in the dessert and close to its namesake. Pointing to the chairs in our room where he wanted us to sit, Solar locked the door and closed the curtains after peering outside for some time. Turning around, he took off his shirt, dropped his pants on the floor and, in jockey shorts, plopped himself on a bed.

"Sandy, did you know I have a master's degree in criminal psychology?"

"No, I didn't."

"Yes, and because of it, I know when people are not telling the truth. So, I want you to tell the truth. Tell Peggy and me how many people you've had sex with."

"Excuse me? Why do you need to know that?"

"DON'T QUESTION ME! THERE'S ALWAYS A HIGHER PURPOSE FOR EVERYTHING I DO! You need to confess this to be free of your past. Now, how many people have you slept with?"

"I guess about fifty."

"Fifty? Are you sure?"

"Yes, I guess." *How should I know? I've never counted.*

"Not 'you guess.' Either you did or you didn't. Yes or no?"

"Yes." *What's the big deal?*

"You're a slut and a whore! Peggy, did you know that Sandy answered the door in the nude?"

"That was only because I knew it was you. Don't you remember that my roommate and I didn't wear clothes inside our condo?"

"Quiet! Don't contradict me! I didn't ask you to bring up anybody from the past, did I? I ought to beat you for that."

"I don't understand," I mumbled.

"There's nothing to understand! You're a fucking whore and a failure! You were a slut before I met you, and you're lucky I rescued you from your fate! You were suicidal, weren't you?"

"Yes."

"Like I said, a failure and a whore." He turned to Peggy and in a booming voice asked, "Did you know that Sandy had sex with men *and* women?"

"No," she demurely replied.

"She was a real slut. And now I'm trying to help her purify herself and leave her filthy past behind."

His tirade continued, disclosing all that I was ashamed of and had confided in him while he comforted me. Once so uniquely validating of my experiences, he now denounced them as despicable acts worthy of shame and disgust.

Peggy got the same treatment when Solar focused on her, berating her for her life choices and turning what she had told him against her. We had both disclosed to him early in the relationship our deepest regrets, surrendering to the comfort of his compassion and encouragement.

"I'm trying to help you get closer to God. You were both failures before I met you. Look at what you did with your lives before I met you! You're both pathetic."

"I'm sorry I did all that," I offered.

"I don't know why I bother with you two; you're both so negative. It's going to take a lot to release you from your past so you can achieve your goals."

"I'll do whatever it takes," I said.

"You couldn't even spread the message you were given! That proves you're incompetent, a failure, and just plain evil."

I guess he's right. I couldn't even get my family to embrace my message, and I left the people I loved working with in Peace Corps before my tour was finished. I ended up in debt from my landscaping business and was asked to leave est.

I'm not going to fail again.

Solar interrupted my thoughts. "I'm the only one who can help you now. Trust me; I know what I'm doing."

The air conditioner groaned in the background, shoving stale air into the room, masking Solar's raging voice.

NINETEEN

After a week of berating us at the Giant Rock Motel, Solar moved our trio into a modern, one-bedroom condo in what was called Grasshopper Flats. Now, in Sedona, he left us alone each day to work in his metaphysical bookstore, which he named Seventh Heaven.

I never saw it, since we were not allowed to go anywhere—the outside world did not exist for us.

Both Peggy and I had shared the vision of creating a place of love and peace where people could study and expand their consciousness. Solar said this place would be the "Mother Light Center," and the Program was the initiation we needed before we could build it.

My personal nemesis continued being "the past," and I was punished for each passage I made into it. My purification, my salvation, would come only when I no longer thought about or interacted with the past—when I had total mastery over my mind. My thoughts, words—spoken and written—and even my dreams were now strictly regulated.

Solar was the only person I communicated with directly. I was not allowed to read any mail sent to me, and my correspondence to my family was conveyed through robotic, tersely written postcards Solar dictated and sent sporadically. He did not want my family calling the authorities, and had me write the postcards to placate them. The sparse correspondence also served to delude me into believing that soon I would re-emerge as a new and enlightened being, totally cleansed and able to march forth to save family and the world from imminent destruction. But sending the postcards reconnected me with what Solar called the "past" or my "dark side," and had dire consequences for me every time. My "past" was supposedly capable of making me "possessed" since it was all deemed negative and unworthy of being referenced or remembered.

Physical abuse followed writing the postcards to "clear" me of the "demon possession" my past represented.

> Dear Family,
>   I am fine. I am editing Solar's books and enjoying myself very much.
> Love,
> Sandy

"I'm only sending them to prevent your family from calling the authorities. You are not to think of them after this. They do not exist for you now! Do you understand?"

"Yes," I replied.

He slapped my face. "I said stop thinking about them!"

He slapped the other side of my face, and then again. Shocked, I escaped even deeper into my trance.

While we were living at Grasshopper Flats, Solar put me in charge of the household chores and cooking. Very pregnant, Peggy was responsible for sewing him a new wardrobe of shirts. Since I had known him, his stomach had continued to grow. To hide his girth, he started wearing oversized corduroy shirts with cowl hoods and embroidered symbols on the front. Made entirely by hand, they were tailored by Peggy to Solar's whims. Since no one wore hoodies in the 1980s, Solar resembled Rasputin or some science-fiction character.

I continued assisting him in compiling his books. He wrote three in all—although much of the information in them was plagiarized. Rejected long ago by my father, and estranged from my mother, I craved love and was vulnerable to Solar's occasional compliments. He would offer them until I had regained some modicum of confidence, and then unexpectedly eviscerate me for the smallest of infractions.

"You are the only one I can trust with my books. You're doing such a good job of compiling all the information. Now go fix us some dinner. I want fish sticks with the usual. Hurry up."

As I scurried around trying to feed his demands, Solar's impatience found fault with my attempts to please him. "How much longer?"

"Well, the oven isn't heated enough to put in the fish sticks."

"Put them in anyway; I'm starving."

"I don't think they'll turn out okay if I do. The directions say that the oven needs to be pre-heated to 475. It's now only 325—not even close yet."

"Don't argue with me, do as I say."

Several minutes later I served his fish stick sandwiches as requested.

"Aaaaah! These are awful; they're not even fully cooked! Can't you do anything right? I can't eat these! Fix some more and *you* eat these."

"I tried to let you know the oven needed more time to heat up before putting them in."

"Don't refute me. Hurry up and fix my sandwiches, and you better not give me raw fish sticks this time!"

My sense of self and reality became increasingly malleable. The paranormal experiences that had driven me into his lair were not exempt. Surviving the Program became the goal I clung to, as I believed the sacrifice was necessary for finding God.

"You are not to think about what happened to you in South America. Everything that happened to you there was negative."

"What about what I did in Peace Corps? That was helping people, especially the starving women and children I worked with."

Thud. The palm of his hand hit the side of my head, sending me backwards.

"That's for going into your past. How dare you refute what I'm saying, and how dare you mention something from your past? I ought to beat you for that."

"I'm sorry."

"You're lucky this time. You are not to think of ANYTHING before you met me. Do you understand?"

"Yes."

"Your mission is to stay here and complete the Program. Do you understand?"

"Yes."

"What?"

"Yes, I understand."

"Good, so now we're clear. Stay out of your past. Now what is your Mission?"

"To finish the Program."

"That's right, and nothing more. Nothing exists before you met me, do you understand?

"Yes."

With constant repetition reinforced with threats or actual battery, his words became my truth.

Peggy and I spent our days together in the bedroom, not talking or inter-acting with one another. The waterbed we all shared filled most of the room, which measured only about 300 square feet. Although only dim light filtered through the room, Peggy sat in her corner sewing. I was usually at a small table where I worked on Solar's books and wrote my "accounting"—the required details of the minutia Peggy and I engaged in while Solar was outside of the room, including any thoughts I might have entertained of my past.

One evening, Solar barged in, announcing:

"Your grandmother wrote you a letter. She's worried about you and had a dream you were bitten by a rattlesnake and are in some kind of danger. You need to call her and let her know you're okay. I don't want the authorities coming to our door."

Stretching the phone cord as far as it would go, Solar dragged the phone into the hallway and brought me out of our room to make the call.

"This is what I want you to say: Tell her you're okay and that she doesn't need to worry about you. And that you were *not* bitten by a rattlesnake. Tell her you're helping me edit my books and are very happy. Do you understand? Now repeat back to me what you're going to say."

After parroting my lines back to him several times, I dialed her number. My chest ached as we spoke, but I did not veer from my scripted dialogue even though I desperately wanted to linger in conversation. After delivering my sparse sentences of reassurance, I disconnected and cradled the phone while Solar glared at me.

"Don't think about her, or your family, or you will be forsaking your quest to serve God. Let them go! THEY ARE IN YOUR PAST. LET THEM GO!"

Oh God, I miss them. I hope Bruce is okay. I allowed myself to feel before slinking back to the cave we inhabited. *But I need to sacrifice and prove my worthiness; then they'll love me just like Solar says. I'll save them by sticking with the Program.*

That was the last time I spoke with my grandmother for almost three years.

The day after the spring equinox of 1980 heralded an escalation of the insanity that had become our everyday lives.

"I'm dying; I'm leaving this body," a prostrate Solar gasped from the waterbed. "Aurora gave me moldy cheese; she purposely poisoned me. I told her I was allergic to mold, and she told me afterwards she'd cut off some mold from the cheese she brought to the bookstore."

Gluttonous Solar had probably consumed more than a healthy serving before discovering that the cheese was moldy. As was true for all his bookstore patrons, we never knew or met Aurora. We would not have known about the equinox celebration except for his sickness, which he claimed was fatal.

"You are to bury the placenta when Peggy gives birth," he ordered with labored breathing. "I'm dying."

I held one of his hands, Peggy the other. His chest quit moving. I looked at Peggy, who shrugged.

After a minute, Solar gasped and began breathing normally. Minutes later, still lying down, he spoke in a normal voice.

"The body of Larry just died, and now I am truly the embodiment of Solar. I am no longer impeded by the human personality I was born into."

From that point forward I witnessed the blossoming of a cruel, paranoid, and gravely disturbed individual. He brutalized me physically, emotionally, and mentally worse than ever. He now insisted that while we were sleeping next to him he had to be touched at-all times, and we were strictly forbidden to sleep on our backs "because the dark forces can have sex with you."

References to my past were now responded to with worse and worse physical battery "to cleanse this dark side" out of me.

"What are you thinking? Is that from your past?" If I was caught off guard and not immediately responsive, his fists continued the conversation.

"Don't lie to me!" He would pound on my chest and stomach, beating down the words I might have said in my defense. "You must have been thinking about your past or you would have answered me. I have to discipline you to cleanse your dark side out of you, since you are now demon-possessed."

If I leave, I reminded myself each time, *I'll be turning my back on God.*

On April 4, Solar and I served as midwives for Peggy as she gave birth to his second son, born exactly eight years to the day after his first child by a different mother.

It was my job to cut the umbilical cord and tie it with the sterilized shoelaces I had readied. For this occasion, we sat on the "contaminated" floor, with Peggy lying on a bean-bag chair while Solar and I assisted. I had scrubbed and disinfected the entire bathroom for the delivery. Unlike the rest of the rooms that were never heated or cooled, this room was warm and toasty for this occasion only.

As the baby crowned with matted hair looking very strange, Solar glanced at me in horror. Fortunately, with another push, baby was delivered problem-free. Solar named him "Boy" and announced his birth time as 4:44 in the morning.

Boy joined his mother and me in the seclusion of our room, and thereafter Peggy, like me, was subjected to physical beatings whenever she violated Program rules. Both of us suffered dearly for every diaper mishap and any other issue with having an infant.

Not allowed to leave the room for groceries, we depended on Solar for supplies. He brought home oversized diapers that hung on Boy and constantly leaked.

"What is that liquid running down his leg? Oh, my God! Is that poop? Get him off the bed immediately, he's contaminating the bed."

"Solar, he can't help it. His diapers are way too big for him. We need the right size diapers so the contents don't leak out."

"I told you that's all they had. It's your responsibility to keep him clean and make sure his diapers don't leak. How dare you blame me for the mess he's made?"

Solar rushed over to me, picked me up and tossed me like a rag against the closet doors. "Now do something to clean it up, and don't refute me again. Boy is not to be on the bed until you can keep his diapers from leaking. Do you understand?"

TWENTY

After Boy was delivered, Solar traveled often, leaving the rest of us sequestered inside the condo for days at a time. After one such trip, he walked into our room with an attractive blond woman behind him. "This is Brenda; she also wants to help build the Mother Light Center, and has decided to join me. She's agreed to be in The Program to cleanse and purify herself so she can work with me. She's from Oklahoma and will be staying with you in the room."

A few days later, another woman, also attractive, blond and our same height, joined us. Acacia and her husband, John, had visited Solar while we lived on Mohawk Street in San Diego, and had apparently decided to follow him to Sedona.

There were now four women, including myself, and an infant sharing this small space during the day while he was at his bookstore. Even though the newest two women were married, Solar was sexually involved with all of us, but I never knew how those arrangements were made.

No matter how many of us were there, we never conversed or made eye contact with one another. Solar was the only person we could speak to, and we were forbidden to look directly at him.

"Sandy, you're in charge. Make sure no one makes any mistakes. No talking to each other or leaving the room, and make sure no one gets too close to the toilet. You all need to leave your pasts behind to become purified and able to move forward in your growth and evolution. Remember, this is a necessary step in order for you to leave the illusion. And you cannot do it without me. I am your path to salvation, to your Creator."

My daily accounting now included reporting on the others and their success with the newest taboos. Meals and cleaning were also my responsibility. We were allowed use of the toilet twice a day, and had to keep our clothes from touching it when we did. Needing more visits was considered a "mistake." Dropping something on the floor was also a violation of the Program rules.

The waterbed accommodated only four, so whoever fell from favor with Solar was relegated to sleeping on the cot as punishment. Since I was held responsible for the mistakes anyone made, I usually slept on it. I didn't mind. Despite my unwavering allegiance to Solar, I welcomed the distance from my persecutor.

Apparently, Brenda's husband had followed her to Sedona, bringing her children with him. She had left him a goodbye note, indicating she was leaving with Solar. In Sedona, her husband met with a reporter who wrote a piece about the Mother Light Center Solar was proposing to create. The "Prophet of Doom" article was picked up by the wire services and received limited national coverage. Sedona's local paper ran a version with a picture of Solar in his trademark appearance, shrouded in a hooded shirt with his waist-length hair and long beard. Brenda's parents hired a private investigator, who traced her through the article, and knocked on Solar's door to bring her back home.

We never had contact with either of their husbands, but soon afterward Acacia also abruptly left our room. Solar's only comment on these mysterious women, appearing and then disappearing within days, was, "Anyone who leaves The Program is unworthy. I have over a hundred-people following me. I even have sponsors from the underworld who want to buy refuge. People from California and other states are coming here to follow me."

This seemed plausible. Edgar Cayce and other psychics of that time had predicted that "earth changes" would begin by the year 1984. Many had feared that California would fall into the ocean after the expected monster earthquakes. Capitalizing on fear, Solar promoted these notions, blatantly plagiarizing Cayce and others for material to fill the covers of his own books that touted him as "God's God."

I knew why *I* was with him, but never understood why the others had joined; he was always so full of judgment, anger, and condemnation for anybody who lived with him.

Soon after Brenda left, Solar burst into our room: "We're moving to a house. Before we go, I want you to rip up every one of my books. Here's a box of them; now get started, and don't stop until every single one of them is destroyed. Rip them like this so no one can read them. Do you understand?"

"You want me to do that right now?"

"You heard me!" He left as brusquely as he had come in.

Why would he destroy all his books? I wonder if someone confronted his plagiarism.

We relocated to the master bedroom of a large one-story house in Sedona. After I sealed all the windows with aluminum foil, not even the tiniest speck of light entered. Also mandated was that I clean our living quarters from ceiling to floor for our sequestration.

Unbeknownst to me, after returning home with her family, Brenda and her husband had packed up their belongings and returned to Sedona, settling into a home close to where we had relocated.

Waste excretions had become increasingly repulsive to Solar, who already had issues with bodily functions. Progressively, his infant son's care, feeding, and hygiene needs became functions that Solar reacted to with increasingly restrictive and punitive standards. Most normal activities were increasingly ritualized and challenging.

A load of laundry once took 24 hours to wash and dry. The process began when Solar pounded the outside of the door to our bedroom with his foot. "Get ready, we're going to do the laundry! Don't forget you're going to be weighed."

"Okay." Registering more than one hundred pounds on the scale, even while wearing shoes and soaking wet clothes, would merit a beating. At five feet six, I hovered precariously at ninety-eight pounds.

Launching into high gear, I showered and washed my clothes and put them back on wet. His rules forbade drying off.

"Toilets are contaminated, and so are towels because they hang in the bathroom next to the toilet." We got hurt every time we came too close to a toilet or touched our clothes against one. When any part of my body or clothing came too close to the walls, doorways, cupboards, or the outsides of the washer and dryer, there were consequences. "Your mistakes prove you're demon-possessed. I have to cleanse the dark side from you," Solar would justify during the battering.

Previous mistakes doing laundry had taught me to slick back and pin down my long hair and to roll my shirt-sleeves above my elbows and my pant legs up to my knees. Solar always loaded in the clothes. "They're too dirty for you."

After finishing the first step, I inched away to the side—maintaining a safe distance from the doorway that separated kitchen from laundry room.

"Stop!"

I held my breath. *Bam!* My right temple throbbed; then the left. I staggered, my brain spinning.

"You fall to the floor and I'll kick you and beat you harder! You got too close to the doorframe! Now you're dirty! Go get cleaned up again and wait for me."

The sequence of "mistakes" and "cleansing" and "purification rituals" repeated for several hours, when I painstakingly arrived at being ready to extract the clothes from the washer—without touching them to the white inside rim or center post, or anything else within close-proximity. "Wash up to your elbows" was Solar's rule. I held my forearms up surgeon style and inched towards the washer.

"Stay away from the center post."

"Okay," I whispered. I had already failed several times to extract a cotton blanket without grazing some portion of it against forbidden surfaces or coming too close to the cupboards above. Exhausted, soaking wet, and in pain, I stared at my nemesis.

He shook his head. "I can't believe you're not able to do this simple task. Even a moron could get the clothes out of the washer without touching the dirty parts. AND YOU CAN'T DO THAT! I see why you failed at so many things. Ungrateful bitch! I rescued you from going crazy. It's a wonder your family didn't commit you! You haven't succeeded in doing anything right in your life!"

With silent clarity, I snapped awake. "This is insanity! Enough is enough! I'm leaving."

"They'll lock you in an asylum and throw away the key. Look at how you're dressed! You have no money, no place to go, and your clothes are soaking wet."

"It doesn't matter!" I slogged toward the door, puffy eyes straining to focus. It was dark outside—probably three in the morning. Daylight had been shining through the kitchen windows when we started.

Solar jumped in front of me: "If you leave, you turn your back on God and condemn your soul to burn in hell forever! Everyone in your family will burn along with you and you'll prove just how evil you really are!"

I stopped, frozen and mute. *I do have to complete the Program so my family will love me and I can find God. How can I possibly risk condemning them to eternal damnation?* The fierce pounding of my heart beckoned me toward reality, but I wrestled down its call. *I cannot deny God or sacrifice my commitment. I cannot fail again.*

Locking away this self with her brief awareness, I retreated into the trance.

Standing in front of the washer, I lowered both hands inside and slowly rolled and twisted the blanket into a long tube so I could remove and safely place it inside the dryer. Holding both ends tightly, I lifted the beast, bending it, and myself, to conform . . . for my survival.

Solar rarely frequented our living space, but when he did spend a night with us, it was always a painful experience. He would hurt one of us—usually me—but his infant son and Peggy were not exempt from beatings.

"I'm coming in for the night" was the announcement that meant we were soon to be at risk. After showering in the bathroom next to ours, he would kick our door to be let in. When I opened the door, I had to move quickly into position beside Peggy, who held Boy in her arms, standing as far from the door as we could. Solar walked immediately into our bathroom to resume his rituals before he felt "clean enough" to spend the night.

In the morning, he would ask, "Did you remember your dreams?" Whether awake or asleep, I was to refrain from thinking about anyone or anything familiar, and had successfully programmed my brain to shut off any recall of dreams so I could honestly answer that I did not remember them.

"I'll know if you're lying. It's much better to take your punishment than lie to me."

Sometimes when he spent time in our room, he dictated our Spartan postcards. I had to stare at the floor when handing over the three lines of printed words, as we were still not allowed to look him in the eyes.

The postcards were now signed "Sandy and Solar."

As Solar's control over us grew, his obsessions took on monstrous importance. To him, many natural behaviors held tremendous negative potential, affecting his life almost as much as the ubiquitous "dark forces" that threatened his every movement. His increasing fears and obsessions gave rise to a plethora of behaviors intended to prevent the dark forces from manipulating him or "his energies," and he passed these behaviors on to us with strict enforcement.

Along with toilets and all bodily fluids, anything that touched the floor was now considered "contaminated." A hierarchy of "clean" and "dirty" arose to further complicate our lives. We allowed Solar to determine every piece of food we ate; how we walked, sat, stood, slept; and how close we could come to objects like walls, doors, fixtures, him, and each other. He controlled how much liquid we consumed and how many times we could use the bathroom. Endless rituals evolved around the simplest of tasks. All our hygiene activities—showering, hand washing, and laundry—became strictly regulated and enforced with physical battery.

My daily routines still involved taking "notes": in-depth reporting on everybody's actions, including whether we had spoken to one another. When we began traveling, paper was no longer available, so my "accounting" became an oral narration.

"You are to be spiritual nuns," Solar announced during one overnight stay. "Your physical, mental, emotional, and verbal mannerisms are to reflect that. Peggy, I want you to sew closed the space between the buttons on your shirts. Leave only enough room for your heads. Do you understand?"

After that, year-round, day after day, I wore turtlenecks underneath high-necked, long-sleeved blouses that Solar purchased. Peggy sewed shut the spaces between the buttons, tacking down the material to make it a solid piece with just enough space for our heads to squeeze through. We were not allowed to sit with any space between our tightly clasped legs. We ate in our room and were expected to write our assignments or follow through with the "discipline" that had been ordered for our transgressions.

At the end of each day, Solar checked in with us, kicking our door to be opened from the inside, where we stood at attention and answered his interrogation of us individually.

"What problems did you have? What mistakes did you make today? How many times did you think of your past?" Any and all of these were reasons to be disciplined. There were periods of time when being punished was a daily occurrence. When he stayed in the other part of the house, we were insulated from his blows, but assigned "discipline" from the doorway.

"Hold your hands up in the air for an hour. You need to be punished for being so evil."

Reaching for the ceiling with elbows locked and hands extended, the offender was allowed no sagging. Programmed to expose one another's transgressions, we stood guard over each other to enforce compliance with the punishment and thus ensure that his control over us continued. He was adept at creating new opportunities for "mistakes," and frequently changed the rules, making them increasingly more difficult to follow.

When not holding her hands up in the air, Peggy held her infant son, as he was not allowed to touch the "contaminated" floor. I spent most of my time cleaning, preparing meals and writing notes. I threw the pages across our threshold to Solar or delivered the notes verbally.

"This will help you learn how to control your mind over matter, so you'll grow spiritually," he often repeated.

Subjected to both sleep and food deprivation, I never knew what day of the week it was, or even what year it was, for aluminum foil always covered the windows.

In the Sedona house, I was renamed "One," and Peggy was called "Two," denoting the order of our succession in The Program. Solar's renaming of me would continue throughout the years I was with him. I progressed from One to Lea, Terra, Terra Lea, San Demon, and eventually Santania.

Growing up, I had been called different names in jest, or when I was in trouble. Agnes, Gertrude, and Samantha were the most common ones used by my mother. Eventually "Sam" stuck, and became a term of endearment used by my immediate family and some on the ranch.

Solar constantly blamed our "pasts" for damaging us. "You're so negative because of how your parents treated you! They are the enemy, not me. At least I'm up front about hurting you to cleanse all your evilness from you. They had their chance and only hurt you; they did not help you. That's why you need to cut yourself off from them. They're responsible for your pain and suffering. Do you understand?"

"Yes," we agreed.

He did not need to chain or lock us in the room; our fear kept us in bondage, more securely immobilized than any physical restraints could have ever done.

TWENTY-ONE

The outside world is filthy and contaminated with dirty energies. I want you to create an energetically pure environment for Boy. As an exalted being, he needs to be protected from dirty energies. From now on, put the groceries I toss you into a pan of soapy dishwater. Then shower before you clean them again, removing all the labels, as they're also contaminated." Solar made his latest pronouncement from the threshold of the room, his belly protruding over Jockey shorts—his favorite outfit.

Since the Program did not allow interaction with the outside world, Solar did our shopping. His ritual began by first showering in the bathroom next to ours.

Pound, pound. He announced his arrival. With our door opened from the inside, he walked into our bathroom to wash his body again and again. It was my job to wait in the room for him until he finally emerged, soaking wet.

"Toothbrush!"

I handed it to him and squeezed paste onto the bristles as his dutiful valet.

"Comb!"

I exchanged the toothbrush for a comb, and then a hooded shirt for the comb. Next were his pants, which I held open at the waist for him to step into since he had decided he could not touch the waistline of his pants to maintain his "clean" state. He didn't use towels and never wore underwear under his Levis, so when he thrust a leg in, his wet body made it difficult. As he hoisted his stomach so I could cinch his girth into the pants, invariably pubic hair and genitals would accidentally catch in the zipper.

Thud. He hit my head for the mishap.

"Gloves."

I slipped bright yellow latex gloves over his upheld hands. After guiding his feet into flip-flops I had washed, I opened the door for him. Gloved hands held aloft, long hair streaming behind, he exited our room—ready to do our shopping.

One day Solar proclaimed, "I've been thinking: toilets are completely contaminated. The toilet connects directly to the sewer, and so I want the lid kept down at all times, and you need to shower each time after using the toilet. Since you'll be leaving your clothes on the floor, you'll need to wash them out and wear them wet until they dry. Do you understand? Bathrooms are dirty!"

"Okay," I said, "I get the connection between toilets and the sewer. But what about the fact that I fix your food on the bathroom vanity?"

"Don't question my authority. I do not have to justify my actions, as they are divinely guided."

At the time, we didn't know who lived in the other rooms of the house in Sedona, but I learned, much later, that in 1981 Brenda and her children had moved in. They only stayed two or three months and then left again. John, Acacia, and Solar shared the other rooms and, while in our house, and even though they were no longer in the Program, Brenda and Acacia were still involved with Solar.

Peggy, Boy, and I remained in the master bedroom, and almost a month passed before Solar came to our door and announced that he was coming in to spend the night. He was sore, and explained that he had totaled my car.

"I hit a patch of ice and ran into a snow bank. The car turned upside down and trapped me inside. I had to shrink my body down to crawl through the window, or I would have died."

This was another of his "miracle" stories; supposedly using extraordinary powers to squeeze his large body through the window, by his account an impossible situation.

I was not surprised to learn that he had lost control, as he drove hard and fast. Years later, I got to see my car, or what was left of it. Flattened and terribly misshapen, it lay entombed in Sedona's wrecking yard—looking very much like my soul at the time.

Solar recuperated from his injuries, and a month later announced: "We need to leave Sedona because the energy of the red rocks has turned against me. I know that because my guides would not have allowed the car accident."

What we didn't know was that Brenda had left again, and finances had forced Solar to close his bookstore.

I obediently prepared myself for another move, packing a steamer trunk with our necessities. The rest of our possessions were jammed into the hatchback Solar had purchased. Three adults with a sixteen-month-old baby and a car filled with the remains of our household hit the road.

"Both of you keep your eyes closed, and Peggy, you hold Boy on your lap. We're going to the power centers of the western portion of the United States."

Starting at Four Corners, where the boundaries of Colorado, Utah, Arizona, and New Mexico meet, he took us to Ship Rock, New Mexico, through Colorado, and then over to Mount Shasta in Northern California.

During the journey, my cleaning routines changed considerably, for now I was to wash our clothes by hand during the night while everyone slept. As we drove to the next destination, I would nod off in the front seat, sandwiched between Solar and Peggy. I was usually beaten several times a week, sometimes daily, as I attempted to sneak around the room without making a sound while doing my cleaning routines. Normal noises disturbed the sleeping beast, who lashed out with his fists when roused from his slumber.

One night, as I scurried around, I accidentally bumped something, making a noise.

"What's that?" He leaped at me, furious. As he hit my chest, pounding my sternum—ten, fifteen times—I detached from my body; my mind hovering above as it had when, as a child, I had nearly died from gastroenteritis. Thuds resounded in me and searing pain raced through me with each blow. My heart fluttered and I could not breathe. *Oh, thank God; I'm dying and leaving this.* Instead, I gasped out loud, "My heart, it's stopping!"

He ceased hitting me and I cried, sobbing deeply.

"Stop crying or you'll get more!"

Obediently I stopped, stuffing all the pain deep within my being, adding more mass to that black pool of anguish inside me.

Soon, not even my tears would show.

As we traveled from motel to motel, Solar pared down our possessions. He claimed we didn't need cooking utensils, or more than two sets of clothes each.

"They're just things, and you can't take them with you when you die. You need a fresh start, and the more personal possessions you own, the more you're ruled by materialism—the opposite of spirituality!"

There was usually one percent truth in whatever he told us, but we consumed his pronouncements as gospel. Soon the steamer trunk held all our worldly possessions; the rest had been destroyed. Necessities consisted of a set of clothes for each of us, diapers, formula and a bottle, paper towels, bars of soap, large garbage sacks, gallon food storage bags, Pine Sol disinfectant, and sea salt. The disinfectant was mixed with the salt to cleanse away negative energies and to clean everything in our motel rooms. With each nightly stop, I hauled the trunk from car to hotel room, cleaned the room, washed our clothes and all the contents of the steamer trunk, only to reload and carry it back to the car in the morning. The cycle would repeat that evening.

Every night, our routine was the same. After preparing Boy's formula, I changed his saturated diaper from the entire day—and then bathed him before starting my other routines. Solar insisted on always eating fast food so we could "avoid interacting with dirty people and public energies." Even our money had to be washed in disinfectant every night to cleanse it of "all the negative energy." I never knew who Solar's financial sponsors were, but at that time he never lacked for money. He usually carried several thousand dollars in hundred dollar bills, all freshly laundered and reeking of Pine Sol.

I want to be clear that my suffering paled compared to the plight of Boy, who was neglected and confined to his mother's lap all day without the stimulus of toys or interaction with anyone, including us. He was so malnourished that his diapers sagged on his skinny legs.

"How much formula are you giving him?" Solar asked me one night, not long into our trip. "I want you to cut back so he doesn't have dirty diapers while we're on the road."

I blankly stared back at him. "He's so skinny already, Solar. He needs to eat more than once a day."

"If you feed him, he'll poop in his diaper and I can't stop to get a room just so you can get cleaned up after changing his diaper until the night. That's just the way it is!"

I shrank away in compliance as Solar glared one of his "I'm going to beat you" looks. I had already endured abuse after protesting his refusal to change Boy's wet diapers until we stopped at our nightly motel room. The idea of changing a diaper without all the showering and obsessive rituals was impossible to Solar.

Peggy secretly gave Boy bites of her hamburger during the day, but he had no formula until we stopped for the night. Peggy was not able to produce enough milk of her own, and his formula consumption was severely restricted by a psychopath who prioritized his own obsessions over the proper care and feeding of his newborn son. Boy cried incessantly from hunger, but no matter how hard we pleaded, we weren't allowed to give him more.

Peggy and I each weighed less than one hundred pounds, and for several years I never menstruated. On the other hand, Solar was both bulimic and hugely overweight. He gorged himself at every meal and then purged into a food storage bag that he tossed out the window as we drove away.

As I powered through my chores, my internal struggles were many. *Why is it so difficult to fulfill your will for me, God? I don't understand why I'm so evil that I deserve all this punishment.*

Solar had an answer, as he reminded me on a regular basis: "You are being tested. You need to prove your faith and your commitment."

I was convinced that if I walked away from Solar, all would be lost. When I found myself doubting the necessity of The Program and all the brutality, I reminded myself of my past failures. *I didn't finish college, failed in my relationship with Graham, left the Peace Corps early, failed in my business, and failed to spread the message given me. I even failed to get my family's approval and to share with them my experiences. I am NOT going to fail in this; I will complete The Program successfully—whatever it takes.*

This is my last chance.

TWENTY-TWO

We drove north to Mount Shasta, where Solar booked a small motel room for a couple of nights. I was having trouble completing my chores as per his demands, and he grabbed his belt and swung it across my face.

"I'M ONLY DOING THIS BECAUSE YOU'RE SO NEGATIVE AND DEMON-POSSESSED YOU NEED TO BE CLEARED! Now go get cleaned up, you evil bitch!"

I staggered into the bathroom, my face aching terribly. When I wiped the smudged mirror, the image I saw horrified me. My nose was bleeding, flattened and broken. *Why, God, am I so evil that I deserve this?*

Despite the pain, I was to clean myself and then wash the clothes in the bathtub. I pounded them with my fists and threw them against the sides of the tub, gnashing my teeth and writhing about, sobbing and silently screaming. *Why? Why, God?*

Listening to an alarm inside me, I quickly finished and exited the bathroom, my arms laden with our cleansed, dripping clothes. *I hate you even though you claim to be God's messenger. Look at what you've done! I'm disfigured, all for your stupid Program. I hate you more than I've ever hated anyone in my life.*

After I finished hanging up the last of the wet clothes, Solar called me over to the bed. Still seething, I turned and glared at him.

Instantly he leapt out of bed and pounded my ribs. "YOU'RE STILL DEMON POSSESSED! SOME DAY YOU'LL THANK ME FOR THIS!"

"I can't breathe," I gasped.

"I don't care how much pain you're in; you brought this on yourself. Now finish the cleaning and take care of your chores and go wash the demonic energy off you. You better come out cleansed of this negativity."

Each time I took a breath the pain was unbearable as I labored to accomplish my tasks. I lost my grasp on the few remaining strands of reality. Everything became a cloudy blur—I couldn't even find my hatred.

The next day when we left the room, I could scarcely breathe, and as I walked to the car, the outside world felt very strange and alien to me.

Solar drove for an hour or two and then stopped, turning off the engine. Instantly the car began to get cold inside.

"We're in Mount Shasta. We're going to live here."

It was really Grants Pass, Oregon, but neither Peggy nor I knew this at the time, since we could never open our eyes while in the car. Solar often drove around aimlessly to disorient and deceive us about our whereabouts.

We were ushered into the master bedroom, past unknown others we heard living in the rest of the house. Due to the severe cold, for the first time ever, Solar gave us sleeping bags to use on top of our plastic patio furniture—chairs by day and beds by night.

"The hot water is contaminated," Solar lectured as we settled into our room, "so you can only use cold water for your showers. You need to learn how to detach from your bodies. Mind over matter. Learn how to master both, and you'll overcome your dependence on your bodily needs. Besides, it's just the shell you live in right now. Soon you will not need it, when the earth changes come."

The thought that my body would soon be obsolete helped me maintain my commitment to the Program. Death by God's hands seemed a sweet deliverance.

As usual, we had no heat in our room. Every night I shivered myself to sleep; sleeping bag tightly wrapped around my wet clothes. Some days my entire day was spent clothed in wet garments. My cotton jeans, blouse, and turtleneck were slow to dry, keeping me perpetually cold. Sometimes, to ease my blue hands and feet, I used the "contaminated" warm water, even though I felt terribly guilty for breaking Solar's rules.

He never came into our room. I'm not sure how long we had been there when he kicked at our door and waited for me to open it and step back.

"I'm going to travel for a month."

"We don't have enough diapers and food for a full month," I said.

"There will be enough, and you'll make it last until I get back. If you have any emergencies, there's someone in the other part of the house you can contact, but only in case of an emergency. Don't talk to her otherwise."

I began worrying the moment the door closed behind him. I started eating a tablespoon of Miracle Whip a day to save the rice and cheese for Peggy and Boy, and supplemented my spoonful of processed blubber with a mixture of brown sugar and powdered milk. I discovered this cocktail not only staved off my hunger, it also numbed awareness of my body and helped to ease the cold.

Although our food supply continued to dwindle, my biggest concern was that we were running out of diapers. It was my responsibility to care for Peggy and Boy's welfare, so I wrote a note to Peggy, asking what she thought I should do.

"Maybe we should go buy some," she wrote back.

It was my first direct communication with her. I certainly could not have suggested such an obvious solution on my own, being the one who was usually beaten for whatever problems there were.

Solar had left money and a car with us in case of emergencies. Prohibited from speaking to each other or anyone else, Peggy and I continued to write notes back and forth. We decided we would all go, find a store, purchase diapers, and then return. We prepared for our junket, and I wrote a note for the stranger living in the other part of the house.

Opening the bedroom door, with heads lowered, down the hall we went. We heard a shuffling noise, and someone got up from the floor. I shoved the note out at arm's length with my printed message: "We are out of diapers and are going into town to buy more."

I never looked at this person, who said nothing in return. Spying the door, I led the way outside, with Peggy following, Boy in her arms. It was freezing outside, and we were dismayed to discover it was Christmastime. There were lights everywhere, reminding us of a custom and season long forgotten in our cloistered environment.

I started the car, and we shivered without jackets as we eased out of the driveway, tires crunching through the snow. Without knowing where we were or where to go, I decided a right turn was in order. After a few minutes, we luckily cruised into civilization, clueless that it was two o'clock in the morning—another hazard of aluminum-foil-covered windows and trusting the clock Solar had placed in our room.

Finding a beacon of light in the surrounding darkness, I pulled into the brightly lit parking lot of a convenience store. For a good ten minutes, I sat in the car, screwing up my courage. Finally, I opened the door and we walked into the shop. Without making eye contact with anyone, I found diapers. Clutching them, I pushed freshly laundered money toward the clerk and collected my change without looking at who was behind the counter. Retracing our route, we diligently remembered every turn and crept back to our darkened house.

Seeing ourselves as champions, safely returned with nary a problem, I was confident Solar would be pleased that we had procured our bounty. It never occurred to me to buy extra food, even though we were running out. Diapers were the only justifiable reason to leave our cloistered environment.

By the time Solar returned later that week, I had used quite a few of the extra diapers we'd purchased. We knew he was home because we heard him yelling at the top of his voice in the other part of the house. He stomped toward our door and thumped hard at it. I opened it and stepped back.

"YOU'VE RUINED EVERYTHING! YOU BROKE THE PROGRAM

FOR DIAPERS! HOW COULD YOU RUIN EVERYTHING OVER DIAPERS? HOW COULD YOU BE SO DEMON-POSSESSED? YOU FUCKING HEATHEN BITCHES! CLOSE THE DOOR!"

Then he left.

With the door closed I stole a glance toward Peggy. When her eyes met mine, they were filled with shock and terror.

We heard more ranting in the other part of the house and then bathwater being drawn next to our shower. He always took disinfectant baths—very warm baths, I'm sure.

His moaning drifted through our wall. "They left to buy diapers. They broke The Program to buy diapers. They ruined everything to buy diapers. How could they annihilate all my efforts to save them and raise their consciousness to a higher level? All over diapers . . ." Over and over he lamented this rant until his foot pounded again at our door.

Naked and dripping wet, he entered the room, still raging.

"This is for desecrating The Program and everything I have labored so hard to create. You're evil to the core, you fucking black bitch!" He had grabbed his belt and hit my buttocks and legs until they bled.

"TELL ME EVERYTHING YOU DID, FROM THE MOMENT YOU LEFT THIS ROOM UNTIL YOU GOT BACK!"

I recounted it all, and then faced more humiliation when I told him I had eaten the jar of Miracle Whip to conserve my portion of rice and cheese for Peggy and Boy.

"You think that's some kind of valuable sacrifice that you ate Miracle Whip? Why didn't you make the diapers last like I told you to?"

He continued. "I left someone in charge so you wouldn't have to leave, and this is how you repay me. Well, she's leaving. Fucking bitch is unworthy of being in The Program. She will never benefit from the salvation I can offer her. Heather is also unworthy of The Program. I told her *she* had to leave. I can't stand being near you. I'm leaving. Open the door and close it behind me!"

Nothing made sense. I had been shamed and denigrated for what I thought was a shrewd choice and a noble sacrifice.

I don't know who these women are, but I envy them their freedom. How much worse is being condemned to hell compared to our plight?

The next day, Solar came to our door again. "Now that you've ruined everything, you need to pack the steamer trunk with our belongings. We're heading back to Arizona."

Flagstaff welcomed us with deep snow and freezing weather. At the motel Solar found, he insisted on changing rooms every week. With each move, I carried the trunk as I trudged through the snow in flip-flops.

Solar was gone all day, every day, and when he returned we had to keep our backs to him as he walked straight into the bathroom, doffing his clothes at the door. Once he was in the bathroom Peggy and Boy could sleep while I stood at attention to wait for him to finish, after which it would be my job to clean the bathroom, wash his clothes and perform my usual routines.

While waiting, I bore witness to more of the obsessions developing within Solar.

"From now on, you're to use the 'dirty bar' of soap to wash your feet and up to your knees, and then use the 'middle bar' from your knees up to your waist. The 'clean bar' is for above your waist, your head, and hair."

Solar lathered each bar of soap into a frothy cream and scrubbed his anatomy, progressively moving from his feet to the top of his head as he worked through each bar, wearing it down in the process.

"Feet, feet, feet," pause, "feet, feet, feet, feet" was his litany. Turning the shower water on and off three times and then leaving it on signaled his rinsing off. His next step was also out loud:

"Thing, thing, thing," pause, "thing, thing, thing, thing," he chanted as he scrubbed his penis raw.

No part of his body went unnamed as it was lathered and rubbed and lathered and rubbed again and again and rinsed only after the shower water had been turned on and off another three times. Sometimes the repetitions continued incessantly, for if someone happened to run water in the adjacent room, he would start all over again, assuming the toilet had been flushed and he had been "contaminated." His showers were an hour-long process, or longer.

"The toilet and the shower water use different pipes," I ventured to explain once, and was rewarded with a beating. Never again did I try to challenge his beliefs with logic or reason.

I usually ignored the sounds of running water in another room, but if he heard it, I was proclaimed "dirty" and sent back to repeat the rituals.

While in Flagstaff, I feared I would never dry out or warm up. We slept in wet sheets that had to be washed each time he arrived home because he had "contaminated them" as he walked to the bathroom. Simple functions in life had become almost impossible to perform.

With all the showers, my hair became so matted it was impossible to comb. Since I always carried a baggie filled with dish soap into the shower for washing our clothes, I started using it on my hair, preferring the straw-like texture to having it matted and crusty with soap residue.

After a couple of months of this routine, Solar decided we were leaving. I packed up the trunk, we piled into the car, and he drove us to a warmer climate.

"Okay, get out. Don't look around."

What? We're at the ranch!

He herded us through the gate and onto the patio. My grandmother, looking very surprised, pushed the screen door open.

"Hello, Mrs. Judson," Solar said. "May we come in?"

"Why, yes. Welcome, come right in." Her warm smile touched an ancient place, jostling me a bit from my trance. It had been almost three years since I'd last seen her.

We found rocking chairs in her large kitchen area. Solar held Boy on his lap while he played with a bar of soap—his only "toy."

I can't believe I'm sitting in my grandmother's home.

"I brought Sandy, Peggy, and my son here because I was hoping you'd let them stay for a short time," Solar told my grandmother. "I have some international traveling to do, and cannot take them because it would be very difficult to travel with my infant son. Would you be willing to let them stay here?"

"I would be happy to have them live in my home for as long as they need," she smiled in return.

"Great. First, we have to visit some power vortexes, but we'll return shortly. I need to travel to the Great Pyramid in Egypt for my spiritual work."

Traveling around the world with Solar had been a perk he had used to motivate both Peggy and me to join him. But once we had committed we were told, "You need to be in The Program first, and since you can't interact with the public, neither one of you can travel with me."

As it was, the domestic traveling we did was so awkward and painful I could not imagine being in a foreign country with him and all his obsessions.

We followed my grandmother upstairs to the "west bedroom," where we were invited to stay. In front of her, Solar announced to me: "You cannot be in that room with all of that furniture and energy from your ancestors. Ask your grandmother to remove it or you cannot stay here."

"I'll have the room emptied before you return," my grandmother said.

"Thank you, Gramma," I responded.

TWENTY-THREE

On Valentine's Day of 1982, Peggy, Boy and I moved into my grandmother's home. I carried our paltry possessions upstairs and hesitated at the bedroom door. My grandmother had emptied the room, as Solar had requested. I hadn't realized the west bedroom was so vast without its three beds and various furnishings.

Solar said, "You have to tell her she's to stay out of your room once you get it cleaned. Do you understand?"

"Yes," I reluctantly answered. *What have I done, bringing Peggy and Boy and our weird customs into Gramma's life?*

I watched Solar close all the doors and windows of the other upstairs rooms. He removed the curtains from the bathroom and our bedroom windows and covered them with masking tape and aluminum foil.

"Make sure there are no cracks or holes where any light might enter. Remember, you're emulating the masters who sealed themselves into the meditation caves of the Himalayas. Pour sea salt along the doorway of each room to keep the spirits of your dead ancestors from wandering around and entering your psychic space." Then he added, "You may talk with one another."

Stunned, I asked him what he had just said.

"That's right; I said you can talk with one another now."

"Thank you, Solar," Peggy and I said in unison.

"Just keep your room cleaned with disinfectant and sea salt. Remember, your grandmother is not to enter. You are never to go outside unless it's to do the laundry—and only for that purpose. Do you understand?"

"I don't know how I can tell my grandmother she can't come into a room of her own house," I protested.

"She's dirty, like the rest of the world. If you want to stay here, you'll find a way to keep her out of your room. Do you understand?"

"Yes," I sighed. I watched his long hair stream behind him as he gave his final instructions. "Clean the door handles after I leave."

I followed him downstairs to obey his orders. As he left, he assured my grandmother, "They'll only be here for a couple of months."

"That's fine. They're welcome for as long as they want."

I retreated to our room, and soon my grandmother came upstairs. She brought us flowers she had picked from her garden. "These are for you," she said, handing me a beautiful bouquet of roses.

"Thank you, Gramma." I inhaled deeply the forgotten sweetness of garden-fresh flowers and her generous heart. I lingered with her, wanting to run into her arms, but my fear of Solar's recrimination kept me from budging.

"Well, I'll let you get settled," she said, and went back downstairs.

I cannot believe I'm in my grandmother's home—my safe-haven of childhood sleepovers with cousins, my refuge, where my family gathered so many times. Thank you, God, thank you!

I ran downstairs. "Gramma? Gramma?"

"Yes?"

"Would you like to have dinner with us this evening?"

"Why, yes. Thank you. That would be lovely. What time do you want me to return?"

"We'll be eating at six. Do you mind sitting in a chair in the hallway?" She looked at me curiously.

"I'm sorry, Gramma. Thank you for understanding."

As she walked away, my heart sank.

I busied myself preparing our starchy meal on the hot plate we used for cooking. I heard Gramma come back upstairs and walk down the hallway. She stopped at the threshold of our doorway and from behind me I heard an unfamiliar voice say, "Hi, Becky."

I turned around to see Boy standing and grinning at my grandmother from his playpen. No one had used Rebecca—her name—let alone "Becky" in his presence. Although he was two years old, he did not speak much, having been raised in a world filled with silence except for outbursts from his father. "Urry up" and "mmm, mmm" were his first words, imitating his father shouting "Hurry up!" every morning as I scrambled to get us all out the door of our motel room. No matter how early I started us in our routines, Solar always consumed any spare time I had created, resulting in a chaotic and frenzied rush to leave before we were "contaminated" by a maid cart parked too close to our door. "Mmm, mmm" was Boy's signal that he was hungry.

Amazed, I looked at Peggy, who shrugged and then turned back to watch my grandmother pull her chair up to the threshold, an imaginary barrier separating our "clean" status from the rest of the world. My grandmother graciously received the food I passed over "the line." Her acceptance eased my guilt.

I cooked on the storage shelves we had brought with us. Everything we ate was prepared on a hot plate. Rice and cheese, macaroni and cheese, and peanut butter and jelly sandwiches were the full complement of our diet.

Peggy fashioned various pieces of cardboard into a changing table that added to our scant collection of furniture, which included two chairs and a playpen. She had covered the changing table with aluminum foil so I could keep it clean, and as time passed, we had saved enough cardboard from our boxed food and diapers to make a table for ourselves.

On Sunday evening, my grandmother called up from the bottom of the stairs. "Sandy? Solar's on the phone for you."

"Okay, Gramma. I'm coming right down. Can I take it in your room, please?"

To avoid seeing anyone else who might be in the house, I walked into her bedroom through a side door from the parlor. Picking up the phone on her nightstand, I waited for her to hang up the one she had answered in the other room.

"Hi. Have there been any problems?"

"No, Solar."

"Is your grandmother staying out of your room?"

"Yes. I served her dinner, and she stayed on the other side of our threshold. It wasn't a problem and really nice to offer her a meal."

"You are not to do that again. Do you understand?"

"I didn't see any harm in it."

"Don't do it again."

"Okay."

The conversation ended with his usual admonitions: "Don't go outside and don't talk to anyone from your family other than your grandmother. Do you understand?"

"Yes. I won't. I understand."

I hung up and returned to our upstairs den.

As usual, Peggy and I were sleeping on the lawn chairs that served as chairs by day. Boy was relegated to the playpen, as his father had instructed us he was not to touch the floor.

"The floor is dirty even if you scrub it—the floor will never be clean enough; do you understand!?"

Recognizing my resistance to his orders, Solar's face twisted into one of his hateful looks, pressuring me into compliance.

He had also taken the opportunity to instruct me about the rules for doing the laundry at my grandmother's. I dreaded asking all that of her, but complied with child-like obedience.

"Gramma, Solar suggested I ask you to open the doors for me so that when I'm bringing out our laundry, I won't get it dirty." I dared to look at her; her face wore a puzzled look.

"What do you mean?"

"Well, I'm supposed to bring out the dirty clothes through the back door and if you could please hold the annex door open for me, I could then put them in the washer and then walk back in through the back door without touching the door handle." I waited and then continued without recognizing the absurdity of what I was asking. "And then when I'm bringing the clean clothes back, would you mind please opening the front door for me so that I can bring them through it and then walk directly upstairs with them?"

"Well, I suppose so. Is that all really necessary?"

"I'm sorry, but it is. I hope that's okay."

"All right," she sighed, and indulged my requests each time I washed our clothes, opening and closing the doors about 15 times each laundry session. Furthermore, Solar had instructed: "The machines are to be cleaned before and after each load. You are not to touch her door handles, since they are all dirty with worldly energies."

My grandmother purchased our groceries, but had started gifting us much more as well.

"Gramma, we didn't ask for these." My eyes widened in appreciation for such luxuries we had not eaten in several years.

"I know. But you need fresh fruits and vegetables."

I felt embarrassed about our diet. "Thank you so much." Her kindness touched me deeply.

"This is the last bag. Sandy, it's a beautiful day outside. Don't you and Peggy want to take Boy and go out into the yard? He could play on the lawn; it's so lovely outside. The fresh air would do you all some good."

"Thank you, Gramma, for the offer, but I can't. We're not allowed to go outside for the time being, as we're cleansing and purifying our minds for God."

"Well, okay. Suit yourself, but it's really a beautiful day."

Solar was calling now almost every Sunday night. His whereabouts were a mystery; I didn't know if he had gone to the Great Pyramid as planned. I wasn't allowed to ask.

"Have you seen anyone in your family other than your grandmother?"

"No."

"Have you gone outside other than to do the laundry?"

"No."

"Has Peggy gone outside?"

"No."

"What have you and your grandmother talked about?"

I failed to mention her suggestion about going outside, and instead focused on what I considered more important issues. "She bought us fruits and vegetables along with the rest of our groceries."

"You didn't ask for them, did you?"

"No, but Solar, my grandmother is buying all our food and paying for our utilities, which I know have doubled because of all the showers we take."

"I don't care. You are not to pay her. Do you understand?"

"Yes, but it's not fair."

"She agreed to this. You are not to give her any of the money I left with you. Do you understand?"

"Yes."

"Have there been any other problems?"

"She has to bring our groceries from her car in the garage into the house all by herself. She's eighty-two years old. Can't I help her?"

"No! You can only go down to the bottom of the stairs to get your groceries. Do you understand? You are not to go outside, and you are not to break the rules of The Program. I'll talk to you next Sunday. Goodbye."

Defeated, I retraced my steps upstairs. *The amount of hot water we use is staggering with our showers, the laundry and all the cleaning. My grand-mother didn't ask to be paid, but I know we're a burden to her—physically and financially. We have money—Solar left us a thousand dollars in cash.*

I don't get why this is necessary for me to complete my spiritual training. Somehow I'll make it up to you, Gramma.

I shared the conversation with Peggy.

"Solar said I cannot pay my grandmother for our expenses."

"He must have his reasons."

"I don't like how he asks me to treat my grandmother. It's not fair that she's paying for all our food. She told me her electric bill has doubled—probably because all the showers we take for the cleaning he demands we do of everything."

"Hmm," mused Peggy.

Even with the freedom to converse with one another, Peggy and I never discussed our "discipline" sessions or how Solar treated us. I felt privileged to be able to speak with her at all, and did not deem this freedom of speech a right. Instead, we mostly kept to ourselves, chatting occasionally, learning about our histories and what had led us to Solar. All the mandated cleaning consumed most of the time in my days. I did the laundry, washed the walls and the floor every week, as well as every grocery item.

There were so many rituals, I had little time to think through my situation, and shamelessly took advantage of my grandmother's love, patience, and benevolence. There were so many strange behaviors she accepted and allowed—maybe hoping we would come to our senses.

The next time she brought in the groceries, I apologized for not helping.

"That's okay," she softly replied.

She also honored our request that she stay out of the upper portion of her home. She never forced herself upon her houseguests—one of them her granddaughter.

For six months, she did all this and never complained.

In July, my conversation with Solar began with news. "My grandmother said relatives are coming to visit soon."

"Can't they stay somewhere else?"

"No, they come to visit my grandmother every summer."

"You are *not* allowed to interact with them. You are not to see them or let them see or interact with you. Do you understand? Try to keep them from coming upstairs. You're to remain in your room until they leave, no exceptions."

"What are we supposed to do about the bathroom? There's only one, and we have to change Boy there and use it ourselves."

"You can only use it in the middle of the night when they're all asleep. That's an order."

"Okay," I responded automatically.

"Have you seen any of your relatives, other than your grandmother?"

"No."

"Have there been any other problems?"

"No."

"Have you gone out outside other than to do the laundry?"

"No."

Back upstairs, I shared my frustrations with Peggy. "I can't believe we're still here and faced with this. We should be able to live normally or not be here at all."

"Are you going to ask your grandmother to keep your family from coming upstairs?"

"I don't know how that's possible, but I'll ask."

My grandmother's shocked response was, "Why, I can't ask them that!" She had drawn a line.

By another of Solar's mandates we kept the bedroom doors, including ours, closed. No fresh air entered or left our personal space except when I went downstairs for laundry or to get the groceries. The sealed bathroom window added more humidity with each shower. Without access to fresh air or being able to use the air conditioner, the temperature upstairs progressively rose as the weather outside warmed up. Despite three fans, our "sanctuary" eventually grew to an unhealthy and humid 100-plus degrees. Many times, out of desperation, I opened our door and fanned it back and forth.

"Do you think that's okay?" Peggy asked.

"I don't think it's okay to die of heat prostration. Maybe I should open a window."

"Are you sure? Isn't that what Solar specifically told us not to do?"

"Yeah, I guess it's better to roast now than for an eternity," I lamented.

My relatives arrived and filled the other upstairs rooms. Peggy and I locked ourselves in our room, sneaking out in the middle of the night to satisfy our bathroom needs. Not being able to converse with loved ones so near was extremely difficult for me, and I struggled to remain in The Program. My grandmother's kindness and the familiar surroundings tugged at me, and yet I remained loyal to Solar, honoring his cleanliness standards and other rules. I felt powerless to change my circumstances.

After a week, my father's sister and her family left, but more extended family came to visit shortly afterwards.

"Sandy, Donna is here. Don't you want to see her?" My grandmother asked at the foot of the stairs.

My heart sank. Another dear cousin I had to shun.

"No, Gramma. I can't. Please give her my love and tell her that I'm sorry."

"Okay, but I don't understand you," she sighed into the empty hallway.

After she left I shared a secret with Peggy: "I've been thinking a lot about what life would be like to not be in the Program."

"Do you know what you'll do when you're out?"

"No, but this is really hard. It's like when Solar would give us a rule and then change it without letting us know. That always seemed so unfair."

"Yeah, I know what you mean. All he has to do is look at me and I freeze in terror."

"I never knew that finishing the Program so I could complete my mission was going to be so difficult. It's hard for me to be here in my grandmother's house and not go outside or visit with her. I felt so badly not being able to see my relatives and my cousin Donna when she came. I couldn't even say 'hi,' just because of Program rules. I mean, we're here in the middle of my family's ranch where I grew up. Everyone comes here to visit and I can't even go outside to talk to them."

"Do you think your grandmother would let us continue living here if we weren't in the Program?"

"I don't know, I could ask her. She has a very generous heart, but we couldn't take advantage of her. We'd have to do something to support ourselves."

"I've been thinking about that."

"Yeah, me too." I hesitated. "I don't think I want to be in the Program anymore, Peggy. What about you?"

"I don't think I want to be in The Program anymore either. Do you think your grandmother would allow Aaron and me to stay here?"

"I don't know. I don't know anything right now."

In August, my brother broke one of the latches we used to secure the downstairs doors. I could hear him talking as he walked upstairs and approached our door.

"Sam, I just want to talk with you. Please open the door."

"I can't, Bruce. Please go away. I know you don't understand, but I can't open the door."

"I just want to talk to you. Come on, open up the door."

"I can't, Bruce. Please go away." I was shaking violently, terrified of facing Solar if Bruce walked in, but falling apart as my heart broke, wanting so badly to see my beloved brother.

"Sam, I don't understand. I just want to talk to you for a minute."

"I can't, Bruce. Please go away."

"Okay, fine!" he said as he walked downstairs and slammed the door at the bottom of the stairs.

My grandmother had been away visiting relatives in Hawaii, and returned a few days after Bruce's visit. I was nervous as I waited for Solar to call, dreading having to tell him about my brother's visit. The call came at our usual time, but my grandmother did not call me downstairs. I could hear the phone ringing incessantly. *It's rung fifteen times and no one is answering. I hope Gramma is okay.*

After another long pause, the phone rang another ten times, and there was a pause and then fifteen more rings. *What's wrong? That's strange; she would have had time to answer the phone by now.* The phone rang again, and this time my grandmother called me from the base of the stairs.

"Sandy, the police are here and want to speak with you."

I went downstairs and stared at the floor as two officers from the San Diego Police Department interrogated me.

"We have a complaint from someone named Solder that you are being held hostage and that your family is trying to kidnap his son. Can you explain what you know about this?"

"His name is Solar. No one is holding us hostage. We've been staying upstairs in my grandmother's house."

"Is there a young boy with you?"

"Yes. I don't understand; you said that Solar called the police?" I was distracted for a moment as the phone started ringing again.

"We're here because someone called in a complaint that you or your family is trying to kidnap his son."

"What? I'm not kidnapping anyone."

"Okay. We'll be back. We need to go check something out."

They walked over to where my grandmother was standing in the kitchen. I could hear the phone ringing, accentuated by the bell mounted outside, chiming in unison as the ones inside loudly announced the unanswered call.

I raced upstairs. No sooner had I explained to Peggy what the police said than my grandmother called me from the bottom of the stairway.

"Sandy, Solar is on the phone for you."

I ran downstairs and opened the door to the parlor—and took a step back. My mother was sitting in one of the chairs.

"No, don't go that way," my grandmother said, leading me around through the dining room. My father was sitting in the kitchen. *What's going on? What are they doing here?*

I picked up the phone in my grandmother's bedroom.

"Solar?"

"You and Peggy have to get Boy and get out of there now! You're in grave danger—your family is trying to keep me from you. They wouldn't let me talk to you and they want to kidnap Boy."

"What? They wouldn't do that!"

"You heard me; your grandmother wants to kidnap Boy. You need to get out of there immediately. I've called the police and they're on their way to escort you out of there. Now get going! Pack up everything and leave as quickly as possible. Don't leave anything behind. Smash your furniture so nobody can use it."

"I don't understand. Solar, the police have already come."

"Get going—you have my orders! They're there to get you safely out."

I was confused, but hung up the phone and stumbled back upstairs, where I told Peggy everything Solar had said. Then, feeling sick, I squashed our cardboard furnishings. *No one in my family would want to use this stupid stuff. I don't get you, Solar. They're not going to use our energies against us.*

Looking as dumfounded as I felt, Peggy started rotely packing the steamer trunk.

Then I heard my grandmother at the bottom of the stairs.

"The police want to speak with you again."

I flew downstairs.

"We're going to help you get out of here," one of the officers said.

"I need to pack up our things before we can leave."

"First we need to make sure your car will start."

"Okay. Let me get the keys."

I returned, out of breath, with the keys in my hand. Leading the way outside, I breathed the fresh sweetness of the cool night air for the first time in six months. While walking through the gate into the outer yard, I noticed a tall figure standing in the darkness by the gas pump, but was more focused on getting to our car. I stopped in front of the driver's side door to unlock it.

"Keep walking!" one of the policemen barked at me as he opened the rear door of their patrol car, which was jammed up against our bumper.

"What do you mean?"

Suddenly one of them was behind me, restraining my arms. He pushed me toward the car as his knee gouged into my back. I lost my balance and fell onto the doorjamb.

"Okay! Okay! You don't have to hurt me," I blurted. Jerking me off the doorjamb, he pushed my face onto the grass. Handcuffs locked on my wrists, I was lifted upright and shoved into the patrol car.

"PEGGY, DON'T LET THEM IN, THEY'RE GOING TO ARREST YOU!" I screamed as loudly as I could. To no avail, for soon we were both sitting in the backseat of the car, arms cuffed behind us. One of the officers held Boy in the front.

We were driven to County Mental Health, or CMH, and escorted into a small, dingy room. The officers started out the door with Boy, who screamed in protest. Tears streamed down our cheeks, dripping onto the floor from our downturned heads. Boy had never been away from either of us since birth.

Our grieving was interrupted when we realized somebody else was in the room, walking straight for us. Peggy and I moved into a corner and the visitor started toward us again, laughing as we two-stepped away each time. He danced and flittered about, taunting and almost running into us as we moved around, from corner to corner, trying to avoid him.

"Stop pestering them!" someone yelled from another part of the room, and he stopped. We cowered in our corner—two cardinal Program rules required not looking at strangers and avoiding being touched, even by accident.

We heard a "come here," and our tormentor left the room. A minute later, Peggy's name was called, and she was ushered through the same door. I waited in the middle of the room, staring at the floor.

"Goodbye. They're letting me go home."

I looked up to see Peggy leaving as she followed someone out through the door we had come in. *I wonder if she's going to stay with her parents in LA.*

"Follow me!" I was ordered by someone in a green uniform, who ushered me through an open door. "Go in there."

I walked inside the darkened room.

"Have a seat," a man directed from behind a large desk.

"No, thank you. I'm in a non-interaction program, and that chair is contaminated with public energies. Therefore, I cannot sit in it."

"Okay. Why don't you look at me when you're talking to me?"

"To grow spiritually I have chosen not to interact my energies with the public, so I can cleanse and purify myself. Looking in someone's eyes is a way to connect energetically with them."

"Well, regardless of what your so-called program says, your family has requested lifetime commitment for you. We're going to find a facility closer to where they live. In the meantime, you'll be staying here at CMH. Any questions?"

"What do you mean by 'CMH' and 'lifetime commitment'?"

"This is a mental hospital and you're being committed. You'll be relocated to a facility closer to your family. I'll talk more with you tomorrow."

"Where are Peggy and Boy?"

"Who is Boy?"

"He's Peggy's son. I'm in charge of taking care of him."

"Well, Peggy has been released, and the child you call Boy is in protective custody with CPS. Someone from the FBI will be interviewing you tomorrow, and we'll talk again then. Go with her."

With this news crashing down on me, I followed a woman out of the office and through thick metal doors that locked behind us.

"Put out your right hand." She strapped a white plastic band around my wrist. "You'll be sleeping down the hall, in that room." She pointed.

I began to walk toward the room but was stopped as I passed the nurses' station.

"Where do you think you're going?" a husky voice asked.

"To my room."

Out of the corner of my eye, I could see his head shaking. "Put these on and leave your clothes here at the front desk." He shoved a pair of pajamas toward me.

"Now?"

"Yes, now!"

In front of this man, I disrobed and then donned my uniform for those without choices. My body and mind had become public property, open to scrutiny and display. Not much different from life with Solar, except now there were many men, not just one, controlling and judging me.

It was Friday the 13th, 1982, around midnight.

Why was Peggy released? Why didn't they hold HER? *Boy is hers. Obviously, the police didn't listen to Solar—but who called them in the first place?*

TWENTY-FOUR

The next morning, Solar called me at the public pay phone inside the lockdown unit. "You've ruined everything. You've broken the Program rules and destroyed all my hard work. Everything is lost; the Master has left Boy forever. All his protection is gone, and the dark forces will take him over now. You're responsible for this!"

How can that be, Solar? You're the one who called the police! And what do you mean that the Master has left Boy?

"Did you hear me? Say something!"

"I'm here."

"This is all your fault! It's up to you to get yourself out of there. I'm not going to help you."

"How am I supposed to do that?"

"ACT NORMAL; START INTERACTING AND TALKING TO PEOPLE!" he shouted, and hung up.

"Are you Sandra Judson?" one of the medical personnel asked.

"Yes."

"There's someone here from the FBI to speak with you. Please follow me." She led me into a vacant office where a tall, blond man asked me who had tried to kidnap a small boy. He looked rather imposing and had a distinct air of authority. I felt nervous at first, then looked directly at the man, took a deep breath and began.

"No one actually tried to kidnap Boy, the young child who was taken away from us. His mother and I were living in an upstairs room at my grandmother's house because his father was travelling and could not take us along with him. We'd been staying with my grandmother for over six months when my family apparently decided to prevent Solar from speaking to me. I guess they thought that he was controlling me too much and tried to intervene. We're in this 'non-interaction' program designed to increase our spirituality.

"Anyway, when my family didn't allow Solar to talk to me, I guess he panicked and called the police, accusing my family of kidnapping his son. They would never harm Boy or us, they were only trying to help. The rest you know about."

I watched his face soften as he responded.

"There's nothing here to follow up with, so I'm dismissing the investigation. There's no reason to pursue it any longer."

He left, and a nurse approached me.

"You can challenge your life commitment by petitioning for a battery of psychological tests that will prove your sanity. When you have your second interview with the psychiatrist, you can request them. May I sit in on that meeting?"

I looked deeply into her dark eyes and saw genuine caring.

"Yes, thank you. That would be nice. I have nothing to hide."

"You can also sign a petition for a writ of habeas corpus, which will be filed on Monday, so they cannot detain you against your will for more than three days after that."

"How do I get a writ of habeas corpus?"

"You'll have to wait until Monday when the patient advocates arrive, and they'll help you through that process."

"Okay. Thank you so much."

As I watched her walk away, I felt a strange sensation inside me. Eventually, I realized what it was: support.

Not long after, another staff member informed me that I had visitors, and I was shown where to meet those willing to visit our locked quarters. As I walked toward the area, I hesitated and then continued towards the man whose love I had always longed for. I sat down in front of my father, his cheeks blemished and face sagging. *He looks so much older.*

"Hi! What happened to your nose?" he asked.

"I was in a car accident and hit the front dashboard." Countless times Solar had had me rehearse what I was to say, his fists reinforcing my lines.

"Looks to me like someone hit you in the nose and broke it."

I could not lie to him again, and looked at the ground. *Everything is so wrong. What have I done to deserve being here?* Remembering that my father was waiting for a response, I looked up—his face wore a quizzical look.

"How's Gramma?" I asked.

"She's not happy with you. Rhodes and Margaret are visiting with her now."

Oh God, that's not good. Uncle Rhodes and Aunt Margaret haven't been to see Gramma in over ten years.

"I'm . . . I'm sorry Gramma is mad at me."

"Yeah. Well, I don't understand you. Guess I'll be going. Still think someone broke your nose."

He left, and before I could digest our visit, a former lover walked in.

"Jane, what are you doing here?" I asked.

"Your mother asked me to come see you. We all want you to know that we're praying for you. You're such a loving presence; you'll get free of this."

"You don't understand why I'm here, do you?"

"I know that you've gotten mixed up with something very self-destructive and that you need to see your way through this."

"I've got to complete my mission and spread the message I was given. Don't you remember?"

"Yes, I do. But is this the way to do it?"

"My family put me here."

"Maybe that's not the entire story. I'll come back to see you soon. I offer you my prayers and love. May you see your way clearly through this."

After she left, my mother walked in. "Hi, honey."

"What do you mean by committing me for life? What do you think you're doing?"

"We placed you here for your own good, to keep you safe. I've asked them not to medicate you and to treat you fairly."

"What's with the lifetime commitment? Who gave you that right?"

"We felt we had to take matters into our own hands to keep you from hurting yourself. We don't know what Solar would ask you to do."

"You're the one who's crazy, wanting to commit me for life. I cannot talk to you now. Please go."

"Sandy, we're only trying to help you."

"I don't want your help. Please go, you're only making matters worse." I burst into sobs.

A nurse came to my side. "Are you okay?"

"No, I don't want to talk to her." And my mother was escorted out of the room. "I don't want her near me. I don't want to see her; she's the reason why I'm here."

"You can ask that she not visit you; that's your right."

"I don't want to see her."

"Okay, consider it done."

I watched my mother, still at the nurse's station, handing a thick manila envelope to someone at the desk.

Before that day ended I had my second psychiatric visit. A different man sat behind an expansive desk, holding a stack of papers in his hands.

"Your family has asked for your lifetime commitment. We're arranging to move you closer to where they live, but in the meantime, you'll be staying here. Your mother has given me letters written to her by some Peace Corps volunteers who knew you, along with some poetry and letters you sent to her. Your friends were concerned about your sanity, and in this poem, you've written 'sanity is a straightjacket.' Any comments on this?"

"The letters were written by some people I knew in the Peace Corps. I told them about my mission and why I was leaving Peace Corps, and they completely exaggerated the events that occurred. The poetry I mistakenly shared with my mother while I was high on cocaine and questioning the patent answers I had blindly embraced. I do not believe it's fair evidence of who I am today. I no longer do any drugs, and even though I have acted in some strange ways, I would like to prove my sanity by taking a battery of psychological tests. Maybe I'm a bit eccentric, but I have a right to my beliefs."

"Not when you endanger the life of a young child."

"You're right. . ." I agreed, my voice trailing off.

"Okay, I'll see to it that you're able to take the tests. They'll start on Monday."

"Thank you," I said, and walked out through the door, looking at my nurse ally, who nodded at me. I wanted to hug her.

I was being normal, acknowledging people whenever they addressed me, looking them in the eyes and not worrying about how close they were to me. I was no longer in Solar's non-interaction program, and although I had experienced many bizarre events in my life, I was witnessing an aspect of humanity previously unknown to me.

Daily I listened in horror as fellow shut-ins were forced into physical restraints even as they protested this abuse with much yelling and cursing. *I wonder what happened to her,* I mused as I walked around a patient frozen in her catatonia in the middle of the sidewalk. She stood there erect for hours until they removed her. Recognizing that resistance to any staff directive would land me on the ground and strapped into bondage, I chose to fully cooperate and was treated well.

The next day was Sunday, and I watched the staff turn my mother away, preventing her from seeing me during visiting hours.

Able to look around now, I watched with curiosity when three men ran up to the coffee cart that had just been left in the common room. I smiled in recognition as they grabbed handfuls of sugar packets, ripped them open and dumped the contents into their mouths. My obsessive struggle for survival with the Program had kept me distracted from the reservoir of hurt and pain deep within me. Memories of cold, wet clothes in Oregon flashed through my mind. *I know, guys, it's an easy way to self-medicate.*

We were not allowed to go to our bedrooms during the day, so it was either the TV room or the quad where I spent my free time. I was there when someone summoned me to the visiting area. Linda, my childhood friend, was waiting.

Embarrassed, I sat down. "Hi."

"What have you gotten yourself into?"

"I don't think you'd understand, but I failed in my mission to spread my message, and now my family wants to keep me here for life."

"Don't you see they're worried about you, that this is not healthy for you?"

"All I know is I'm only trying to fulfill my mission and warn people about the changes we need to make. So far everything I've done has failed; this is my only hope."

"I'm sorry, but visiting hours are over," a staff member said.

"This is not the way—you might want to rethink what you're doing," Linda added as a parting note.

Nobody understands me. They weren't given the message I received. Solar's right; they don't honor or respect me.

On Monday, I filed the writ of habeas corpus and started the tests, completing them as quickly as the psychologist would allow. He was a very busy man, sometimes needing to speak with his stockbroker while I stared at inkblots. I censored my imagination, thinking it would help me get out of there.

The entire battery of tests took a day and a half. Tuesday after lunch, I was talking with Solar on the pay phone when the psychologist came up to me.

"That's not your family, I hope?"

"No, why?" I covered the receiver.

"Well, your family is the reason you're in here, and we cannot keep you.

You're not insane. You need to leave today."

"When will that happen?"

"We need to go over the results of your tests first. Can you talk right now?"

"Yes. I need to go, Solar. They're releasing me," I said into the phone. I hung up and followed the psychologist to his office.

"The MMPI, which stands for the Minnesota Multiphasic Personality Inventory, revealed that you're a nonconformist, but there's nothing in these test results to justify holding you any longer."

"Well, the great thinkers in society were nonconformists, right?"

Unimpressed, he blankly stared at me. "You cannot stay here any longer. You need to make arrangements to leave today. Go see the front desk and they'll tell you what to do."

I walked to the front desk and used their phone to call my father and ask him to pick me up. After we arranged our rendezvous, the staff handed me a clean set of street clothes that Peggy had dropped off for me. I changed, turned in my pajamas, and thanked and hugged the nurse who had been so helpful.

As she escorted me to the door, an impulse came over me. "Just a minute, please, I want to say goodbye." She followed me as I walked into the common area to announce my departure. Waving my arm, I shouted, "Goodbye everyone, good luck!"

"Goodbye! Come visit us!" was shouted back to me as I turned to leave. *Free at last.* I walked through the heavy metal doors into a transition room.

"Let me see your wrist," a male staff member requested. I put out my arm in front of him, and huge scissors snipped off the plastic band. "Here is your medicine," and I took the bag of pills for a massive kidney infection I had developed, perhaps due in part to how hard the officer's knee had hit my back as he wrestled me to the ground before cuffing me at my grandmother's.

As I started to leave, I asked, "Who's the president of the United States?"

"Ronald Reagan."

"You're kidding."

TWENTY-FIVE

At the rendezvous point, I watched a car slowing to a stop. My father was sitting in the passenger seat; Peggy was in back—and my mother was driving.

What's SHE doing here? I called Dad to get me!

"What's wrong with Dad?" I asked as I slid into the backseat, looking to him for an answer.

"I asked your mother to drive because I'm not sober enough to do so. Is that okay?"

His voice sounded strange, and I realized he was drunk. "Thanks for coming to pick me up," I said. I sat back and glanced over at Peggy. Her lips were pursed. The drive back to my grandmother's house was a silent one.

My mother dropped us off at the ranch, and my father followed us inside.

"Hi, Gramma." I felt hesitant as I entered her home. "We need to get our things. May we go upstairs?"

"Yes, of course. Are you okay?"

She seems different.

My stomach tightened as I walked up the stairs. Every door and window was open. I stopped breathing when I walked into our room; our crippled cardboard furniture still lay on the floor where I had stomped it.

A cool breeze gently lifted the curtains. *She put them back. Oh God, look at the mold and mildew on the window frames and screens!* Bright daylight revealed faded images on the wallpaper—my cleaning had scrubbed the pattern off.

Not able to take in any more, I packed our things into the chest, dissembled the shelves, and carried everything downstairs to the car. I had orders from Solar, and returned to the house to relay the message before we left.

"Gramma, Solar said that you tried to kidnap Boy."

I instantly regretted my words as I watched my grandmother's face cloud with pain.

"I don't understand why you'd say such a thing. I can't have you stay here. I'll give you some money for a hotel room because I can't let you stay here."

She left me standing in the kitchen as she retreated to her bedroom for her purse. My heart sank, and I felt a door slam shut inside me.

Peggy and I left the ranch and drove into town to find a motel room. Once settled, Peggy made a collect call to Solar. It turned out she had been speaking to him the entire time I was at CMH.

"You're to drive straight through to Colorado tomorrow," he told me. "Peggy knows what to do when you get here. Don't talk to anyone along the way, and only stop for gas and food. Do you understand?"

"Yes, Solar."

"Anything else? Did you tell your grandmother what I said?"

"Yes. She asked us to leave and gave us money for a motel room."

"Okay. Good."

The next morning, we headed to Colorado, where we would discover that Solar was living with Brenda and her family, as well as with Lori, his latest convert.

When we pulled into the address, I remarked, "It's cold here."

"Solar said we're to go in this entrance."

I knocked on the door. Solar opened it and stared at me.

"You're completely possessed with negative entities you picked up at the psych ward. You need to soak in disinfectant to cleanse them from you. Do you understand?"

"Yes," I responded, my face pointed at the ground.

"Leave all your clothes on the bathroom floor, and Peggy will have a change of clean clothes waiting for you when you get out."

Solar turned on the water to fill the tub, and poured in an entire bottle of disinfectant. "Get in."

I soaked for several hours in a quart of Pine Sol concentrate until Peggy spoke from the doorway: "You can get out now." My skin reeked of disinfectant.

We waited for Solar in a darkened room, but could see stairs leading to the basement.

"He's doing laundry," Peggy whispered, and almost as if on cue, we heard Solar shouting downstairs: "CAN'T YOU DO ANYTHING RIGHT?", followed by the muffled sounds of body blows.

Peggy and I looked at each other as we listened to Solar slugging Lori in the basement.

Solar gave us his orders and we left for Arizona to obtain Boy's birth certificate, since his arrival into the world had never been registered. Peggy needed the certificate to regain custody of her son, who was now in foster care.

In Phoenix, Boy officially became Aaron, with Solar registered as his father.

We drove back to California, where Peggy and I set up housekeeping in a duplex on Reynard Way in San Diego. Aaron was in Foster Care in nearby Coronado.

Those were painful days. On our first visit, Aaron did not recognize us, and ran away crying. His long hair had been cut, and he was wearing shoes—both for the first time in his life.

But each visit got easier, and over time he remembered his mother and me, his caretaker.

Peggy and I furnished our apartment in anticipation of getting custody of Aaron. Functioning independently of Solar, we spent many hours discussing our situation and desire to be free of the Program and Solar's control and abuse. Accepting defeat in fulfilling my mission, my love for Peggy and Aaron became my focus as we planned our future together as a family—living away from Solar. Terrified and yet convicted with my dedication to the two of them, we decided our next call to Solar was when we would announce our emancipation from him.

"We love each other and want to raise Aaron out of The Program."

"Let me talk to Peggy."

Handing the phone to her, I covered the receiver and whispered. "He wants to talk to you."

"Yes, that's right." Peggy said and then fell silent as she listened to Solar for several minutes and then with downcast face, handed the phone back to me.

"We'll see about this. I'm coming to California; you two are not to make any decisions on your own or you will never see Aaron again. Do you understand? Do nothing until I get there."

I hung up the phone and Peggy's voice shook as she related her conversation with Solar. "He said that he would fight to take custody of Aaron away from me, proving that I was an unfit mother; that I would never see my son again."

Still spell-bound and frightened of Solar we waited in fear when several days later, he barged into our quiet household unannounced. Next to Solar was a slight blond woman, emaciated and beaten down—the Program look well-known to Peggy and me.

CPS was still visiting to keep tabs on us, and even though Solar hid Lori in the back bedroom, the agency wisely decided that with Solar now on the scene, Peggy had to move back with her parents to regain custody of Aaron. Her parents agreed to the arrangement, and she soon left. I seized the opportunity.

"Solar, now that Peggy and Aaron are living with her parents and you no longer need me to take care of them, I'd like to return to my family."

"You can't go home; I need you here to help me with Lori, who's in The Program now."

"But, Solar, please. I don't want to be here anymore, and I don't want to be in The Program."

Wham! My head was spinning. I hadn't seen that one coming, and was still reeling when he slugged my temple, right ear, and then left ear. My ears went numb; everything was muffled until Solar stuck his face in front of mine and shouted: "YOU ARE NOT DONE WITH YOUR MISSION! I DON'T CARE WHAT YOU WANT, YOU'RE DONE WHEN I SAY YOU ARE. RIGHT NOW, I NEED YOU TO STAY HERE BECAUSE LORI'S IN THE PROGRAM. YOU CAN'T LEAVE UNTIL SHE'S DONE. DON'T GET ANY IDEAS—YOU LEAVE WHEN I SAY YOU CAN LEAVE! I KNOW WHERE YOUR FAMILY LIVES, AND WILL COME GET YOU. YOU DON'T WANT THEM TO GET HURT BECAUSE YOU FAILED TO COMPLETE YOUR MISSION AND LEFT BEFORE YOUR TIME, DO YOU? IF YOU LEAVE BEFORE I SAY YOU CAN, ONE OF THEM IS GOING TO GET HURT!"

I nodded, holding my bleeding head.

The cleaning, laundry, and food preparation for Solar and Lori became my responsibility. Since Lori was in the non-interaction Program, Solar controlled her every moment just as he had done with Peggy and me—it was the only way he knew how to be in a relationship.

Feeling sorry for Lori, I started sneaking her extra portions of rice and cheese. The first time I gave her more food than Solar had ordered, I looked directly into her eyes, glanced toward the room where Solar was, and silently moved my head to signify a "no." Nothing needed to be said, for we both knew that discovery meant a beating for both of us.

Lori and I had to wash our clothes and wear them wet after each of our once-a-day visits to the bathroom. Our showers were limited to when it was convenient for Solar, not our bodies, and Solar still showered only once a week, when he needed to move his bowels.

Grocery shopping offered me relief, for I could breathe fresh air and move about on my own accord. No longer under the watchful eye of CPS, Solar had sealed the windows with his usual aluminum foil. The humidity inside was so intense, the ceilings started dripping with condensation. Lori drew cartoons about my attempts to swab the ever-present drips from the ceiling. But it wasn't funny, as eventually a black fuzzy mold moved in.

"Go buy a gallon of bleach and use that to clean off the mold," Solar commanded one day.

Armed with Clorox, I attempted to slay the furry intruder, swabbing the walls until I had to stop because I was in so much pain. Remembering that chlorine is deadly, I feared I was going to die from all the toxic fumes. I protested, breaking down in tears despite the risk of a beating.

"Solar, I can't breathe. My arms, hands, and lungs are burning, and I can't open my eyes, they sting so badly. Please don't make me do this anymore. I can't see and I can't breathe."

"What a baby! Go get cleaned up and go to the store and bring back some antifungal spray. I'll show you how to clean this up, because you're so incapable."

I returned with the mold spray and Solar marched into the bathroom. Not wanting to scorch my lungs any more than I had already, I tried to hold my breath.

"I CAN'T BREATHE!" Solar was soon shouting.

Practically running to the front door, Solar threw it open and stood outside in his underwear as he inhaled the fresh air. Not wanting to breathe in more fumes, I started to follow, with Lori behind me.

"Stay where you are! Don't move!" He fanned the door, having to break one of his cardinal rules rather than asphyxiate us. I put my shirt up to my face, breathing through it until I no longer smelled the fungus spray.

When Solar came back inside, he closed the door behind him and I noticed his eyes, arms, and hands were burned red. "We need to move. Go find us another place to live!" he ordered.

After much searching, I found an apartment where the three of us could live. On Christmas Day, we moved to a place near San Diego State University where Solar could sequester Lori.

After we settled in, I was driving along Interstate 8 on a food run when fireworks in the sky jolted my memory of a world that included pleasure and celebration. *It must be New Year's Eve.*

A few days later, I was losing the battle for marathon bladder control. My clothes had not dried all day as I slogged around doing Solar's bidding, and I was chilled to the bone from the cold outside. Seeing the apartment complex pool, I stepped in fully clothed and relieved myself as I walked through the shallow end. *I hope someone cleans the pool before they swim in it when the weather warms up.* Being as irrational now as Solar, I still had not realized I could urinate in the shower while washing out my clothes and he would never know. Equally forbidden was finding a bathroom in which to relieve myself; I believed I could not take that risk.

As the months went by, I continued begging Solar to let me leave to be with my grandmother. Every time, he responded by pounding my head, and each time I temporarily lost my hearing. One time, my hearing did not return by the next day, and my ears were oozing blood.

"You still have medical benefits, don't you?" Solar shouted.

"Yes, I was on Medi-Cal at the mental hospital."

"Then go see an ear, nose, and throat doctor."

I nodded in gratitude and found a specialist in the phone book. I drove there without an appointment and waited several hours until I was seen.

"How did you lose your hearing?" the good doctor asked me.

"I picked up an unexploded M-80 firecracker," I said, repeating what Solar had ordered me to say.

"How did you get those bruises on your face and neck?"

"Oh, I guess that must have happened when I fell."

"Your ears are infected from a percussion injury. You may have suffered permanent hearing loss. Take this medicine as prescribed and come back next week for a follow-up exam."

"Thank you." I took the antibiotics, but Solar didn't want me going back. After my infected ears healed, I pleaded again to return home. He slugged my face several times, avoiding my ears.

Several days later I developed an excruciating toothache. "Solar, it's been four days and my tooth in back hurts so badly, I can barely open my mouth."

"Well, I guess you better go see a dentist then."

He had never been so generous before, or offered to send me for medical care. Perhaps he was willing now because he knew I might leave if overwhelmed with pain.

Away I drove, this time to a dentist. "Your molar is fractured. Medi-Cal will not pay for a root canal and crown; I'll have to pull it."

Braced for more questions about the bruises on my face, I was not prepared for the shock of losing a tooth. Clenching my jaw when Solar slugged my face had prevented further chipping of my front teeth, but I'd never imagined that my back teeth would crack as they absorbed the brunt of his blows.

Tears welled in my eyes. *I've never lost a tooth. Even in the Peace Corps I took excellent care of my teeth. God, are my teeth like everything else—Solar's property that he can just destroy?*

On my way home, as I slowed on the freeway off-ramp and rolled up to the light, my heart ached. The deed was done. I opened my door to spit out the blood pooling inside my mouth, and watched horrified as the pavement turned red.

Is this serving God? Apparently, it is.

Slamming the door shut, I drove further into oblivion.

Not long after I received that beating, Lori mentally drifted away to some distant place. Solar decided he knew the cure.

"I'm going to take you to Sedona and Ship Rock, New Mexico. The trip will restore your commitment to The Program and your spiritual growth. Sandy, you stay here and make sure no one comes into our apartment while we're gone. Do you understand?"

"Yes." *What a relief not to have to go with them. Finally, something good is coming from his paranoia.*

Alone, I exercised my freedom by lying on the bed, watching endless TV, and eating when I wanted to. I behaved as Solar did every day, except that he always peed into food storage bags.

I'm not contaminating myself, I rationalized, urinating into the toilet at will and avoiding touching the seat or any part of it. These forbidden behaviors felt luxurious.

I was basking in my brief escape when I heard someone coming up the stairs. I was not expecting their return, for Solar had indicated their stay was to be longer. Fear raced through me. *He's going to know that I haven't been showering after using the bathroom.*

A moment later Peggy stood in front of me. "Solar is downstairs waiting in the car with Lori and Aaron. He wants you to join us because Lori 'lost it' on our trip."

"What?"

"He's taking her home. He wants you immediately."

I eliminated evidence of my rebelliousness, followed Peggy downstairs and climbed into the backseat of the car.

Solar turned around to face me. "I cannot work with someone who's mentally unstable. We're going to drop Lori off at her parents' home. I need you to come with us."

Can this be true? Do I finally get my freedom because Lori's going home? Solar promised me I could go home when she was no longer in the Program. Thank God, and thank you that he did not discover the liberties I took while he was gone.

I felt elated as I waited in the car while Solar walked Lori to her front door, but did not dare watch him return.

"I left her at their front door," he said. "We'll wait a few minutes, then drive by to check on her." He started the engine, drove slowly past the house, and then pronounced, "She's nowhere to be seen. They must have let her inside. Let's go."

He drove Peggy and Aaron back to her parents' home in Downey, but kept me for several more weeks, claiming he needed me for cleaning his rooms while moving from motel to motel around the Los Angeles area.

I prayed daily to be released. *Lucky Lori!* I constantly thought.

"Before I send you home, Sandy, you need to contact Lori to make sure she's all right."

I know you want her back. You once told me you could never live alone. Coward, let her go; and let me go home.

After collecting Peggy to aid him on this mission, Solar parked the car across the street from Lori's home.

"Sandy, go ring the doorbell nonstop for a full five minutes, or until someone answers. Don't come back until you talk to Lori."

I walked up to the front door and rang it several times, pausing in between. *No one's answering. Maybe I should look through the peephole. I see someone behind the door, but why don't they answer?* I pressed the button and held it down, counting out five minutes.

I returned to the car. "Solar, I rang the doorbell for a full five minutes and no one answered."

"Go back and ring it another five minutes."

I walked back and did as he asked. *This is rude! I've never done such a thing before; it feels creepy.*

I reported another unsuccessful attempt.

"Get in the car immediately!" Solar snapped. "Don't say anything; let me do the talking."

I climbed into the front seat next to Peggy—and the next thing I knew, policemen were surrounding us and shining their flashlights inside the car.

"We know who you are; we've been warned about you," the officer closest to us proclaimed. They walked around the car but stayed about six feet away as they circled us.

Solar spoke to the cop nearest the driver's side. "My fiancée is in that house, and I believe her parents have kidnapped her and are preventing her from seeing me."

"They called us to demand that you leave. We know you use some kind of mind control, and you need to leave now," said a husky voice behind the flashlight. "We know you call yourself Solar and that you have Sandy and Peggy with you, and that they're victims of your abuse. You have no right to be here and need to leave immediately."

Since domestic violence was not yet a criminal offense, they could not arrest Solar, even though they knew he was abusing us.

"But they're holding my fiancée hostage and keeping her from me," Solar pleaded once again.

"Sir, you are being ordered to leave NOW! We will arrest you if you choose to remain here after being asked to leave."

Solar started the car and drove cautiously down the street, looking all around to make sure he was not being followed; cursing the entire time. "Fucking cops and fucking Lori. She must be totally demon-possessed by now. I know she's been completely taken over by the dark side if she called the police on me."

He continued complaining about how the dark forces had foiled his plans as he drove us to where Peggy's parents lived in a different section of Los Angeles. Once he had dropped her off, we headed south to the ranch.

He stopped in front of my grandmother's house. "I promised to let you go home once Lori was out of the Program. We're here."

"Thank you. 'Bye." I hopped out and bolted across the lawn and through the gate before he changed his mind.

I turned to close the latch behind me, and watched the back of his car disappear down the driveway in a cloud of dust. I breathed in the fresh air as a soft breeze rustled the trees surrounding my grandmother's home. *I'm free! I'm free!*

As I pivoted to face the house, I thought, *Please God, let her welcome me to stay with her; help her to forgive me for what I said and did the last time I saw her.*

Ordinarily, family walked in through the back door without knocking. But because of our last encounter, I didn't know if I would be welcome; especially since Gramma had asked Peggy and me to leave. It had been almost four years since I had relinquished my life to Solar with the express intention of deepening my connection with God and discovering how to deliver the message given me in South America. Believing that I had finished the Program, I now reached through the years of that foggy nightmare, held my breath, and knocked.

TWENTY-SIX

The inside door opened, and with my next heartbeat Gramma opened the screen door and smiled at me.

"Well, hello, Sandy. Come in. Are you alone?"

"Yes, Gramma, I left Solar. Could I stay with you while I figure things out?"

"Yes, of course! Come in, come in," and she ushered me into her open heart. I walked into her arms and cried softly, and then entered the kitchen with its familiar smells. The furniture I had known welcomed me back, and the same pictures of family members on the refrigerator greeted my return. Gifts and mementos adorned her mantel and bookshelves, and I instantly felt safe and calm.

"Please sit down," she said, motioning me towards a rocking chair. "Where are the rest of your things?"

I dug my driver's license from a pocket and placed it on the counter. "This is it; I only have these clothes. I don't even have my glasses; they got broken." I could not explain that long ago Solar had slapped my face, sent the glasses flying, and then stomped on the lenses.

We made light conversation as she caught me up on the family news and, eventually, suggested I make myself comfortable in a room upstairs.

I left her sitting in her chair and walked up the familiar carpeted steps, remembering how we kids had ridden down them atop her window seat cushions and worn the carpeting bare. Heartfelt relief rushed through me as I remembered my forbidden "past" and the people who had shared it. *What was so awful about that?*

The west bedroom where Peggy, Boy, and I had encamped still caused my stomach to clench, so I backed away and walked into my aunt's room. I sat on the bed to test its comfort, then walked into my father's room and chuckled at my Goldilocks behavior as I sat on his bed too. Deciding my aunt's felt better, I returned to her room, sat down again . . . and stared at the wallpaper. *Now I can speak with whomever I wish, touch or get near anyone, eat and eliminate when I need to...*

My eyes filled with tears. I blew my nose and announced: "I can wear clothes of my choosing, and do whatever I want. Why, God? Why was all that necessary and so brutal? Please explain all of it to me. Why? Why?" I collapsed onto the bed, sobbing.

Eventually, my tears lessened and I stood up, motivated to start putting my life back together even though I still lacked answers to justify all the abuse I had sustained.

I stared out the bedroom window until I felt ready to rejoin my grandmother. I walked deliberately as I entered the kitchen, noticing how much lighter I felt. *I am no longer going to be punished or restricted for my mistakes.*

"I looked through my closet for some things I thought you could wear." My grandmother pointed to clothes on the back of the chair I was going to occupy. "You need something to wear until you can get some clothes of your own. They might be too big for you, but will have to do for now. I'm going to give you some money to buy some that will fit you better."

I walked over to hug her. "Thank you, Gramma." Choked with her generosity, I picked up the clothes and took them upstairs to hang in the closet.

The next day I still felt dazed, and decided to fill my free time by reading. I discovered that my grandmother had a fascinating array of *Time* and *Life* magazines and book compilations reflecting current events. She read two newspapers every day, and I took full advantage of her supply of educational books and magazines, inhaling volumes of glossy images of politicians, world events, and movie stars—all unknown to me. *Madonna, the Iran hostage crisis, violence in El Salvador, the Pope shot and the AIDS epidemic. What is that? I've missed so much.* Satiating my curiosity and trying to erase my naïveté, I plowed through the information commonly known to everyone else. "Good grief" escaped my lips as I read about the wars and conflict in the Falklands, Lebanon, Grenada, Iran, and Iraq.

"Princess Grace and John Lennon died. How could that happen?" I asked aloud in wide-eyed amazement. My sequestration had created the illusion that nothing was changing, but life had continued in my absence from society. *People all over the world are facing their individual and collective struggles, except mine seem so unfair.* In my self-absorption, it was difficult for me to recognize that none of it was fair.

Not long after I arrived, my grandmother ventured to ask, "What do you plan on doing?"

"I don't know."

"Well, if you'd like, Franklin has work he said you could do on his property in Ramona. They bought some acreage when they left the valley, and he said the caretakers have neglected his trees."

Sixteen years earlier, Franklin had rescued me from the ranch, and was again offering me a lifeline.

He picked me up and we drove to the property in Ramona they had purchased when forced to sell their land because of the water rights lawsuit with the City of San Diego. He and his wife were among the thirteen family members of a total of seventeen plaintiffs who had sued the city for violating their water rights with the construction of the Sutherland Dam that caused the water tables to drop. The dam harnessed the Santa Ysabel River, one of the three that flowed in San Pasqual. Even though they won damages against the city, everyone ultimately lost their land when the city condemned it through eminent domain.

They had been awarded a million dollars in damages in the judgment against the city, quite a lot of money in the 1950s. However, when forced to sell their land, they were given a pittance. Ever since that event, our family farms had been owned by the City of San Diego.

Toiling in the foothills of Ramona to save my Uncle Franklin's trees and my sanity, I pleaded for answers from God as I worked. I was relieved to be outside in nature and spent my breaks kneeling in prayer, desperately begging for understanding.

"Why, God? Why did I deserve all the abuse? Tell me, please. I was given that message and thought Solar's Program was your answer to my prayers. Solar claims he was sent to save us; that he is 'Source.' Is that true? How can it be true? He also claimed I deserved the abuse because of my sins, that I needed to atone for them. Am I so evil that I deserved the beatings and deprivation? Please God, tell me. Am I evil? Solar says I am. Solar says I'm among the lowest and most evil of people who have walked the planet—and that is why I deserved the beatings. God, is that true? Please, tell me."

Over and over I begged for answers. I cried and prayed throughout every day, attempting to purge my grief and make sense of all I had experienced. I never got answers to the questions haunting me, but the daily physical work was a relief.

One day as I drove into the ranch after work, I found my brother Bruce working on the dune buggy he was constructing.

He looked up to ask, "Do you know how you're going to get transportation when you finish with Uncle Franklin's work?"

"No. I hope to have enough money to buy a junker, because I do need something."

"Why don't you look for an old VW and I'll help you renovate it? Then you can sell it and get an even better car with the money."

"Oh, wow, Bruce. You'd do that? I'll start looking."

Less than a week passed before I found an ad in the paper for a cheap VW Beetle in the San Diego area.

"What do you think?" I asked Bruce.

"Call to see if it's still available, and ask them to hold it so we can see it."

As we pulled into the seller's driveway, we could see a worn 1963 VW Beetle covered in black house paint. The tires were bald and the interior thrashed. Bruce tinkered a little with the engine, got in and started it, and asked to drive it around the block. I stayed with the owner until Bruce returned, shut off the engine, and crawled out.

"Sam, come here a second." I walked up beside him, and he spoke to me with his voice lowered. "I think you should get it, but don't offer them as much as they're asking. It's salvageable but needs a *lot* of work. The body is solid and the tranny is good, but you're looking at a new engine, new seats and interior upholstery, plus tires. Not to mention new paint." We both laughed. "Basically, we're going to have to completely refurbish it."

"And you think it's worth it?"

"Oh yeah. I can drop in a used engine, and the rest is a piece of cake."

The price was negotiated and the pink slip signed and handed to me.

"Let me drive it, since it's not very safe," Bruce offered. "Just follow me in case it stops." He folded his six-foot six-inch frame into my "new" car and, with knees against his chest, eased out onto the road. I followed in our grandmother's Thunderbird.

Bruce and I labored together, reconnecting with one another as we renovated my Beetle. The ranch was an ideal place for our project, with an ample supply of tools and space and our shared love for it.

One day while we were working on the car, our grandmother came outside. "Sandy, someone from the Employment Development Department wants to speak with you."

I shrugged at Bruce as I got up to follow her back to the house.

"Hello, is this Sandra Judson?"

"Yes, that's me."

"I'm Officer Brown, an investigator with the California Employment

Development Department. I need you to come down to San Diego to answer a few questions for me."

"Am I in trouble with the law?"

"No. You're not in trouble. I just need to ask you a few questions. When can you come to my office?"

I borrowed Gramma's car for the drive. A large, burly man stood up to greet me as I was escorted into his office.

"Thank you for coming. I'm a fraud investigator for EDD. Do you recognize this man?" He held up a copy of a driver's license.

"Yes, that's Solar. Why do you ask?"

"I hope you're not involved with this man at the present time."

"Oh no. I moved back home and am trying to get my life together. I want nothing to do with him. Why?"

"You know a Lori—?"

"Yes. Is she okay?"

"Yes. She and her family have pressed charges against Solar for illegally using her unemployment benefits. Do you know anything about that?"

"Oh, man. Yes, unfortunately, I do. Solar had me impersonate Lori to get her unemployment benefits. She was in this non-interactional spiritual program that did not allow her to leave the apartment or to interact with the outside world, and so I became her surrogate. Solar had me bleach my hair, perfect Lori's signature, and use her license to obtain the benefits. Am I in trouble for that?"

"Well, young-lady, actually, you're not. But you know that what you did is highly illegal and would constitute fraud if Lori had wanted to press charges against you."

"Oh, wow. Lori said she wanted the benefits, and Solar insisted I impersonate her. He controlled us both."

"I am well-aware of this. Lori and her family have filed charges against him with the district attorney in Los Angeles. They want this Solar arrested for his mind control tactics. Unfortunately, I'm afraid we lack sufficient evidence to prosecute him. Lori shared her concern for you and your safety. I hope you steer clear of this man; he sounds very dangerous. Are you willing to write a sworn statement that you are no longer involved with him and did all that under his control?"

"Oh, yes, absolutely."

Bruce and I were outside working on my car when our father drove down the hill from his house and onto the ranch. He nodded his hat at us and went inside to visit with his mother. Not long after, he came back out.

"You impersonated someone?" he said to me. "I knew there was a reason why your hair was bleached blond. This is not good. You were lucky this time."

"I know, Dad. I don't plan on doing anything like that again."

"I sure hope not. Maybe you've learned your lesson this time."

"Yeah." I looked at my brother, whose eyes were filled with sympathy. "I've been thinking; I want to get away from here. Solar knows where I am. I don't feel safe, and the thought that he could come around is scary. I spoke with our cousin Donna about moving up north to live with her, and she was thrilled. You know she's divorced now. She said she could use my help."

"What about your car?" my father asked.

"It's almost finished," Bruce offered, "and when it's done, she's going to sell it and buy a better one."

"Something that can handle the snow," I added.

"Well, I guess Donna will keep you honest. She's always been good for you. Try and stay out of trouble this time."

"I will." It was the longest conversation I'd had with my father in many years.

"What's so good about where Donna is?" Bruce asked after our father left. "Have you ever been there?"

"No, but she says it's in the middle of nowhere about an hour outside of Redding. It sounds like a paradise. You know Donna and I gardened together when I returned from the Peace Corps and was staying with Gramma. We spent a lot of time together, and she helped me get through my 'culture shock.' She was even open to the earth changes that The Manuscript spoke about."

"Oh, yeah?"

"Yes. You know the Adventists believe the world is coming to an end soon."

"Do you still believe that?"

"Yes, if we don't do something to change. But I don't know much about anything else right now. I need some time and space to figure things out."

"How will you support yourself up there?"

"Donna said I could work for my room and board. She basically lives off the land, and I plan on helping her out as much as I can. I need to get a job at some point, but I don't feel able to do that just yet. I'm still pretty confused about everything that's happened to me."

"Well, I hope you're done with that man."

"I don't plan on ever seeing him again. Now, how much is left to do on my car? It's really looking good."

A few weeks later, we stood admiring our handiwork.

"It looks so good; I almost hate to sell it," I said. "I'm so grateful to you for all your help."

I showed the car at my mother's home and it sold quickly. After the new owner drove away, my mother asked me to come inside.

"Sandy, I have something to discuss with you." Her tone was serious.

She handed me some photocopied pages of text.

"What's this?" I said.

"Lori sent it. Please read it. Now."

Lori had written in the margins:

> This is taken from the book Thought Reform and the Psychology of Totalism—A Study of "Brainwashing" in China. This chapter contains the eight criteria used to determine whether a group is, in fact, a cult. Knoblock will be using this, so I thought it important

for you to become familiar with it. Solar fit all eight points. I've underlined pertinent parts and made notes describing the specific techniques to which Sandy and I were subjected...

Specifically, Solar controlled all forms of communication. He seldom allowed us to listen to anything or anyone but him, or to communicate with each other. We were required to tell him every thought, dream, or action and this on a daily-basis. When Sandy, Peggy, and Boy lived at Grandma's, he called constantly and insisted that they tell him what they had done each day and everything they had said to each other. He had us write "DAILY ACCOUNTING," detailing every aspect of our experiences.

When we lived together and Sandy did the shopping, he forced her to tell him every single aspect of her day under constant threat of beatings or worse: separation from him or eternal non-existence. Beatings were "necessary" to help rid us of "negative" entities. Solar was "chosen" by "Source" to help the twelve to return to spirituality. We believed all that Solar did was out of love and that we could improve. We believed in the HIGHER PURPOSE of becoming "aware" and helping save Humankind from imminent destruction. The betrayals included lying to our families, lying to authorities, hate letters home, fraud (forgery, etc.).

The ultimate-goal became releasing ego and separateness from Source. We were to "merge" with Solar and trust all that he did or said. We were constantly made to feel shame over our past and guilty that we had been unable to become "spiritual." We were told we had failed but that by staying with Solar we could still "improve."

In this regard, he was most merciless with Sandy. She was "black," "negative," "evil," that her constant desire to return home and give up the "spiritual quest" was evidence of her fallen nature. But, if Sandy would only "be good," and give Solar "harmony," he could "allow her consciousness to live after her physical death." Sandy always talked about how low she was, how "stupid and negative," how "unworthy" of Solar's "love and forgiveness and help." She viewed herself as being worse than a "HOLOGRAM," a "LIGHTWORKER" gone bad.

When Solar insisted that we "confess" or "expose" our lies or "negative actions," we would often confess to smaller things while guarding the larger "betrayals." I did this often and I know Sandy did, too. Confessing a little bit helped to partly dissuade our guilt over keeping secrets. Solar would force us to hear each other's confessions and join him in judging. Of course, we always said what we knew he wanted us to say. It is obvious to me that this was extremely painful for Sandy and me. I hated saying anything bad about her, but the fear of Solar forced me to do so. If I disagreed or supported Sandy, he flew into a rage.

We believed that through Solar we had found the ultimate truths of the Universe, yet when so often these truths were changed and we questioned the inconsistencies, we were beaten and verbally abused for doubting. We were told we were too stupid and negative to possibly understand. The guilt and fear became unbearable at times. We worked so hard to try to understand and learn and be worthy . . . Sandy has a wonderful command of English. If she used words Solar didn't understand he would become irate and forbid her to use them, or tell her she didn't know what they meant. He constantly put her down as being stupid, ignorant, a "hick."

Our pasts were gone over time and again and distorted. We were made to confess to our worst sins, and then Solar would blow them up. Soon, I couldn't tell reality from Solar's paranoid imagination.

So often Sandy expressed the desire to help people, to eat health food, etc., but she was always quieted because these things were "unspiritual." . . . In Solar's paranoid schizophrenia, he truly believed that HE was the only path to perfection. We were threatened with the death of consciousness after physical death. We would cease to exist forever...

Dear Sandy,
   I love you.
Lori

"It's not like that," I blurted.

"It's brainwashing!" my mother said. "You've been beaten and brainwashed. Are you going to deny that?" She was angry. "Lori said she was professionally deprogrammed, and thinks you could benefit from that as well."

"Well, you wouldn't understand. I was given a mission in South America. Anyway, I'm away from Solar now—it's over, so let's forget about it."

I left with the money from my car.

TWENTY-SEVEN

A few days later I was driving north with a new car and a full heart, feeling confident about my fresh start. *Everything's going to be all right.*

As I drove, my thoughts drifted to memories of all the times Donna and I had spent together gardening, baking, and worshiping. When I'd moved in with my grandmother after leaving my mother's house, Donna had been living in one of the family's original homesteads with her husband and two sons. Our connection had deepened as we worked and worshiped together. We had even started our own community co-op, buying our food in bulk from several places on the coast and distributing it among our neighbors.

Donna shared my passion for gardening. Since we'd lived on some of the richest farmland in San Diego County, we took full advantage of this blessing. She'd taught me all the gardening tricks she knew and tutored me in canning, freezing, and how to dehydrate fruits and vegetables. A master baker and fabulous cook, she had also mentored me as we made candy and baked pies, pastries, and every type of bread one could imagine.

If only the starving families in Cartagena had land like we did in San Pasqual to grow their own food. It all seems so unfair. I wish I were still there to help them. Why was I given that message? I didn't ask for that; if only that had never happened. I wonder if Donna is still open to hearing about my paranormal experiences. We used to pray together about Biblical prophecies. What is her faith like now?

My cousin's directions led me through a forested area north of Redding, California, almost in the shadow of Mount Shasta. As I descended the driveway to her backwoods retreat, she came out to greet me.

"I thought you'd never get here," she said as she squeezed me tight.

We unloaded the oranges and avocados I'd brought from the ranch, and then she gave me a tour of her place. I followed her behind the house, along a small path that led across a plank footbridge with a creek running under it. Walking into the trees lining the creek, she stopped and pointed to a small building. "You can stay here in the guest cabin. Can you hear the river?"

"Yes! You have a creek *and* a river?"

"They feed into the Sacramento River. Pretty cool, huh?"

We walked up the stairs and through the screened porch. Donna pushed open the heavy wooden door to reveal a small, cozy room, completely furnished. "There's electricity but only cold water in the kitchen sink. You can use one of the chamber pots or hike up to the bathhouse over there. That's where you can shower."

"It's perfect! Did you bring your furniture from the house in San Pasqual?"

"Yup. Even the wallpaper is the same—it was here when we bought it. Weird, isn't it?"

"It feels like home!"

"Now it's your home. Come on and I'll show you the bathhouse."

I floated behind Donna as she headed to a square red building nestled between the cabin and main house.

"This is so amazing." I inhaled the brisk air and took in the stereophonic rushing from the river and little creek.

"Let me show you my garden."

We followed the path into a high-fenced area half the size of a football field. She was growing something everywhere—trees, plants, vines, vegetables, fruits, flowers. She introduced me to every section while pointing out upcoming weeding and planting projects.

"This is a so wonderful!" I cried. "Thank you so much for letting me stay here." *God, thank you. If I had to go through all that with Solar to deserve this, then it was worth it.*

Life with Donna was tied to the land and the simple pleasures that brings. Her boys, the vegetable garden, fruit and nut trees, grapes, flowers, chickens, dogs, and the wildlife kept us occupied. I was glad to help with the chores, and although exhausted at the end of each day, I felt a sense of accomplishment and was filled with peace and gratitude. The land was not as ideal as in San Pasqual, but Donna had created good soil through rototilling and composting. The abundance of rocks served as garden wells for raised beds. We couldn't grow twenty-three different varieties of melons like we had before, but we tried several varieties nonetheless. With a shorter growing season and uncooperative weather, her greenhouse helped keep seedlings alive until the frosts stopped. The Northern California climate made gardening more challenging, but our efforts were not without rewards, for which we gave many thanks.

The summer months whirled by as we gardened, canned, and froze the produce, and in the fall her grapes ripened. We squeezed and canned quarts and quarts of juice and made fruit leather and jelly with the rest. When the last of the food preparations were done, we stacked firewood for the winter.

But as the year waned I began to feel uneasy, the way I'd felt with Solar when he was beating us all the time. I called Peggy to make sure she and Aaron were okay.

"We're fine. Aaron is growing, and talking up a storm. Where are you?"

"I'm staying with my cousin in the woods away from everything. I love it here."

"I'm glad you're happy. Can I have your phone number in case I need to get in touch with you?"

"Sure," I said, and gave it to her.

Even though Peggy and Aaron were fine, my sense of anxiety remained. I meditated and prayed, hoping to discover the source of my discomfort. I decided to hook up my tape recorder, thinking I could ask for and record higher guidance. I left the microphone on my chest as I prayed and fell asleep.

The next morning when I listened to the tape, I was mortified to hear my voice say, "In the very near future, you will rejoin Solar because you are not done with your mission."

This can't be! How could you want me to return to him, God? Why do I have to go back to the bowels of hell?

Upset, I decided to use a technique Solar relied on to get a "sign" when he was in doubt. I found three coins for my challenge.

"One Heart, One Mind, One Spirit. God, please give me a sign whether, or not that tape-recorded message is true. Heads I get to stay here, tails I need to return to Solar to complete my mission." I threw the pennies into the air, then peered at them. All three were tails.

Dazed, I walked to the house.

"What's wrong?" Donna asked.

I played the message on the recorder.

"Well, let's pray about this. That doesn't necessarily mean you have to do what it says."

Together we prayed, and yet I remained disconnected, trudging through my days, thrashing against the fear that was swallowing me.

A few days later I got a phone call. "Hi, Sandy. Do you know who this is?"

"How did you get this number?" I demanded.

"Peggy gave it to me."

"I never want to see you again. I'm very happy where I am, and I don't want anything to do with you." I hung up.

"Who was that?" Donna asked.

"Solar. Peggy gave him my number. I can't believe she'd do something like that."

"I'm sorry. Is she still hanging around him?"

"Apparently so. Too bad—she has his son, you know. Let's go get some weeding done."

Several days later, I woke up with a throbbing tooth. I ignored it, but the next day I noticed a sore at the base of my gum.

"Will you look at this?" I asked Donna, who had worked as a dental assistant for years.

"It looks infected," she said. "You need to have it looked at."

"I don't have any money for a dentist."

"I know, and unfortunately, neither do I. Do you think your mom would help you out?"

I phoned my mother, who told me she would pay for my dental work—if I went down to San Diego to have it done. "She doesn't trust me with the money," I explained to Donna.

"Let's load up your car with apples you can use to barter for oranges and avocados for when you return. I also have some things for everyone down south."

I had arranged to stay with my grandmother. Once I settled in, I visited the same dentist who had previously pulled out my molar—she was the only dentist I knew.

"The tooth is abscessed," she told me. "You'll need a root canal and crown."

"What do you think caused the abscess?"

"Well, sometimes teeth get infected . . . but trauma can also cause them to dislodge and become abscessed over time."

As she said it she looked right at me, and I felt that she was referring to the cracked molar she'd removed before. Avoiding her gaze, I said nothing.

The dental work would take a couple of weeks to complete. During that time, away from the isolation and protection of my cousin's retreat, I felt extremely vulnerable.

Just before my crown was completed, Peggy called. "Solar and Brenda are living out of a broken-down truck at a rest stop in Arizona. They haven't eaten for days. I bought them a replacement car, but after I take it to them I'll need a ride back to Los Angeles. Will you help me?"

It had been only six months since I'd escaped from Solar. Out of love and concern for Peggy and Aaron, I felt obligated to help her . . . but not Solar. Of course, they would have to wait until my dental work was completed.

Shortly before we departed, Lori sent another letter to my mother, dated October 31, 1983:

Dear Alice,

I received a letter from Jim Knoblock in which he stated that you still had not been able to find help for Sandy. This saddens me. I wish for her the joy of freedom and peace of mind that I have found since I was released from those clutches of Hell in which I existed for so long. I know your frustration.

Mom, Dad, and I have just returned from a three-day conference held by CFF [Citizens Freedom Foundation]. I wish you could have been there. It was moving and enlightening, to say the least. I've enclosed some things I thought might help open some doors for you. Also, in case you have not spoken with these two individuals, I am sending their numbers and addresses. They are cult exit counselors. Mark Blocksom, Specialized Counseling Services, Inc., P.O. Box 1014, Mesa, AZ 85201 (602) 835-7954. And David Clark—Court-certified Cult Expert (215) 544-5830—Northern Virginia. (David specializes in "scripture groups" or bible (sic) cults. Since Solar used the bible (sic) I thought this young man might be helpful. If nothing else, either one can open some new doors for you.)

The special investigator from the unemployment dept. came to the house and let me read Sandy's statement. From her tone, it is obvious to me that she is still in the grips of devastating mind control.

We have had our phone number changed, and I am not at liberty to give it to you, for obvious reasons. Please feel free to correspond with me through letters, if you wish. I think of you often.

Good luck,

Lori

Without knowing about Lori's letter and her assessment of me, or the information she had shared with my mother, I left my grandmother's house with a trunk filled with oranges and avocados. After driving through LA to meet Peggy at her home in Downey, I followed her as she drove the "replacement car" to Solar.

Peggy eased into the rest stop and pulled up next to a nice looking truck. I parked far away and watched from the safety of my car as Brenda and Solar climbed out of it. Brenda held onto Solar's arm and stared at the ground; she was obviously back in The Program. *Look at how emaciated she is.* Solar glanced in my direction as they talked, and then Peggy walked over to my window.

"He wants to talk to you."

"Well, I don't want to talk with him."

"Please, just get out and speak with him. He's really changed."

"No. I have nothing to say to him. I only came here to help you out."

"He said I couldn't leave until you speak with him. Please, just get out and talk to him so we can go."

Reluctantly I climbed out and stopped about six feet in front of Solar and Brenda. *Things don't seem to change with you—same old flip-flops and flannel shirts over Levis.*

"How have you been?" he asked, Brenda still clinging to his arm.

"Fine, thank you. I only came here to help out Peggy."

"What about your incomplete mission, the work you promised to do, and your commitment to God? And what about the message you received? When are you going to complete that?"

"I don't know."

"You know I'm your only hope to do it. You'll be turning your back on God again if you walk away and don't complete your mission. Don't you care about your family and their salvation?"

"Of course I do!"

"Well then, how do you think you're going to get your work done without me? Have you thought about that? What have you been doing the whole time you've been away from me? Have you done anything important related to your mission? Doesn't look like it. You're worthless without me. You need me to complete your mission; otherwise you're lost."

I said nothing.

"You know I'm right. If you love your family, you'll finish what you started. If you want them to love you, you'll complete this—the most important work you've ever undertaken. For once in your life, you'll be doing something important, something that has higher spiritual meaning."

Why does my brain feel so foggy?

"I think you need to consider your incomplete mission," he said. "How are you going to face yourself and your family if you don't finish?"

"I haven't figured that out yet." I was responding automatically now.

"Where are you headed after you leave here?" he asked.

"Back to my cousin's after I drop Peggy off."

"Why don't you take her and Aaron with you?"

"Because I have work to do when I get back."

"If you don't take them, I promise you'll never see them again."

"All right. I guess I can take them," I said, and walked back to my car. Peggy talked with Solar a few more minutes, and then got in my car. Our trip back to Los Angeles was silent.

After we picked up Aaron, I drove the three of us back north to my cousin's. Donna was thrilled to meet Peggy and Aaron, and gave them the same hospitality she had shown me. For the first time in his life, Aaron frolicked and played in snow.

I struggled to sell all the firewood I had cut, and decided it wasn't worth the effort. During that period Solar called several times, each time adding more pressure on me to "complete my mission."

I listened. The truth was, part of me already knew I was bound to fulfill the prophecy I'd left myself on the tape recorder: I would return to Solar.

When I told Donna this, she tried to talk me out of it. "You don't have to go back to him; you can stay here. I don't understand why you feel it necessary to take up with him."

"I believe I was given a mission, and Solar is my only hope of accomplishing it."

"Oh, Sandy. How can I get you to see that what you're doing is not good for you?"

"You can't."

Soon after that Peggy and I drove south, dropped Aaron off at his grandparents, and turned east toward Arizona.

Later, as I listened to Solar and Peggy talking to one another, I realized he had never stopped controlling her life. Furthermore, although I had managed quite well without Solar controlling my every move, I found his ultimate authority was somehow a relief to me. It felt familiar and by embracing it, I no longer had to wrestle with the uncertainty of my life.

Still pursuing his "divine quest," Solar drove Peggy, Brenda, and me up to Montana. He frequently traveled there, since returning to his family was still his default solution when he ran out of money or people to support him.

On a frozen and wintry day, shortly after we settled in a motel in the Big Sky State, the law caught up with Solar. The four of us had been staying in a motel for several weeks while Peggy ran errands and bought our food and groceries. Even though she paid for our lodging with freshly laundered one-hundred-dollar bills reeking of Pine Sol, we had not aroused suspicion until housekeeping reported Solar's usual departing chaos.

The temperature was below freezing as we slogged to the car through the snow in wet clothes. Brenda sat in the front seat, and Peggy and I in back. My clothes stiffened with ice, and I began to shake uncontrollably while waiting for Solar to start the car.

Click, click, click.

"God Damn it!" He had ground the battery dead. "Get out now, before we freeze to death! Hurry! We need to cross the street and get another room. Go, get going."

Walking in the snow, I left a trail of blood as the frozen straps on my plastic shoes ground the skin off my bare feet. Solar opened the lobby door, and I welcomed the blast of heat from their fire. As we huddled around it to thaw, Peggy secured another room, returning with a key she handed to Solar.

"Go get the battery jumped or buy a new one," he ordered as he shoved the car keys and money into her hands. Then he ushered Brenda and me to the room. No sooner had he closed the door than someone knocked.

"Open up, it's the police."

Solar signaled us to move back, and opened the door. Two officers walked in.

"We have some questions for all of you," one of them said. He pointed at me. "You stay here with me, and they'll go in the other room with him."

Solar and Brenda followed the other officer, and the first one turned to me. "The housekeeping manager of the hotel where you just stayed reported that you guys left the room in shambles. Why did you rip up the phone book and all the tourist pamphlets and hide them underneath the bed covers in the bathroom?"

"Oh, that. Solar has a thing for cleanliness, and he feels those things are 'dirty' and 'contaminated with public energies' so he puts them in the bathroom before leaving a room."

"Why did he take the toilet paper holder off and place it under all the towels and a mountain of trash?"

"Those are more things he considers dirty."

The officer stared at me in disbelief.

I wish I could tell you he does that in every room. You have no idea how obsessed he is with cleanliness. If I could only tell you . . .

But I couldn't. Fearing that my eyes might betray me, and the repercussions I would face if I told the truth, I looked away.

"And the paper towels by the door? Was that more of the same?"

I nodded.

"Okay. I'll be right back." He left to join his partner in the other room with Solar and Brenda. I could hear them talking, and then after a few minutes they walked them into the room where I was.

"Well, there is nothing here we can arrest you for. We're done here," one of them said as they walked towards the door and left.

Solar closed the door behind them and turned to me. "Did you look them in the eyes like I told you to do from now on?"

"Yes, I did."

"I want to know everything he asked you and what you said."

I started repeating the policeman's interrogation, but before I could relate my response, Peggy knocked.

"I got the battery jumped, and the car is locked and running now."

"Okay, let's get out of here," Solar responded and began herding us out the door. I followed closely behind, feeling relieved that I did not have to recount my conversation with the policeman. Solar would have most likely found it incriminating and therefore deserving of punishment.

We left this room in dry clothes—a first for us—without all the rituals, cleaning, cursing, and melodrama that usually accompanied motel stays.

TWENTY-EIGHT

You and Peggy need to work," Solar announced while driving toward Los Angeles. "We need the money."

"We could work for a temporary agency until we find something permanent," Peggy suggested. "There are lots in LA."

"Okay. We'll start here, in Sun Valley. Go get us a room, Peggy, and I expect you guys to find a job tomorrow."

Through an agency, I found work at a television studio as a temporary assistant. I loved this job and the people at the studio. When my time was finished, Cat, my boss, approached me.

"*Mama's Family* was picked up by a network, and I'd like you to come work for me as my personal assistant. You'd need to travel with me—can you do that?"

"Thank you, I'd love to!" I blurted before realizing I was not free to make my own decisions. "Well, I need to think about it; I'll let you know tomorrow."

"Fair enough," she replied, and I left, ecstatic but unsure how Solar would take this new development.

He shut me down. "You are not to take that job; do you understand? How can you finish your mission if you do? You'll be done when I say you're done or when we run completely out of money and support for the work I'm doing. That will be a sign that my quest is over."

The next day, I returned to the temporary agency and interviewed for a different position with the Mirisch Agency. Hired on the spot, I left feeling triumphant and returned to Solar with this good fortune.

"You can't take that job! I don't want you working directly under a man! Go back and tell them you need a different one!"

I was to start the next day, but returned to the agency. "I'm sorry, but I cannot accept the job after all."

"Are you crazy?" The agent who had hired me looked shocked. "You don't turn down a job with this agency and expect to get anywhere in this industry."

"I know, and I'm very sorry to have wasted your time, but I cannot accept the job."

"Fine. Suit yourself. There's the door."

As I walked out, thoughts drifted through me. *My stomach hurts. Is this destiny I'm walking away from? Or is it my destiny to complete my mission? I guess I'm doing what I'm supposed to do and should ignore what's happening inside me.*

True to what I was told, the temp agency didn't have any more jobs for me. Solar interpreted this to mean it was time for us to leave Sun Valley. "Peggy, I'm taking you back to your parents. You need to take care of Aaron and get a job in Los Angeles. Brenda and Sandy are coming with me to Phoenix."

Lucky Peggy! I envy you being able to stay home in a normal environment, wearing dry clothes and living as you please.

As we drove back to Arizona yet again, Solar mused, "We'll be safe in Phoenix. The earth changes will begin this year."

I did not respond. *That's right, it's 1984—the year that Edgar Cayce and other psychics predicted that Phoenix would become a coastal city on the Pacific. If the big quakes are coming, God, please let me be in one. What a great way to die.*

Within days, we had moved into a furnished "snowbird" rental in Phoenix. As we settled in, Solar stated my next task: "Go get a job and don't come back until you have one. Stop at every office building until someone hires you."

Walking to the door, I glanced toward Solar and Brenda lying in bed. "Goodbye," I said, and reached for the door handle.

"STOP!" When I turned around, Solar was striding toward me. *Thud*; his fist found my stomach. "That's for contaminating yourself before you left. How dare you mix our energies with the outside world! Now go and clean yourself and DO NOT SPEAK TO US OR EVEN LOOK IN OUR DIRECTION WHEN YOU LEAVE! DO YOU UNDERSTAND?"

"Yes," I gasped. As I washed, showered, and disinfected, I anguished over the insanity of it all.

Why, God? Please, tell me why I need to do this.

An hour later, I walked successfully out the door. As I flip-flopped my way along the sidewalks of downtown Phoenix in the midday sun, my clothes quickly dried. Relieved to be on my own, I tried shaking off the morning's events.

Downtown Phoenix is a mecca of office buildings—all potentials in my quest for a job. I applied at each high-rise I came across, but to no avail. As I crossed the threshold of yet another, I watched the receptionist's reaction as she caught sight of my blue flip-flops. My plastic jellies had fallen apart with all the cleaning rituals, and Solar refused to buy me shoes.

"No, we don't have any jobs; we're not hiring right now."

I knew it. I tried to warn him. "Solar," I said when I returned, "my clothes are passable but no one is going to hire me wearing flip-flops."

"What's wrong with them? I wear them."

"People don't wear flip-flops to an office job."

"You will when they hire you! Now get going and don't come back until you have a job."

Again, and again I asked, and was told each time to come back in a couple of weeks. I kept looking until I developed blisters on my feet. My desperation grew at the thought of returning without a job. *Please God, help me—*

A man walking past interrupted my worried thoughts: "Hey baby, I like you."

"FUCK YOU!" I shouted as I swirled around. As he walked away, I stood in shock at my behavior. Not even in Colombia with all the groping and grabbing had I reacted like that; I was accustomed to holding my anger inside and complaining to God.

That evening when I gave Solar my daily accounting, I conveniently left out that story, and any other detail that would have merited "discipline."

At the time, I never questioned how learning to lie to avoid a beating equaled becoming more spiritual.

After several days of rejections, a temporary agency hired me for secretarial work despite my attire. My first job led me downriver along the Channel. The Salt River and I got acquainted as I walked to work, eating breakfast along the waterfront. One peanut butter and jelly sandwich was my meal allotment—three times a day. Solar ate bologna and cheese with the crusts cut off. Instead of discarding them, the crusts became my smuggled contraband—adding bulk to my paltry staple without showing when I flattened them inside my sandwiches.

"You're like Job," Solar told me in response to my complaints about the heat and my aching feet, "needing to prove your love for God through suffering. You'll be tested and purified through it."

Accepting his words as truth, I complied, walking everywhere loaded with groceries and supplies but without hat, sunglasses or shade.

I worked unnoticed at my temporary job until one day another secretary in the office put her hand on my shoulder.

"Oh! Your blouse is wet."

I said nothing. What would she think if I told her I was living with a madman who beat and starved me and kept me up until 4:00 a.m. every night with his cleaning rituals? A man who, after work, required me to disinfect the walls, floor, bathroom, and kitchen—showering in between each chore. According to Solar, these areas were all "dirty" because he and Brenda occupied the bed, and their sexual energies had "contaminated" everything.

I slept in a chair with my legs propped up to reduce the swelling. I had to be at work by eight, after fewer than four hours of rest.

What chains are greater than those imposed by the beliefs in our minds?

I continued bouncing from job to job until I was offered work "up the river," where I stepped into the frontier world of computerized communications.

The company was New Vector, AT&T's response to its forced breakup. Engineers from around the country were flown in, and Lincoln Continentals and Cadillacs filled the parking lots; rented for their cigarette lighters. Mobile communications—cellular phones—was an idea AT&T wanted to manifest, and Motorola was at its heels. Meeting after meeting the other temps and I sat poised at our typewriters, earphones in place, transcribing reports and data gathered as the engineers roamed the streets of Phoenix, attempting to talk to one another on their prototype phones.

In this race against the competition, our work hours were not limited as the engineers wanted their meetings promptly transcribed. Solar insisted I work eighteen-hour days while maintaining The Program rules. He forbade me to drink coffee to stay awake, but allowed me a dozen No Doz tablets a day.

As usual, I was expected to wait until I returned to our apartment to use the toilet. But after a few days of ingesting so many pills to stay awake, my intestines rebelled with violent contractions. I had to use the bathroom at work. I left the stall shaking with fear and dread as I contemplated confessing my submission to carnal needs. By Solar's standards I was now contaminated—but chose to continue working, and accept the consequences later.

Before leaving work at my usual two in the morning, I called for a taxi. On the ride home, the driver kept staring at me in his rearview mirror. "You're working late. You want some company? I can take some time off and stop by your place for a while. How about it?"

I ignored him until I noticed we were a few blocks away from our apartment. Solar had instructed me to "never get out in front of our door."

"Let me off here." I shoved money at the driver and scrambled out, ducking around the corner until he drove off.

I grew angrier as I walked to our apartment in the dark. *How am I supposed to tell Solar what the driver said? I'll get beaten although I've done nothing wrong. It's not my fault I have to come home at this ridiculous hour. . .*

"Were there any problems today?" Solar asked when I was inside.

"No." I held my breath, waiting to see if he detected my lie.

"Okay. Tell me your accounting."

I did, going through the recitation of everything I had done, eaten, drunk and thought all day—except for details like using the "forbidden" bathroom and my interaction with the taxi driver.

"Okay," Solar said. "Get going. I'm hungry."

I walked toward the bathroom to begin the rituals. *So much for you being an all-knowing highly evolved being who can tell if I lie to you! I can't believe I've been telling you the truth all this time without realizing you're clueless. I'm just waiting to finish your Program so I can spread the message I was given.*

To keep up the maniacal pace Solar expected from me, I joined the other secretaries in accepting the engineers' invitation to partake of the food delivered each day. There was more than enough for all of us and my three, peanut butter and jelly sandwiches, even with his added crusts was horribly inadequate, leaving me hungry and weak. I liked being away from Solar for so long, able to get my fill of food and freely use the bathroom—but the gold mine dried up when the engineers at New Vector perfected their prototype cell phones.

In response to this news, Solar announced, "We're going back to LA. Peggy got a job as an editor. Sandy, I want you to work there too. From now on, call me JW, as I'm changing my name to Jonathan W—."

As I packed up our belongings, a memory of walking the streets of Phoenix raced back to me. I had picked up a twenty-dollar bill from the sidewalk, even though it was on the "contaminated" ground. Thinking how I could spend this fortune without having to account for it excited me, then ebbed into such a strong fear that I regretted finding the bill. Clutching it, I wished whoever had lost it would return so I could give it back. The weight of my fear and guilt slowed my gait to a halt as I grew frantic. *How am I going to get rid of the money? Oh, is that a church? Yes, I'll go in and leave it as an offering.*

What's this? Churches aren't supposed to be locked. I'll just stuff it into this crevice in the door. Dear God, please accept this offering and answer my prayer to be released from my bondage.

Standing in front of this citadel of faith, I stared at the money, repeating this prayer until I was convinced my plea for freedom had been heard. I had vowed never to speak of this to Solar—another deception I gladly entertained.

TWENTY-NINE

S oon Brenda, JW and I rolled into Los Angeles and found a motel room. "Sandy, I want you to find work again." Solar announced.

Suddenly fed up with working long hours only to come home to be the maid and ritualized cleaning queen, I ran out of the room, dashed across the parking lot and found refuge in a car wash.

What am I going to do? I don't have any money—no identification. Maybe I can find a phone booth and call my grandmother. Yes, that's what I'll—

I looked up to find Brenda standing in front of me. "Sandy, JW asked me to come find you. Please don't run—he's not going to hurt you. It's going to be okay. He asked me to bring you back. He's going to call Peggy, and we're all going to live together. It's going to be okay."

I followed her back.

Before long we had all settled into a townhouse in Buena Park. It was right next to Commerce, an industrial complex where Peggy worked at Parker & Son Publications, Inc., one of the few remnants of a large family-owned empire established in 1898. A thriving niche business, it published legal texts and the directory of lawyers for California. In the mid 1980's, the publishing world was rapidly changing with the transition to computers. To keep up with the latest technology, the company was expanding.

"Sandy, you like to write," Solar said.

"Yes."

"I want you to go to work with Peggy and get a job. They'll hire you."

"What? I don't have any formal training in publishing."

"Yes you do, because I say you do."

"Okay. I'll give it a try."

"No, you'll get a job."

I hope I do. I could escape from JW every day. Now he has Brenda to keep him occupied—it would be just like Phoenix.

Peggy and I wore the same size clothes and shoes, and I borrowed from her wardrobe for my introduction to Miles, the editor in chief. He asked me to start work that same day.

While living in the townhouse, Brenda left again to return home. I was never aware of the reasons for her departure. Nonetheless, we vacated our residence and Peggy and Aaron moved back into her parents' home. JW decided I was to sleep in the car with him and find a motel for the two of us every Friday. My first Monday with this new arrangement JW dropped me off straight from the motel room where we had stayed the weekend.

"Did I miss the rain? You might want to take an umbrella next time," my boss commented—visibly shaken by my soaking wet clothes and hair.

"It's a long story," I said, evading further questioning about my unprofessional appearance—unlikely, since it hardly rains in Southern California. After I reported this encounter to JW, he started dropping me off at Peggy's house so I could shower and show up at work with shoes and dry hair and clothes.

Every Friday and Saturday night, week after week, we stayed in a motel room following the same routines. First, I needed to be his witness next to the car while holding our garbage sack of food and supplies.

"Locked, locked, locked," pause, "locked, locked, locked," pause, "locked, locked, locked, locked," pause, "locked, locked, locked. You saw me lock it, right?" JW had turned the key in the car door, pulled it out, and had to lift the handle countless times until his afflicted brain let him recognize that it was indeed locked. Again, and again, he repeated his ritual: "Locked, locked, locked, locked," as his brain looped through the same litany.

"You saw me lock it, right?"

"Yes, I saw you lock it. It's locked."

"Are you sure? Check it again."

And I would, and then he needed to repeat his ritual again several more times.

When his fears had finally been satiated, we moved on to the next excruciating step. Following him to the room, I held my breath as he opened the door to peer inside for inspection.

"Okay, this will do. Step aside."

He always paused to briefly stare out the window before shutting the drapes, overlapping and fastening them together with safety pins. All books and printed matter were tossed into a corner and buried under the wadded-up bedcovers and blankets he whisked off the beds. Surveying the room, he would then strip off his clothes, plop down in a chair, and turn the TV to a deafening volume.

"Hurry up!"

The encampment had begun. I scurried around the room dousing and cleaning all the furniture and then tackled the bathroom. Numerous rituals later, I emerged, clothes dripping wet.

"Okay. Everything's cleaned and ready."

"Stand over there."

I held my position. Bowel movements were major events for him; sometimes a couple of hours passed before he finished. Emerging dripping wet and scoured red, JW pawed through the food bag, grabbing candy bars, baked goods, and a soda. This was the only time he considered himself "clean enough" to go through it. Otherwise, it was my job.

"Get going. The toilet is clogged."

Gathering my supplies, I headed for the bathroom. *I feel so sorry for the maids who walk into the maelstrom we leave behind. How many boxes of Kaopectate did you take this time? You've got to be kidding; the water in the*

toilet is inches from the brim and it's filled with mounds of toilet paper. God,
please release me from this burden, please set me free . . . and please, please help
me unclog this toilet.

With nonstop self-indulgence, JW "held court" in bed, alternately napping
and eating, with the television blasting whatever movies he could find filled
with action and drama. He remained mesmerized until our departure day,
when the rush began. The routine was always the same, week after week;
year after year.

"Hurry up!" was constant during my thirty minutes of scurrying around
after his showering and preparations. Feverishly "removing our energies"
with all the cleaning rituals, I finally wiggled into my just-washed clothes.

"Hurry up! Are you ready? Disinfectant sprayer. Here!" He doused the
door handles with his "hand sanitizer" and then cracked it open to examine
our exit paths.

"Fucking maid carts," he grumbled. "One Heart, One Mind, One Spirit,
please help us leave this room without interference. Come on, let's go!" And
he bolted from the room with me following close behind.

Once safely locked inside the car, JW prayed. "One Heart, One Mind,
One Spirit, let our energies and vibrations be cleansed and purified and
released from everything we touched and every place we were. Thank you
and Amen. One Heart, One Mind, One Spirit." Fearing the "dark forces"
would use our energies against us, this was his ritual for everything we
touched and everywhere we stayed. It was repeated after any interaction
with the outside world and especially when we relieved ourselves outdoors,
since we were never allowed to use public bathrooms.

"Make sure we didn't drop anything" was my signal to watch carefully
as he drove forward and back several times from the same parking space.

"Okay. It's all clear," I would say.

"Make sure we didn't drop anything!"

I looked again as he backed up and then pulled forward into the same
parking space.

"Look! Look! Make sure we didn't drop anything!"

"It's all clear. We didn't drop anything." *Please let's just go.*

Eventually, finding a room clean enough for JW's obsessive standards became impossible. Anaheim, Orange, and Buena Park were teeming with motels—all close to Disneyland and Knott's Berry Farm. But JW never frequented the same room twice, and often a motel was declared off-limits due to some speck of dirt on a wall he claimed was fecal material. He started bringing Peggy along because she knew the area as we extended our search into nearby Stanton, Cerritos, and Garden Grove.

"Peggy, ask for a key first. I want you to inspect the room before you bring me. It needs to be clean and no shit on the walls. Do you understand?"

"Okay, JW." Even when the room was passable, JW often found something wrong with it, and then beat us for subjecting him to such "lowly and degrading filth."

Working at Parker & Son was delightful. I had forgotten how rewarding it felt to be passionate about a job. Very soon, I was promoted from assistant editor to production manager, relieving the vice president of operations, who wore many hats at the time.

He mentored me in creating a separate department responsible for typesetting and printing their titles, along with producing the binders that held them. The burgeoning legal mandates handed down by the California Legislature required constant revisions to these publications. The Editorial and Production departments interfaced with one another as well as with the lawyers writing these texts.

It was a fast-paced, deadline-driven world of stress and the normal glitches of a production process. I thrived in the management of this outer chaos, completely distracted from the insanity of my personal life as I developed collaborative relationships with my printers and vendors. Pulling together as a team, we met our deadlines, and I was generously rewarded for my efforts. Work fed my suffering self-esteem as it became a conduit for me to overcome the angst and emotions generated by the abuse I endured with JW—all for the cause of fulfilling my mission of saving the planet and serving God—sacrifices that were to deem me worthy enough to earn my family's love.

"Everything is disposable and unimportant," JW said, "—especially our bodies. It is all part of the 'illusion,' and we are to leave all this behind as we evolve in consciousness and fulfill our missions." I lost track of how many times I heard that; each time reinforcing my own belief in its veracity.

Cars were traded in or trashed, just like everything else. No matter how valuable, they were used without relief until they fell apart from lack of maintenance.

JW's current transportation was a classic he called the "Bomb;" a deep canary yellow Oldsmobile in prime condition. Filled with all the bells and whistles of long ago when it was a luxury automobile in the 1950's, we enjoyed this delightful car until everything suddenly changed.

Peggy, Aaron and I emerged from her parents' house and walked towards the car, parked in the driveway.

"GO AROUND TO THE PASSENGER SIDE; DON'T GET IN ON THIS SIDE!" JW screamed.

We all looked at each other and obediently herded to the other side and slid into the backseat.

"Peggy, your goddamn fucking neighbor just sprayed dog shit on the car with his garden hose! He just contaminated the entire driver's side. You can never get in on this side. Do you understand? It's been contaminated with dog shit!"

"Okay." Peggy hesitated. "I'm sure he didn't mean any harm by it."

"Don't contradict me! Are you calling me a liar?"

"No, I just don't think he meant to spray the car with dog poop."

"Well, he did, and the car is now contaminated. Do you understand? That side has been forever contaminated! You are never to use the door behind me! It's now off-limits."

"Okay," she quietly responded. The air crackled with anticipation of who would be punished for this latest development. Yelling was not enough; he usually discharged his anger by hurting someone. Aaron was least likely to get hit, as JW usually vented on the women who lived with him. It was only a matter of time before he exploded.

"You took us the wrong way, Peggy!" His arm flew into the backseat and his hand grabbed her hair, using it to wrench her head against the back of the front seat. As his massive fist moved back into the front seat, he shook out a bunch of her hair. Fearing I would be next, I held my breath, hoping I could escape this one time.

"How many stops did we make yesterday, and how much have we spent so far, Sandy?"

Still in charge of the accounting, whether it was my behavior, that of the others, or all our expenditures, I had to keep a running total of everything in my head. I was not allowed to open my eyes at each stop or inquire what had been purchased.

I said, "We made three stops, two for food. You spent fifteen dollars and thirty-one cents the first time; nine dollars and twenty-six cents the second, and you didn't tell me how much you spent on the third stop."

He pounded my head against the window. "Each time we stop you're supposed to ask me! That's your responsibility. Understand?"

"Yes." *You never said that before. You told me you'd let me know how much you spent each time because you didn't want me looking around.*

When JW left on one of his numerous road trips, I happily stayed with Peggy in her parents' home. Otherwise, I slept in the car with him at a regional park off the 91 Freeway. Monday through Friday, JW waited for me after work. I crawled into the backseat, essentially my cage, and recited the day's accounting as he pounced on my freedom that had taken flight while away from him. After finding a fast-food restaurant that was "uncontaminated," he would drive us around to kill time, and then silently roll the car past the ranger station when the post was empty.

We left at dawn to avoid paying the fee, ate a fast-food breakfast, and then I had to fill his gas tank, because it was on the "contaminated" side of the car.

I could not get back inside, and walked to Peggy's house with JW following me until I was at her door. Kicking it with my foot signaled her to let me in. Once inside, I showered, changed into clean clothes, dried my hair and rode to work with Peggy. I would not see JW until the end of my work day, when he picked me up and we went through the same routine. Interspersed in our interactions would be his rants about how the prevailing influences of the "dark forces" had thwarted his predictions and spiritual work.

Except for the paltry amount he allowed me to spend on hot dogs for dinner and sandwich makings for lunch, my entire paycheck was his. Blessedly, Peggy's mother kept their dinner leftovers on the stove so I could forage and supplement my allotment. No one ever said anything, and I was never questioned when I stayed in their home or cleaned up their leftovers. Had there been questions, I probably would have lost my refuge.

Despite the weekend drama, I flourished in my job as the months passed. Developing collaborative relationships with coworkers and vendors, I felt recognized for my positive contributions and was relearning to trust myself and growing in self-assurance. By day, I lived in a world apart from the craziness, and ever so slightly was moving away from JW's control. Over the weekend I would retreat again, battered for a dirty motel room, or not cleaning correctly, or some other contrived infraction.

"You have that job because of me!" JW constantly reminded me. "Everything you've gained is because of me and who I am. I am your Source and don't forget it. I came here to release you from your karma and free you from this illusion. You are nothing without me!"

Whether it was the job Brenda's husband had while she was with us, or any of ours, JW bragged that our accomplishments were always because of him. I didn't care that he took credit for my success. I loved my job, where I could be open and genuine. I appreciated their simple gestures of kindness—a refreshing change from JW's vicious judgments and harsh criticisms.

Before the Christmas holidays, we were given bonuses and two weeks off. "See you next year," my supervisor said as he handed me the check.

"Thank you." My smile faded when he left the room. *Wow, this is generous, but I can't enjoy it, since I'll have to give it to JW.*

"We were given bonus checks today and told we won't return to work until after New Year's."

"Give it here. Why aren't you working until then?"

"The publishing industry back East traditionally shuts down their presses until the first of next year."

"Hmm. I've been thinking, because you've been working so hard, I'm going to let you go to your Grandmother's for Christmas."

I was shocked. "Thank you, JW."

On Christmas Eve, he drove me to a store on our way down south.

"Go buy your grandmother a Christmas gift."

"What shall I give her?"

"I have no idea. She's not my grandmother. Don't spend over fifty dollars."

I wandered through the store until I found gifts I hoped Gramma would enjoy.

I spent two glorious days with my family, filling up with their love, especially my grandmother's. After I watched her open my gifts, she walked over to me and placed a package in my hands. Inside was a stunning pink cashmere sweater.

"Gramma, this is so beautiful. Thank you!"

I had arrived unannounced and had not expected to receive any gifts, but because the sweater was from her, it was especially precious. I planned on guarding it from JW.

That night I offered to sleep on the sofa in the dining room, remembering JW's instructions: "You are to sleep in your clothes, and don't you dare sleep upstairs with your cousins and their husbands." I was forbidden from coming in close contact with any male relatives, let alone risk seeing them in their pajamas.

Several different family members approached me on my makeshift bed, asking, "Are you sure you'll be comfortable enough?" They had no idea that I was accustomed to sleeping bent over in the backseat of the car with my feet firmly planted on the "contaminated" floor; the sofa was luxurious for me.

After tearful goodbyes, JW picked me up as arranged. He drove us to a motel and I remained silent, preferring to relish my visit, rather than automatically launching into my "accounting." Being around so much love had loosened more of his control over me.

I clutched my new sweater under my arm as we entered the room.

"What's that?" JW asked.

"It's a sweater my grandmother gave me." I paused. "I'm leaving you and want to return home. I just came back to get my clothes from Peggy's. I'm not willing to live like this anymore."

"How dare you defy me and talk like this!" He wrenched the sweater from my hands and ripped it to pieces. "Your fucking materialistic family with all their wealth. They think they're so powerful. Well, they're going to find out in the end what happens when you disregard the spiritual life. Trust me, they'll regret it."

As he destroyed my sweater, I started to cry, growing louder with his words. "Stop!"

My grief and despair were so deep I continued sobbing. Reaching over, JW grabbed one of my nipples, then the other, and furiously pinched and twisted them.

"STOP CRYING OR I'LL HURT YOU MORE! DON'T MAKE ANOTHER NOISE! STOP OR IT'LL GET WORSE! STOP! STOP!"

I gasped and yelped. He pinched harder. Trying to squelch myself, I clenched my teeth and held my breath, but the pain was so great that noises escaped. I stuffed cloth between my clenched teeth, trying to muffle my whimpering as I convulsed with pain.

"YOU ARE DEMON POSSESSED! THIS IS HOW YOU REPAY ME FOR LETTING YOU VISIT YOUR FAMILY? YOU CAN'T LEAVE

UNTIL YOU ACCOMPLISH YOUR MISSION IF YOU WANT TO SAVE YOUR GRANDMOTHER AND FAMILY."

He pounded my back with his fists, and I bit down harder. The pain was so intense I started drifting away. I disappeared to a place where the pain did not matter, nor my desire to leave him.

Floating above my body, I was free.

I returned to work, but JW's attitude toward me had changed.

"Production Department, Sandra speaking. May I help you?"

"Why do you have to be so nice? Is that the way you always answer the phone?"

"Yes, JW. This is my job. This is how I'm supposed to answer the phone."

"Well, you don't have to be so nice about it!"

"I interact with vendors and publishers all day. I'm not sure what I'm to do. How am I supposed to answer the phone?"

"Well, I don't want you to be so friendly. You're never to go anyplace or out to lunch with anybody. Do you understand? You haven't done that, have you?"

"No, JW. I keep turning them down."

"Make sure you do."

"Right. I'm sorry, but I have to get back to work," I said.

That Friday, JW summoned Peggy to join me in the car after we left the office.

"Peggy, get in after Sandy. Sandy, you're not going back to work on Monday. Peggy, you're to tell them on Monday that Sandy went hiking over the weekend and fell off the trail and broke her jaw. Tell them that she can't talk because her jaw is wired shut. Do you understand?"

"Yes, JW," she answered, not daring to look over at me.

To me he said, "You have to prove your worthiness to me if you want to return to work. You're not going back until you show me you're committed to fulfilling your purpose."

For that, I was required to wait thirty-six hours before emptying my bladder. All the women in The Program usually had two opportunities every day to void—before dawn and after nightfall. JW urinated whenever he desired, peeing into the same food storage bags he used for his purging after each meal.

I accomplished the feat as he drove us around to all his favorite haunts, which he called "power vortexes." Chanting and praying at each one, he communed with his "guidance," asking "Spirit" to reveal to him his next step. *I just want to go back to work and the people I care about. I love my job; just let me go back, JW. I passed your test.*

On a visit to collect money from Peggy, she gave him an update. "JW, work keeps asking why Sandy hasn't called or submitted any doctor bills. They're holding her position for her but they're worried. What shall I tell them?"

"Tell them she still can't talk and won't be back to work until she can."

Six months passed before he needed money and decided I could return to my job. Peggy was only giving him a portion of her paycheck, since she needed to support Aaron and herself.

"I'm sending you back to work, but you are not to leave your office, even to make copies, without taking Peggy with you."

"Okay, JW," I desperately agreed. *Please God, just let me return to work.*

"You are not to speak with any male vendors unless Peggy is patched in on the conversation. Do you understand?"

"Yes."

I returned, but was visibly anxious and unable to perform my job as effectively as before. I felt trapped and frustrated; JW's new rules were totally impractical. Even so, desperate to stay at work, I tried.

While away with my "broken jaw" a shipment of binders I ordered had arrived. They were all defective and had been dumped outside, scrapped and awaiting my return to deal with the problem. I contacted the company and a representative flew out from New York to inspect them.

"These are definitely stamped incorrectly," she confirmed, walking around the pile as she picked up several to examine. "Hey, do you want to grab some dinner tonight, my treat?"

"Uh, no thanks. I really can't."

"Okay. But what's wrong? You don't seem like the same person I've been dealing with over the phone. Are you mad at me about the binders?"

"No, that's not your fault."

"Are you okay?"

"I'm okay," I lied. "Thanks for asking—it's complicated. I really can't explain."

"Well, would you like to go with me to see the Boss? He's here in LA and I have tickets. I thought we could go to his concert after work. I'd like to try and make up for this mistake."

"No, that's okay; you really don't need to do anything other than re-stamp the binders with a better dye process. Who's the Boss?"

"You don't know who the Boss is? You haven't ever heard of Bruce Springsteen?"

"No, I'm sorry, I haven't."

"You're kidding."

"No, I'm not. That's complicated too." *I wish I could explain why I can't go with you and don't know about the Boss. If only I could explain my mission to you, maybe you would understand.*

Without sharing my silent conversation, I just shook my head, and we parted after arranging to fix the order.

The next week, Linda from Human Resources asked to speak with me to talk about my "accident."

"How long were you in the hospital? Don't you have doctor bills you need to have paid? I can file a claim for all your medical bills if you just give me the paperwork."

I feigned having to respond to a work need, with assurances I would get back to her. Our benefits would have covered all my expenses, but of course

I had nothing to show for my time off. As I stumbled through my excuses, I hoped she would drop it.

That same week, other coworkers approached me to share how glad they were for my recovery. With natural curiosity, they asked about my accident and I bluffed my way through.

When JW returned from his trip that Friday, I shared these work conversations with him, hoping for a way out of my dilemma. "What do you want me to say to them when they ask these questions, JW?"

"It doesn't matter. You're quitting that job and will never return."

"What? What do you mean?"

"We're going on a quest called 'The Journey.' I need to seed the Continental United States with crystals, and you are going to be my witness. The Space Brothers have told me we need to cleanse and purify the negativity from the power vortexes across the planet. We're focusing on the United States because the Northern Hemisphere was the heart of the supercontinent that once encompassed the planet millions of years ago before the continents drifted apart."

"Oh." I could barely speak. *What is he talking about? I've never heard him mention space brothers before.*

"The Space Brothers are going to send a beam of laser light into the crystal packets we leave and supercharge them with love energy. This will cleanse and disperse the accumulated negativity from all the years of suffering caused by humans preying upon one another."

Could this be how I fulfill my mission and spread the message? I know my emotions have always controlled me, and bogged me down. Maybe releasing people from their emotional bondage will help transform humanity and end our suffering. Maybe this could prevent us from unconsciously destroying our planet.

I don't want to lose my job, but maybe this is the way to finish my mission and gain freedom from JW. If I fail to accomplish my mission, I'm doomed.

As always, my belief that I had to save the world took precedence over everything else.

PART V—THE JOURNEY

We would rather die in our shame than climb the cross of the moment
and have the illusion die.

—*W.H. Ogden, Age of Anxiety*

'

THIRTY

The next day, JW officially stripped me of my job as production manager. I never knew what Peggy told our bosses, or how my departure was explained.

The isolation I reentered was reminiscent of the pervasive and all-encompassing restrictions of my original days of The Program—sequestered and cut off from any information, influence, or stimulus other than JW himself. Although afraid of what was next, I was fiercely determined to fulfill the purpose I believed to be mine.

"To cleanse the vortexes, we need a crystal to conduct the energy the Space Brothers beam down. You and Peggy are to find one in that store and buy it for our Journey."

As we walked inside a store specializing in Earth's mineral treasures, I was dazzled by the array of crystals with their rainbow of colors. Walking down row upon row, Peggy and I found one of the clearest and largest crystal points I had ever seen. After exiting the store to share our find with JW, we returned with his permission to purchase this single point from Brazil, weighing sixty-six pounds.

"I'm naming it Baby," JW announced as we hoisted it into the truck. "Using the phantom leaf effect, we're going to seed all the vortexes with a chip of Baby so they'll get the full effect of the crystal. For each seed, we'll need a piece of gold, copper, silver, and iron to represent all the ages of mankind. Sandy, you need to combine all those into something I can use in our quest. This will create the same effect as if the entire crystal had been used. Here's a hammer. Now get busy and break Baby into small pieces so I can start the seeding process."

"How am I supposed to combine all those things?"

"I don't care how you do it, just get it done."

"How about some Scotch tape? I'll wrap it around the piece of Baby and secure everything else with it."

"Okay, good idea, that should work. Peggy, go get us some tape. You'll make them in the back. We'll call them 'combos'."

I crawled into the camper shell, where my knees sank into the foam pad Peggy had purchased for the truck bed. There was a single blanket and dark curtains JW had instructed Peggy to sew, obscuring visibility through the shell windows and cab opening.

Peggy's last errand was to purchase our groceries. After passing them through the crawl space, we hit the road. As JW drove, I reluctantly shattered Baby with a hammer and a knot in my stomach. To each small piece I taped a link of sacrificed gold and silver jewelry, a piece of iron, and a penny for the copper. (In 1986, pennies still contained copper.) At first, JW pelted the combos into areas where there was water, or would be water in the future. "The Space Brothers said we needed water to help conduct the energy they are going to beam down into the crystals," he explained while driving.

Is this how I'm meant to spread the message I was given, God? I hope so.

But it did not take long before JW became as obsessive about seeding the combos as he was with everything else he did. As fast as I could make the combos, JW threw handfuls of them out the window, marking our route with these Scotch-taped bundles.

As "vortex plumbers," we started our trek around the United States in a new Mitsubishi Mighty Max truck purchased with my credit. Filled with grandiose purpose, we headed north, crisscrossed California, passing through Yosemite, then on to Oregon, the Puget Sound area in Washington, and to

Montana and Wyoming, through Yellowstone and the Grand Tetons. This became a favored route of JW's, repeated countless times over the years, until the very last days of my time with him.

As we continued our maiden trek, we encountered snowstorms and freezing temperatures without benefit of jackets, scarves, sweaters, shoes, gloves, or anything practical for colder weather. JW had his customary red flannel long-sleeved shirt that hung loosely over his Levis. He wore flip-flops and mine stayed in the cab for my morning and evening exit to pee outside. I had long cotton pants and my proverbial turtleneck under a long-sleeved blouse.

"You don't need to have special clothes for the weather."

"Okay, but could you please open the curtains a bit so I can get warm?"

"You need to learn how to use mind over matter. I don't want you looking around, and besides, I can't risk anyone seeing you or what you're doing."

He littered land and water with our combos as we crisscrossed the continental United States. At first he tape-recorded each significant turn of the odometer or digital clock. He also requested that I note where he had left such and such combos with "special numbers." He considered certain sequences of numbers, like 11/11, 144, 123, and 222, to be magical. He always looked for them, or for 4/4, the birth date for both his sons, and 5/5, his own.

The temperature inside the aluminum-framed shell, which had no insulation, was like the temperature outside. I discovered that tucking my bare feet under crossed legs kept them warm. Making combos kept me busy and distracted from my cold body.

"I'm not sure where we should head next, down south to Arizona, New Mexico and across to Texas, or towards the East Coast. Any ideas?"

"No, not a clue."

"I'm going to pull over because I need to find out before we come up to the junction. Stay where you are while I throw some pennies to get guidance." He slowed and then eventually pulled off on a side road. I could hear the coins rattling in his hands.

"Heads. The East Coast it is. Spirit wants us to head towards the Badlands. You better get busy and make more combos."

After crossing the Dakotas, we headed into Nebraska, Minnesota, and Wisconsin and continued through the Midwest, generally finding rest stops to park. Starting the engine to run the heater warmed us during the night, but as we drove into the more densely populated states we met a different challenge with a lack of rest stops. JW started parking in hotel lots but could not start the engine for fear of being detected and asked to leave. Layers upon layers of thirty-gallon-sized garbage sacks wrapped over our clothes served to insulate us from the freezing weather.

For a short time, I possessed a sweater gifted to me by a woman named Patti who had allowed us to stay with her in Virginia Beach. Another kindness was extended to me when Mary Lou Keller, someone JW had met while running the bookstore in Sedona, gave me a pair of insulated boots. While visiting her, she noticed my blue toes and offered the boots for our travels to the Northeast. I enjoyed their comfort until JW insisted I wade into the Atlantic Ocean with them, when they fell apart.

At least once a week, JW would order me to "Start praying—there's a cop following us." He feared the law more than most, and rightfully so. He was constantly engaged in criminal behavior. Regularly trespassing on private land, he destroyed personal property, jettisoned trash out the window, violated common decency and lacked moral integrity. He did not hesitate to deceive store clerks into taking back merchandise he had sabotaged, and could not tell the truth if his life depended upon it. When he was in doubt, his form of praying for guidance consisted of the usual— "One Heart, One Mind, One Spirit, please use these coins to guide us. Heads means . . .; tails mean . . ."

I started soliciting help through prayer, not just to keep us out of trouble but also to herald support for myself. Once, in the middle of the night, JW snarled through clenched teeth: "You better start praying because we're going to freeze to death if we don't get some help. I'm too tired to drive, and I can't start the truck to warm up because if I do, they'll call the police. Start praying or prepare to die!"

Letting me drive was out of the question for JW, so I began desperately begging God for assistance. I continued until JW rustled me from my fervent praying.

"Look, the ice is melting. Don't say anything, just keep praying."

I choked back tears of gratitude as the inside of the camper shell warmed. Ice that had formed on the ceiling was melting and dripping on us.

I witnessed being rescued numerous times after beseeching God for intervention. Whether stuck in some field or stranded alongside the road, help arrived. It seemed to me those prayers were answered. Thinking my sins were keeping me bonded to my daily nightmare, I prayed constantly to be released, to no avail. *I must be evil and unworthy like JW said, or my prayers would be answered. I already left once and got pulled back, so I guess I need to finish the Journey before I'm free to go.*

Since JW insisted on washing the car every time we got a motel room, the Midwest and East Coast were especially challenging. After returning from the car wash, he accompanied me as I rubbed paper towels soaked in our disinfectant and sea salt solution over everything in the cab—dashboard, steering wheel, gearshift levers, mirrors, and seats.

Soaked doors that wouldn't close in the freezing temperatures weren't the only problems.

"The fucking key won't turn in the lock!"

"Why don't you use the spray bottle on the key hole?" *I'm sure the sea salt in the disinfectant will thaw the locks.* It worked, but he never acknowledged me for knowing anything of value.

Due to the extreme cold, JW eventually invested in an extra set of clothes for both of us, but I still had to wear wet clothes to the Laundromat.

"You need to be clean enough to wash our clothes," was his reasoning.

Driven by survival, the extreme cold forced me to adapt. I bent his rules to avoid perishing. Leaning against the dryers to warm my wet body, I ignored quizzical eyes staring at me. Eating a chocolate candy bar also helped me stay warm. I added the expense into the cost of doing laundry, believing staying alive justified these indiscretions. If JW knew my clothes had touched the "dirty" dryers, I would have been battered, and spending money without his permission was also grounds for a beating.

What you don't know won't hurt me, JW.

Once again my weight dropped to a little over a hundred pounds. Our fast food diet was complemented with peanut butter and jelly sandwiches, Little Debbie cookies, and sodas. JW never drank water. I was allowed three peanut butter and jelly sandwiches a day or a thirty-cent MacDonald's cheeseburger. On days I had not been punished for past or present sins, I was rewarded with a fish filet sandwich and a cookie. For years, one twelve-ounce can of soda was my daily quota of liquids.

To survive, I learned how to steal as well as lie. Since JW hated interacting with the public, he often sent me into a store to purchase our food and supplies while he hovered in the parking lot. Walking through a store as I gathered our groceries, I usually gobbled down a stick of cheese and a candy bar.

One day a store manager followed me out the door in upstate New York.

"I saw her shoplifting! She ate some cheese in the store and left the wrapper! See?" he shouted at JW as he held up the evidence of my transgression.

JW shot out of the truck, beseeching the clerk. "I'm sorry, sir. She's mentally ill and doesn't know what she's doing. I'll pay for whatever she took. Please don't call the police."

"I don't believe you for a minute."

"Please, sir, I'll pay for whatever she took. Get in the car, Sandy. NOW!"

Violently shaking, I crawled into the cab while he paid the manager and then screeched the tires leaving the parking lot. Driving down the road, I paid for that stolen plunder when he released his anger onto my body. When JW told the store manager I was mentally ill, he was correct, for who else would have stayed in such a situation?

Not long afterwards, while still in upstate New York, we were pulled over by the police.

"Get out of the truck and stand with your legs spread, hands on the truck." The curtain was shoved open and I watched the cop as he surveyed the inside of the camper.

"Good God! Get out!" he ordered, and I scrambled over the front seat and staggered to stand on stiff legs, next to JW. It was the first time I had seen him in many days since he had been sleeping in the cab while I stayed in the back. My eyes met his gaze and I was shocked to see how much fear his face betrayed. His deeply set eyes were bloodshot from all the No Doz tablets he had taken to stay awake.

The policeman busily searched the cab and then scooped something into his hand. Shoving it in JW's face, he demanded: "What's this? This looks like crack!"

"Those are just pieces of a quartz crystal, Officer."

"Eh?" He tasted the contents. "I know you're doing something illegal, I just can't prove it. And this?" He held up a brown paper bag filled with combos I had made.

"More of those quartz crystals, Officer," JW replied, strangely meek.

"I don't get you; I know you're up to no good." The officer rolled the Scotch-taped little bundles of trinkets, rocks, and pennies in his fingers.

After more searching, insisting that JW open the tailgate, he declared, "Get going! I can't find anything, but I know you're up to no good."

As I crawled back into the camper shell, perhaps I saw it for the first time, remembering how the police officer's face had looked when he peered into my hovel. Garbage sacks hung loosely taped from the ceiling—my attempt to prevent the condensation from dripping onto me as it melted each day.

The foam mattress was covered in cardboard and paper sacks salvaged from our groceries. I had saved every scrap to use as insulation since the condensation that froze around the inside frame of the camper shell melted during the day and dripped down under the foam, only to be wicked up into its interior. At night, the moisture inside the mattress would freeze.

After the officer left us, JW continued driving, but kept dozing off. "I'm falling asleep, and we're on a fucking country road with no place to pull over. Fucking New York! It's raining and I don't want to get stuck! Come up front and sit next to me."

"Okay." I crawled through the curtained window.

"Come closer and put your left leg on the accelerator and steer from where you are."

"What?"

He hit my head. "You heard me! Don't argue with me and don't question me! I'm falling asleep! Do you want to die?"

"No."

"Then do as I say!"

Sliding next to him, I lifted my left leg over the transmission hump and eased my foot onto the accelerator. As I took the wheel, I started praying. *Dear God, please help me steer this truck safely and protect us from danger. Please hear me, please keep us safe, especially in this rain.*

"Why are you slowing down?"

"Because it's raining hard, and I've never steered from the passenger seat, and want to be safe."

"Well, don't go so slow."

I waited until he nodded back asleep and slowed down again.

Despite the rain, I drove for miles, steering as I sat alongside him and waking him whenever he needed to brake. *I don't get it. You let me drive to the Laundromats and grocery stores, but cannot give up control to let me drive now, even though this is incredibly dangerous?*

In Massachusetts, as we entered Boston for the first time, we were pulled over again.

"Sandy, you better pray we don't get hassled."

I was in the front seat when two policemen approached his window.

"Let me see your licenses and registration," one of them ordered. With our papers in hand, they walked in front of the truck, got into their patrol car, and sped off, leaving us waiting alongside the road. Twenty minutes later, they returned and gave us back our identifications with no explanation.

"I know we're being tailed by the government," JW commented after they left. "I constantly see their white vans. They're spying on our conversations and every movement we make. That's why they needed our IDs.

"We're going back to New York and getting out of here. Besides, we need to visit all the historical places important to recorded history, and landmarks of people who were famous. You know I was Joseph Smith in another lifetime, and was murdered?"

"No, I didn't know that."

"Well, I was, and we need to go to where the Angel Moroni revealed the golden plates to Smith, who transcribed them into the *Book of Mormon*. We'll go to New York and then Nauvoo, Smith's original settlement in Illinois. Because he was murdered, we need to release the negative energies and vibrations."

You seem to have been everyone who was important in history, haven't you?

Compliance with JW's rules frustrated my very existence, especially when the rules changed to suit his needs only. Moving our bowels was still not allowed until we had taken refuge in a motel room. In between, JW consumed voluminous amounts of Kaopectate to stop his own natural bodily processes. Invariably, he took all the pills we had, leaving me without such stopgap measures.

While waiting in the truck for JW to return from seeding crystals in whatever locale we had parked near, my body usurped control. In sheer panic, realizing I could no longer control my bowels, I pawed through the trash.

Finding an empty mayonnaise jar, I pooped into it, wrapped several layers of garbage sacks around it to obscure the smell, but now had an even worse problem—how to dispose of it without getting caught. JW went through our trash regularly, and I could not imagine surviving this transgression.

Using every instinctual-sense I had, I slipped into the front seat with my garbage sack of "wrong doings," sneaked out of the truck, tossed my guilty evidence, and returned to my lair.

When the truck door opened, I had calmed myself. With the passage of so much time, I knew he had not seen me, for JW was impulsive and would have pounced on me immediately if he had. I didn't know our whereabouts, and he seemed unsure of our next stop. "I'm going to ask Spirit where we're going next. Don't talk to me and be quiet. … One Heart, One Mind, One Spirit, please give me a sign. Heads we go to Virginia Beach, tails we go back north. Heads. Okay, we're going to visit Edgar Cayce's center in Virginia Beach."

From there we drove to Washington, DC, and peppered the area near the Capitol buildings with crystals. We drove around in circles so many times it's a wonder we were not stopped and apprehended.

Every battlefield and burial ground—whether Native American, civilian, or military—received our combos. This country has a very rich and diverse history, and since negative energies were to be transmuted by leaving the crystals, we crisscrossed the United States for several years. Peggy was sending him money to fund this quest, and later, I learned that JW still had a few wealthy donors regularly giving him money as well.

Spiritual communities were favorite stops, especially the one in Kingfisher, Oklahoma that provided food and lodging to like-minded seekers. Its founder had successfully produced giant, buffalo-sized milk cows through genetic engineering and then sold his center to the Association for Research and Enlightenment (A.R.E.) in Virginia Beach, the organization responsible for safeguarding Edgar Cayce's archives.

Our first time in Kingfisher, we stayed in one of their trailers. JW was away all day and returned in the evening. In hopes of rescuing my kidneys,

I started drinking more than my allotment of water and sneaked an extra bathroom break right after he left in the mornings, since I never knew when he would return. One morning, as usual, I waited and then peered down through the bathroom window to see if the coast was clear. JW was standing directly below, staring up at me.

A moment later he flew through the door and kicked me with his new hiking boots until I was writhing on the floor. Since I was cloistered from those who paid for JW's "spiritual readings" at the Kingfisher center, no one was the wiser. Especially since JW hid behind a mild, meek front with his monk-like frocks and gentle manner.

When the readings dried up, we left Kingfisher and Brenda joined us again. We drove west across the Dakotas and through the Black Hills, stopping in Los Angeles where I again seized the opportunity to attempt another escape. I made it all the way to my grandmother's home after calling her to pick me up from the train station in Oceanside. But minutes after we arrived at her home, JW knocked on the door, claiming we had to leave immediately, that my visit had to be cut short due to an emergency Peggy had.

Once again, as if responding to some deeply seated hypnotic suggestion, I followed him out the door.

"Why did you leave?" JW asked me as we drove away.

"I no longer want to accompany you on the Journey. You don't treat me with respect. If I'm doing God's work, it shouldn't be so difficult and painful."

"What about your mission?"

"I'll find a way to complete it."

"You've never succeeded before. You know you can't do it without me. If you go home before I say you can, I'll hurt your family. You'll be very sorry and they'll deserve it if they prevent you from doing your mission."

"They won't prevent me from doing my mission. I just don't want to be with you any longer. I'm done."

"You cannot leave until you complete the Journey with me. That is the mission you agreed to do; afterwards you'll be free to leave, but not until then."

I was not immediately punished, but physical battering always found its way to our bodies, whether for our sins in this life, or karma, or just because JW was feeling irritated.

Back again in LA, we picked up Peggy, who had been with Brenda, and all of us continued to Sedona. Mary Lou Keller, an ordained minister, was one of JW's supporters from our first days there. He asked her to perform the ceremony, and she accepted. JW and Peggy—Aaron's parents—were officially married.

Immediately afterwards we returned to Los Angeles and settled into a motel room together. One day Brenda was sitting next to JW and said something I did not hear. He jumped up and violently slammed his hands against her ears. "DO YOU UNDERSTAND NOW?"

"I can't hear anything," she responded.

"You'll be okay. That's what you deserve for being so demon-possessed and not listening to what I say."

Brenda was not better the next day, or the day after; her ears throbbed with pain and were oozing.

"Peggy, take Brenda to a doctor and get her ears treated," JW demanded.

When they returned, Peggy shared the news. "Brenda has two perforated and infected eardrums. The doctor said that she might have permanently lost her hearing."

"Then take her to the airport and get her a plane ticket to go home now," JW said. "I can't be responsible for keeping someone who cannot hear."

That was the last time I saw Brenda. Peggy related to me privately that Brenda had told her she was now legally deaf. JW never apologized for hurting her, and her name was never mentioned again even though she had spent seven years, on and off, with him.

It was 1988 and we had logged one hundred fifty thousand miles on the Mitsubishi truck. JW ground it to a halt in Los Angeles, appropriated Peggy's car and decided she and Aaron needed to join us in our return to Sedona, where it had all begun.

His support base in Sedona had all but evaporated, replaced by a burgeoning spiritual community unfamiliar to him with the lone exception of Mary Lou. Gone were the gurus and psychics he had consorted with, like the "Pink Prince" (Prince Hirindrah Singh) and the "Dome Man."

We occupied a rambling condo with commanding views of the red rocks of Sedona. Fully furnished, this beautiful home came complete with dishes and linens but was rapidly transformed into a place of unimaginable stress with JW's rules, prohibitions, and consequences.

"Since there are two bedrooms and two bathrooms, one side will be 'clean,' and the other is the 'dirty' one."

Prostrate on the couch and clothed only in Jockey shorts, he watched television nonstop, taking food and drink as I waited on his every need. Even though I cleaned it each time he left, the couch was permanently indented with his impression and reeked of his sweat; he spent so much time on it. He only vacated his throne every seven days or so, when needing to move his bowels. Until the end of each day, when I collected them, he littered the floor with his bags of urine and vomit, regurgitating after every meal.

As always, he started his migration in the "dirty" bathroom, then crossed to resume more rituals in the "clean" bathroom. As I waited for him to finish so I could begin my cleaning up after him, I cried, prayed, and demanded that God rescue me from my self-prescribed internment. *God, how can you ask this of me? I hate him. He's just using me and he's disgusting! Please God, release me.*

His last set of showers would stir up a wave of fear in me, as I was expected to service his sexual needs after my cleaning. While preparing to enter his bed, I mechanically forced myself into compliance. *I have it better than*

Aaron. He sits at the table for hours on end, playing war with crayons—his only toys. I should be grateful I'm not Peggy—she sits with Aaron at the table with nothing to do except when she escapes to run errands.

One day JW turned to Peggy as she sat at the table with Aaron. "You and Sandy need your third eye opened! We're going to use an incense stick to do it. Peggy, you burn my forehead and then Sandy's. Sandy, you do Peggy's."

To this day, I still have that scar.

When his forehead healed, JW informed us he was going to San Diego for a visit. A new benefactor named Janet had given him thirty thousand dollars toward the "Journey." With this new money and us safely tucked away in the condo, he was free to travel again.

After he left, I broke the rules and called my grandmother. I hated being his slave and wanted out of my nightmare; this was my opportunity to escape. I pleaded with her to send money for a plane ticket home. She agreed.

My next call was a risky one to Janet. We had never spoken privately, but when I met her she had felt like an ally. I had memorized her number and now explained the reality of JW and how he treated us.

"I'm leaving him, and need your help. Will you pick me up from the airport and take me to my grandmother's? I can't be on the Journey any longer. Solar's not like how you see him when he's around you. He's cruel and abusive. He only thinks of himself and is away right now spending your money."

"I'll pick you up. I wondered about this the last time we were together—he was pretty rough with you guys."

I had calculated the days it would take for my grandmother's letter with the money to arrive, and rehearsed what I would do. After feeding Peggy and Aaron, I washed the dishes and then turned to face Peggy.

"I'm leaving. I cannot take it anymore. JW is coming back tonight, so you'll be fine."

Her eyes widened. "You don't know what you're doing. He'll be furious."

"You don't understand—I don't care. I refuse to live like this. It's a night-mare, and it's especially unfair to Aaron."

Peggy said nothing, and I walked out.

There was no money in the condo, but I took the spare mailbox key, my driver's license, and a set of clothes. The taxi I had called was waiting outside.

"Would you please take me to the post office?"

Along the way, I drank in Sedona, since I had never seen the town—my eyes were always closed as he drove around. The driver pulled into the parking lot of a large building.

"Is this the only post office in town?"

"This is it, the only one."

"Please wait for me and I'll be right back."

I found the box, inserted the key, and retrieved the letter with my grand-mother's check. *Thank you, Gramma!*

"Could you please drive me to the bank?"

We pulled up in front of the solitary bank in the community.

"I'll be right back, and then I need you to drive me to the airport."

"The meter's running."

I walked through the door and sat down in front of a teller. Opening the envelope in front of her, I took out my precious cargo.

"This is a check made out to me from my grandmother. May I please cash it?"

"Do you have an account here?"

"No. My roommate does."

"Well, I don't think we can cash this check for you."

"Would you please ask your manager? This is an emergency. I need to get home and don't have any money. My grandmother sent this; see the envelope? She has plenty of money—you can check her bank account or even call her."

"Well, let me go ask. Please wait right here."

"That's fine. I cannot go anywhere, as I need to cash this check so I can pay the taxi driver outside and purchase my plane ticket."

"I see. Well, please wait and I'll check with my manager."

I nodded and watched the clock ticking away the minutes. *Please God. Please let them give me the money. Please.* Over and over I chanted my prayer as I filled with more terror with the passing time.

Fifteen minutes had passed before the teller emerged from the door behind the counter. "Well, just this once we'll cash your check. In the future, you'll need to open an account."

"Oh, yes. Thank you, thank you! God bless you! You have no idea what a good deed you've done."

I took the money from her, wadded it into a pocket, and practically flew outside and back into the cab.

Janet picked me up at Lindbergh Field in San Diego, and we walked along the city's wharf while I divulged details of life with JW—the abuse, his anomalies and phobias, some of which she had witnessed personally. Although a benefactor for JW, she was also my guardian angel, driving me to the safe refuge of my grandmother's house, where I again took up residence.

Janet and I spent a great deal of time together and developed a relationship. Her loving kindness was refreshingly nurturing, and after a couple of months together, I decided to move in with her, find work, and start over in San Diego.

But a few days before I was to leave my grandmother's, Peggy showed up at the door.

"What do you want?" I asked after hugging her.

"When JW returned, we packed up the condo and left Aaron with my folks, who moved to Hemet. Aaron is back in school, and JW's promised not to take him out again. JW is a completely different person now. He said he didn't understand why you left but he's changed. He doesn't beat me, and has promised never to hurt either one of us again. He's even relaxed all the weird cleanliness stuff. He wants you to come back and said he loves you and has always loved you more than me, or the others. He wants to marry you and have a child with you."

"Oh, he does? How does he know that I want to have a child?"

"He told me that you'd said that."

"Yeah, so. But how can I be sure that he's changed? If he hasn't, why would I consider going back to him, let alone having a child with him?"

"He really has. He's told me he can see how wrong he was. He wants to make it up to you by marrying you and treating you the way he should have. We even laugh together now, he's so different."

"I'm done, and in a relationship with Janet. I'm moving to San Diego this week."

"Please consider it. There's also the fact that he said one of us needs to witness the Journey with him."

"I thought that was done."

"No. He said we still have more to do, and one of us needs to be there, so it's either you or me. Please come back." She paused. "I thought I was going to die. After you left, we dropped Aaron off with my folks, then he drove us to Montana. I don't think I can live through another trip with him. I just can't do it again. I don't know how you do it, but you're stronger than me. I know I won't survive if I have to go on another one with him."

"Hmm."

"Please, please come back. He's changed and promised me he's going to make it up to you. He told me to ask you about your mission. How are you going to accomplish it if you stay here?"

Guilt exploded my fantasy. *I love Peggy and Aaron. I couldn't live with myself if Peggy died on the road. Why can't I just be free, God? Why can't I just live a normal life and be free of all of this?* As these thoughts flew through my brain, I desperately grasped for the respite I had tasted. But my freedom struggled for breath.

I truly wanted to believe that JW would love me and treat me kindly. The possibility that my perpetrator would correct the wrongs he had done was manna from heaven for my shattered self-esteem. Peggy, the messenger, kept repeating his promise, reminding me he had been told in his dreams to mend the error of his ways. *I love Peggy and Aaron. What if returning to finish my mission would free all three of us from his bondage? My sacrifice would be worth it. Besides, Peggy promised that he's changed.*

I called Janet. "I'm going back to JW tomorrow."

"What? What on earth for? You can't be serious! I thought you loved me and we were planning a future together. I don't understand!"

"I'm so sorry. I do love you, but I have my mission to complete. I have to do this first."

"You're not making sense. You said you were happy being away from him."

"I have been, but I also need to finish my mission. I don't expect you to understand, but I need to do this. I still have to spread the message that was given to me."

THIRTY-ONE

In his softest voice, one I had not heard since I first met him, JW explained that he loved me and had always intended to treat me well, and was sorry for the way he had been before. "I want you close to me, and am going to show you how much I love you."-

Without violence or shaming for my escape, I was whisked back into the throes of a cloistered life and relegated to JW's bed. Indulged in the sweetness of romance and love, we spent day and night together. I was deliriously happy, believing my life was going to turn out all right after all. What I had gone through suddenly all seemed worth it—my persecutor was now my protector. I had vanquished the beast and was beloved, the favored concubine.

Several weeks passed as I absorbed all his warm affection. Then, one morning as I basked in the afterglow of sex, I shifted my body.

SLAP! SLAP! SLAP! SLAP!

"That's for exposing yourself! You fucking whore! How dare you lift the sheet for all the world to see your naked body! What kind of trash are you to expose yourself to that window and the world outside?"

I searched for proof of my transgression and noticed a window high up on the wall and out of view of any other building. Terrified, I excused myself and headed for the bathroom. Huge clots of blood gushed into the toilet.

"I just miscarried," I announced upon my return.

"Doesn't matter. I'm still going to marry you in Sedona so Mary Lou can perform the ceremony."

Our marriage was chronicled eleven years later, when Mary Lou Keller published her book *Echoes of Sedona Past*. She wrote the following, first commenting on JW's marriage to Peggy when he was still using the name of Solar:

> This marriage lasted for about one year. Then Solar again appeared at my front door with his little entourage and another girl he wanted to marry. In those days, I often performed some rather strange weddings without question. It seems that *this* girl and the first wife were close friends, and at this point in their relationship they decided the second girl should become the wife, while the first wife was to remain friends with both.
>
> I am not too sure I understood all this, but it was not my custom to question people's reasons for doing what they thought they had to do. So, the wedding took place. (Keller, Mary Lou. 1999. *Echoes of Sedona Past.* Light Technology Publishing: Page 141.)

True to the words she wrote, Mary Lou performed our ceremony on top of a dome-shaped rock in Sedona, outside the Cathedral in the Cliffs, a favored place of prayer and ceremony for JW. Just as the ceremony ended, a shooting star fell to the right and one to the left.

"Look, UFO's. That's a sign," professed JW.

It was the fall equinox, September 22, 1988.

Without further ado, we all drove back to Hemet, California and left Aaron and Peggy at the apartment. JW and I continued traipsing around the country for the Journey, scattering pieces of the amethyst pyramid I had reluctantly shattered. It was most likely one that Mary Lou had given him as noted in her book.

A favorite destination for JW was the Grand Canyon. One of the turnouts offered access to the edge, where he would park and wait for a lull in traffic before hurling countless objects over the rim, with much ritual and prayer.

The maze continued, north to south, east to west. Not sure of where to drive next, JW decided to consult his oracles—three coins he would toss in the air while asking for an answer to his question. "Okay, Spirit. I need a sign where we go next. Heads, we head to Texas, tails we go back to California." When the last coin had landed, JW announced. "Heads, says we're going to stay with my mother and stepfather in Dallas-Fort Worth. I need a break and to recuperate. You need to earn us some money. Besides, they don't know I married you. Stay away from my stepfather while we're there. Don't talk to anyone unless I say it's okay. Do you understand?"

"Yes." *Do you think I want to get clobbered just because someone comes too close to me?*

"You are to call me Jonathon from now on. Do you understand?"

His mother and stepfather were kind enough to welcome our unannounced visit. The central office of Pier One Imports hired me and I worked while Jonathon lounged in his mother's small place. He never offered to help her, even when she voiced concerns about their struggle to survive on Social Security and her husband's pension.

Upon returning from work, I fixed our meals while Jonathon bitterly complained.

"This place is so filthy and overrun with cockroaches."

"It's probably the weather," I said. "I'm sure that doesn't help."

"Don't you dare give me food that those fucking roaches have touched, do you understand?"

"Trust me, I don't like them either. I'll never serve you food with roaches in it."

After about a month, his mother spoke up. "I want you to leave. I've had enough of your criticism and you can no longer stay here. You eat all our food, and we can't afford to feed you. Besides, this place is too small for you and Sandy to be here too."

The next morning, Jonathon stormed out with me in tow. I left another job where I was not able to say "goodbye" or "thank you for everything" as I continued to drift with Jonathan, blowing in and out of one locale after another.

"We need more crystals, and I know a place where we can buy them from the mines. They're cheap, and we can sell them when we come back."

I don't care what you do; I just hope you run out of money soon! You said that was the sign that my mission and our work were ended.

We meandered through the States, selling and seeding crystals, and then returned to Sedona. As we drove around fire roads in an underdeveloped area outside town, it was blazing hot, and the car had no air conditioning. Jonathon enjoyed a large, ice-cold soda and then relieved himself into a plastic bag. These luxuries were not available to me as I baked in a turtleneck underneath my long-sleeved blouse that was buttoned up to my neck. I was hot, dehydrated, and urgently needing to pee.

Per his rules, relieving myself in daylight even in the bushes was not an option, but my need was growing extreme. Waves of convulsions shuddered through my body as I struggled against its needs.

"I'm really having a hard time waiting."

"You fucking demon, you know you have to wait until dark."

"I'm sorry, but I can't help it." My voice wavered as my body shook violently in protest.

"FUCK YOU!"

He stopped along the side of the road and, with more cursing, walked around to the passenger side door and yanked it open. "COME ON, DEMON!" Grabbing my long hair, he pulled me out, slugging me as he did so. "Fucking demon-possessed whore," he barked and tossed me toward the bushes. "YOU COULDN'T WAIT UNTIL DARK! YOU JUST HAD TO EXPOSE YOURSELF SO THE ENTIRE FUCKING WORLD COULD SEE YOU!"

I didn't care what he yelled as I let go—shaking with pain and relief.

"You'll pay for this! I refuse to be married to a demon-possessed woman who's willing to expose herself because she couldn't wait until dark to pee. I'm divorcing you!"

We drove back to California, picked up Peggy and Aaron, and turned around for Phoenix. Once the divorce papers were signed and filed, he dropped Peggy and Aaron off at their apartment and traded our worn-out hatchback for her new Hyundai.

I feel immensely relieved and one step closer to my freedom.

"You do know that you have to complete this Journey before you can leave. You're not looking around, are you?"

"No, I'm not."

"Make sure you're not! Now plug your ears, I want to listen to the radio."

Behind closed eyes, I began breaking his cardinal rule of "staying out of my past." Entertaining future-plans, I absorbed myself in a private world filled with prayer and fantasies to keep myself from being swallowed up by despair. *I can't continue being this spiritual vagabond. Maybe Gramma will let me live in the Annex. After all, they lived there while they remodeled their home. I can do art there and even put a shower where the drain is under the laundry tub. I could hang a hammock by the windows, in between her old refrigerator and the upright freezer. Yes, that's it. I can sculpt with clay there—make it a studio apartment.*

Gramma, I love you. Please forgive me; please let me stay with you if I ever finish this and am freed. Will I ever live to see that day?

Mile after mile, I soothed my angst with my silent monologue, looping again and again through my incessant praying, worrying and dreaming of what I would do once I was free.

As usual, the circuit involved passing through St. George and Salt Lake City. After staying until the hospitality of others soured, we headed east to the Badlands and the Dakotas, traveling in silence.

Before turning around and driving west to the Puget Sound area in Washington, Jonathon spoke.

"I'm moving into a new vibration. From now on you are to call me Jon. I am no longer Jonathon to you or anyone else. Do you understand?"

"Yes." *Good grief, another name change.*

After crossing on the ferry to Orcas Island in Washington, Jon stated he was baptizing me in an island pond. Despite my resistance, he insisted I wade into the pond and dunk myself as he stood on the bank, chanting and praying.

I don't mind being baptized, but don't like having to sit all day in wet clothes—they never dry and now they smell like pond water.

"We're heading back down south now. Stay in the car."

I could hear the ferry as we chugged back across the Sound, and he returned just as our landing was announced. It was always his custom to get something to eat while crossing, and, as usual, I remained behind, escaping in prayers and dreams.

I could tell the sunlight was waning, and welcomed the approaching opportunity to relieve myself outdoors.

"Sandy, I'm sick and can't take you out to pee."

"What? What am I supposed to do?"

"Hold it. I'm driving us south and I can't stop for you."

"It's been all day. I can't hold it any longer."

"Then I guess you'll just have to pee in your seat. It's not like you haven't done that before."

"Not on purpose," I breathed out in frustration.

"I'm driving straight through to California and I'm not getting a room until then. I'm sick and need to go to the bathroom, so I'm not stopping."

I could care less that you feel sick. What about just letting me go pee someplace?

A few hours later, my body signaled its immediate need.

"You're really not going to take me out?"

"No, I'm too sick."

I cannot believe this is happening to me again. I gave in and flooded the car seat as he continued driving for hours on end, oblivious to me as he occasionally moaned.

"I'm sick. I don't feel well. And you can't put your leg over to drive because you're all wet."

"I couldn't hold it any longer. I don't know what you expected me to do."

He said nothing until a few minutes had passed. Then he shouted, "GIVE ME MORE KAOPECTATE!"

"We don't have any more. You took the rest of the box, remember?"

"Oh God. I can't hold it any longer." Screeching to a stop alongside the road, Jon jumped out, yanked down his pants, and squatted beside the car.

"I'm so sorry," he cried. "I'm going to contaminate the car and everything in it. I can't hold it any longer. I'm sick, I'm so sorry."

"I wouldn't worry about it. You're sick. That happens sometimes." *If you only knew how many times I've been in your position. You're not going to 'contaminate everything.'*

He climbed back into the car, drenched his hands in disinfectant, and shoved our only blanket at me. "Put this around you, you smell."

I hate you! Don't you think I know I smell like an old church pew—peed on and left to air dry?

Without another word, he pressed on, stopping for gas while I festered in my urine-filled seat.

Finally, he pulled into a parking space, left and returned shortly to the car. "We're here. I got us a cabin on Mount Laguna."

I said nothing as I held the blanket around me and followed him inside and walked directly into the shower with our cleaning supplies. I emerged in wet and washed-out clothes and stood in the back of the room to wait while Jon showered. When I could hear him scrubbing, I grabbed my driver's license and some money, and sneaked out as quietly as I could.

As I followed the trail in front of the cabin, Jon called me from inside the bathroom.

"Sandy? Sandy? Where are you?"

I ran down the path, which led to a general store. Bursting through the door, I searched for someone in charge. "Is there someplace I can hide? My husband is coming after me and will hurt me if he finds me! Please! Can you give me a place to hide?"

The clerk at the register stared blankly at me. Like my clothes, my hair was dripping wet.

"Please? Won't you help me?"

He still said nothing. Turning around, I searched the other faces in the store. "Can't someone help me, please?" Nothing but mute statues. I whirled back to face the clerk. "I need to hide! Isn't there someplace you can hide me?"

He remained frozen and silent.

I've got to get out of here. I ran out of the store and hesitated, spying a pay phone on the outside wall. *No, it's too exposed. Besides, no one is going to help me.* I bolted across the street and into the woods, surprised I had not lost my flip-flops as I sprinted away. *There's a house. Maybe I can get help there, I'll just knock.*

The door opened slowly and a very tall, zombie-like man partially emerged from the darkness behind him.

"I'm sorry. I must have the wrong house." I backed away. *He's scary—not here.* I bolted off, found the path again and ran deeper into the woods until I spotted a rooftop nestled among the trees. Dogs barked loudly as I waited out of view behind a large tree.

"That's enough," a woman's voice called out.

I walked cautiously into the yard. "Hello? Hello?"

"Yes? May I help you?" The woman poked her head around clothes she was hanging on a line. Her kind face looked right at me as she extended a hand.

"Can I help you?"

"I just ran away from my abusive husband. Could I please use your phone to call my mother for help?"

"Oh, yes. Come in. I'm so sorry. Here, come inside." The dogs joined us and nuzzled me as we entered her charming home.

She handed me the phone. "You can sit over there."

"Oh, I'm sorry, my clothes are wet. Maybe I should stand."

"No, that's okay. Sit here."

"Thank you. It's a long-distance call; is that okay? I can pay you."

"Don't be silly. Just go ahead and make your call."

As I dialed the number, I hoped my mother was home and willing to help me. It had been several months since Jon and I had mooched off-of her.

"Mom, it's me."

"Sandy, where are you?"

"I'm in Mount Laguna, and I've run away from Jon."

"Who?"

"Solar. He calls himself Jon now. I'm hiding at this woman's house. Would you please come pick me up? I'm leaving him for good and need a ride home."

"Yes, Sandy, I can do that, but it's going to take some time to get there. Where will you be exactly?"

"I'll wait in the woods across from the Country Store by the Laguna Mountain Lodge. I need to hide from Jon just in case he sees me. When you drive by, go slowly and I'll see you."

"Okay. I'll be there in about an hour."

"What are you driving?"

"The Mustang."

"Thanks, Mom. I appreciate this. I'll be waiting."

I breathed easier than I had in months as I hung up the phone.

My benefactor smiled softly at me. "I know what it's like to be abused. My ex-husband used to hurt me."

"I'm sorry."

"Yeah, me too. I'm sorry for both of us. Please stay here as long as you want. Would you like something to eat?"

"No. No, thank you. I'm not hungry. But thank you so much for your kindness. I need to get back to the store where my mother's going to pick me up. You have no idea how grateful I am. I hope to be able to repay your kindness someday."

"Just stay safe. That will repay me."

Retracing my steps, I squatted behind a clump of bushes near the road and leaned against a tree. Peering through the shrubbery, I prayed: *God, please don't let Jon see me.* I held my breath as a car approached and I heard my name called out: "Sandy, Sandy. Come back. It's okay, I'm not mad. Please come back. Wherever you are, let's talk this over. Please, I'm not going to harm you. Please come back."

I slumped farther into the bushes as he drove back and forth. *Please, God! Make him go away. Please, please make him go away.* I could scarcely hear myself think, my heart was pounding so hard.

"Sandy, I'm leaving now. I'm not coming back. This is your last chance. Please reconsider and come back to me. You'll never see me again if you don't come back now."

By the time his car disappeared down the road, my whole body was shaking. What seemed like an eternity passed, and finally a Mustang glided past me.

"Mom! I'm here! Mom, here I am! Wait!" Leaping to my feet, I hopped over bushes as I ran to catch her, only to see the rear of her car disappear down the road.

Desperate, I stood in the middle of the road, and then a speck of white appeared and grew bigger as she approached, slowed down, and I hopped inside.

"Thank you, Mom. Thank you so much for picking me up! We better go. Jon was driving back and forth looking for me."

She sped off. "Are you okay?" she asked. "Your clothes are all wet."

"Yes, they are and no, I'm not okay. I have welts on my butt from sitting in my own urine."

"What?"

"He was sick and said he couldn't take me out to relieve myself, and so I had to sit in my urine for several days."

"Good God, Sandy. This is no way to live. I hope this is the last time."

"It is. I never want to see that man again."

"I sure hope you're done this time."

"Believe me, I am. This was the last straw. Can I stay with you, please?"

"Yes, but I have someone living with me. Her name is Wendy. She's a physician's assistant and has been with me for a while. She knows about you."

"Oh."

Contrary to my fears, Wendy was very warm and friendly and did not seem to hold my strange lifestyle against me. We became good friends.

"Hey, Sandy, do you want to go see a movie with me?"

"Sure. What's it called?"

"Dead Poets Society."

I was sobbing at the end of the film. Wendy patiently waited for me to stop crying to hear my explanation.

"That father is just like Jon."

"What do you mean?"

"He's oppressive, abusive, and doesn't let us be who we are. I feel like the son who suicides in the movie. I can't tell you how many times I've felt trapped and helpless to do anything about my situation. I've tried running away and I don't understand what happens to me."

I stayed a month with my mother; slowly integrating myself back into mainstream life. One day she invited me to a free lecture for social workers at the hospital. Moira Fitzpatrick, Ph.D., a psychologist, was demonstrating her work with schizophrenics using a dynamic type of psychotherapy called "Bioenergetics." Even though I found group settings anxiety-provoking, I felt compelled to go, and accepted the invitation.

The presentation included a video with Dr. Fitzpatrick and her staff using

Bioenergetics to help the seriously mentally ill patients at Hanbleceya (Vision Quest), the center she had founded. I was so intrigued I waited to speak with her after the presentation.

"Dr. Fitzpatrick, your work is very moving. It seems so important and meaningful, especially for those struggling with mental illness. Thank you for helping to make the world a better place."

"Well, thank you," she humbly replied, searching my eyes.

Another two years would pass before the tapestry woven from these events could be seen.

As I approached the second month in my mother's home, the relationship between us deteriorated. Our old patterns of relating with each other had returned. She started responding to me with the familiar criticism and anger.

"Here, let me do that, I don't want you to cut yourself with that can opener."

"I can open the tuna by myself, thank you."

I pushed back against her by retreating to my grandmother's house.

It was not long afterwards that my grandmother approached me with an opportunity to house sit for a friend of hers. The woman proved to be very kind, and I accepted the job, moving into her house for the duration of her trip. I was given use of her car, and frequently visited my mother and Wendy. Once while I was there, Peggy called and asked to speak with me. My mother handed me the phone.

"Hi, Peggy," I said.

"Aren't you glad to speak with me?" It was Jon.

"No. I don't want to talk to you."

"Aren't you worried about completing your mission? How are you going to fulfill your contract with God?"

"I'm not worried."

"Oh, really. Are you going to turn your back on God, your family, and everyone and everything that matters to you?"

"I don't want to talk about it. Leave me alone."

"Oh, I'll leave you alone to rot in hell along with everyone else in your family because you failed to complete the one thing God has asked of you. Such a simple task and you can't even do that."

"Goodbye." I hung up, shaking.

"Are you all right?" my mother asked.

"No. That was Jon."

"I thought that Peggy called."

"She did and then handed the phone to him."

"I'm sorry."

"Yeah, me too. Did you know that he wrote me a letter?"

"Wendy told me you had a letter from him in the mail. He sent one to me, too."

And she handed it to me to read.

7/17/89

Dear Alice,

I am so sorry for all of the pain and suffering I have caused you and your family over the last 10 years.

I was jealous of the love Sandy felt towards her family and was so afraid of losing her; I tried to turn her against you.

I know now that it was wrong. If I could undo all of the pain and suffering, I would.

Please do not hold Sandy accountable for my actions.

I will be leaving California soon, for good.

I only hope that someday you and Sandy will find it in your hearts to forgive me.

God bless you,

Jon

"What do you think of that?" she asked as I put it down.

"I think he's feeling guilty and trying to ease his conscience."

"That's pretty much what I felt. What did he have to say on the phone?"

"Oh, he reminded me of my mission and a bunch of other stuff. I don't want to talk about it."

"Well, I hope you don't go back to him again."

"No, I'm done."

Uncannily, the next time I visited my mother's, Peggy called again, and Wendy answered the phone, unaware of what had previously happened.

"Sandy, it's Peggy. She wants to talk to you."

"Tell her I don't want to talk to her if she's going to give the phone to Jon."

Wendy relayed my message and replied, "She says it's just her, that she wants to talk to you."

"Hi, it's Peggy. I miss you and would like to see you. Can Aaron and I come visit you?"

"Well, it would be good to see you guys. But I'm not at my grandmother's right now."

"Yeah, I know. Your grandmother said you were housesitting. Where are you staying?"

"I'll tell you, but I don't want you to bring Jon along. Do you understand?"

"It would be just the two of us."

"Okay. I'll give you the address, but I want you to promise you'll just bring Aaron. Do you promise?"

"Yes, I'll come alone. It will be just Aaron and me."

It was dark when I heard a knock on the door. Through the peephole I could see Peggy, and standing next to her was a much taller Aaron. They both looked nicely groomed and weren't wearing wet clothes, so I figured it was safe to open the door to them.

Jon stepped in behind them.

"What are you doing here? I told Peggy I didn't want to see you."

"I came here to apologize. Did your mother get my letter?"

"Yeah. So what? You need to leave! Peggy promised me she would just come with Aaron." I looked at her, but she was staring at the floor.

"I wanted to tell you in person how sorry I am for the way I treated you and all the wrong things I did to you. I wanted a chance to make it up to you."

"You can make it up to me by leaving now."

"Don't you want to see Peggy and Aaron again?"

"Yes, of course."

"Well, if I leave now, they go with me, and you'll never see them again. I've changed. You always said that people should be given second chances to show they've changed."

"How many chances have I given you already, and each time it's the same?"

"I know. I was wrong—very wrong. I'm sorry and won't let it happen ever again. Aren't you worried about your mission and your promise to God?"

"I'll figure that out later."

"I want to help you. I promise that I won't hurt you again. I've changed. Please let me show you I've changed. Just ask Peggy."

"He has. He's relaxed the cleanliness standards, and things are way different. He's been living in Hemet in the apartment with us. We laugh and play together. We're a family now. Jon said the only thing missing is that you're not with us. We want you to come back and be a part of our family."

"I've heard all this before."

"Well," Jon said, "you'll never see them again if you don't give me a chance to prove to you that I've changed. Do you want to take that chance?"

"How do I know you've changed? You've said all that before."

"I'll show you. I want a chance to show you. I've always loved you more than the others. Please let me show you how much I love you."

"Nope."

"Sandy, you know how committed you are to the work and your mission. I can help you complete your mission. I know how important that is to you. You've always said you wanted to do that. It's late. Please let us stay the night and you'll see. I promise you'll see how different I am."

"You can spend the night here only because it's late. But first thing in the morning, you need to leave. I can't have you staying here. I'm house-sitting, and I didn't ask her if I could have guests."

"I understand. It will be just for tonight. We'll sleep in the living room, on the chairs and the couch."

"Okay. And then you'll leave in the morning."

"Promise."

That night, I was awakened when Jon slipped into my bed.

"What are you doing?"

"Please let me show you I've changed." Caressing me, he started kissing me like he hadn't done in years. His gestures seemed so genuine and caring I was soon completely overcome with his kindness.

He continued pleasuring me, and our sex was unlike any we ever had before. Radiating through me was the hope that he was sincere.

"You know I'm the only one who can help you accomplish your mission. I know that you're committed to it. Why don't you let me help you so you can be free? Don't you want to finish the Journey with our relationship like this? You know it's possible now."

"I hope you're telling me the truth. I've always wanted you to treat me with kindness like you did tonight."

"Yes, I know. You deserve that. But I know that you also want to accomplish what you came here to do. Remember your commitment to your mission."

"But my mission can be accomplished without accompanying you on the Journey."

"How do you know that? How can you deny all the signs we've received? Remember the time you led us to that abandoned plantation on that dirt road without looking around or having ever been there? Isn't that a sign that you're being guided?"

"Yeah, that was pretty strange."

"And what about when we were married, and saw the UFOs going in opposite directions? You remember that too? Or what about the time Brenda and I saw the ball of light in Kingfisher? Remember you saw the flash of light from inside the camper?"

"Yeah, I do remember that."

"So, are you going to refute all those miracles and the fact that you still have not completed your mission?"

"No. I guess you're right."

I was totally back under his spell.

I had a commitment with Wendy for the next day, and called to cancel.

She recognized the difference in me immediately. "Sandy, what's wrong?"

"Nothing's wrong, Wendy. Jon came over last night and he's completely different and has promised to treat me with respect and kindness. I'm leaving with him as soon as my house-sitting job is over."

"No! Are you serious? What happened to your decision to never see him again?"

"I know I said that. But all that has changed now. I'll talk to you later, okay?"

"No. I don't think everything is okay. Does your mother know?"

"No, I haven't told her yet."

I hung up feeling a twinge of regret, which I quickly dismissed.

Later that day, Wendy showed up at my door.

"I need to talk to you, Sandy."

"Sure, come in. Wendy, this is Jon."

He offered his hand to her. She did not shake it, and sat down. Jon sat next to me on the couch, draping his arm over my shoulders as he pulled me into him.

"Sandy, I cannot believe that after all he's done to you, you're going back to him. Are you sure about this?"

"Yes, I'm sure. He's changed; he showed me that last night. Jon said he's seen the error of his ways."

Jon nodded. "I know I need to treat Sandy with respect and am really sorry for how I treated her in the past. That's all changed now. Just ask Peggy."

Wendy spoke only to me. "Yeah, but what about how he hurt you? What about that? What about all the things you told me he's done to you?"

"I believe he's really changed. I don't expect you to understand, but I have a mission to do. I have to complete it, and he's promised to treat me with respect from now on."

Wendy shifted in her seat, her irritation growing.

"I'm sorry you don't understand, Wendy, but I need to complete my mission."

She left, frustrated that I would not listen to reason; but I was already gone.

THIRTY-TWO

When the housesitting job ended, Jon drove us to the apartment in Hemet. The moment we stepped over the threshold, he reached out and grabbed my purse.

"Give me that!" He dumped the contents onto the table, separated out my driver's license and new pair of glasses, and destroyed everything else. *At least I still have my glasses. Mom paid a lot for them.*

"Don't move!" I had shifted slightly as he turned his attention to the clothes I had brought. "Just stand there!"

Instinctively, I tightened up as he rifled through the garments. *What have I done?*

"WHERE DID YOU GET THESE?" Disdain dripped from each word as he held up my clothes.

"I bought them."

"HOW DID YOU GET THE MONEY?" Spit flew as his face corkscrewed in front of mine.

"I earned it."

"When you bought these, did you try them on in the store?"

"No."

He shredded the clothes, even the T-shirts I had worn underneath my blouses in-place of his mandated turtlenecks. That alone should have told me something: I still felt the need to wear a garment underneath my blouses, just like he had commanded me to do, even though I thought I was "done forever with him."

"Put this on!" He shoved a dress at me.

"Right now?"

"JUST DO AS I SAY!"

I obediently pulled the dress on over my clothes and stood facing him.

"HOW DARE YOU DEFY ME AND BUY A DRESS!" He tore if off me. "YOU FUCKING WHORE! DON'T YOU KNOW THAT ONLY SLUTS WEAR DRESSES?"

I retreated into a familiar dark, isolated place.

"We're going to complete the Journey together. You gave your word to God you would do this! We leave tomorrow. If you leave me again, I will systematically kill a member of your family until you return to complete your work with me."

I WILL finish this, you demon; you're not going to hurt my family because of me!

Peggy relinquished the urine-soaked Hyundai and bought a small station wagon that was to be our next home. Car rental agencies had blacklisted Jon after he'd traveled from destination to endless destination, raking up countless illegal miles. And after compromising Peggy's and my credit, he had been forced to drive secondhand vehicles with questionable reliability.

As promised, we left the next day, and we were not long on the road when Jon lit a cigarette.

"I didn't know you smoked. When did you start?"

"It's your fault. When you left, I stayed with my mother, and she offered me one. Now I'm hooked."

"Oh. Well, can I have one?"

"I thought you quit."

"I did, long ago, but if you're smoking, I'd like one too." *Maybe it will ease this hell for me.*

"You can only have four a day."

"Okay. Can I have my first one now?"

"Here," he said, giving me one, and I revisited an old habit.

In Los Angeles Jon looked up Barbara, the benefactor who had contributed twenty thousand dollars to his world trip in 1982 when Peggy, Aaron, and I were sweating out the summer in my grandmother's upstairs. It was now 1989 and I didn't know how joyous Barbara was to receive Jon, but she let us stay for a few days. She didn't bat an eye when asking Jon about the food storage bag filled with urine she found under the bed we were using. Looking her in the eyes, he gestured in my direction, claiming I had stashed it due to an aversion to using bathrooms. Even though we had a private bathroom, he had insisted on using the bags. Barbara looked at me and I said nothing, sensing she knew he was lying. *That's right, Jon, blame your phobias on me, like you do everything else.*

While at Barbara's, Jon left briefly, and in that rare moment she shared how they had met in 1982. "He was Solar then, and gave great credence to a book called *The Jupiter Effect*, which predicted that the planetary alignment in March that year would cause catastrophic weather and earthquakes. Solar had organized a group of spiritual seekers to take a trip to prevent these negative events from occurring. He claimed it was necessary to spend the day of the planetary alignment inside the Lower Chamber of the Great Pyramid to disrupt the predictions from happening.

"I'd met him through friends the night his trip's sponsors left everyone waiting at the airport. He asked me to fund the trip. The next day, after a series of coincidences, I agreed to do it. Someone in the deli where we went to eat claimed Solar was the reincarnation of Jesus. I interpreted that as a sign I had to go. I took my son with me and although it cost me my marriage, it was truly worth it."

"So you went into the Lower Chamber with Solar?"

"Yes, he took everyone."

"There were others with you?"

"Yes, a couple named John and Acacia."

"I know them. Well, let's say I've met them, but I haven't spoken with them. Acacia was with us briefly in the Program."

"What's the Program?"

"Jon's non-interaction program for spiritual development."

"I've never heard him mention it. Well, they were there, but Acacia didn't fly home with us. She left directly from Egypt after exploding at Solar over his behavior. You could hear her yelling, 'Fuck you, Solar' all throughout the hotel. She shouted it several times, she was so mad at him."

"Wow. What did he do?"

"Oh, he was trying to control her, even though her husband was there."

"Yeah, he does that—that's what his "Program" is all about. They came to visit Solar when we were living in San Diego when I first joined him, and then they moved into the big house with us in Sedona."

"That's what Acacia said. Our last night was in Mexico City. Even though Acacia left early, John stayed and returned with us. That flight back was when Solar met someone named Lori, who was a stewardess at the time."

"I know her too. She was with us for a while. He claims he dazzled her with his crystal."

"Well, I don't know if that's exactly the way it . . ."

Our discussion was cut short when we heard Jon return from his errand. I kept our conversation to myself, and we left Barbara's place the next day.

Apparently, Jon had drummed up some work, because he announced we were going to do some readings in the Los Angeles area. We spent the night at the home of someone who believed in his vortex seeding; "the Journey" that was supposed to gain me the way to spread my message and accomplish "my mission."

Our hostess came home early the next morning, walking behind a man so tall he shielded her.

"You need to get your things together and get out immediately," the stranger announced.

I cowered, frozen, in the corner. I could see that our hostess was hiding behind this voice of authority. *Maybe she knows Jon beat me this morning.*

"I don't understand," Jon said with unusual softness.

"There's nothing to understand. Get your things together and get out, or we're calling the police."

Those were the magic words. Jon turned to me and, although it would break his cleanliness rules, gently asked me to get our things together as he himself gathered up what I could not carry. We were escorted to our car and Jon backed out the driveway, muttering under his breath and cursing the tall sentinel who oversaw our departure.

Driving around, Jon lit a cigarette and broke the silence. "Want one?"

"Sure, thanks."

"We're in North Hollywood, and I want to find some readings to do."

While I waited in another nondescript parking lot, he returned with good news, having found people interested in his psychic readings. Once we arrived at their doorstep and were ushered inside, Jon introduced me as "Terra" to some famous and not-so-famous celebrities with abundant money to explore their curiosity. It was new for him to bring me along, but, as usual, he limited my interactions. When I was introduced, they responded by calling me "Tarra." I noted the difference, but it seemed insignificant, since Jon had changed my name countless times.

Leaving the Hollywood area, we stopped in San Jose and met the owner of a metaphysical bookstore. She invited us to stay in her home in exchange for our "spiritual work," asking me to guide her in a "soul regression" or spiritual journey. I had never done one before, but had learned to live more intuitively to stay alive and so prayed for guidance and that the best interests of this woman be served. Surrendering my ego to become a conduit to facilitate her quest for expanded self-awareness, I followed the sense that led me through her guided meditation.

Toward the end of her experience, her voice changed; sounding like a stranger was speaking through her. "Your work and sacrifice are recognized and will soon be over," the voice said. I sat dumbfounded, listening to this unsolicited information, feeling it must be a hoax. However, I felt strangely validated and looked over to Jon who was sitting next to us, fast asleep, snoring.

The voice spoke again. "Do you have any questions?"

"Well, yes. Who are you?"

"We are guardians, using this woman's voice for our message to you."

"Thank you for noticing my efforts. I guess I'd like to know how soon I'll be free. Oh, and why people are calling me Tarra now."

"Your work is almost done. The answer to your second question is because that is your true name. You will change your name one final time."

"Thank you." Tears choked my voice; I believed I had witnessed a miracle. *My work is almost done. Can it be true that soon, soon, I will be free?*

I silently digested this experience as Jon continued snoring and the book-store owner awakened from her sleeplike state.

"Do you remember what you said?" I asked her.

"No, not at all. I do remember feeling strange, and many visual pictures, but nothing that I said. What did I say?"

I started to explain, but Jon roused and proceeded to dominate the conversation.

I never shared this incident with him. Being acknowledged—especially being told I would soon be free—was manna to my soul, renewing my strength and determination to see the quest through.

We left the bookstore owner's home and were offered another place to stay in exchange for readings. Two friends listened raptly to Jon wax on about the Journey—how we were seeding crystals in all the vortexes and places of historical significance. One of the pair remarked, "You guys live beyond *The Twilight Zone*!"

If you only knew.

After that, I started working with people interested in our spiritual services, and found that many of those seeking truth and wisdom were suffering from emotional wounds so devastating the individuals had not been able to heal or move beyond the events that caused them. No matter how many times they were told how beautiful their inner being was, it was meaningless until they could feel and experience it for themselves.

I sensed all this in them, but not in myself.

THIRTY-THREE

After the work dried up in California, Jon drove back to Montana. I sat silently beside him, contemplating my San Jose experiences. Predictably, Jon got sick again, and would not allow me to urinate outside even though we both knew I could not endure more than fifteen hours without relieving my bladder. Yet again I ended up sitting in urine-soaked clothes with another blanket wrapped around me to cover the smell. It took a couple of days before Jon felt better, while I sat dousing my seat.

"I'm going to take you to the Yellowstone River so you can clean up before we get a room. But first I need to stop at Pray to leave crystals at the shrine." He frequently visited a Virgin Mary shrine, where he left offerings and performed his rituals.

Alone in the car, I took advantage of this privacy to say my own prayers.

Please forgive me, but I can't go on. Mother Mary, we are here at your shrine and I ask you to please forgive me because I cannot do this to save the planet any longer. I realize now there is only one way out for me, as I have run away countless times and keep getting pulled back. Jon has promised to hurt my family if I leave him again, and I cannot let that happen.

I'm sorry. Please forgive me, God. I love you. Please forgive me.

I peeked through my sunglasses. Jon was still walking around the shrine, so I stole a glance at the mountains in front of me. The clouds above them parted, revealing a face that resembled Mary, the mother of Jesus.

Thank you, Mary. It's so ironic that today is my mother's birthday, and here I am sitting in my own filth, waiting for the decency of cleanliness. I've missed countless occasions without simple gestures of connection and kindness—all forbidden, all sufficient reason to be beaten whenever I ask to acknowledge them. Since 1979, I've missed them all—weddings, funerals, celebrations—and apparently, I'll continue to miss them. I'm not allowed an acknowledgment of anything, including my own physical needs.

I'm trapped. . .

My thoughts drifted to another fully-clothed washing I had endured. That one was in Wyoming; in the dead of winter. Just like now, Jon had prevented me from relieving myself. He'd pulled up to Jenny Lake—snow rimmed its banks. "Here's your bar of soap. Wade out and wash your body and clothes in five minutes or less and walk out. Be sure to bring your soap back with you."

I gasped as I waded in. *I have never been in such freezing water!* Numbly washing myself, I moved slower and slower.

"Time to get out."

"I lost my soap. I'm trying to find it."

"GET OUT NOW!"

I struggled to move out of the water.

"GET OUT NOW!"

Eventually, my hypothermia thawed in the room he got for us. Perhaps he was afraid I would die on him, since I was numb and violently shivering.

And now, once again, nature was to be my bathtub. I started to gently cry.

The car door opened. "What's wrong?" Jon asked as he climbed inside.

"Nothing, I just feel moved."

"Well, we're going to find a place where you can get into the river and clean up."

Clutching the soap, I waded into the Galveston River. Jon added behind me:

"Be sure and wash your clothes, body, and hair."

Waist deep in the river, I turned to face him, let go of the soap, and delivered my speech.

"I can't do this anymore. Please forgive me. I love you." Turning around, I dove headfirst into the river and sucked in a breath of water. Swimming to the bottom, I grabbed a rock. I did not want to risk surviving by floating to the surface and being swept away in the current.

Crouching there, I heard Jon shouting: "SANDY, SANDY! WHAT ARE YOU DOING? YOU CAN'T DO THIS—THEY'LL ARREST ME! SANDY, SANDY! STOP! WHAT ARE YOU DOING?"

I tuned him out and waited for the end. *What's taking so long? I inhaled water when I dove in!*

Then, through the sound of rushing water, I heard a deep, resonant voice, distinctly different than Jon's.

"Tarra!"

Who's calling my name? No matter—I'm ending this now.

"Tarra! You can't do this!"

What's going on? Who are you? I'm trying to die, please leave me alone.

The voice grew louder: "Tarra, stand up! You can't do this! Tarra, stand up now!

Obediently, I let go of my rock and staggered to my feet, coughing out water and wheezing for breath. Jon, hysterical, ran into the water to help me as I inched my way to the river's edge, coughing and struggling to walk.

"Why did you do that? Don't you know they could have arrested me for murdering you? What's wrong? Why did you do that?" His voice was high and tight with fear.

"BECAUSE I CAN'T TAKE IT ANYMORE!" I yelled when I found my breath.

Shrinking back, Jon quietly ushered me to the car. "I'll get us a room. I still can't believe you did that."

I didn't respond, and never told him about the voice that had called my name and commanded me to stand up.

Now what am I going to do?

Jon drove us to Bozeman and rented a cabin in the Angel Motel. He pointed to the chair where I was to sit while he covered the windows with aluminum foil. "I'll get a job delivering pizzas if I have to," he said, and did just that. I never even had to clean up the mess in the car—he did that, too; another first.

Every time he left to deliver pizzas, his instructions were the same: "While I'm away, you are to sit in your chair at the kitchen table. Don't answer the door if anyone knocks. Do you understand? I don't want any problems."

Our temporary home consisted of a single bedroom and bath, a very small living room and a kitchen. It was spacious enough, but cold and drafty. I decided to write children's stories to fill my time in captivity and to ease my dismal surroundings.

Eventually, I completed several I wanted to keep. *Since Jon trashes everything on a regular basis, I need to find a way to preserve them. I'll transcribe them into a microscopic script.*

After condensing pages and pages onto a single sheet of paper, I folded it into an inch square and tucked it underneath the lining of my shoe. I felt empowered by this small gesture of defiance, and grateful to have shoes. They had become a necessary concession when my feet developed calluses that cracked open into deep sores. They had become so painful I could no longer forge through snow and ice in flip-flops, forcing him to purchase shoes so my feet could heal.

I had stashed away a few other things people had given us that I wanted to rescue from Jon's destruction. On every visit to my grandmother's, I tucked mementos I had saved behind a dresser in the room upstairs we used while showering. I planned on doing the same with my children's stories.

Jon's rigid control over my behaviors continued while at the Angel Motel. Each night when he returned, the first words out of his mouth were "Did you get out of your chair? Did anybody come in or knock at the door?" Never did he inquire how I was, how my day had been, or show any interest in my well-being.

Most nights he slept in the recliner in the living room, and I wrapped up in blankets on the floor. My clothes were usually wet and my body cold—my bladder's nemesis. As I watched Jon pee and purge into food storage bags, I decided to use the bags as a source of comfort during the night. Silently, I relieved my stressed bladder into them and stuffed the evidence in my clothes until I could dump them in the bathroom every morning.

Since sleeping on the floor "contaminated" me, my first step was always to shower and wash out my clothes. Sneakily meeting my bodily needs saved me untold suffering as Jon's obsessions continued.

He still considered every fluid or object from his body vulnerable to exploitation by the "dark forces." Beds had lost their function for sleep and comfort, and now were only used for his sexual needs.

"That hurts." There was no longer any pleasure in our sexual encounters.

"I like it when you're tight; it helps me come easier."

I hate you. I hate you. I hate you! Please, God, don't make me do this. Please make him stop. Please! Please, please, please. Praying helped me disconnect, but did nothing to alleviate my frozen resignation. I believed this was my fate.

"Now get going. Be sure and wash the sheets, the shower, and then the walls, and hang the sheets over the bed to dry like before. We can't afford to have any of our sexual energies exploited by the dark forces."

I knew the routine, and even though I could not protest being raped, I found other ways to push back against his control. Treating my clothed body as one unit, I rubbed soap over it, rinsed, and squatted to squeeze out the water instead of taking my clothes off, washing them, wringing them out, and struggling back into them, only to slog on to the next procedure. In my mind, I was asserting myself by refuting his rules. However, I did actually-wash and ring them out for my final washing routine—just to reduce their drying time. I hated them clinging to my body, wet and cold, making it impossible to feel comfortable in my own skin.

Every now and then Jon stayed home—always with the same excuse: "I have a master's degree in psychology; I shouldn't have to deliver pizzas for a living. After all I've done for this world, the sacrifices I've made, and the traveling for the Journey, this is beneath me—the universe should be supporting *me*. Go get cleaned up so you can take notes and record what I say. I want to do some channeling."

I wrote as he rambled and mused about the origins of the universe. Relegated to the kitchen, I transcribed these meanderings into book form while he delivered pizzas. *At least it's something to do. I don't want to write more stories that I need to transcribe for my other shoe. One wad of paper is enough to deal with.*

Jon's brother, who lived nearby, still helped us. One day I heard a knock on the door and the sound of something dropping onto the front porch. When Jon brought in the box of groceries from the local co-op, I felt hopeful. How I craved wholesome and healthy food, and enough to fill my belly.

"It's all contaminated. He left it on the ground. Besides, who wants to eat that shit?"

My heart sank as he tossed the bag into the trash. I craved "that shit," but he preferred jumbo hamburgers, candy bars, chips, and fries. He wolfed down his food, swigging Cokes to wash huge bites down his gullet, and then chewed on his ever-present antacid tablets in between.

One day Jon announced I was to write my grandmother. "Write it exactly as I say! Do you understand?"

"Yes."

> Dear Grandma,
>
> Greetings from snow country. I got your Easter card and the check and want to thank you very much for both. Hope that your Easter was fun. We spent ours at Yellowstone—it was beautiful. There was plenty of snow, and we were even surrounded by a herd of buffalo moving to lower ground, looking for food. They are really incredible animals—totally unbothered by us; they just encircled

the car and escorted us on the road for at least a couple of miles.

We left Sedona because the arrangement with the center did not work. We're having our mail forwarded, but they wait until there's a substantial amount of mail before they send it on. Please don't send any more mail there. We have a P.O. box here in Bozeman and are staying in a motel-cottage until we save up enough for a permanent place.

The car lost a wheel bearing and it was a miracle that we were not killed. The wheel came off on the Interstate on the way to Sedona. Luckily, we were close enough to Sedona to get towed there. We sold the car and bought another vehicle which got us safely to Bozeman. Life has been interesting to say the least.

It has alternately snowed, rained, or hailed here. They were in a drought until we got here—now the weather is catching up. A good thing, since so much of the country seems to be suffering from severe water shortages.

I have almost completed my book [his meanderings] and am looking forward to its completion. I have reworked much of what I left with you and am pleased with how it's coming together.

I hope all is well with you and everyone. I've been following the news and California seems to be having its share of earthquakes. Hope you keep safe.

Please take care and know that I love you. Thank you again for the card and money. You can write to us in Bozeman at P.O. Box 7002, Bozeman, Montana 59771.

Love,

Sandy and Jon

After he finished, I put the pen down and stared at the pages of lies I had just recorded.

"What's the matter?"

"I didn't know my grandmother sent an Easter card," I said.

THIRTY-FOUR

E ach day as I continued wrestling with Jon's oppression, my hatred for him grew. Suicidal thoughts returned.

Dear Gramma,

I know that I have not been in touch with you and I am sorry for that. I have been trying to do my mission—spreading the message that was given me in South America. Because I had failed in my attempts to share it, I entered Jon's non-interaction spiritual Program to develop a closer relationship with God, thinking this would help me with my mission.

I have failed in that too and am writing this note to let you know that I love you and hope that you will forgive me. Thank you again for all your help through the years Gramma and please share this with everyone and let them know that I love them and hope they can forgive me.

Love,

Sandy

I left the note on the table, scooted my chair toward the sink and took a serrated knife from the kitchen drawer. I envisioned how I would accomplish the deed. *When I slice my throat, the blood will flow down the drain without leaving a mess. My head goes here, knife on my neck, now where to cut? There's my jugular—run it down across there. Right there, go. What's wrong? I can't move my arm! Why can't I move my arm? Come on, I'm doing this. Why won't my arm move? Why can't I move my arm? Let go of my arm!*

I sat in silence—my dispossessed arm was out of my control.

Denied escape again, I cried and cried. *All right, I surrender—to whatever this is. I don't understand why I'm stuck here! Oh, man, I should burn my suicide note.* I watched my tear-filled goodbye blacken and curl into flakes until it disappeared in smoke.

I'm going to get more cigarettes since I smoked my quota for today. And I won't even break your stupid rules by getting out of my chair to do it. Clutching the chair to my buttocks, I walked into the other room and helped myself to more cigarettes while stooping over to balance the chair on my back. Leaving my old butts in his ashtray, I stuffed new cigarettes into my mouth and walked back into the kitchen, still tightly clutching the chair until I sat back down at the table. *You won't have any idea I've smoked so many today, and I can honestly tell you I didn't get out of my chair.*

From that day on, I made a regular habit of carrying my chair around as I moved freely into the other room to steal his cigarettes, leaving behind my extra butts. It somehow eased my angst about being held captive.

Soon afterwards, Jon allowed me to write another letter to my grandmother. Perhaps now that she had an address, she was sending regular correspondence. He did not dictate this letter, so I started it with "Dear Gramma."

"Give me that and start over without using a baby name like 'Gramma.' Do as I say or you won't write it at all!"

> Dear Grandma,
>   May today be special and a very happy one for you full of sunshine, love and joy, reflections of your heart. May you know how deeply I care, that my love for you is true. Even though I cannot

be with you and my views are not a part of the reality you choose, your love and acceptance of me will someday help you understand the things you've met in life that never seem to make sense, nor appear a possibility. Yet faith and trust in the Creator will bring us peace, an end to strife.

Happy Mother's Day! I hope that it is a special day for you. Wish I could be there to help you celebrate. Things are tight here, couldn't afford a Mother's Day card. I am sorry. I hope you like the poem. I love you and miss you. Please take care of yourself.
Love,
Sandy & Jon

P.S. I wrote this a while ago, and wanted to share it with you. It's called "Earth."

Oh Earth, with all your glory and might
If only you knew, to the universe you appear such a fright.
With polluted waters and poisoned skies,
The cancer grows on your surface, fed by all the lies.
Humanity—existence, the future never-ending
According to religions, philosophers and theories all contending
The meaning of life, one purpose here, the reason for you and I.
But just wait, humans, when you see the moment you die
Your avoidance of truth and reality has left you totally blind
Realize that, Earth is just one thought in Source's mind.
I love you Gramma

More months passed as I stayed tucked away in the Angel Motel while Jon delivered pizzas. He came home one evening and informed me: "Your grandmother is turning ninety this year. Write her a letter because you're not getting a card to send her. Do you understand?"

"Yes. Thank you."

"Don't thank me. Thank your grandmother."

It must be August. Since I destroyed my suicide note this is my opportunity to let her know my true feelings. At this point, I don't know if I'll ever get away from Jon alive, but hopefully she'll share this with family. It will be my farewell letter if I never return.

Dearest Grandma,

I hope that you have a very happy birthday! I wish I could be there to help you celebrate. Ninety years is quite an accomplishment and I admire you for the way you have lived them. I hope that you know that my heart is with you this day and I also hope that you know how much that I love you.

In your lifetime, you have witnessed the advent of many quantum leaps in science, technology and human awareness; to name just a few. So much change, and so much yet to do. The miracle of life continues on, revealing to us its mysteries in the process. In my life, I have always been troubled with the way things happen to us, many times with no apparent logic or justification. If I had my life to live over again, I would change all of it. I admire the peace which you have and hope that there are no inner-turmoils grinding away at you. I have thus far, been filled with uneasiness, pressing me onwards to seek the answers as to why I have been the person that I am, and was.

My book [the one I was writing for Jon] has been the result of much inner-searching and attempting to understand the incomprehensible. Of course, I know that my beliefs are strange to my family and I do not expect any of you to accept them. I do hope however, that I am accepted as I am and I regret my actions and behavior that have interfered with that acceptance. Because of the things I have done, experienced, have happened to me, et cetera, I had to find a higher order explaining things other than the conventional answers consumed on a mass basis.

In my emotional turmoil of insecurities, anger and resentment,

I have lashed out at the ones I have loved the most. I realize, rather belatedly that I am responsible for my life, although I don't like to look at it, but I have no one else to blame other than myself. My regrets include the way I rejected my father when my parents were in the middle of their divorce. It hurts me deeply that we can never be close again. Unfortunately for me, I patterned many things about myself after my mother. My judgments against her have been my own unwillingness to face myself. She now I know, has **many** regrets about her behavior but I cannot hold her responsible for the results of my life. I love them both and blame them for nothing. I only wish I could show them that somehow.

I have always been able to be open with you and thank you for that. Our bond has shown me much which I feel I did not experience in my childhood. I thank you for that as well.

Life is strange with all of its ironic twists. I am convinced that it is a learning process; a composite of the past, present and potential future; weaving the tapestry of each lifetime, in the continuum of Creation. It is my desire to share what I have learned from my personal struggles, but in the process I have become a stranger. It is only because I have not known myself, nor been willing to look inside; afraid of what I might see. My fears were warranted but not healthy as my distance with myself has translated itself outwardly in my life as well. Sometimes the truth hurts as well as sets you free.

It is not my intention to burden you with my troubles, but only to share some of my personal revelations. I share them with the hopes that you can better understand who I am. We are still in the same house (motel, cottage). It is very comfortable and reasonable, but I am unsure of our future here. Many things are changing and unpredictable at the present time. I had hoped to hear from you but I know that

you do not like to write. We have no phone here. I do wish you a happy birthday and many more. I send you my love, a hug and a kiss, and am sorry I cannot send more. Please take care and know that I love you very much. Happy Birthday!
Love,
Sandy

Jon read it aloud, didn't say anything, and left with it. This was the first time I had written a letter independently and signed it without his name.

I never knew whether he mailed these letters until they were discovered with my grandmother's papers many years later.

Everything continued the same until one day Jon awoke with a dream and insisted I get cleaned up so that I could record it in the kitchen. "Write this down," he ordered from his chair. "I am not to have sex with you any longer. I was shown in a dream it would be like a father being incestuous with his daughter. Just as I awoke, I also heard that I am not to lay a hand on you ever again. You should be glad since you've been asking for these things."

"It's about time but this doesn't change anything for me. I'm only staying with you to complete my mission. I'm leaving you the minute I get my sign I am free to go."

Jon said nothing and a few days later, we left for Utah. Traveling along our predictable routes, he continued leaving his "power objects." We were living in the car again and Peggy had finally stopped sending us her paychecks. All the benefactors Jon had relied upon were also tapped out. No longer commanding large sums of money exposed a rare vulnerability within him. During this leg of our travels, his personal revelations were numerous.

"I'm afraid of being alone. I know that I could never live by myself. Aren't you afraid of living alone?"

"No. I don't think that would bother me particularly. What was it like for you when your parents divorced?"

"My mother used to fix her hair, put on makeup and her fancy dresses, and go bar-hopping."

"Oh." *Maybe that's why you have such a negative association with women wearing dresses. . .*

"When I lived with my stepmother—remember *her* name was Sandra? She put her tongue in my mouth to kiss me one day. She made me sick. I guess she was attracted to me because I was really buff then."

Sometimes, while sitting in a park after having read the newspaper from cover to cover, he had nothing to busy himself with, so I became his confessor. As he waited for time to pass, he purged more secrets.

"Did you know how I lost the hearing in my left ear?"

"You told me your older brothers poured sand into your ear and they had to extract everything, leaving you deaf in that ear."

"Yes. I'm surprised you remember."

I remember everything you've told me about yourself.

He continued, "You know that time when you jumped into the river, I thought you had died. You really scared me. I can't believe you were trying to end your life. Why did you do that?"

"You really don't know, do you?"

"What do you mean? I no longer beat you; isn't that good enough?"

"You no longer beat me *now*, but all those years you should never have beaten me in the first place."

"I thought you believed in forgiveness. I'm also no longer having sex with you. You finally got what you asked for."

"Not until just before we left the Angel Motel and only because your dreams kept telling you not to ever beat me again or have sex with me. I meant what I said in the cabin, that I'm only with you to complete my mission. When that's done, I'm leaving you. Remember when you said the quest was complete when we ran out of money?"

"We're not completely out yet."

"No, not yet." *But you can count on me praying for that to happen as soon as possible.*

Such candid discussions had never been possible before, and would have resulted in a severe battering. I was elated when his dreams forbade him sexual contact or to hurt me, since he always obeyed his dreams. With my safety guaranteed, his frailties became more obvious to me.

"Did you know that when I went shopping in Sedona," Jon said, "if anyone sneezed or coughed in the grocery aisle, I would abandon the cart and start with a different one since those groceries were contaminated?"

"No, I didn't know that, since we never went with you."

"Did you ever abandon a grocery cart?"

"No, and I never had to deal with people sneezing; we always made sure the aisles were empty when we went shopping. I know that's why you've left food at the window or sent it back."

"You don't think that if someone is mopping or sneezes inside a restaurant that it's contaminated?"

"You really want to know what I think?"

"Yes, I do."

"I think that's a little extreme, especially since health codes require people to wash their hands when handling food after doing some sort of cleaning, sneezing, or coughing."

"You'd tell me if someone sneezed on my food, wouldn't you?"

"Yes, of course. I'm just saying I've been lucky it's never happened." *Please forgive me for lying, God.*

Judging by the weather, I figured it must be December. We were back in Montana when Jon confirmed my suspicions: "We're going to spend the winter solstice in Yellowstone. That's when the world is ending. Nineteen-ninety, the date when the illusion will end! I'm responsible for taking all the light workers out of here and back home—back to their Source. Our last night together will be tonight, the winter solstice—here in Yellowstone."

None of your prognostications have ever come true, but you keep making them. Maybe we'll freeze to death tonight. That will certainly release us.

"Here," he said, handing me garbage sacks. In preparation for sleep we wrapped one around each leg and then another bag around both legs, and two around our torsos.

"You can have an extra cigarette," he said, "since it will be your last. We're out of food, but tomorrow we'll be out of here, out of the illusion. Good night."

"Good night." *I hope you're right because I can't take much more.*

As usual, I slept next to him with my feet planted on the floor. He still insisted I touch him while sleeping—a rule he maintained until the end—so I slept with my head on his lap, my body bent at the waist.

My shivering torso awakened me before dawn. Both legs were completely numb, and I could barely move them. I nudged Jon awake to start the engine. As the heater warmed, I began to thaw and so did my brain.

The world did not end.

"Sandy, do you need to pee?"

"Yes."

"Well, get going before it gets light."

"Okay." I sluggishly made my way through the snow to relieve myself while he used a plastic bag inside the car. *So much for his predictions. What's left to do before my mission is finished? Why do I still have to do this?*

Climbing back into the car, heat blasted me as I shook violently with the cold.

"The world did not end," Jon said, "because the 'dark forces' prevented it."

"Oh. Well, what's next?"

"We're heading back to California. We'll stop at your grandmother's and then maybe see your mother. I'm going to call you Tarra from now on, like you asked."

I requested that after San Jose. Took you long enough.

For years, contact with my family had been minimal, but when Jon's support base vanished, we started staying with my mother and grandmother, exploiting their hospitality. When visiting my grandmother together previously, we had been made to sleep in the car, and entered her home only to eat or shower. But this time she relented.

"Sandy, I've decided you can sleep in the rumpus room if you'd like, rather than having to sleep in the car."

"Thank you, Gramma. That would be great."

She gave us blankets and pillows to cushion the hardwood floor. During the night, Jon threw a plastic bag filled with his urine onto the floor. It leaked undetected until the next morning.

"Hey," I said, "one of your bags leaked onto my grandmother's floor."

"So what? What's the big deal?"

"It left a stain! I don't believe you! You are so incredibly inconsiderate and selfish." I got up to clean the spot, showered, and then washed out my clothes.

You're disgusting and I can hardly wait to be done with you. I'm going to throw some coins to see if it's time yet.

One Heart, One Mind, One Spirit, please God give me a sign whether-or-not I'm finally free to leave Jon. Heads I have completed my mission and am free to go; tails I am not done and need to stay.

I watched the coins fall one by one.

Three tails.

After breakfast, Jon instructed me to call people we had previously given readings to in hopes of generating money. No one was interested, but my call to an intuitive was very revealing.

"Diana, it's Tarra. We're in town again and Jon wants to know if you'd like another reading."

"No. I'm not interested, but it's good to hear from you."

"It's good to talk to you too. Can I ask you something?"

"Sure. What is it?"

"Do you sense that I'm done with the Journey? We're running out of money, and he always said my mission was complete when the money ran out. No one I've called wants a reading. I'm hoping I'm done. What do you get?"

"Oh, I'm sorry, but you're not done. I feel that Spirit wants you to take one more trip with him to the East Coast."

"I was afraid of that."

"I'm sorry. Please call me when you're done."

I didn't share with Jon what Diana had said, and reluctantly got ready to leave.

We were walking toward the car when Jon commented, "You're unusually quiet."

For the first time, ever, I raised my voice at him: "I HATE YOU, AND I'M ONLY STAYING WITH YOU BECAUSE I PROMISED GOD I WOULD FULFILL MY MISSION. YOU TALK ABOUT ENDING THIS ILLUSSION. I'LL DO EVERYTHING IN MY POWER TO BLOCK YOUR OBSESSION WITH DESTROYING THE WORLD!"

Surprised at my outburst, Jon said nothing. His flagrant disregard for my grandmother's floor had pushed me over the edge. I always felt more empowered around family, and knew he could no longer hurt me because of the warning from his dreams. Interacting with my family helped me break through his mantle of control, but not enough to liberate me. I was incapable of leaving due to my obligation to "fulfill my mission."

We drove to Carlsbad where we found a bookstore and people interested in readings. Taking full advantage of another person's gracious hospitality, we lingered for several weeks until the work started drying up.

"Do you think your mother would let us stay a night with her?"

"I can call her and ask."

"No, let's just go visit her and find out."

I was surprised by my mother's warmth and her offer to let us stay a few nights. When the time was up and we were leaving, I hung back so I could hug her goodbye.

"Thanks for letting us stay here, Mom. I really appreciate it."

"I'm just glad to see you. I hope you take care. You are always welcome to spend the night and get cleaned up, although I didn't appreciate Jon soaking the carpet."

"I'm sorry. He doesn't believe in using towels. Do you think I'll ever be done?"

"Honey, I guess you have to do this until you don't."

"Tarra," Jon interrupted from the sidewalk, "come on. We need to get going."

I got inside the car.

"We're headed to the East Coast. Don't look around. Before that, we'll be going through Yosemite and Kings Canyon to leave more power objects and release vortex energies before we go on to the East Coast. Didn't you say your cousin lives up north? Isn't she the one you lived with when you went home in 1983? We should go there first."

"Yes, she's the one, but I don't remember how to get there."

"You're lying! I know you are. Do you want to condemn your family to hell? It's important we go there to release your negativity and all your family's negative energies. How do we get there? Tell me now!"

Slipping back into subservience, I led him toward my cousin's. Along the way he stopped in a secluded place to have a snack. "Here, open these," he said, handing me some cans of tuna.

"Where did you get these? They look like the kind my mother had."

"They are."

"What? You took them without asking?"

"She won't miss them; she had plenty."

"You're unbelievable! I'm never taking you back there again. You stole food from my mother. What else did you take?"

"Nothing."

How do I know you're not lying? "Don't ask me to go there again because, if we do, I'm going to tell her that you ripped her off."

"It's just tuna."

"That's not the point! You took something that didn't belong to you without asking."

"Well, then, I guess you won't be having any of it to eat, will you?"

"That's fine." *I hate you.*

"What did you say?"

"Nothing."

The year was 1991.

THIRTY-FIVE

"Oh my, I can't believe my eyes. Sandy, how are you? And is this Larry?"

"Yes, Donna. Except he goes by Jon now. I'm sorry to barge in on you like this, but we were in the area and Jon wanted to meet you."

"Oh, I'm so glad you did. Please come in; it's cold out here. Have you had supper?"

"Yes," I responded, but was overridden by Jon's "No."

"Well, come on in, and I'll fix you guys something to eat."

"Thank you, Donna, but I don't want to trouble you."

"It's no trouble at all. I'm so glad you're here. I can hardly believe it's you. You look different, and you've lost so much weight. Are you getting enough to eat?"

"It has been a long time. Good to see you too."

"You guys can spend the night in the cabin. Sandy, you remember how the hot water works in the bathhouse?"

"Oh yes. Thank you, Donna, but that really won't be—"

"We'd be happy to take you up on your kind offer," Jon interrupted again. The "overnight stay" was extended to a couple of days as Jon poured on his charm. Neither Donna or I suspected he was gathering information to use against us later. He inquired about the time I had spent living there, and my cousin shared pictures of our "Pioneer Days," when we had worn our ancestors' clothes for a church celebration.

"Do you have any other pictures of Sandy when she was younger? I'd like to see what she looked like."

"Oh sure. She was a bridesmaid in my wedding."

"May I see them?"

"Of course." She pulled her wedding album off the shelf, and Jon thumbed through it while listening to her comment on each picture.

The next day while Donna was at work, Jon snarled at me, "We're leaving tomorrow, and there's something we have to do before we can go. Where are the clothes you wore to church? We need to burn them to release your negative energies from them."

"What? Those are antiques and family heirlooms. Our aunties wore them, and they're priceless to my cousin."

Eyes blazing at my defiance, he swung his arm back like he was going to strike me. "GET THEM! IF YOU DON'T TELL ME WHERE THEY ARE, YOU WILL CONDEMN YOUR COUSIN TO HELL AND *YOU* WILL ROT THERE ALONG WITH THE REST OF YOUR FAMILY!"

I led him to the clothes, which he cremated in her wood burning stove.

I can't believe I've brought such horror to my dear cousin. I hate myself; I hate my life. How will I ever tell her what we've done?

We were sitting in her living room when Donna walked in. "Hi guys. What's that funny smell? Did something happen to the stove?"

"No," Jon lied. Nothing unusual happened."

I hid behind my self-hatred. *I AM a failure. Jon smokes in her cabin even though Donna asked us not to smoke in it. What a nightmare, me bringing him here. How can I ever face her again?*

As we got ready to leave the next day, I balked at his latest request.

"Smearing Pine Sol on her antique furniture will destroy it."

"HOW DARE YOU DEFY ME!"

His twisted face spit rage and sputum on me. I noticed his tightened fist and automatically dropped my head.

I drenched her furniture with disinfectant and sea salt as we left.

We drove to Yosemite, and I pressed my eyes closed as mandated. Retreating into the darkness, I entertained my silent soliloquy of self-hatred.

I was jostled back to reality with Jon's shouting: "GOD DAMN IT! THE CAR STOPPED AND WON'T BUDGE. GET OUT!"

"What?"

"You heard me! Get out! Pack up everything. Get some garbage sacks, double-bag them, and put everything inside them. We're leaving the car. It's going to be dark soon, and we need to get out of here or we'll freeze to death."

Gripping our thirty-gallon garbage sack suitcases, I surveyed the home we were abandoning. A Good Samaritan drove us to the nearest pay phone, miles away from the car. This was fortunate for me, since Jon had thrown out my shoes and I was once again wearing flip-flops.

After our savior pulled away, Jon barked his orders: "Call your grand-mother. We need money for a bus to Bozeman. Then call your cousin and ask her to come get us."

"What? You expect her to help us after you burned her clothes, smoked in her cabin, and left disinfectant on her furniture?"

"DON'T ARGUE WITH ME! JUST GET US OUT OF HERE!"

My grandmother agreed to wire money. Swallowing hard, I tried to push down the lump in my throat as I dialed my cousin. *Oh, God. My chest hurts.*

"Hi, Donna? It's Sandy. Could you please come pick us up? We're at a gas station a few miles from Yosemite. The car broke down and we need a ride to the bus station. My grandmother has agreed to wire us money so we can buy bus tickets to Montana."

"Yosemite? That's at least six hours away."

"I know. I'm sorry to have to ask this of you, but it's important. I'm doing God's work, and we need to get to Montana. Would you please come get us?"

"Sandy, everybody is telling me not to do this because I'm enabling you."

"You don't understand how important this is. I have to do this."

"All right. I'll come get you, but only because I love you."

"Thank you, Donna. I know you don't understand, but I've been given a mission by God."

"My God is a God of love."

I was speechless. The world hushed to a stop. I gazed up into the sky as this seed of truth rooted itself deeply within me.

Donna picked up a friend to keep her awake, then drove for over six hours to pick us up. We climbed into the back seat and she immediately turned around to head back home. My cousin and her friend talked to each other during the ride, interrupted only by coffee and bathroom breaks.

Once, after I let Jon know I was squirming, he allowed me to use the bathroom with them.

Donna confronted me. "I know you guys smoked in the cabin. And when I went to get the sheets, I noticed all the disinfectant on the furniture. Why, Sandy? I don't understand."

"I'm sorry, I'm so sorry." I was reeling with shame and could only stare at the floor, unable to say more. *I don't know what will happen when she finds out we burned the clothes. I hate myself. Why God was that necessary?*

When we arrived at Donna's place, she bustled around and then handed me a large bag. "This is for you guys for the bus ride. There's enough food for three days. That should get you to Montana, and here's a suitcase for all your stuff." She pointed to a medium-size green suitcase on the floor. At Jon's nod, I transferred our things into it from the garbage sacks.

We piled back into her car and rode silently to the bus station, an hour's drive away. Jon never expressed a sliver of remorse or an apology to Donna, but at least added a "thank you" to my profuse gratitude as she left us at the bus station.

We purchased two one-way tickets to Bozeman, Montana. Once on the bus, Jon commandeered the food bag and gobbled down everything

Donna had packed for the entire trip. Thereafter, we ate candy bars and smoked cigarettes to abate our hunger. At four thirty in the morning, our bus rolled into a dark and snow-covered winter landscape in Bozeman.

"We have to walk to my brother's store," Jon said. "He'll help us."

"I hope so; we're going to freeze to death in this weather."

"Be quiet and keep walking. Don't look around. I'll help you carry the suitcase when you get tired."

I wish you hadn't thrown away my shoes. "I'm tired, would you please carry the suitcase now?"

"You're so weak. Give it to me."

His brother's store was a mile or two from the bus station and was closed when we got there. We stomped our feet and walked around to keep warm, but I was so cold I needed to relieve myself. Since it was dark, Jon allowed me to pee behind the store. It would not bode well with his brother if I had wet my pants.

Hours passed before his brother—a resource Jon tapped every visit to Bozeman—arrived. As we waited, I remembered the last time we parachuted into his brother's life. *He was kind enough to share the rooms he rented downstairs in that lady's home. George introduced us to his Christian community, and they insisted you bring me even though you didn't want to. I don't know what they looked like since I wasn't allowed to interact with them. Back in the corner of the room, I couldn't even hear what you shared or how you prayed in their Bible studies.*

Oh, and I remember when I was standing in the corner of the kitchen, while everyone snacked and sipped their tea. That teenager cornered me when he opened the silverware drawer. I knew I was in trouble when you caught my eye and motioned me to follow you outside. For a moment, I thought everything was going to be okay on that path next to the stream. But when the trees blocked their view of us you whirled around. "That's for getting too close to that kid!" It hurt so much when you kicked my legs and slugged me in the stomach. I tried to explain what had happened. "Shut up! I don't want to hear your excuses!"

Back inside, I heard people murmuring behind me. You told them I was not feeling well and walked me out to the truck. "Stay here, demon!" Locking me inside. I wonder if they ever knew?

My thoughts were interrupted when a truck pulled into the space behind the store. "Come on," Jon ordered and I followed him to the back entrance. George opened the door. I followed Jon inside, keeping my distance. Pleading with his brother, Jon shared that we were homeless and half-frozen, but this time his brother did not offer help. Instead, he suggested we visit one of the local churches that gave charity vouchers for hotel rooms.

We left and began trudging downtown as Jon cursed his brother. Tuning him out, my thoughts drifted away. *Maybe George remembers the croquet game we played with his kids the last time we were here. Wonder what he thought when you ran over to me, grabbed my mallet and tossed it? All because I was defeating you.*

The streets of Bozeman were lined with snow as we stumbled along.

"Come on, they might be able to help us find someone interested in readings." I followed as Jon ducked into Lair's Bookstore, which looked like it had just opened for the day.

The warmth inside was overwhelming. Jackie, the owner, offered her phone to Jon as she handed me a cup of hot soup. "You look familiar. Tell me about yourself."

"You look familiar, too. I'm sure I've never met you before, but it seems like I have." My hands thawed while cradling the soup, and her caring nature and kind face warmed my heart.

A minute later, Jon sat down next to me. "Well, I got through, but the Crow Indians won't help us."

"I know of someone who takes in God's soldiers," Jackie offered, scrutinizing our one suitcase and snowcapped feet in flip-flops.

While she made a phone call, Jon reached for my soup and asked me what Jackie had said. She returned before I could answer.

"Marilyn has agreed to meet you tomorrow. I'll take you up there. She may be able to offer you a place to stay for a while."

After thanking Jackie, we left to find the church that George said offered vouchers. They gave us enough for a room and food. As agreed, the next day Jackie drove us to Kelly Canyon and parked the car in front of Marilyn's home, an architectural wonder. With floor to ceiling windows, the house curved around a wooden deck that we now ascended. Jackie knocked and Marilyn, a very tall and elegant woman, opened the door. Jackie stepped inside with Jon behind her.

As I walked past Marilyn, who was holding the door open for us, I caught her gaze. She rolled her eyes at me, and I felt like somehow, I knew her.

The beauty of her home with its artwork and furnishings wrapped me in a spectrum of color and light, wonderful in its generosity and comfort. She directed us to a lush purple couch where I sat next to Jon, who gushed stories about our "divinely guided journey," slipping in our present need for a place to stay.

I basked in the light streaming through her giant windows opening to a view of nature and solar energy collectors. Marilyn's intensely green eyes focused on Jon as she spoke. "I can let you stay here until you get back on your feet. I often accommodate the overflow crowd of devotees who attend pilgrimages to CUT."

"Oh, what's that?" Jon demurely asked.

"Church Universal Triumphant. It's the church Elizabeth Claire Prophet founded, located between Livingston and Bozeman. The Royal Teton Ranch is its headquarters. They have so many seekers the locals in Bozeman call them the 'purple people' because of their wardrobe. Everything is purple. Jackie said you do past-life readings. I can probably line up some people who would like one of your readings. You can do them here if that will help."

Over the next few days, we did many readings and soul regressions for Marilyn's friends and residents of CUT. I wanted to help Marilyn to show my gratitude, but Jon insisted I do only the cleaning he required. She had given us our own private suite, and even though we ate her food and stayed with her rent-free, he never paid her any money.

I fixed Jon's food and washed our clothes, but was prohibited from interacting with Marilyn without him present. He had relaxed some of his standards, but they were still far from reasonable.

"You will not use the toilet here unless you shower afterwards." Every night, he still took me outside for my nightly pee, until one night when Marilyn had overnight guests.

"You will not go out tonight."

"It's been all day, Jon."

"I don't care. You've gone thirty-six hours before."

"I'm sure I can't do that anymore."

"You will, or face the consequences."

Needless to say, I soaked the comforter I had wrapped around me.

"You have to take it into the shower and wash it there before loading it into the washing machine. Do you understand?"

"Yes, but what if Marilyn sees me?"

"She won't. She's not up yet. Get going."

I wadded up the comforter and silently walked past the kitchen. Marilyn was standing there, looking at me quizzically, and her jaw dropped. "Tarra, are you okay?"

"Yes," I whispered back. "I had an accident last night and have to wash this out before putting it into the washing machine."

"You really don't have to do that."

"Oh, yes I do. Jon has some strange cleanliness beliefs." My candor shocked me.

"Yes, I've noticed. Do you really need to do this?"

"Yes, if you only knew. I'm not even supposed to be having this conversation with you."

"Okay, Tarra, but if you're ever free of Jon, you're always welcome in my home. I would love to talk with you more."

As I continued to the bathroom, I noticed a strange sensation inside me—our secret conversation had felt nurturing.

After that, whenever the chance arose, I stole more bits of conversation with Marilyn, never reporting my interactions and closely guarding my budding friendship. Marilyn constantly reiterated the same message. "You don't need to be subservient to Jon to serve God or fulfill your purpose in life."

"You don't understand how negative I am. Jon calls me a demon because I've been very negative. He claims that all the times he 'disciplined me' were to 'cleanse the sin' from me."

"What?"

"Disciplining me was when he used to beat me. He doesn't do that anymore but he calls me Santania, twisting Sandy, my birth name, into 'Satan's bride.' San Demon is another favorite. He claims my last name, Judson, means 'son of Jude.' And since Jude betrayed Jesus in the *Bible*, he says I'm a traitor to Jesus, and that makes me evil."

Marilyn's face scrunched in disbelief. "Tarra, I don't see how you could believe all that."

Knowing Jon was waiting for me, I left her to walk back to our room. *You don't believe me but why do I get pulled back every time I escape? I know it's because I absolutely must complete my mission. When I do, I'll be released from my sins, be freed and will gain my family's love.*

Jackie left her bookstore to visit us. "I'd like to share some information with all of you that I have been asked to convey. Do you mind?"

"That's fine," Jon agreed.

Marilyn nodded, and we gathered in her living room. Jackie closed her eyes and the room fell silent. Within minutes, Jon began breathing heavily, and I opened my eyes to see his head resting on his chest as he slept.

"I am Quan Yen," Jackie said, "and use this entity often to share information that is needed. I have a message for the traveler. You can serve God and do not need to defer to this man. There are many ways to serve God, and perhaps you need to look at how you are having to defer to this man to pursue your path. This is not necessary."

I knew that Quan Yen, or Guan Yin, was a mythical Chinese Taoist immortal known as the Goddess of Mercy, or the Virgin Mother of Compassion, in the Buddhist/Oriental world.

Jackie came to visit us several times, and each time, her message was the same. Jon always fell asleep. Had he heard the content of the messages, I'm sure he never would have allowed me to participate.

Jackie's messages planted seeds of hope within me that the end of my time with Jon might be close. At the end of the summer, we had earned enough money to purchase another secondhand car. It was a cruiser reminiscent of what Jon had been driving when I first met him.

Since we still had not completed the final East Coast trek, we headed down to Salt Lake City, to look up people Marilyn had suggested would be interested in our work. The owner of a metaphysical bookstore arranged a place for us to stay, where we passed several weeks doing readings and healings. We were also given referrals in St. George and stopped there.

Sherry was like so many: openhearted and trusting. She graciously housed and fed us while we worked that area until the interest dried up.

On the road again, we drove north to the Dakota Badlands, over to the Atlantic Seaboard, and then dropped down through the Midwest. Our circuit usually passed through Arkansas. Like before, Jon decided to purchase more crystals that he planned on hocking for a profit. Thinking the Church Universal Triumphant people would want more crystals, we headed back to Bozeman. This time Marilyn was not interested in talking with Jon or buying crystals from him. And even though the CUT people had purchased several large slices of Brazilian geodes previously, they were not in the market for what he was peddling.

"I don't suppose we could stay with your cousin Donna?" Jon asked one day.

"You must be joking! You burned her clothes." *Not to mention, you told me later, all the photos of the two of us, including her wedding pictures.* "You're something else!"

"It needed to be done."

"You'll never convince me of that. You had no right!"

"Well then, we're going to Sedona. Mary Lou Keller will help us out.

I'm going to use that Brazilian amethyst geode I gave you as collateral for a loan from her. I know I gave it to you, but we need the money and you're not done with your mission."

"Right." *I want that geode, but I'll gladly let it go. Maybe he needs to pawn everything we own before he recognizes the journey is over and it's time to let me go.*

We landed on Mary Lou's doorstep again, and she gave him money for the geode—a huge, beautiful domed structure. She offered us a place to stay, and later wrote about our visit in her book:

> Much later these two would come back to see me, both of them in a sad state of affairs, not only totally broke but also very disturbed emotionally. So I put them up in my guest room for the night.
>
> It seems this young man (Solar/Jon) had lost his connection with the aliens . . . His wife was not doing well, either. She would sit all day in my guest bedroom, refusing to speak or participate in any way. Meanwhile I was buying all the groceries, preparing the meals and working full time at my office while they made no effort to help. After two weeks of this uncomfortable arrangement, I realized I must ask them to leave. At my age, I did not need to take care of two capable young people who were making no effort to take care of themselves. By this time in my life I was not bringing in enough income to support more than myself.
>
> It was an extremely unpleasant end to a long and interesting friendship, and I have always regretted that it ended that way. However, I realized I owed it to myself not to take on problems that belonged to other people. After a lifetime of serving others, I finally came to the realization that now my first commitment had to be for my own welfare and happiness (*Echoes of Sedona Past*, pages 142, 143).

As usual, Jon had prohibited me from helping, and felt it beneath him to do so. He never offered to pay Mary Lou or anyone else who fed and housed us, believing they owed it to us as we "were doing God's work."

When not staying with others, we showered every week or week and a half, stopping at motels because campsites were "too dirty and exposed." Eating exclusively from fast food restaurants, driving around incessantly, and running the engine to keep warm, was an expensive lifestyle. Jon blew about a hundred dollars a day on food, snacks, and gas.

Mary Lou's money did not last long, and his support was tapped out.

"We're in Phoenix, and I'm going to apply for aid. You stay here while I go inside and get us some food and vouchers." Phoenix had the largest homeless population in the U.S. at that time. An entire city block was filled with tents and cardboard shanties—makeshift homes using whatever shelter could be scrounged.

After an hour of waiting, Jon returned. "Since we have a car, the Salvation Army considers us 'transient homeless.'"

Great, besides battered wife and spiritual vagabond, I can add "homeless" to my résumé.

"They gave us a cash grant and this commodity food. It's all crap!"

He tossed it into a large garbage sack filled with trash, and my hatred grew, along with my judgments against him. *I would gladly eat any of that food rather than choke down the thirty-three-cent cheeseburgers you get me.*

Jon had one more option when we exhausted this money—his trunk full of quartz. "I'm going back to Los Angeles to sell these crystals." In LA, he left me in the car when he knocked on Barbara's door.

"Barbara doesn't live here," he announced back in the car. "Her son said she's moved and we can't stay here."

Years later I would learn that Barbara had informed her son not to let us stay there, and had indeed moved away. Uncannily, she had connected with Lori at a seminar where the two exchanged Solar stories.

When we originally left her home, Barbara called Lori to let her know we were in town and had just left her place. The next day, in a conversation with a friend, Lori discovered that we had landed at her friend's house. That was when her friend took reinforcements to remove us.

Still struggling to find another place to stay, Jon made some inquiries. After several stops, he returned to the car beaming. "I found out there's a Whole Life Expo going on now, with all kinds of booths and vendors. I'm going there to sell my crystals."

At the Expo, he parked in the shade, but it was so incredibly hot he allowed me to wait with the window down—another first. I watched the people walking around, gladly breaking another of his rules. *I wonder what it would be like to be able to come and go as I pleased. Uh-oh, here he comes. Doesn't look like he was very successful.*

"I couldn't sell any of them because I don't have a booth, and it's too late to register for one. I don't know what to do because we're out of money. We can't even afford to get a motel room to get cleaned up. Do you think your grandmother would let us stay for a few days?"

"Sure." *This is the end of the road—you're out of money and options. God, please give me confirmation that I'm finally going home.*

I remained silent the entire drive to San Diego, barely able to contain the elation growing inside me.

On November 18, 1991, we rolled into my grandmother's driveway.

"Go inside and ask if we can stay for a few days."

My flip-flops scrunched across the lawn, and I glided through the familiar wooden gate opening onto the patio. My feet barely touched the flagstones as I hopped onto the upper patio and knocked on the screen door. Family always walked through the back- porch door without knocking, but I had forsaken that right.

"Well, hello. Come in, so good to see you." Gramma opened the door wide for me.

I hesitated before walking in. "Hi, Gramma. I'm here with Jon, and

I was hoping you would let us stay here for a few days. Please say yes."

"Well, of course. You can stay in the rumpus room."

"Is it okay if we shower and get cleaned up first? It's been a while."

"Oh yes, of course."

"Thank you so much. I'll go get Jon."

I retraced my steps back to the driver's side. "She said we could shower and stay in the rumpus room."

"Okay. Bring in the suitcase and get your cleaning stuff out. You'll go first and then I'll shower."

I placed the suitcase in my father's old bedroom, which was closest to the bathroom. I showered, washed out my clothes and continued with my plan, knowing Jon would take at least 30 minutes.

Jon still sought divine guidance by throwing coins, and I decided to use pennies once again as my oracle, in hopes of getting a "sign" about being free to go.

I nervously jingled six pennies between my hands. *The last trip to the East Coast is done and we're out of money. Jon's financial support has dried up. Please, God, give me a sign to confirm that I am now free to leave him. Heads mean yes and tails is no. I promise to honor the coin toss. Heads mean yes; tails no. Here goes….*

I tossed each penny into the air until all six had landed on the bed. When the last one fell, I held my breath.

Oh, my God! Oh! Thank you, thank you, God! I'm free! I'm free!

Six heads stared up at me. An electrical charge raced through my body, and I stealthily began separating our belongings, putting mine in a different room and Jon's into the suitcase. Then I snuck downstairs and asked my grandmother if I could stay with her because I was leaving Jon.

"Why, of course!"

"Thank you, Gramma! Thank you so much! When Jon finishes showering, I'm going to tell him my decision. Please call my father if he resists leaving."

I crept back up the stairs, but one of them creaked.

"Tarra, is that you?"

I said nothing and sped back into the room. Within minutes he was standing before me, drenching the carpet. Once he was dressed, I put his comb and toothbrush inside the suitcase, closed it, and handed it to him.

"Goodbye. I'm staying and you're leaving."

"I don't understand."

"There's nothing to understand! You're leaving and I'm staying. Goodbye. You need to leave now. My grandmother is waiting downstairs for you to leave. I've put all your things in the suitcase. You need to leave now."

"You must be possessed. You're making a big mistake. What about your commitment to anchor the ray in Hawaii?"

I pointed toward the stairs. "You don't have the money, and that's my sign we're done."

"What if I get the money? You made a commitment."

"If you get the money for air fare and hotel for you, me and a third person, then I'll go. I'm not going with just the two of us, and that's that! Now please leave."

"Do you realize what you're doing?"

"Yes." Trying to hide my nervous shaking, I gently pushed him toward the stairs as he walked around the banister. I followed him down the stairs and through the dining room. He stopped in the kitchen and turned to face me.

"You're making a big mistake."

"Sandy, do you want me to call your father?" my grandmother asked.

"No, thank you, Gramma. That won't be necessary because Jon is leaving right now." I again pointed to the door, and gently pushed his arm as he walked through it. Closing the door behind him, I slid the dead bolt.

"Thank you, Gramma, for helping me and letting me stay with you. Do you mind if I go upstairs for a few minutes to gather my thoughts?"

"No, of course not. Do you need anything?"

"No, not right now. I just need a few moments." As I climbed the stairs, I tried to process my freedom. *I got my sign; I'm free. Why do I still feel so much fear?*

It was dark outside, and I turned on the light and sat on the bed to steady myself—my entire body was shaking. As I gathered my wits about me, I heard Jon shouting from outside.

"Tarra, reconsider what you're doing—remember the miracles, the work you committed to do; the ray we have to anchor in Hawaii. What about your mission and your family? They'll be condemned."

I turned out the light and walked to the window. Jon was standing just outside the gate. Both dogs were facing him. *Keep him away, Wendy and Ears.*

"Tarra, please don't leave me. How can you turn your back on God? You're making a huge mistake. Tarra, please listen to me. Don't do this."

I closed the window, pulled down the shade. *I can't listen to you anymore; I don't have to listen to you ever again.*

Within minutes, I heard a car rolling down the dirt driveway. Jumping up, I walked into another room to watch through the curtain as Jon's car left the ranch. Even after it turned onto the bridge I stood guard until the taillights disappeared.

You're not welcome here anymore.

Dropping to my knees, I prayed for direction, and that my liberation was mine to keep. Tears came easily as I wept in gratitude.

Realizing I had not said goodnight to my grandmother, I gathered myself together, washed my face and walked downstairs.

"Do you have pajamas to sleep in?" my grandmother asked.

"I only have the clothes I'm wearing, a comb and my driver's license. I gave Jon our only toothbrush and toothpaste."

"Oh my. Well, there are supplies in the upstairs bathroom you're welcome to, and I found these pajamas that I think might fit you. Would you like to borrow some clothes?"

"Yes, thank you; that would be great." I waited for her until she returned with her arms full of clothes. I put them on a chair and hugged her close.

Walking back into the room I would live in, I sat on the bed as a wave of fear washed over me. *What if I lose my freedom again?* I sat on the bed praying for guidance, and once again a wave of peace and gratitude washed over me. After running my hands over the bedspread, I pulled it back and burrowed my face in the pillows with their freshly laundered smell. The sheets were smooth and my hands drank in their softness. Feeling more settled, I changed into a set of my grandmother's pajamas and slowly edged into luxury.

A real bed with clean, dry sheets! How long has it been? Twelve years of being dragged back again and again. I've finally escaped from Jon's control—I got my sign—I'm free!

PART VI: WILD WOMAN WILDEBEEST

Your vision will become clear only when you look into your heart. Who looks outside, dreams. Who looks inside, awakens.

—Carl Jung

THIRTY-SIX

At the age of ninety-one, my grandmother gardened, was a world traveler, volunteered with the hospital auxiliary, socialized with family and friends, and played bridge on a regular basis. She had been born by the light of a kerosene lantern, with a midwife assisting, on her father's ranch in San Pasqual Valley on August 22, 1900. Her family first lived in the Clevenger House, the first home built by settlers in the valley. Her grandfather, Amos Davis Trussell, had moved his family south from Sierra Madre to San Pasqual, and her father, Ray Trussell, bought the dairy and another in San Marcos from his father. In 1905, to accommodate their growing family, my grandmother's father and grandfather built a new two-story home where she and her eight siblings would grow up. That house presently stands among citrus trees that replaced the fields and cows of her day.

Electricity and running water would come to the family before indoor toilets, and horses were the usual mode of transportation. Her sister Mary rode a cow to Escondido, and during my grandmother's first year of high school, she and her brothers drove a horse and buggy to "town." Depending on which horse they used, the trip would take anywhere from an hour to an hour and a half.

Beginning her sophomore year, they drove a Model T, as did my future grandfather, Charlie, although his was slower. The road into Escondido was dirt with a deep herringbone curve as it climbed the grade. Not wanting to eat the other's dust, my grandmother delighted in racing ahead and holding the lead. She would weave back and forth, hogging the road to prevent her future suitor from passing. It became a daily contest to see who could grab the preferred dust-free lead.

Years later when the two decided to marry, they drove their cattle together, raised two children, boarded workmen who slept in the bunkhouse, and lived the hard rancher-dairyman's life.

Now she had another child to raise. With a broken body and crushed psyche, I felt that my life was a wasteland of unexamined insanity.

I awakened the next day to hunger and fear. Besides regular meals, I stuffed my emaciated body with coffee cake, doughnuts, cookies, and ice cream. Food and sugar became my drugs of choice as I put on ten pounds and jumped two sizes in clothes.

I had never experienced insomnia, but now suffered from an extreme case of it. I had missed more than a decade of history and cultural changes and attempted to jump-start my awareness into the 1990s, using my sleeplessness to absorb as much printed information and television as possible.

As before, my grandmother had a plethora of journals, magazines and archives of material chronicling the world, cultural, and familial events I had missed. I consumed them all, falling asleep in my chair and then awakening to shuffle upstairs to collapse into bed each night. I started remembering my dreams again, and would lie awake in bed absorbing my new reality.

One morning a familiar baritone voice spoke in my head: "Write to Louise Hay and share some of your information with her. Give her one of the pieces of the Brazilian amethyst geode you saved from the Journey."

What? She doesn't even know me. How did you know I stashed some of those geode pieces before our last trek to the East Coast?

I didn't hear a response. I had read Louise's first book, "You Can Heal Your Life," and followed an advice column she wrote for one of the alternative healing magazines available at health food stores. Trusting the voice, I wrote her.

"Hello, Tarra, this is Louise Hay. I'm very interested in the information you sent and would like to invite you for a visit."

She gave me her Solana Beach address and received me warmly when I arrived. After introducing me to her guests, she guided me to her extensive backyard. I sat on a bench next to her and surveyed the lush surroundings, including the huge amethyst geodes gracing the garden. I held out the small piece of amethyst I had brought with me. "I was instructed to bring you this."

"Thank you very much," she said as she took my gift.

"But I feel ashamed because you already have much better amethyst geodes here in your garden."

"That's your stuff," she added, pegging my core shame.

"Yeah, I guess you're right." *I am very judgmental against myself.*

"I'm very pleased to have this, and I appreciate that you were willing to bring it to me."

Several days later I received a lovely card from her with a personal hand-written message thanking me. I treasured the card and began practicing the message printed on the cover: "The point of power is in the present moment."

I was beginning to integrate myself back into everyday life, and soon realized I needed help in sorting through my experiences. Most of my behaviors had helped me to avoid long-suppressed emotions that rumbled inside me. I wasn't sure where to turn, but realized that all my intellectual and spiritual pursuits had not helped me avoid someone like Jon. *Maybe psychotherapy would help; I've never tried it before.* I mentioned this to my mother one day while visiting her.

"Do you remember the psychologist we saw at the hospital after you rescued me from Mount Laguna?" I asked.

"Dr. Fitzpatrick. Would you like to talk with her? I consulted with her after the last time you left. She was very helpful; she does Bioenergetics. She had me conduct a funeral to let you go because there was nothing I could do until you decided to return on your own. If you're interested in seeing her, I'll pay for you to have some sessions."

I made the appointment and drove to San Diego, filled with anxiety.

After the first two visits, I felt better, even though I did not understand exactly why. My mother had offered to pay for nine two-hour sessions, so I continued driving to San Diego for this intriguing experience.

"Are you angry?" Dr. Fitzpatrick asked me the third time I saw her.

"Yes, very much so. Every day I'm discovering more anger about how Jon treated me. It just doesn't seem fair that he could hurt me the way he did—not to mention what he did to the others."

"Would you like to start working free of it?"

"Yes, I think I would."

"Here is a piece of garden hose and a phone book. Why don't you try hitting the phone book with it?"

"You want me to do what?"

"Just try it. Try hitting it a couple of times." She demonstrated, striking the phone book with the hose end.

Whack! Whack!

"Okay, I guess I can do that."

Whack! Whack! The sound was very loud, but I continued for a few minutes.

"Now, what are you noticing?"

"Well, strangely, I feel better."

"Good. It's helpful to allow expression of your anger in a way that does not hurt you or another."

A week later I received a letter from Jon and brought it to my next session.

"He says he has the money to pay for our 'last mission.'"

"You told me you were done and felt you'd accomplished your mission with him."

"Yes, I know. But while on our last trip to the East Coast, we made a commitment to someone named Solara to help support the anchoring of rays of enlightenment being directed to Earth on November 11. Solara asked us to anchor one on January 11 on Maui, in the Hawaiian Islands. Jon and I both agreed to do that."

"Yes, I know where Maui is. Are you planning on traveling there with him?"

"When these rays of light are introduced they'll serve to shift humanity's consciousness." I paused. "When I made Jon leave my grandmother's house, I told him that if he got the money for airfare and accommodations for me and one other person to go to Maui I'd do it; otherwise, no deal. I wasn't worried about it then, now I feel obligated to follow through with my promise. I don't want to sabotage any possibility I might have of helping and contributing to the expansion of consciousness on this planet."

"Are you sure you have to go? You've said that you tried to leave him several times before and were not successful. What is to prevent him from swaying you to stay with him again?"

"Because I got my sign that I was through. This is the only part of my pledge I haven't completed, and I don't want anything left undone that would require me to rejoin him. I want to be completely done!"

"I can understand that. That's good, but are you sure you need to do this trip with him? How do you know you'll be safe?"

"That's why I insisted on him bringing a third person. I don't know her, but I doubt she'd allow him to bully or mistreat me. I'm going to go, but I'll return and continue with my treatment."

"What does your family think of this?"

"No one likes the idea. I'm sure they're all afraid that I'll pick up with him once again."

"I hope you can see why they would feel that way."

"Yes, but no one understands how determined I am to be done with this man and all of my supposed work with him. I have no intentions of staying with him."

THIRTY-SEVEN

J oann was a Texan, fair-complexioned, about my age, and a little shorter than me. I liked her friendly manner and instantly felt she would be a good ally. She was a friend of the benefactors who had donated us a week with all expenses paid so we could complete our last "mission."

Jon's hair was shorter than when I had seen him last, and he appeared to have aged. Otherwise he looked the same with his bearded face, flip-flops and oversized shirt hanging over Levis. I did not speak to him on the flight over to the Big Island, but en route to Maui, he jockeyed himself in between Joann and me. I felt his gaze and looked over to see him glaring at me—a familiar tactic I recognized from my Program years.

Looking directly at him, I said, "Your scrunched-up face really looks ugly with that scowl on it. And your attempts to intimidate me are pathetic. I'm not afraid of you anymore."

"I can't believe the way you're acting. What kind of a person are you to keep your eyes open on the plane, looking around and even staring at men? I am appalled at your behavior. I cannot believe how negative and demon-possessed you're acting right now."

"I'm no longer in your so-called Program. You don't control me anymore. I'll look around and look at whomever I want to."

Joann had witnessed this exchange. "Jon, I'm shocked at what you just said to Tarra. You're not the person I met in Texas. Your behavior is controlling and cruel, and you're making me uncomfortable. I think you should stop. My friends didn't pay for a trip where you get to treat her like that, so stop it, please."

Jon sank back in his seat.

Thank you, Joann—the very reason why I needed a third person to accompany me on this trip.

But it wasn't over. Unlike before, I watched with eyes wide open as Jon used every trick he knew to intimidate, shame, and control me. While on the crater rim of the volcano in Maui, he threw in some crystals and then turned to face me.

"You're not supposed to be looking around at people and the sights."

"I can look at what and who I like."

He glowered. "It's clear you are completely demon-possessed by the dark side and you don't care what happens to me or any of the light workers here. There's no reason for me to continue living if you're going to be such a black witch. I'm just going to end it all now by jumping into the volcano."

"If you're serious, I'd like the car keys and the plane tickets first so we can leave," I responded as Joann and I walked back to the car.

We waited, and fifteen minutes later he walked back from his fiery death threat. Jamming the keys into the ignition, he drove us off without a word.

Since the "light energy ray" was to be anchored in the village of Hana, we drove there for that purpose. After we conducted our ceremony a rainbow appeared, followed by fireworks the locals had set off.

As I stood next to Jon on the pier, a turtle swam under us, and Jon took my hand in both of his. In his softest voice, he lobbied, "Tarra, we've accomplished what we agreed to do. Remember, we were promised a rainbow at the journey's end, and a million dollars."

"Yeah, I remember." I pulled my hand from his.

"Well, there's our rainbow, and the fireworks mean the money is on the way. Please don't leave me; let's celebrate this victory together."

"I'm done. I've completed everything I promised God I would do. We're through."

"I can't believe you're going to turn your back on God after all the signs we just saw."

Without another word, I walked away and climbed into the car with Joann. We waited until he drove us back to the hotel in silence.

In our shared hotel room that night, Jon made one final attempt with a so-called card reading he performed. "Do you agree that if you see a Queen of Spades that you're forsaking your promise to serve God because you left me?"

"What do you mean?"

"I'm shuffling the cards and am going to lay them out. If the third one is a black queen, it will signify that you've turned your back on God. Now watch." He placed the cards one at a time on the bed where he was sitting; the third one was the Queen of Spades.

"Joann, do you agree that means that I'm turning my back on God?"

She shrugged. "I don't know. How should I know something like that?"

Fear seared through me. Recognizing the familiar emotions of doubt and shame growing inside me, I retreated into the bathroom. Locking the door, I crawled into the shower and collapsed—sobbing and praying for help; afraid I was somehow forsaking God.

After the crying subsided, my mind cleared and I began to take possession of myself again. *He has no right to say what is best for me. I don't care if I risk being condemned for eternity, I'm not joining him again, and that's final!*

I emerged from the bathroom. "You tried to trick me into doubting myself," I said. "You did that all the time when I was with you. From this point, forth, Jon, I'm ignoring you."

When I boarded the plane the next morning, I grabbed the window seat. "I don't want him near me," I told Joann. She obliged, but I could feel Jon's eyes on me. Leaning forward, I looked directly at him. "You're the epitome of evil. I want nothing to do with you ever again. Stop looking at me, and don't talk to me."

Nothing more was said until we landed in San Diego. My mother and brother met our plane.

"We were worried you wouldn't come back again." Bruce walked next to me as Jon struggled to keep up. As we strode through the parking lot, I could hear Jon whining behind us: "Tarra? Tarra? Aren't you going to stay with me?"

I stopped and whirled to face him.

"I'm going home with my mother and brother. Goodbye, Jon. Goodbye, Joann. Thank you for making this trip possible, and please thank your friends."

"Take care," Joann said, and we hugged.

Jon walked toward me. I put my hand out to stop him. "Goodbye, Jon." And I turned to follow my brother, not looking back as we walked toward the car.

I climbed into the back seat behind my mother, who was driving.

"I brought Bruce along for support to prevent Jon from convincing you to stay with him," she said. "We were so worried he'd overpower you again. Did you know that Gramma cried the entire time you were gone? She was afraid he'd pull you back under his control."

If you only knew how close he came to doing that. But he didn't. I'm free for good! Finally, there's nothing else I need to do—I'm done!

I returned to therapy and related the events of the trip to Moira, processing what it was like to stand up to Jon. For my last session, I had a request: "I'd like to experience more Bioenergetics."

"You've been doing Bioenergetics, but I think I'll ask you to lie on your back over this breathing barrel. Twist this towel in your hands like this, and ask God 'Why?' Just keep asking *why* over, and over again."

"That's good because that's my biggest concern. I'm still struggling to make sense of the abuse and my commitment. I was supposedly serving God, but it didn't feel like it."

"Well then, why don't you go ahead and do the exercise." She helped me lie on my back over a padded barrel and handed me a small towel.

I asked "Why?" as I exhaled and twisted the towel with both hands. "Why?" I breathed out again, and after about the third or fourth "Why?" I began to sob, letting myself go into the depth of my sadness. My tears continued, and with closed eyes, I began a silent dialogue. *Why? Why, God? Why all the abuse and suffering when I was supposed to be serving you? It doesn't make sense. Why? Please tell me.*

As clearly as if I were in conversation with someone, I heard the following: "You need to get a job, transportation, and go back to school and study psychology."

I opened my eyes and repeated the instructions I'd just received.

"Well, that's great," Moira said. "I encourage you to do that."

"How do I find out more about Bioenergetics?"

"There's a San Diego Institute where they offer workshops, exercise classes, and trainings. Would you like the number of the office?"

She handed me a piece of paper with the information, and we said our goodbyes. As I drove home, I realized I had a newfound purpose.

THIRTY-EIGHT

After a thirty-year hiatus, I obtained copies of my transcripts, brushed the dust from my intellect, and enrolled in National University. My grandmother was very supportive of me returning to school. She herself had spent a couple of years after graduating high school lobbying her parents before they finally allowed her to attend Redlands University. All her siblings had attended college or some form of advanced education.

When I moved back to the ranch with my grandmother, a cancer research foundation was using the milk barn and surrounding pastures to house sheep for culturing their treatments and remedies. I found work with the foundation as a shepherd, and shared responsibility for tending and feeding the sheep, cleaning their pens, and midwifing the babies during lambing season.

It depressed me to see how the ranch had fallen into disrepair. The barns, corrals, workshops, and sheds all needed much attention and major cleaning. I found an outlet for my anxious energy as I cleared out the bays and pens on the part of the ranch still available to us. After clearing out the debris, an old calf pen became my carport and I adapted the other work bays for my art projects.

"It looks better around here all the time," my father commented one day as we sank new fence posts to restore a corral. He was donating time and materials that allowed the foundation to expand operations on the property as we renovated it.

Although he was considerably warmer towards me, he still insisted that he would "never forgive me and will not allow myself to love you again. You betrayed me!"

It was true that I had intervened where I did not belong. I had been in the middle of their marriage for years, attempting to keep the peace and them together. Every time I had visited him from San Diego before meeting Solar, he gave me the same message.

After their bitter divorce, he moved into the adobe home where we had lived as a family. Depressed and brooding on the demise of his marriage and the dairy, he lived like a hermit on his hill above the ranch. I was determined to find a way back into his heart this time.

It was 1992, less than a year after I'd left Jon. Since my last therapy session had been so powerful, I decided to explore Bioenergetics further in search of more breakthroughs. I called the number Moira had given me and a gravelly-voiced man answered the phone.

"San Diego Institute for Bioenergetic Analysis, Bob Jacques speaking."

"Hi. My name is Tarra, and I'm interested in finding out more about the kind of Bioenergetics activities you're offering."

He read several names and activities, including "There's an exercise group led by Eugene Bischoff and myself, and Barbara Thomson is offering a study group. What are you looking for?"

"I'd like more information about the study group, please."

I arrived late to the first class without knowing the room number. As I sat in the waiting room, hoping someone would show up to use the bathroom, I struggled to stay awake. Even though I had gotten plenty of sleep the night before, I faded in and out of consciousness.

When someone finally came, I followed them back to join the group. A presenter was discussing the personality characteristics of people who had sustained emotional wounds in early infancy, while another adjusted herself to mimic the kinds of postures they would unconsciously adopt in their bodies as defense mechanisms. *I don't understand why I feel so uncomfortable with this discussion. I wonder if it has anything to do with why I was struggling to stay awake in the waiting room.*

"Infants and children need to feel safe and loved by their parents. When their emotional or physical needs are not satisfactorily met, there are behavioral and emotional consequences that compromise their developmental progress."

"The repetition of these environmental patterns over time reinforces core false-beliefs, certain bodily adaptations and neuronal pathways in the brain that generate internalized emotions like fear, anger and shame. These emotional deficits manifest in the brain and body of the child and later the adult."

Hmm. When I was born, I spent time in an incubator and was surrounded by death and grief. Is this where some of that stuff came from?

"In this course, you will learn about the importance of these developmental stages and how adverse circumstances affect the infant, the child and adult—mentally, emotionally and physically. The body is just as important as the brain and often shows when that person's development was compromised or where they are holding trauma."

This is too much. If what they're saying is true, then the emotions I struggled with way before I met Solar could have been because of the stuff that happened to me in childhood. But how could it be as simple as that? Bruce and I weren't happy, and our parents certainly weren't! I wonder how that affected us?

In the study group, I learned about the profound effects trauma has on humans during our lifetime, and was given the keys to understanding the bedrock of my foundation. With a depressed mother, my infant and childhood traumas, medical procedures, molestations and having internalized the criticism directed at me, I perceived rejection by both parents. The template for my adult-self relationships was shame-based and held within the neuro-muscular structures of my body. These encoded experiences drove mental and emotional disturbances, and my self-hatred that left me vulnerable to

336 | tarra judson stariell

substance abuse, dysfunctional behaviors and someone like Solar.

My history was not as devastating but strikingly parallel to stories I would later hear as an intern when I worked with battered women, substance abusers, probationers and the homeless. Even the best of parents are sometimes presented with stressful events beyond their control that generate emotions and reactions that adversely affect their children in their adult life. Unfortunately for my brother and me, our home life was not particularly happy due to the many issues contributing to the growing dissonance between our parents. As the heir-apparent, my brother was treated differently and acknowledged the contrast when he later told me, "Sam, you and I were raised in different worlds."

Affirmed for his gender, Bruce resembled our mother's beloved father and was named for him and our father's founding patriarch, five generations before.

Despite this new information from the study group, emotions continued to flood over me. Recovering from the insanity my time with Jon represented seemed overwhelming. Self-compassion was beyond my reach with all the shame and anger I was harboring. Studying my psychology textbooks exacerbated my regret and self-loathing as I became more aware of the healthy choices I had not pursued.

I feel so naïve; how do I apply this knowledge to heal myself? How do I use it to stop hating myself so much for what I did and allowed Solar/Jon to do to me?

My grandmother's love and emotional support were an oasis to my broken self, but I needed to heal the brainwashing, violently driven into the deepest recesses of my psyche. I wrestled to sort fact from fiction with the distortions of reality that lurked inside me, driving unhealthy behaviors even as I attempted to regulate my emotions rather than allow my raging to destroy me or be aimed at others. In the end, I would need all the love, support, caring, and understanding my grandmother; loving friends; my therapists; mentors, family—both related and the Bioenergetic community— could offer me as I reclaimed myself and healed.

THIRTY-NINE

I now had a job, was studying for a profession in psychology and working very hard to turn my life around.

I began approaching the contents of my life with the belief I could restore myself to functionality. With the same fervor that had propelled me into The Program I strived to uncover the hidden mysteries that had plagued my lifelong efforts to experience a sense of wellbeing and fulfillment.

Every so often I had glimmers of that driving force that had kept me bonded with Jon. Even though I was feeling better all the time as I interacted with family and connected with friends—some of whom I had met while with Jon—all was not as it seemed. Underneath the surface a force to be reckoned with was pushing its way from my depths to daylight.

I first became aware of this surging energy while driving home from visiting a friend in Encinitas. After stopping at a convenience store, I left the parking lot, making a right turn onto the road. Out of nowhere, there was a car tailgating me. Before I could move over, it passed me and then pulled directly in front, forcing me to brake. The driver raced ahead but I noticed two small children in the backseat. I was furious he was driving so recklessly with children in the car. When we stopped at a light, I pulled alongside him and rolled down my window.

"You should be more careful when driving with kids in your car."

He jumped out, ran over to my door and yelled through my open window: "YOU PULLED OUT IN FRONT OF ME!"

"You must have been speeding because there was no one when I pulled out," I said.

"IT'S YOUR FAULT! I DID THAT BECAUSE OF YOU!" He shook his fist at me.

I numbly sat there, stunned at his yelling until he leaned through the window, still shaking his fist. Something snapped inside me.

"FUCK YOU! FUCK YOU! I'M CALLING THE POLICE!"

He jumped back, bolted to his car and sped off. The kids' faces looked terrified as he raced ahead.

Shocked at my behavior, I didn't move my car until someone behind me honked. As I drove home, I reviewed the scenario over and over until finally I decided the man was a crackpot—and conveniently dismissed my own inappropriate anger.

I forgot about the incident until one night, after crashing in bed around midnight, I heard an old clunker drive up into the ranch. Jumping out of bed, through my window I could see a car slowly driving around.

I bet that's Jon.

By the time I threw on some clothes and got outside, the dilapidated car was down the driveway and moving up the old cow manger road, which had no outlet.

I was on a mission as I slipped into my rubber boots and grabbed the large flashlight hanging in the porch. I breathed prayers as I strode up the road. There was one overhead light left from the days when my father had milked his herd twenty-four hours a day, and I stood under it.

Waiting, I clutched the flashlight on my hip as if it were a loaded weapon. The car turned around and slowly made its way back through the ruts and gullies, its bumper within inches of my knees as it rolled to a stop. Walking around to the driver's side, I tightened inside as I saw my mistake. It was not Jon but a car filled with very seedy characters.

"Do you know you're trespassing?" I said, sneering at the driver.

"Uh, no."

"Well, people around here shoot first and ask questions later when they see strangers driving around where they don't belong."

"We were just looking around."

"You don't belong here, and you need to leave immediately."

I stepped back so they could drive away, but the deep ruts in the road forced their exit to a creep. Walking behind them, I impulsively kicked the rear bumper with my boot.

"Hey, don't kick my car!" the driver said, leaning his head out the window.

"That's not all I'm going to kick if you come back here!" I belted out. They drove away, and I walked home, shaking violently as I realized how much risk I had subjected myself to.

Racing upstairs, I called the sheriff, but speech was difficult—my voice was vibrating with fear. He arrived shortly and informed me they would check out the license plate I had memorized as I walked behind the car.

The next day, I related the story of my brash behavior to my father.

"Could I please have a shotgun to keep in the lockup in case it really is Jon who shows up in the middle of the night?"

"No, I'm not giving you one. You're dangerous and might shoot someone."

I did not embrace the full reality of that statement; I was so terrified Jon would stalk me at the ranch. His barrage of letter writing was unrelenting and even though a little more two years had passed since I had said goodbye to him, Jon was still writing occasionally. With morbid curiosity, I read his letters, but never acknowledged them until he sent me a birthday card with a sapphire ring, supposedly to replace the one my parents had given me that he destroyed. I returned both card and ring. This was his response:

Winter Solstice '93

Dear Tarra,

First of all, I want to wish you a Merry Christmas. How are you? I don't know why you sent back the birthday card. When you went home you said you wanted time away and that in a couple of years you would be back at my side. That is why I am writing. Is it totally over between us? Why can't you say so? It was cold to send back the birthday card with no response. We witnessed so many miracles together. Just the other day, the music started playing in the vents again, Silent Night. I remembered the Grand Canyon when we stood there on the full moon. I will never forget it. Things are not working out between M and myself. I don't want a lover, I would like someone to travel around with and lecture. I have plenty of resources. I would like to have someone to love, but so far it has not worked out. You were the only one that I can honestly say I loved. Please write and tell me how you're doing. If you can find it in your heart to forgive me, I would like to be your friend. If you never want to see or talk to me again, please just tell me. It's the not knowing that hurts. Just spell it out for me and if it is your desire that I never bother you again I will oblige. I do still care about you. Please don't send this back with sea salt. The last card left a trail in my P.O. Box. Just destroy it if you must. If you write and tell me to leave you alone, I will never bother you again. Just please write.

Love,

The PX

The Phoenix? Since when are you "the Phoenix?" What next? I hope you got my inside joke since you always used sea salt to cleanse and release negative energies and vibrations. I'm going to ignore your letter, maybe you'll get the message—I NEVER said that I was coming back to be with you—you're totally delusional!

His letters continued, alternately bribing, threatening, and pleading with me. His purpose was always to get me to rejoin him and stop "turning my back on God." One day I made the mistake of reading one before leaving for school. He had written that my family was "doomed to hell and beyond" for my behavior, that I had "forsaken God," and so on. His blathering infuriated me, and I grew more enraged as I drove to San Diego. Pounding my fist on the dashboard, as my anger escalated, my driving became more erratic.

"GOD! HOW CAN YOU LET HIM DO THIS TO ME? HE HAS ABUSED ME, BROKEN MY NOSE, MY TEETH, TAKEN ADVANTAGE OF ME, AND EXTORTED MONEY FROM ME! HOW CAN YOU LET HIM CONTINUE THREATENING ME AND ABUSING ME LIKE THIS? THIS IS WRONG!

"GET OUT OF MY WAY, ASSHOLE! CAN'T YOU SEE I'M PISSED?"

I tailgated and cursed whoever got in my way until I noticed flashing red lights behind me. I pulled over and fumbled for my license.

"Do you know you were speeding over eighty miles an hour?"

"I was not going that fast!" I blurted above the traffic noise. "I was not speeding."

The officer's hand instinctively touched his gun. The gesture brought me back to my senses.

"I'm sorry I just yelled at you, officer. I guess I didn't know that I was speeding; I apologize."

"Slow down and drive more carefully, will you?"

I took my speeding ticket from Officer Green and gingerly drove to school. *I think I have an anger management problem.*

It was rage, but I wouldn't discover that until much later.

Sitting in class was difficult; I felt so ashamed of my behavior. *I need someone to help me work through this stuff. I wonder what this professor would be like as a therapist?* During each class that week, I scrutinized my instructors, trying to ascertain who could help with what was boiling up inside me. In the meantime, I penned the following and shared it with my writers' group:

I no longer effort to swim upstream.
And yet my passage still turbulent remains.
I gasp and choke in between breaths,
As I'm slammed against the rocks of my past.

Rolling like pebbles, the river piles high these boulders and stones,
Crashing and churning, pushing me through rapids and foam.

I want to stop, but the force carrying me is not done.
Reaching out, I claw the darkness groping for a branch, or someone.

To my fear I succumb, plunging to the depths of who I am.
And although lost and weary, to the surface I return, once again.

Angry at my folly, I yell, I scream and pound with my hand.
"Damn it, God Damn it! This black joke needs to end."

FORTY

After realizing that none of my professors felt like a good fit, I recalled the mysterious curiosity I had felt about the organizer of the Bioenergetics workshop series I had attended.

With my mother's encouragement, I called the organizer to ask about being her client, and returned to the location of the study group for my first session with Dr. Barbara Thomson. It was intimidating, for now I was the center of attention, something I had desperately sought in my life and then suffered severely for during my years with Jon. Sitting cross-legged in a chair opposite her, I blurted out the chronology of my history, dropping tidbits of the abuse along the way to watch for any adverse reactions.

Without blinking, Barbara responded, "Well, I'm glad that you're here."

"Can you help me?"

"Why, yes, I believe I can. It's going to take some time, so would you like to schedule another appointment next week and we'll continue this discussion?"

I had the most profound experience of settling into my body with a peace I had not touched in decades.

And so, began a very nurturing and loving therapeutic relationship, lasting many years. Painful at times, but transformative and lifesaving.

It is impossible to narrate the hundreds of hours I spent in therapy working through the brainwashing and trauma. Stored within me over my lifetime were the formidable energies of shame and self-hatred.

Twice weekly therapy became a lifeline. School and the seminars and workshops I attended and ongoing interaction with my family were recreating healthier relationship models within me. Working with the sheep forced me to drop into my body as they pressed up against me. Caring for the infant lambs and their mothers served to warm my heart and loosen emotions—thawing my frozen disconnection from myself, and the world. Day by day I was learning to stay in the here and now, rather than disconnecting and living in my head with my traumatic memories—eviscerating myself for what was done.

My grandmother's love was an oasis, and my compassionate therapist helped me clear out the violence lurking in my mind and body. None of my recovery would have been possible without the collective support from them, my immediate and extended family, and friends-both old and new. Expunging the twisted memories made room for love and forgiveness. My greatest obstacle would be the most difficult—to forgive myself.

As self-destructive events poured out of me, I noticed gratitude and felt a sense of awareness of the blessings I had. I never knew that anything so wonderful could come of something so destructively negative and painful. That option seemed to present itself consistently.

During one of my psychology classes, I shared about being a victim of domestic violence. The woman sitting next to me touched my arm. "I'm sorry. I know what that's like."

We swapped stories at a break, and I noticed how validating our conversation was and I felt a little less shame about my history. Barb, my therapist, had encouraged me to write about my experiences as an adjunct to my healing, so at home later that evening I penned the following—intending it for the beginning of this book.

> I did not willingly walk through the gates of hell,
> But once across and beyond that fiery threshold,

I discovered what God is and what God is not.

I entered that experience searching for a deeper connection with my Creator.
Convinced I had been called, I was committed to that purpose.

The knowledge I came away with I would have willingly paid a lifetime for
And in a sense, I did.

For who I was, is now gone
'Though her memories with me still remain.

I am her future,

Created from the ashes of dreams
And hopes spent for naught.
The magnificent quest to make the world a better place
Through which I forgot and buried my personal space.

So deeply wounded, misunderstood, and totally caught
Was I, in the game of what could, or should have been.

As I walk the road before me now, shaking off the dust of my past
How long a lifetime of torment; how sweet the peace—mine at last!

So full my life, this one time, seems more like ten;
These mistakes have laid the foundation of who I am.

And my sincere prayer is that it all will lead in the end
To a way for others to find their own divinity within;
The cornerstone, I believe, to be life's way with woman and man.

FORTY-ONE

My insomnia had lessened but I had not been able to stop my revived cigarette habit, another reminder of my time with Jon. One day as I walked upstairs to my room, I found myself gasping for breath. *I know I'm courting disaster. My lungs were damaged with Valley Fever, and I cannot imagine what inhaling all those bleach fumes did to me. This is ridiculous—I need to quit.*

I did not realize how much smoking numbed my emotions until I tried to stop. So strong was my addiction, that I would stop for a day or two, then give in and buy another pack—smoke some, and then in my guilt break the rest of the cigarettes into pieces. Later, when the cravings again became unbearable, I would smoke the broken pieces I had rummaged from my trash.

After cycling through this behavior several times, I realized that breaking the cigarettes was silly, since I was smoking them anyway. I had even tried soaking the broken pieces in water, but would just dry them on my window ledge and then smoke them.

Another time, I unraveled the pack into piles of ground tobacco—then, in crazed desperation, searched the top drawer of my grandfather's desk in hopes some of his roll-your-own cigarette papers were still around.

After many false starts, I finally succeeded in getting through several months, smoke-free. I knew the battle was over one morning when I awoke from a dream with total recall of seeing myself having a cigarette. Walking up to my smoking self, I grabbed the cigarette and threw it onto the ground. While stomping it out, I told the smoking me, "You're not doing that anymore."

Another remnant of my self-destructiveness was laid to rest.

My grandmother's house required lots of maintenance and repair, and even though the city of San Diego owned the property, the city took little part in its upkeep. That responsibility fell mostly upon my father. Growing up, I had watched him repair tractors, farm equipment, and whatever was broken on the ranch. He would disassemble something to discover its inner mechanisms, and then restore it to working order.

Thirty years later, I accepted the invitation I had yearned to hear as a child. "Stick around, kid, and you might learn something," my father told me one day.

Whenever possible after that I worked with him, learning many skills through a series of broken pipes and household mishaps. As I fetched tools and provided an extra set of hands, we also repaired our relationship.

My father's alcohol consumption, overeating, and forty-five years of smoking had compromised his health. But now he was trim, smoke-free, and exercised regularly, feeling better than ever.

"Your brother told me he didn't want me smoking around his kids. He even went through the program with me. That's why I take everybody to dinner every year—a way to spend the money I would have wasted on cigarettes."

"Do I get to go this year?"

"Yeah. Now hand me that wrench, would you?"

At my father's next smoke-free dinner, I sat next to him.

"Sam," he said, "I'm proud of you for stopping smoking. I know it wasn't easy; I still crave them."

"You're kidding. I can't stand to smell cigarette smoke now."

"I guess that's where you and I differ. By the way, are you registered to vote? You know the election is coming up soon."

"Yes, I registered as an Independent."

"You did what?" His face turned red with anger.

"I registered as an Independent."

"There are only Republicans at this table!"

"Well, I guess I'm the only Independent."

"Move! Go to another table; you can't sit here."

"What? I will not move!"

"I don't want you sitting here if you don't have enough sense to vote the right way."

"I'm not moving, and I have a right to vote the way I see fit."

"Hmm! Stubborn kid."

"That's right. Just like you in that respect."

"Oh, no! You got your stubbornness from your mother because I didn't give any of mine away."

Even though our relationship was healing at glacial speed, he was helpful with some of the difficulties between my mother and me.

"Do you know that Mom sometimes yells at me over the phone?" I shared with him one day.

"No, I didn't know that. Maybe she's still angry with you for the way you were."

"I get it, but I can't talk to her if she's going to get so angry all the time."

"Well, have you tried letting her know you're going to hang up if she starts yelling?"

I tried it, and only had to hang up once before my mother and I could have conversations that did not escalate into anger.

FORTY-TWO

Even as I recorded my story and began feeling better, I still had times when negative emotions would flood over me. I disclosed my struggles in therapy and, as per that discussion, subsequently purchased a heavy bag filled with sand. I suspended it from the rafters in the milk barn where it towered above a long, narrow pit where years before milkers had systematically connected cows to vacuum tubes that sucked their udders dry of the mother lode. Now, instead of acting out my anger on myself or anybody else like unsuspecting drivers, I used the heavy bag as a regular part of my routine—hitting, kicking and slamming it with my body.

During one episode of punching, yelling and screaming my hatred and anguish, I noticed a faint bleating noise in the background. As it grew louder, I stopped to investigate. Walking up out of the pit, I found all the sheep crammed into a corner, pushing and shoving against each other, trembling and crushing those in the corner. With tears streaming down my cheeks, I inserted myself into their huddle, reassuring, soothing, and stroking their bodies to calm them. "I am so sorry—my yelling and screaming was not aimed at you. You've done nothing wrong, I am so sorry, I was wrong. It's okay, it's okay, you're safe now, it's okay."

Like innocent children subjected to a parent's raging behavior, they were frightened and trapped in their attempt to flee. Realizing how I had traumatized them, I resolved to conduct my purges only when they were turned out and not within earshot. Far too many had suffered already from rage and unconscious behaviors driven by anger; I did not want to pass on more hurt and pain.

Living in the natural habitat surrounding my grandmother's sanctuary, I was healing and could sleep and relax again. A family of owls had nested in a very tall palm tree outside one of my bedroom windows. One morning, the squawking of a fledgling owl awakened me. "Aack!" was followed by its mother's more mature and calm "Hoo, hoo, hoo." "Aack!" and again a "Hoo, hoo, hoo" would follow. Over and over, this continued until the fledgling finally mastered "Hoo, hoo, hoo." My heart swelled as I witnessed this gentle mentoring process, mother to child. It reminded me of how Barb, my therapist, had been with me.

Several days later, instead of being awakened with the usual chorus of "Hoo, hoo, hoo," I heard a rustling of the palm fronds and lots of screeching and commotion. When up and dressed, I investigated—and there at the base of the palm tree was the baby owl lying next to its nest—dead.

"Caw, caw."

I looked up to see a big black crow taunting me from where the nest had been.

You bastard!

I stormed into the house for my keys and ran out to the lockup where we kept the shotgun my father had entrusted to me since I was acting more rationally because of therapy. Unlocking the deadbolt, I grabbed some shells and the .410. Jamming in earplugs, my eyes locked onto the crow as I pushed a cartridge into the barrel and snapped it shut. Easing back the hammer, I stealthily approached the palm tree.

Bam!

The crow dropped. Crying, I nudged the perpetrator with my shoe. Revenge did not feel sweet as I eyed the lifeless fledgling next to it.

When I related the story to my therapist, she winced. "It would appear you felt the need to champion the owl's death."

"Yes. I hate crows and how destructive they are."

"Did you identify with the baby owl?"

"Yes."

"And perhaps you wished that someone had rescued you?"

"Yes."

"There might be a difference between you and the baby owl. The crows are just trying to survive."

"Well, they didn't have to do it by killing the baby owl."

"That's what they do. Survival of the fittest in nature."

"They are disgusting. We have to fish out pieces of dead animals all the time that they drop in the water tanks for the sheep."

"Have you ever considered that there are those who might like these birds?"

"No."

"In some cultures, crows are sacred."

"Well, I don't like them."

"Does that give you the right to kill them?"

"Hmm." I still could not see how divided my thinking had become. I had decided there were good and bad animals and good and bad people. Owls, the sheep, horses, and so on were "good." Ravens, crows, squirrels, and coyotes that threatened the lambs were "bad." Those who loved me were "good." Jon was "bad." Acceptance of "what is" without judgment was still beyond me.

FORTY-THREE

The Bioenergetics study group had taught me how the body stores memories and emotions from our negative experiences until they are processed consciously. I experienced this firsthand when I elected to repair my broken nose. I hated looking like a professional boxer, and on November 23, 1993, underwent my first of the four surgeries that would be necessary to patch, repair, and bridge a very damaged and badly scarred nose.

While recovering from each surgery, I was haunted by visions of the battering that broke my nose. Although it would be greatly improved, the surgeons said complete repair was not possible; my nose had too many layers of scar tissue inside. Jon had often given it "healings," pressing so hard on my nose each time that tears spontaneously filled my eyes. Apparently, his "healings" had made matters worse.

After my nose had genuinely healed, I was in a therapy session processing some of the damage done to my body. During my narration, I sat with my hands clenched and my arms pressed in against my torso.

Standing next to me, my therapist asked, "What are you feeling right now?"

"I'm furious!"

"I noticed your arms and shoulders are tight. Would you like to express some of your anger?"

I nodded and she handed me a tennis racket, which I grasped, hitting a pillow she had placed before me on a futon. The strength of my anger drove my arms hard, striking the pillow with a "whack" each time. Rage found my voice.

"YOU DEMON! BASTARD! HOW DARE YOU BREAK MY NOSE! YOU'RE EVIL! YOU'RE EVIL! YOU HAD NO RIGHT TO HURT ME! YOU DEMON! YOU HAD NO RIGHT TO BREAK MY NOSE! I HATE YOU! I HATE YOU! FUCK YOU! FUCK YOU! I HATE YOU! YOU HAD NO RIGHT TO HURT ME LIKE YOU DID!"

I collapsed in a heap on the floor, sobbing and powerless to correct my disfigured nose and everything else that had transpired with him. I clasped my hands against my face as I wailed. Barb came over and put her arms around me, wordlessly cradling my body. Her contact soothed my despair, and I eventually stopped crying. Sitting up, I pulled away my hands.

"My nose is bleeding. I never get nosebleeds. It bled when he broke it."

"The body remembers," she softly offered.

Because of the tremendous support I was receiving from my therapist and the Bioenergetics therapy she practiced, I decided to enroll in the training program. My four-year commitment began in January 1994 as I finished my studies on the undergraduate level at my university. The Bioenergetics community was filled with very gifted and deeply spiritual individuals, therapists and trainers who became a second family for me. Through their empathic mentoring and support, I internalized their healing connections— adding to the community of healthy models forming inside me.

To begin the training, we were asked to tell a little about ourselves. I wrote this poem for that assignment:

I See None and No One

And only feel pain welling up within my heart;
From this insanity in my mind.

Where is the tenderness I once felt?
Overwhelming me to be kind?

This place within me, covered by hate,
Fed with emotions—my padded cell.

Is this anger mine, do I own it,
Or disclaim what I find in this private hell?

Buried in misfortunes, I am deaf
To an inner voice gagged and restrained

With all the stuff from a lifetime
Of failed attempts—grandiose and vain.

This training accelerated my recovery as I continued to discover how life with Jon had exacerbated the fragmentation within me that had started long before I met him. My trauma and subsequent separation most likely began in the incubator during the first week of my life and continued growing during infancy with my mother's grief and depression. My father's own ambitions were not realized, and his resulting depression increased his withdrawal and subsequent alcoholism. Compounding it all was the accumulated trauma of being molested and hospitalized several times. Rejection and the shame that accompanies it continued as others and myself failed to accept my bisexuality. My struggles to save innocent people from their culture's oppression, and the paranormal experiences and prediction about the future of our planet, all combined to push me over the edge.

At one point during the training, a realization hit me like a speeding train. I started gathering my things, and when Mac, our trainer for that semester, looked at me quizzically, I started crying.

"I just realized that I can never be a therapist and don't deserve to be in this training, because I've participated in child abuse."

"What?"

"Do you remember when I told you I was in a cult? Well, there was a baby boy who was my responsibility. I allowed him to be undernourished and not properly cared for. I'm so ashamed of myself and hate myself for what I've done. He was just an innocent baby...." My tears choked off the rest of my words.

I'm not sure when Mac picked me up, but he was holding me tightly in his long, gentle arms as I cascaded into the deepest self-hatred and shame-filled hysteria I had ever experienced. I stopped breathing and then began hyperventilating.

"Breathe, Tarra!" Mac was insisting. I continued hyperventilating, not able to catch my breath when his voice commanded, "Exhale, hard! Like this," and his voice made a forceful "Aahh!" sound. I opened my eyes to see his looking deeply into mine. Filling up with his empathy, I tried to exhale.

"Again!" And he made the same sound. I forced more air from my diaphragm to his command, and again, until I began to catch my breath.

"You weren't the same person that you are now, Tarra. You were doing the best you could. You were living with a madman; you were fighting for your life. You were doing the best you could. You're not the same person now."

FORTY-FOUR

Some of the people I had met in Bioenergetics invited me to a lecture, and I agreed to attend. But the day of the event, I resisted driving all the way to San Diego; however, a feeling inside pressed me to go. I eventually surrendered.

The speaker asked for volunteers for a demonstration, and several people stood up. I blinked as I tried to focus on one of them. *That looks like Fortune. Could that be possible, all these years after Peace Corps? How long ago was it that Gwyn and I met her in Encinitas when she returned from Colombia?*

At the seminar's end, I pressed my way through the group.

"Excuse me, are you by any chance Fortune?"

I was standing directly in front of her as she looked at me for an instant and then grabbed and hugged me. "Sandra, how are you?"

A sweet reunion came of that, and we are in touch to this day. I learned that even though my mother had forwarded correspondence from her to me, Solar had destroyed it all.

Living on the ranch gave ample opportunities to reconnect with lost friends and family. A lovely retreat, my grandmother's home was a longstanding gathering place for most holidays and special occasions, as traditions ran deep in our family. The common thread among the descendants of our two pioneer clans, she was diligent in gathering us together in love and celebration.

Bruce continued to return, bringing his family out to enjoy the bounty of the ranch. Off-road vehicles were his passion, but I preferred tooling through the orange trees and in the riverbed in the Foundation's golf cart with his kids aboard.

After one such jaunt together, we were enjoying a meal together when Bruce asked Gramma, "Do you know where Grandpa's gun is that was left on the back porch?"

"No, I haven't seen it in years. I keep a golf club by the backdoor now."

Remembering a story she had recently told me, I interjected, "Is that the shotgun you used to protect the chickens? And got that day the salesman was here?"

"Yes, that's the one."

"What's that?" Bruce asked.

"You tell it," Gramma encouraged.

"I guess there was a hawk circling over the chicken pen, and Gramma raced back to the porch for the shotgun. As she opened the screen door with gun in hand, a salesman who had just entered the yard saw her, wheeled around, leapt over the picket fence, and ran to his car. He sped off without a word."

We enjoyed a good laugh.

"Bruce," I said, "there's the .410 in the lockup that Dad leant me to scare off the coyotes during lambing season. Is that what you're referring to?"

"No, it's another one."

"Oh. Did you look in the cupboard with the bridles and halters? I remember Grandpa used to keep one there."

"Yeah, and it's not there. I found the musket in Dad's office but not that one."

"Oh."

Bruce got up to look through the office and back porch again. I didn't pay attention to the rest of the conversation regarding the gun's whereabouts, but something inside me rumbled a little.

Later that week after a therapy session, a memory rushed back to me. Several years ago, Jon had dropped me off at my grandmother's house with instructions to "bring back money or you will pay dearly. I don't care if you have to steal something; you had better come back with some money."

Until my brother had inquired about the gun, I had not remembered how, crazed and desperate, I had taken that same rifle into town and hawked it for a hundred dollars.

I realized that at some point I needed to share this, but felt paralyzed with fear. I finally felt like a member of my family again and had been trying to clean up the messes I had created, and was desperately afraid of losing everything I had worked so hard to regain.

Riding heavily on my heart, guilt overwhelmed me for another day until I could share this with my therapist, who encouraged me to tell my grandmother. Another day passed before I found enough courage. I ended my narration with "I hope you can forgive me."

"I don't think I can," she quietly responded.

"Oh." My heart sank and my despair deepened with every step as I trudged upstairs. *I can't take this. I need help; I'm going to call Barb.*

She did not answer the phone.

"Hello, Barb," I told her machine. "This is Tarra. I told my grandmother about the shotgun, and she said she couldn't forgive me for what I did. I don't know what I'm going to do. Please call me; I cannot believe how awful I feel right now." I left my phone number and sat there waiting.

With each crushing minute that passed, I was less able to tolerate my feelings. *That's it—I give up. I cannot do this any longer. I have tried to exonerate myself and make sense of my life but I can't struggle any more.*

I called my therapist again and said goodbye, thanked her for everything, and explained I could not deal with the pain of my grandmother's rejection.

I had made a pact with myself that turning my life around meant I would never deceive anyone again—especially my grandmother. Now I faced the unfathomable—my benefactor had lost faith in me, and could not forgive me. The finality of her decision pierced me. For too many years I had lived with my father's inability to forgive me, and now her. I could not bear the pain of her rejection, too—not now.

Walking downstairs, I glanced at my grandmother sitting in her chair as I headed for the back door. Reaching into the basket with our keys, I grabbed the ones for the lockup outside. As I unbolted the door, my grandmother flew out of her chair and was by my side in an instant.

"Where are you going this late?" She was blocking my exit, and I tried to hide the fact I'd been crying.

"I'm going outside to sit in the barn."

"Why are you going out there?"

"Because I need to think."

"But why out there in the cold?"

"Because I can't live with myself if you cannot forgive me. Gramma, please get out of my way, because I need to go."

"If I let you go, what are you going to do?"

I wish I hadn't taken that vow. "I'm going to shoot myself; I can't live with myself if you can't forgive me. Please move out of my way." And I opened the door.

"Tarra! Sandy!" She pulled the door shut and blocked me. I was not about to push her aside and, instead, slumped down against the door, sobbing.

Please just move out of my way.

"Sandy, I've been thinking. I was wrong. I'm sorry you feel this way; I'm sorry about the things that happened to you. I was mistaken, I *do* forgive you."

I looked up into her eyes. "Do you really mean it?"

"Yes, I do! I forgive you," she said as she reached down for me. I stood up and hugged her as we cried in each other's arms.

"Gramma, I'm so sorry. I'm so sorry for everything I've done."

"I know, I know."

When her comforting had calmed me, she suggested I go upstairs and rest. I numbly went up to my room and sat down.

My phone rang and through the answering machine I could hear my therapist's concerned voice. "Tarra, this is Barb Thomson, please pick up the phone. I need to speak with you right now."

I did, relating what had transpired, and she asked for my word that I would not do anything stupid. I agreed to behave and to see her the next morning.

Sitting with her, I was still very distraught and fragile.

"Tarra, we care about you. That's not what you do to people who care about you. Do you know how hurt your family and I would have been?"

"I'm sorry. I never thought about it that way. I just hurt so much and am so tired of feeling like shit."

"Yes, well, it isn't easy I'm sure, but suicide is not an answer. You need to promise you will never try that again."

Later, when I divulged the incident to my father and then to my brother, they both asked me to consider how my suicide would have impacted my grandmother. I had no desire to inflict further pain and suffering on her or anyone else in my family, but had not been able to weigh those consequences during the pain of her rejection.

FORTY-FIVE

For a shepherd, lambing season is a particularly stressful time, especially when the babies fail to successfully enter our world. One night, I struggled alone with a breech birth. Our vet was on an emergency call, and the other shepherd was gone. I called our supervisor, but her cell phone kept dropping my calls. Finally, we had a connection.

"Call your father," she instructed.

I had never involved him with the lambing process, but no one else was available. Even though I had turned the lamb, it was delivered stillborn. Now the ewe was starting to fail. I could barely get through my call.

"Dad, this is Sam. Could you please come down to the barn? I need your help."

My father walked in and, realizing the situation, sat silently beside me on the straw. I was holding the ewe's head on my lap, crying as I stroked her. Life was rapidly slipping away for one of my pets.

"That's too bad. I'm sorry," he said in the softest voice I had ever heard him use. In all those years ministering to the cows, he had appeared impervious to emotional responses. But now as I grieved the dead baby and its dying mother, he offered compassion and kindness I had never known from him.

"Do you think I caused her death?" I asked through my sobbing when her breathing stopped.

"No, I think that sometimes no matter what you try, it does not help. Life and death have their way with us." His voice was soft and gentle.

"Thank you, Dad. You don't know how much that means to me, and that you're here. Thank you." In a rare moment of heartfelt connection, he hugged me.

Through my grief I noticed the irony that in losing the ewe, someone precious to me, I had gained something even more important.

Even while cobbling together all the support I was being given, I began to realize that no matter how loving my family and others were to me, it would never be enough to heal the dark emotions residing deep inside me—that would have to come from me. If I wanted to continue getting healthier, I needed to find a way to accept and forgive myself for my behaviors and insanity.

Self-compassion was difficult as I assessed my absence at the weddings, funerals, and births involving the people I had left behind. Even though my tribe had accepted me back, I struggled to drop the guilt, shame, and sadness I felt about my choices. I had missed my brother's marriage, the birth of his first two children, the funerals of numerous dear aunts and uncles—and so much more. The heaviness in my heart was forcing a deeper look, now that I was away from Jon's restrictive cloak.

As with my return from Peace Corps I was awakening to how strange my culture had become to me. My searching continued, but this time for integration of the concepts, innovations, and historical events that most people took for granted. Jon had shielded and interpreted my awareness—locally, nationally, and globally. I had been allowed to watch two movies while with him—the first *Star Wars*, and *the Never-Ending Story*. Printed material was off-limits, although I had secretly devoured a few religious books he kept in the back of the truck.

Family often visited my grandmother, and when Donna came to visit, I shared the grim news that Jon and I had burned her priceless antique clothing and irreplaceable wedding pictures. I cringed as the hurt traveled over her face.

"I hope that someday you can forgive me," I said. "I cannot tell you how sorry I am, but I know that does not bring back what we burned."

"Sandy, I know that you were not in your right mind when you did that. I forgive you because if we don't forgive others, then God will not forgive us for all our mistakes."

"I just hate him so much for all he did to you, the others, and me; how he took advantage of your generosity and then violated you the way he did."

"Well, it was amazing how you just changed. I remember talking with you and you seemed like your old self, and then when he came into the room, you changed abruptly, and I watched you get anxious and uptight. I couldn't believe how quickly you changed and how different you became."

"I was so afraid of him because he had hurt me so much and I thought he was some exalted being."

"Well, we're just so glad to have you back. Mom prayed for you every day, and she had a whole prayer circle going all the time to get you back."

"Your mom is the greatest. I'm sure all your prayers helped. I hope to be able to repay you for all your love and support."

"Sandy, God has a plan for you. Look at all the people you can help with your experience."

"I can only hope and pray that's so." I marveled at how easily Donna could let go of what we had done.

My seething hatred for Jon had grown with each procedure to repair my nose, teeth and body in general. Painful memories locked into my anatomy had resurfaced with each correction. I also hated myself for allowing him to batter me.

As my dissociation thawed, memories surfaced—bringing so much rage with them I felt like I could have killed him with my bare hands had he been in front of me. As it was, hitting pillows, my heavy bag and a foam futon helped purge those murderous energies from me. How ironic that his battering of me, meant to cleanse the "dark side" out of me, had filled me with such negative energies.

Raging about it all in therapy, I eventually emptied out the toxic emotions and discovered compassion for myself. Along with it came a different way to regulate my emotions and accept my reality. The separation from being so engulfed with emotions assisted me in recognizing that was then, and that now, I was making different choices—learning from my mistakes.

Barb, my therapist, accepted my emotional purging with compassion. Her validation facilitated my internalization of self-acceptance—so necessary before I could move on from my trauma-induced trance. The more aware I became, the more honest I had to be with myself. I had always struggled to love myself, and now recognized that Solar/Jon was merely the external representation of my internal condition. I could either continue hating him and myself, or stop the madness by working through my emotions and finding a place of acceptance and forgiveness.

A novel and refreshing option began to take root within me, creating a foundation for self-compassion and forgiveness.

ODE TO MY INNER CHILD

My dear, dear little one within,
How precious and yet lost to me you have been.

I have allowed you to be broken, beaten, and abused.
How sorry I am, that your pleas for help I refused.
Your pain I deeply feel, especially now,
I pray that someday you can forgive me, somehow.

Please let me hold you close and cuddle you to my heart.
Let us go on from here together, never again to be apart.

Your innocence, spontaneity, and enjoyment of life,
I lost in my efforts to heal and erase the pain and strife.

Alone again I am faced with you and all the aspects of us.
I need you and the others; I want you back if you will trust

That now I love myself, what I was, and all we've ever been.
Let's end the pain and separation that's torn us apart again
and again.

My dear little one, I love you—I love you with all that I am.
Please join me now in my heart—please, take my hand.

FORTY-SIX

Jon continued to sporadically pester me with letters, so I wrote him back with an itemized list of money I figured he owed me. I included the medical and dental expenses I had already incurred; added in the cost of the three cars of mine he had appropriated and trashed; all the monetary gifts given me over the years that he took and never told me about, and my land money he confiscated instead of paying off my debts as we had agreed. It was a very conservative bill, totaling over one hundred thousand dollars, but I capped it there.

He responded by calling my grandmother's phone to tell me he was coming to Escondido to give me the money. "I have the money you asked for; in fact, I have over a million dollars now. Would you meet me at the motel where Mary and I will be staying?"

I agreed to it, although I felt a wave of fear pass through me at the thought of seeing him again. *I think I'll be safe if he has someone with him, even though I don't know who this 'Mary' is. I don't know if I believe that he has a million dollars and plans to repay me. We'll see.*

Walking up the stairs to his motel room, I assessed my exit routes and laced my car keys through my fingers. After knocking on the door, I stepped back and a familiar bearded Jon opened the door. I waited before entering, observing that his demeanor and wardrobe were the same. He walked over to the bed and sat next to someone. *That's different, he's never sat on the bedspread, or let anyone else do so.*

When my eyes had adjusted to the dim light, I stepped inside, leaving the door ajar behind me.

"There's all your money on the table," he said. "Have a seat. Why don't you tell Mary about all the miracles while you're counting your money?"

I sat down and started gathering up the one-hundred-dollar bills spread across the table. "You want me to tell Mary about all the miracles?" I said quite deliberately as I gathered up the money. I looked at her. "What I can tell you is that the road back to recovery from living with this man is a long road back from hell. I hope you get some help when you find it within you to leave."

Mary looked shocked, and Jon immediately jumped up from the bed. "Well, I think we've heard about enough."

I hopped to my feet, stuffing the money into my pockets as I opened the door and bolted outside. He never got close to me as I rushed down the stairs. Racing to my car, I looked up as I reached for the door handle. He was standing at the railing on the balcony.

"I don't understand why you're so angry. What about all the miracles we witnessed?"

I shook my head. "You don't get it, do you? Goodbye, Jon. I don't ever want to see you again." I got into my car, locked the doors and drove away. Glancing in my rearview mirror, I could see he hadn't moved.

I had not told my grandmother where I was going, but related my story when I walked in.

"Did he pay you the money?" she inquired after I had explained everything.

"Not all of it. I got a couple thousand dollars, but then he stood up and I ran outside. I'd taken too much of a chance already."

"My word. Well, I'm glad you're safe now. You're not going to see him again, are you?"

"Nope. Not ever again, thank God."

"Good. I don't think he's a very nice person."

Now that I knew that Jon had found another convert, when Marilyn told me she had seen him walking down the street in Bozeman, I decided we should pay his brother, George, a visit on my next trip there to visit Marilyn. We wanted to warn George about how dangerous his brother was, and I also wanted to set the record straight with George about all the times Jon had taken advantage of him.

The location of George's store was etched in my memory after our snowy trek from the bus station, right before we landed on Marilyn's doorstep in June 1991. George was alone when we walked into his store. I introduced myself and Marilyn to him, explaining that I could now shake his hand and look him in the eyes because only Jon's rules had prohibited me from doing so before. "They were all part of his Program, Jon's excuse for his mind-controlling behaviors. He designed this Program to keep us isolated and submissive. I left him three years ago. Because I'm studying psychology, I feel obligated to share what I have learned about his behavior, especially since I know he's with another woman now. Have you seen her? Do you know if she's safe?"

"No, I haven't seen her since they first came here."

"Did you know that he beat all of us to keep us under his control? She could be dead right now, for all you know."

"No, I didn't know that." George looked shocked.

"He's capable of some pretty amazing things," Marilyn chimed in.

"He's known for his violent behavior," I added.

"Hmm. Well, I'll take that under advisement. Do you think he's a paranoid schizophrenic?"

"Oh, most definitely. But he also has a narcissistic personality disorder and OCD, to name just a few of the things he suffers from. I suggest that your family intervene on Jon's behalf to support him in finding professional help."

George cleared his throat. Some customers had walked into the store.

"Well, thank you for coming in and telling me these things." His gaze shifted to the people standing behind us. Sensing the conversation was over, we left.

"Do you know where the Angel Motel is?" I asked Marilyn as we got in her car. She cruised by the crude little cabins scattered on the property, and I bade farewell. I smiled, remembering how I carried my chair around to sneak cigarettes and could honestly say that I had not gotten out of my seat.

Thank you, God, that I started becoming a person again in that miserable cabin with all his senseless rules. I get now why Linda said I seemed "evil" when she visited me in the psych ward. Being self-destructive truly IS evil; I was out of my right-mind.

FORTY-SEVEN

I earned my bachelor's degree in behavioral sciences in 1994. Fortune, my brother, and both parents attended my graduation. Next would be graduate school, but life was full during my break. I realized that my mother and I had not addressed our mutual pain surrounding the time I had spent with Jon. She was angry with me for what I had done, and my anger with her was very old. Having returned to my roots time and again, I was now realizing that my work had always been to heal the relationships with my family—most specifically my parents. Still feeling distant from my mother, I was convinced she didn't understand the depth of my suffering or the misguided commitment I had to martyring myself to "save" my family and experience their love.

To help sort through emotionally charged and polarized feelings that neither of us could calmly hear from the other, I invited her to some therapy sessions. During that process, I learned how painful it had been for her to be completely disconnected from me, knowing I was with someone who controlled and abused me.

"I had no way of writing to you, or calling, or even knowing whether you were safe," my mother told me. "I feared at some point you might have been rolled out of the car onto the side of the road, dead."

During subsequent talks, I learned how she had consulted numerous psychologists, specialists, religious leaders, and others in hopes of finding a way to rescue me from the madness and emotional bondage she feared would kill me or keep me permanently estranged.

Tragically, many of the professionals she consulted were ignorant about brainwashing and mind control. One psychologist even told her, "Your daughter is a loser and you should forget about her."

In our joint therapy sessions, I learned how to listen to my mother, and my love and appreciation for her deepened in this process. With this softening, I could take in her perspective of our shared drama. With an anguish filled voice, she related her accumulation of voluminous notes and files in search of solutions and a way to help me.

"The worst part of it was I could not get through to you even when I would see you. I could not reach you—Jon had you so deeply under his control. I'll show you everything; I saved it all."

The research, anti-cult, and brainwashing organizations she had contacted in her attempts to extract me from the throes of Jon's mind control were impressive. Letters and information Lori had sent were among them, including copies of chapters from Lifton's *Thought Reform and the Psychology of Totalism* mentioned earlier.

Just before I had moved up north to live with Donna, Lori sent my mother a letter naming my dissociation and obvious layers of denial that were evident from my interview with the Employment Development Department: *October 31, 1983. The special investigator from the unemployment dept. came to the house and let me read Sandy's statement. From her tone, it is obvious to me that she is still in the grips of devastating mind control.*

Because my mother was helpless to intervene, Lori's information only fed her distress. I had not intended to punish her or my father, but characteristically demonstrated my anger towards them by hurting myself with it. Our joint therapy sessions also served to facilitate the collective unraveling of my mother's and my history. We discovered common factors that had contributed to compulsive and self-destructive behaviors within each of us. She was also a molestation victim, only hers had been by the man next door, who had exploited her loneliness and vulnerability.

Both of our lives had begun in death zones. When my mother was born, her maternal grandfather died, followed immediately by the death of her maternal grandmother's brother. Shortly thereafter, her own mother's sister passed away, leaving behind a very young cousin who then lived with my mother for several years. My maternal grandmother was angry and depressed when my mother was a child, and my own mother later struggled with anger and depression when she herself had children. The deaths of her parents, one after another, two miscarriages, and a stillborn baby exacerbated her emotional chaos.

After conjoint sessions with my mother, our relationship started healing significantly. I finally experienced her love, reminded by my therapist that "We are wounded in relationship and healed in relationship."

FORTY-EIGHT

Before I entered graduate school, Marilyn, whom I continued visiting, arranged for me to meet Alan and Mary, a couple she knew from Montana. After several days of in-depth conversations with them while staying at the Sundance resort, I returned with my heart expanded, feeling inspired to find a way through the guilt and shame still crippling my self-esteem. Alan and Mary became dear friends after that, facilitating a renewal in the conviction I felt to continue my intrepid path toward emotional wholeness.

My first day back from this trip was incredibly hot, so I proceeded to water my grandmother's yard. I noticed water bubbling out of the ground.

There must be a broken pipe under there. I better call Dad.

I reported the problem, but his voice sounded different.

"Are you okay, Dad?"

"Well, either I'm having an asthma attack or a heart attack. I'm not sure which one. I'll talk to you later."

I heard a click as he hung up.

What? I started toward my grandmother's room to share this, but then turned around and waited in the kitchen while she finished in the bathroom. The phone rang again.

"Hello?"

"Would you please take me to the hospital?"

"Yeah, Dad. I'll be right up! Gramma, my dad's having a heart attack! I'm taking him to the hospital; I'll call you once we get there." I yelled through the closed bathroom door, and ran out to my car.

I raced up his driveway and my father was staggering outside to meet me. I strapped him in and we sped into town. There were no emergency responders in the valley then, so I put on my lights with flashers blinking as I broke the speed limit. My father's breath rattled as if he were under water.

"Dad, hang on." I touched his knee and punched the accelerator. I feared he was going to die next to me, since the hospital was still miles away. *Focus on driving. Dear God, please let us get there in time.*

"Don't kill us," I heard him softly say through his gasps.

"I'll get us there safely; you stay alive," I said, choking back tears.

I parked in front of the emergency room and helped him walk in, expecting a gurney and medical staff to rush toward us when we came inside. No one budged.

"He's having a heart attack!" I announced, and the room filled with help.

While they wheeled him in, I moved the car into a parking space and recalled an incident between us several months before.

While working to repair a different broken pipe, he shared some disturbing news.

"My doctor said my heart is not healthy and won't last much longer without surgery."

"You're going to get it, then, right? Especially since the Judsons have all died from heart issues."

"No, actually, I'm not going to get the surgery. I don't think it will be worth it."

"You've got to be kidding! Don't you want to live?"

"I'm not going to talk about it!" Offended, he stomped away toward his truck.

Oh, right. Walk away as usual and refuse to deal with it. Like that's going to make it go away.

"Well, I still love you and so do your grandchildren and your son!" I shouted after him. "Those should be reasons enough to get the surgery!"

He drove away without a word. Instead of surgery, he elected to have chelation therapy and had enjoyed several months of excellent health until now.

Like you've always said, I must have gotten my stubbornness from my mother, since you certainly didn't give any of yours away.

He was immediately scheduled for bypass surgery, and Bruce and I were both there. Right before they wheeled him in, he had a few choice words for us:

"You both have been a pain in the ass."

"Yeah, well, we love you too, Dad." I bent down and kissed his cheek, raising my eyebrows to Bruce as he rolled his eyes. Seeing Bruce's eyes fill with emotion, I nodded to him. He bent down and gave our father a kiss on his cheek.

"I love you, Dad."

We watched him disappear through the double doors.

"That's Dad," Bruce said.

"I know. It's always been difficult for him to express positive emotions; even with the pre-op anesthesia he couldn't do it."

"Such a kid."

"Yeah, maybe that's why Donna calls him 'Boy.'"

"Did you find out how this happened?"

"He was digging a trench for Uncle Amos in that 103-degree heat a few days ago and started feeling poorly. I guess the next day was even hotter when he returned to finish the job. The doctor said that's when the attacks started."

"Why did he go back to dig some more?"

"You tell me."

Our father underwent quintuple bypass surgery, and when he was released from the hospital, Bruce and his wife, Lynn, moved him into one of their spare rooms for his rehab. Bruce had gone to our Dad's house to collect some of the things he would need, and invited me over for a barbecue so we could discuss the situation.

"Well," he said, "now I understand why Dad never let anyone visit him. I spent four hours cleaning and didn't make a dent. I helped him fix the roof a couple of times. It was messy but never this bad."

"Yeah, I think his health was just getting worse and worse until he couldn't do anything at all. I spoke with Gramma, and she agreed to help us pay for a crew to go in and clean up."

Our father's life would never be the same now that his hermitage was exposed. Depression is cruelly disabling and offers no motivation for order and cleanliness. Suppressed negative emotions cloud awareness and push us into the recesses of our minds as we retreat from the accumulated pain stored in the body. Our father had contracted so deeply within himself that his home had become a reflection of the clutter and chaos of a heavy heart and mind filled with the crushing weight of pain and regret.

"Those were the happiest days in my life—living with Bruce, Lynn, and the kids," he mused as I drove him home many months later.

After school that night, I bought fresh fruit and vegetables for him. Walking in with the groceries, I stopped, shocked at the sight before me.

"Dad, what have you done?"

"It looked naked."

The counters and furniture were completely covered (as before) with the contents of the boxes I had neatly organized, packed, and labeled. I thought he could open one at a time, sort through and eliminate all the things he did not want or use.

Sometimes people do not change until our relationship with them or our judgments about them do. Hearts fill and expand with love and joy, heal with kindness, and can break with hurt, anger, and pain. It's the latter that slowly destroys, or kills, whether the pain turns to hatred for self or others. My father still had many lessons of the heart to teach me—this was one precious moment of many. His unresolved pain was increasingly more obvious to me; mine was still not fully revealed.

FORTY-NINE

Feeling more confident, I approached my now healed father with a request I had long wanted to ask but had been afraid to.

"Dad, will you please teach me to weld? I've always wanted to know how, and thought of repurposing the old tractor and machine parts lying around the ranch, creating art from them."

Ten minutes later, he had given me short lessons in acetylene and arc welding using the equipment left over from the ranching days. Armed with my burgeoning creativity and passion for art, I fashioned my "Wounded Warrior" with movable arms, cow chains for his beard and hair, oil pan for his chest, tractor parts for his stilt-like legs, cow tags for the trophies he carried on his arm, and an old bucket for a helmet. I identified with his broken and rigid structure. His hollow face reflected vacant eyes after witnessing so much terror.

My process continued as I welded smaller sculptures, a busy box for my nephews and niece, and then eventually graduated to my "Goddess of Rebirth." She began at my height, but after studying an anatomy book, I realized that she needed major structural changes. I removed the round discs I had originally given her for feet, and anchored her to a large piece of solid steel.

"Is that a scraper blade you welded her feet onto?" My father asked.

"Yes."

"Where did you find it?"

"It was lying there on that pile of iron."

"That's tempered steel. You've ruined a perfectly good scraper blade. And that pile is full of angle iron. Looks like you used that too."

"Yes, I did. I didn't think anybody was ever going to use it, since we don't have the ranch anymore."

"Oh, boy." And he walked away, mumbling under his breath.

Undaunted, I continued to fashion wings all around the goddess's body as she evolved. Finding an old block and tackle rusting in a heap, I hoisted it onto a beam above my workshop and was now able to raise and lower my goddess as I worked on her. She grew to be over seven feet tall.

As I sculpted my metaphor, my mother offered her input. "What is this?"

"She's my 'Goddess of Rebirth' to symbolize my own rebirth and reclaiming of myself."

"Oh. Are those her hips?"

"Yes."

"Well, they're too big, aren't they?"

"No, I don't think they are."

"Well, they're too big—they're not in proportion to the rest of her."

"This is my art project, and they're exactly as big as they need to be. She needs lots of room; she's fertile and holding lots of creative energy."

When a neighbor adorned her with a pair of red sunglasses, my goddess became community art. Another placed an American flag in her hand; and one day when I came out to work on her, there was a plastic heart hanging next to hers—a cog from another piece of machinery. With uplifted arms beseeching God, she sported wings on her back, legs, chest, and arms. Her breasts were exposed, with a circular chain running from her heart down to her pelvis. Wrapped around her feet (anchored to the scraper blade) were large strands of rebar I had bent and attached, representing the briar bramble holding her back and out of which she was bursting.

The act of bending steel was exhilarating and felt empowering as I heated large coils of rebar left behind from some ancient construction project. Twisting them into the obstructions encompassing her feet and what she was leaving behind her, I felt elated I could represent her movement out of what had previously entrapped her . . . and me.

FIFTY

A master's degree from Chapman University was my next step. Even though my student-loan debt was mounting, my education would be to no avail without a master's and a subsequent license to practice psychotherapy. One of the admission requirements to enter the psychology program was to write my autobiography.

The more I learned about myself and human behavior in general, the easier it became to understand how I had been hijacked by my need for self-worth and driven by the events of my life.

My relationships with family were greatly improved, but sometimes my father's old behaviors would show up. The bypass surgery had given him a new lease on life but his body was still suffering from years of abuse.

I was working in my garden at Gramma's one day when Dad walked over, propped his leg up and lifted his pant leg to reveal the skin above his ankle.

"See this?" He said and poked a finger into his leg, leaving an indentation that indicated his heart was not pumping properly.

"Are you going to let your doctor know?"

"No, and don't worry about me."

I started blankly at him, feeling he was playing with my emotions. *You know I'll be worried and want you to see your doctor. I can't believe you're pulling such a familiar stunt with me.*

"You ornery son of a bitch," I said, enunciating every word as I looked in his eyes.

"I've been called worse by better," he retorted, and walked away. Three steps forward and two steps back was sometimes the dance I did with my father as he taunted me to care about him, wanting and resisting it at the same time.

Fortunately, I had my brother to bounce off these difficult interactions. He had learned much earlier than I not to get hooked by the emotional double-bind our father used: "Help me, help me"; and when we offered to help, "Don't help me." Therapy and the courses I was studying were shedding light on how such interactions might have contributed to me losing touch with my feelings and therefore myself.

As I continued in the Bioenergetics training program, I felt the need to dispel any notions I might have that the founder was some sort of guru or charismatic leader looking for a following. Alexander Lowen was one of two psychiatrists who had created Bioenergetics in the 1970s. He had studied with Wilhelm Reich in the 1940s and '50s, and based much of his theory on the work and discoveries of Reich.

A fellow trainee shared my desire to see Dr. Lowen, and so Barbara Potts and I flew to Pauling, New York, for one of his presentation-workshop series. Before leaving, my therapist warned me, "Lowen does not do transference; he is not concerned with the relationship between you and him so much as facilitating change within you." I did not expect to engage with him at that level, but did need to meet him and see what he was all about.

I stood in front of Dr. Lowen, a slight but muscular white-haired and bearded man looking much younger than his 84 years. In gym shorts and a sports bra, I was astounded that he could narrate my history just from looking at my body. We had never met but he was uncannily accurate, stating that it appeared I had spent a great deal of my life frightened and unable to find adequate resources.

"You have tendencies toward depression, anxiety, and dependence and most likely had a problem with drugs or alcohol in your life."

Hmm. How did he see that? I smoked marijuana day and night for years.

"You have probably struggled to support yourself in a healthy manner. One of your strengths would be your strong will, but because you relied so much upon it, your life would most likely entail much difficulty and effort. How am I doing so far?"

"Very accurate, I'm afraid."

"Would you like to do some work?"

"Yes, I would."

He gestured for me to lie down on a mattress on the floor in front of him.

"Okay, now start kicking. And as you do, let out a 'no' or some sort of noise from your voice."

On my back, I lifted my legs up one at a time and hit them on the mattress while he sat in a chair next to me.

"Kick. Yes, that's right. Kick, kick." And soon his face got very close to mine, mirroring the agony I was feeling as I bellowed out a loud "NO!"

Overcome by his show of empathy, I stopped kicking and started crying.

When my crying stopped, he put his face even closer and softly asked, "Would you like to put your hand on my cheek?"

"Yes, I would."

He took my hand in his and gently placed it on the side of his face. As I gazed into his clear blue eyes filled with compassion, I cried softly, drinking him in as a peaceful feeling washed through me. My breathing deepened.

In the workshop portion of this conference, I was assigned to a group with Carol Bandini. After I summarized my childhood, she framed it as "a death zone," more validation of the trauma I had sustained.

Upon returning to San Diego, I continued pondering the relationships between trauma and my behaviors, and noticed a much lighter attitude toward myself. I also felt increased energy that was lifting my depression and accelerating more healing.

There were twelve of us in the Bioenergetics training program. Jim Lair worked as a therapist at Juvenile Hall and invited me to become a "Volunteer in Probation." Watching him work with those incarcerated adolescents was an inspiration. However, the first time I walked inside the lockup unit I felt like my stomach had been punched; the energy was so staggering and intense. I could identify with being incarcerated, although my imprisonment had been self-imposed.

The youngsters' stories reflected distracted or poorly informed parents not able to attend properly to their children's emotional needs. I witnessed first-hand how parental support, or the lack thereof, is pivotal and formative in a child or adolescent's life. The significance that gangs held for these abandoned and neglected youth reflected the depth of their unmet developmental needs. The level of violence inherent to their lifestyle and activities was indicative of the deprivation and abuse they had experienced at home. Research has shown that well over half of the incarcerated population had dysfunctional childhoods with exposure to some form of trauma.

Wanting to gain as much experience as possible, I accepted the invitation from another colleague in our Bioenergetics training group to work in a program to support the rehabilitation and recovery from substance abuse of homeless veterans. Barb Potts, who had gone to New York with me to see Dr. Lowen, was supervising therapists working with these vets healing from the horrors that humans perpetrate on one another.

Learning from her gentle mentoring, I witnessed the vets' resiliency and wrote of my time with one such individual whose life was unique to him but mirrored aspects of my own struggles. His recovery was yet another inspiration propelling me toward wholeness. A Vietnam veteran, he was homeless and addicted to drugs until entering the program where I volunteered. For him the war had not ended, as he battled to make sense of risking his life for a cause previously scorned.

His confusion and love for country had been no less than how he felt for his mother and father. They too had abused him and his siblings in their own way. Growing up, hunger was familiar, his belly gnawed with emptiness as did his heart, for the want of an absent father. This boy in a man's body yearned for a mother who did not beat him with a vacuum cleaner hose and a father who rarely returned. Would they ever learn how much their son needed them and craved their love?

A good soldier he had become, risking his life for those who asked him to serve. He was so easy to love, but could not see that beyond the shroud of memories and shame. His abandoned heart doubted his worth and held close the angst of rejection.

Living in neighborhoods of makeshift tents strung between tree branches and cardboard walls between sidewalk beds, he and his buddies made a pact. They wouldn't forget each other as their country had done; leaving them to shift from here to there, looking for the lives they'd lost and could not find again. They would gather for stories and remembering the dead. Numbing was their shared recreation and favored antidote for the festering pain inside. Drugs masked it all, giving relief—but with a price.

He came to me, opening his duffle bag of wounds. Sometimes our room was filled while others used the space, so we sat on sidewalks in between walking. An occasional tear would sneak down his cheek; I wore a sun hat, leaving my eyes open so he could see them filled with respect as he emptied his heart.

One day, he hobbled in with a broken foot and sank into the chair. Crutch in hand, he hit, cried, and screamed until the anguish of injustice left him spent. Seeking but not finding the judgment he feared would show on my face, he loosened further his tide of grief.

With each betrayal that he unveiled, my heart opened to him more. His courage kindled and grew, as did my love and respect for this man of great strength.

Week after week he chose to change, leaving behind the drugs and despair. When he left the program and my care, he felt like a son to me. I said goodbye as he moved forward and rejoined his fellow-soldiers in the field. Only now the battles were for recovery, assisting them to heal from the ravages wrought when woman and man turn against their own.

FIFTY-ONE

I graduated with a master's degree in psychology in 1997. With three thousand hours of internship ahead of me before I could sit for my boards, I took a job working with pregnant and parenting adolescents on probation. They were substance abusers allowed enrollment in a diversion program held in the heart of City Heights, at that time a problematic neighborhood where two of the largest Southern California gangs engaged in regular turf wars.

The staff offered ancillary services, and together we provided a comprehensive treatment program for these courageous young women. They were an inspiration, yet one of the more difficult aspects was recognizing that even though they were highly motivated, they invariably returned home to a substance-abusing parent or to drug dealing in the garage next door or down the street.

Sometimes a home visit was in order, and I drove there myself. These ghettos reminded me of the ones I had walked while working in Cartagena. I had never expected to witness such abject poverty and cultural impoverishment in my own country. Again, I grappled with how a nation with so much abundance could have citizens with so little. Even so, I found this work fulfilling as I accumulated the requisite hours.

One day, while I was catching up with paperwork, my desk phone buzzed.

"Tarra speaking."

"Aren't you glad to hear from me?"

"Who is this?"

"Jon. I'd like to take you out to dinner to make it up to you."

"What makes you think I would want to eat dinner in the same restaurant, let alone at the same table, with someone who beat and abused me and took advantage of me and my family? You have to be the most demented person I know!"

"What about the mission you have not fulfilled? You have turned your back on God!"

"You're disturbed and a sick, sick man. Don't ever call me again, or I'll tell the police about you and not stop until they find you."

I hung up and immediately called my mother; she was the only one who had my work phone number. "Mom, Jon called me here. Did you give him my number?"

"Oh dear. I am so sorry—I had no idea. A woman called me claiming she was a friend of yours from Sedona. She wanted to get in touch with you, and so I gave her the number. I'm truly sorry; I had no idea it was someone connected with Jon."

Later, I warned everyone about his stunt, and to be aware of any future intimidation tactics. I felt grounded when sharing this information, no longer afraid of this man who used to be my jailer. I did not feel the slightest desire to know how he was or what he was doing. The fear he had used to mold my consciousness and do his bidding was no longer there.

Thank you, God! I seem to have found something that is working!

I was phasing out my shepherd work, having gone from full time to part time. Now that I was earning enough money to support myself, I entertained the thought of moving out on my own. My grandmother was ninety-seven but still very healthy, active, social, and continuing her service work and gardening. We enjoyed many lively discussions, and during one of them I learned of her fears of being moved into a rest home and becoming dependent in her declining years.

Our conversation stirred my awareness of how deeply I loved her and how much I appreciated her for all that she had contributed to my life. I decided a small gesture demonstrating my gratitude would be offering to care for her until the end of her life.

It was one of the best decisions I ever made. I knew my father and aunt loved their mother very much, and never felt like I was competing with them for her love or a place in her heart. She had room for all family members, and even those who weren't related but had asked her to be their grandmother!

And so, we decided that I would share her home and life until the end of hers. She maintained that a healthy attitude, eating right, and hard work were the cornerstones to a long and fulfilling life. Her outlook on death was equally balanced.

One day, she was apparently looking towards the future when she descended the stairs with a disgusted look across her face.

"Is everything okay?"

"I was just in Louise's (my father's sister) room, looking at the cedar chest I made. I climbed into it, thinking it would be a great coffin to be buried in, but I'm sorely disappointed I did not fit."

FIFTY-TWO

Continuing my work with the adolescent mothers on probation and maintaining a small private practice on the coast helped me power through my intern hours. I was on my way to licensure and a profession. Having completed the academic portion of the Bioenergetics training, certification in that was next. Life was easier now, and I was feeling much better about myself and my future.

Just before Thanksgiving in 1999, our mother was diagnosed with colon cancer, requiring immediate surgery.

She returned home from the hospital with her cancer successfully removed, and that Sunday my brother, his wife and children went to visit her. I was in San Diego with my training group for our monthly process group meeting. It had just ended when I received a page from my mother. I called her while walking to my car.

"Bruce had a heart attack and was taken to the hospital! Where are you?"

"I'm in San Diego for my meeting."

"Please call Dad and Gramma and let them know."

I took off, speed-dialing my father's number. The call dropped several times before going through. No answer. I called my grandmother's number.

"Hello?"

"Gramma, Bruce just had a heart attack!"

The call dropped.

"Damn cell phones!" I called again and got through. "Gramma, please tell Dad to meet me at the hospital."

"He's already left."

"Okay. I'm driving back from San Diego. I'll call you when I get to the hospital."

"Drive carefully."

When I got to the ER, my sister-in-law and father were waiting in a family room. Very shortly my father's cardiologist came in.

"We're trying to revive your brother but aren't having much success. I wish I'd given him the cardiac belt when I saw him."

I looked at my sister-in-law because I was not aware Bruce had seen a cardiologist. She nodded.

"Please don't give up on him," I said. "Go back and keep trying to revive him." I dropped to my knees and silently prayed for Bruce's recovery, begging God to spare him. *Surely my service to God counts for something; people survive heart attacks all the time, and Bruce is only forty-six and very fit.*

Not long after, the doctor returned to announce they had called my brother's death.

This news stopped our world. *How can this be? His children are only six, nine, and twelve, and he and Lynn love each other very much. Bruce, how can you be dead? God, how can you let this happen?*

My father was so disoriented when leaving the hospital, I had to escort him to the parking lot and to his truck. Overwhelmed myself, I could not drive and sat in my car as I called Barb, my therapist and lifeline. I remained immobilized until she phoned. Her empathy and support helped to reorient me back into my body.

When I finally arrived home, my grandmother was sitting in her chair looking very worried. No one had called her. After I related my sad news, we held each other as we cried.

"Why do these things happen?" she said.

"I wish I knew, Gramma," I said, holding her tight.

I had never felt such pain as when my brother died. Our childhood had bonded us deeply; we liked similar activities and had explored together the natural space around us. He had brought me soup and crackers when I was sick; sitting by my bedside to talk with me. When we were much younger—before he grew up to become a "gentle giant" at six feet six inches—he would crawl in bed with me on weekend mornings with our dog Pudgy in the middle, also underneath the covers. As our parents' marriage disintegrated, I passed the criticism meted out to me on to Bruce. When our mother was absent over the weekends, I bossed him around, taking on her role.

"You can't order me around—you're not my mother."

I slapped him above the waist since I could not reach him any higher; at the age of twelve he was already six feet tall. Looking down at me, he took my arms in his hands and pushed me back into the laundry corner. "Don't ever do that again."

"Okay," I meekly replied, and a new realm of respect began between us. From then on, I bottled up my anger instead of taking it out on him, but he never took advantage of his height over me; he was incredibly kind and loving.

Part of me died along with him. My faith was shaken, for I could see no good reason for his demise. Eventually, I realized that understanding his death was not for me to discover, but I still struggled to accept it and remained angry with God for quite some time, still thinking God was responsible for such tragedies. I love Bruce and still miss him; his loving presence is very much alive in my heart today.

FIFTY-THREE

I wrestled to embrace how unalterably changed our lives were now. I had never felt such grief, and I could not believe how the rest of the world continued, blind to my family's pain.

Before Bruce passed away, I had changed jobs to work for an agency operating a teen center closer to my home. My past supervisors had been gifts, and my good fortune continued with more excellent mentoring as I worked with another troubled population—adolescent males with substance abuse issues and/or gang affiliations. I was not long at this job before being recruited for a grant program with Columbia University, the Robert Wood Johnson Foundation and the agency where I had completed my practicum before graduating with my Masters. This privately funded project focused on discovering the best method for the rehabilitation and return to work of chronic welfare mothers with substance abuse issues.

The results were staggering, showing across the country correlations with poverty, chronic welfare dependence, domestic violence and substance abuse. The most effective outcomes addressed their learned helplessness through collaborative efforts that provided a caring and supportive structure for this population lacking a core foundation of loving and emotionally stable resources in their developmental years.

The grant ended as I approached licensure. After passing my boards, I entered the private sector in 2001.

Several months later, my father asked me to accompany him to a nephrologist. I squeezed his hand as the doctor confirmed kidney failure and the need for immediate dialysis. A whirlwind of medical procedures followed with a pacemaker, two additional surgeries, extended hospital stays and eventually moving Dad to a rest home. Except for his time in the Army and university, his life had been spent entirely on the family farm.

At the rest home, we worked through more of the anguish and grief between us. I helped with his final dialysis treatment of the day and he plowed over my boundaries less and less frequently.

"I need all these things by tomorrow and want you to run these errands," he demanded one day, shoving a list towards me. I blankly stared at the items needing my immediate attention, wrestling with how and when I could squeeze them all in by his deadline.

"Well," he said, "I guess it all doesn't need to be done by tomorrow. Maybe when you have time would be okay."

"Thank you, Dad." *He's taking my needs into consideration.*

Inch by inch, he began validating me as I became a real person to him with my own needs, thoughts and feelings; with my own rights that he was learning to honor.

One night as I was leaving, I said my usual, "Good night, Dad. I love you," and he mumbled something.

"What did you say? I didn't hear you, Dad."

"I said I love you too."

Despite failing health, he truly enjoyed the last portion of his life. His high school buddies, friends and family visited him on a regular basis. No longer reclusive, he formed relationships with his fellow residents, the staff, and owners of the care facility. He was even successful in healing his relationship with my mother.

That had truly started while Bruce was still alive. Both of us wanted our parents to behave more maturely and get along for the sake of their grandchildren. For a while, it felt like World War III was starting whenever they shared space together, yet Bruce continued to invite both parents to events, and once even stood up to our father, who was ranting and protesting the presence of his ex-wife at a family affair.

"I can invite anyone I want to family gatherings. My kids have a right to see their grandmother too." My brother possessed far more self-confidence than I did at the time. Grumbling under his breath; our father had reluctantly conceded.

But it wasn't until after the bypass surgery that his relationship with our mother changed dramatically. She gave him a small bear holding balloons as a get-well gesture, but after she left, he tied the balloons around the bear's neck. "My ex-wife gave this to me. This is what she thinks of me," he joked to everyone who visited.

Again, I mediated. "Dad, how do you think Mom felt when she came to visit you and saw that you hung the bear with those ribbons? I believe she was just trying to be nice to you. The least you could do is return the gesture."

The next day, the ribbons were gone from around the bear's neck. He asked me to send her flowers and when he left the hospital, the bear sat on the window ledge above his bed.

In and out of the hospital, our mother visited him daily. Dedicating herself to his care, she shuttled him to doctor appointments and helped attend to his needs. As his health continued to decline, she stepped in more.

One December night, I walked into his room to see the staff huddled around him.

"What's wrong?"

"I can't breathe. I'm having trouble breathing."

I watched as he was loaded into the ambulance, and followed him to the hospital. He was kept for observation and I stayed until he ordered me to go home. My mother spent the following day with him, and I visited in between work. He seemed in good spirits, but didn't look well that night.

The next morning, my mother left a voice mail. "Dad's not in good shape—he's having more mini-strokes and wants you here."

I immediately left my seminar and raced to the hospital. When I walked into his room, he struggled out of his chair.

"Sam, I don't think I'm going to make it out of here alive."

"Oh, Dad."

He reached for me. I folded my arms around him, and we cried in each other's embrace.

Too weak to stand any longer, he sat down. "Lynn brought the kids by yesterday to see me and Louise and Bud paid me a visit afterwards. I signed the papers giving you the adobe," he said. "It's all done now; I'm glad you changed your mind about it."

"Thank you so much, Dad, but let's not talk about that right now. I'd like to know how you're feeling."

"Scared."

Just then a nurse walked in, scolded my father for sitting up, and then helped him back into his bed. I was still moved by his openness, feeling overwhelmed with love and gratitude. Never, had he let me so deeply into his heart. Although desperate to help, I was also powerless to lessen his fears, and that saddened me.

As he lay in bed, he grew restless and asked us to help him sit up more. With my mother on one side and me on the other, we gently held him as he struggled to move up in bed and onto his pillow. He froze and winced. He'd had another stroke; this one severe and extremely painful. I called for help and the nurse responded immediately, giving him an injection.

"He's asleep right now from the Dilaudid and is not feeling any pain. You should ask for a brain scan and X-rays to determine how extensive the damage was from the stroke."

Soon my father was wheeled back with the doctors following behind. They reported the damage to his brain was so severe that he would never recover.

Instantly, a memory pushed its way into my consciousness. Several weeks previously, Dad and I had been discussing his mini-strokes and what he wanted done if he had a massive one. "I don't want to be revived if I'm going to be a vegetable," he'd said, and then his voice had trailed off into silence. I had filled the empty space: "Don't worry, Dad, I won't let you suffer."

Now the choice was here, but I found it extremely difficult to voice his wishes. I phoned my aunt and uncle, my sister-in-law, and the others who had been standing by.

Thank God you saw everyone yesterday except Gramma, Dad. I don't have the heart to tell her now. This is it, isn't it? Please God, help him; help me and all of us deal with this. I love you, Dad. . .

On December 7, 2003, we waited for my father to ebb away after pulling all life-sustaining measures. We continued waiting throughout the day and late into the night, sitting in silence. I was mentally conversing with my father, letting him know how much I loved and appreciated him, and how sorry I was that he had to suffer so much in his life.

Eventually, everyone who had been visiting went home except for my mother; Patti, our neighbor; and me. My father's pacemaker and oxygen had been unhooked hours before, and massive amounts of morphine had been administered. He continued breathing on his own, and when the hour grew later, I started worrying. *Did I make a mistake? I thought this was what you wanted. What's wrong, Dad? Why are you still here? Dear God, what is wrong? What shall I do?*

As suddenly as I had asked, it occurred to me that my mother needed alone time with him. I helped her lie next to him, and then left with our neighbor to walk down the hall.

Patti was talking to me when I felt a pressing need to return immediately. I walked into the room just in time for my father's last breath.

"He's gone," my mother softly announced. "As soon as you left, his breathing slowed, and I sensed Bruce standing at the head of his bed. I'm sure he came to help him."

"Bruce is here now?"

"Yes. Now they can go fishing together again."

I helped her out of his bed, and when the nurse came in to confirm his death, I asked for time alone with him. In between tears, I said my final goodbyes.

I love you very much Dad; I'm so grateful for the healing we experienced. I'm so grateful for everything.

After the services, my dear Montana friends Alan and Mary invited me north, to join them on their docked boat. Their support soothed and held me for several days as the gentle swaying and bobbing of the boat comforted me.

The holidays felt somber. As usual, Christmas Eve was spent with family at my grandmother's, and the next day my sister-in-law opened her home for dinner with extended family. Driving home, I passed my garage and stopped in the barnyard to gaze upon the giant cross my father always lit on his hill. I had continued the tradition for him and now offered silent prayers. "You are missed, Dad. I hope you know you're loved."

As these final words tumbled out, a light arced from one tip of the cross to the other.

FIFTY-FOUR

At 103 years, old, my grandmother, Rebecca Harriet Trussell Judson, had outlived all her friends, siblings, her son, and one of her two grandsons. She now spent more time sitting in reflection than reading. Previously she had consumed several books a week. Her only outings were having her hair done, and even those ceased when we brought that service to her.

Unlike her son, my grandmother harbored no regrets, and lived her life with the grace and ease of a wise sage. With amazing gusto, she had embraced all the good and bad that walked into her life. She happily vied with others at family Easter egg hunts in her extensive yard, and had enjoyed camping in the woods, adventure and travel. She loved spending time with her family and spoke with gratitude about her full life with all the love and joy she felt, an attitude that eased her surrender to a body that gradually gave way to life's natural conclusion—the transition into death.

Our relationship was easy; she was an extraordinary human being who never had a cross word to say to or about anyone. Although she no longer canned five hundred quarts of fruit a summer or froze homegrown vegetables, she continued working in her yard for as long as she could. She now slept in until a leisurely eight in the morning. I left before she got up, but she usually came into the kitchen to greet me and then returned to bed. A gracious lady to the end of her days, she never lost her sense of humor.

I slept very lightly, awakening when she got up or roamed in the kitchen for a snack. One night, during a thunderstorm, lightning cracked outside the house, and I got up to check on her, as it sounded like it had struck the tree next to her bedroom window. I found her standing by the back door, leaning on the counter, peering out the window.

"Are you okay?"

"Yes."

"Did you hear the thunder?"

"Oh, that's what it was. I flushed the toilet and heard this loud noise and wondered what had happened," she laughed as her quandary was explained.

The Santa Ana winds—we called them "East Winds"—and earthquakes shook the house, but I believed some wonderful force looked over my grandmother. After my father's death, hurricane winds whipped through our area, imploding the hay barn and splintering it into millions of pieces. A huge eucalyptus branch cracked off and crashed through our fence, falling within two feet of her bedroom. It easily could have been pushed by the wind into her window or onto the roof, or caused another tragic scenario. As it was, four of us with chainsaws spent hours cutting up the massive branch so we could open the garage and enter the house through that side again.

Once, parts of the house were without electricity. The electrician pointed to an outside light that had burned on its wooden block mounted onto the garage—also wood.

"It's a mystery that the fire went out and did not torch the entire garage," he added, shaking his head in disbelief.

"Yeah. I think it was the work of guardian angels that look out for my grandmother."

Now, in between working, much of my spare time was focused on renovating my father's home and grove. Although both were extremely compromised, I tackled this project with passion. The grove had been my father's godsend, and I felt protective of his trees. After he sold the cows, he had become a farmer with nothing to care for.

One day, a stranger named Gabor showed up looking for land to grow experimental fruit trees. My father offered his vacant land, and Gabor would return from his travels with new varieties of avocados, cherimoyas, macadamias, and other exotic fruits. One year he stopped showing up, but my father continued fostering the seedlings into trees for over twenty years. He expanded the grove and planted an orchard behind his house.

I spent close to three years repairing and remodeling my inheritance. The house became my canvas as I worked to transform memories of familial dysfunction into a healing, nurturing space.

As the completion approached, my grandmother's self-efficiency lessened, with simple tasks becoming more difficult for her. Sitting in her expansive kitchen, we still enjoyed casual conversation and a fire together.

"How old am I?"

"You're almost 106 years old, Gramma."

"I am not!" she countered.

"Yes, Gramma, I'm sorry to say that you are. But look at how well you're doing, and everyone loves you. How old you are doesn't really matter."

"Oh, that's too old!"

The conversation did not continue, since it was her bedtime and she needed help getting out of her chair. Incredibly, she still walked without assistance of a cane or walker, but after sitting all day, her legs needed help in loosening up so she could stand up and walk.

The day came when I had to call the paramedics. Now only minutes away, the volunteer fire department responded. I spoke with my aunt and uncle and they met us at the hospital. She stayed for five days, with precarious health for several. One evening she kept insisting I was a neighbor from long ago, calling me her name, reminding me "the children [my aunt and father] are upstairs."

"Gramma, I'm Tarra; I'm Sandy. Don't you recognize me? I'm Sandy."

Her mind remained stuck in the past that night, and I left saddened and disturbed that I had not been able to penetrate her fugue.

The next night was extremely difficult for my youngest cousin, Pam, who spent the night with Gramma at the hospital. I stayed late to keep them company and tried to calm my grandmother before leaving.

"I want to go home, I want to go home, I want to go home. I want to go home and go to bed," she repeated.

"You're already in bed," I softly responded.

"No, I want to go home and sleep in my bed that Charlie and I slept in."

"Well, Gramma, I can't take you home tonight, but I promise if the doctors say you are better tomorrow, I'll take you home." *I hope you forget by morning.* I glanced over at Pam and gestured to her that I was leaving.

Pam later told me how our grandmother kept waking her up: "Pam, go upstairs and make sure Sandy is home safe and in bed."

She had lapsed into calling me "Sandy" again, and even though Pam reassured her I was home and in bed, she continued to worry.

The next morning, I was called to bring a set of clothes, and that Gramma had miraculously recovered so much the doctors were discharging her to a rest home.

Until that morning she had been unable to get out of her hospital bed. However, we watched her stroll around the hospital hallway, beaming her beautiful smile and using a walker for the first time in her life. She positioned herself in a chair with her daughter and granddaughters gathered around and we swapped tales and reminisced about our times together on the ranch. Everyone had flown in to be with her, and we laughed and shared the wholesome, loving experiences we had all enjoyed.

Our grandmother was radiant.

Later that morning, Pam and I took off, leaving the others to keep her company. I was meeting Linda, who had agreed to help me arrange my furniture in the living room, the only room that was finished in my adobe home.

We had just sat down to admire our efforts when my cousin Candy called. "Come quick, Gramma's having trouble breathing."

Linda locked up the house for me as I sped to the hospital. On the way, my cell phone rang.

"Hello?"

"Tarra, this is Pam. Where are you?"

"I'm still in the valley but I'm coming. Where are you?"

"I'm just leaving Mom and Dad's, and entering the freeway. I went there to rest."

"I'll pray for easy traffic. Drive carefully!"

We hung up, and several minutes later, Pam called back, shouting into the phone. "Bruce just told me he was going to help Gramma!"

"What? —Bruce? My brother?"

"Yes! He told me he was going to help Gramma."

"I wonder what he meant? Drive safely and I'll see you at the hospital. I'm almost there."

Minutes later I ran into the hospital, got an elevator, and saw Pam walking into our grandmother's room. Gramma was lying in her bed, alabaster white. *Oh, no, I'm too late!*

"What happened?" I asked.

"Gramma said she couldn't breathe, and then she died. You know she had a DNR," Candy said.

"Bruce told me he was going to help Gramma," Pam said.

"You mean Bruce Faulkner?" Pam's mother asked, referring to Pam's brother-in-law.

"No, Bruce Judson."

"I'm not sure I understand what you're saying."

I overheard Pam begin to relate the sequence of events, and rested my head on my grandmother's chest, crying softly until something jerked at me and I suddenly stood up.

"I have to go!"

"Are you leaving?" Pam asked.

"No, I just need to take a walk. I can't explain it, but I need to go for a walk."

"Do you want some company?"

I nodded, and Pam and I walked down the hall to the stairway door. I pushed it open and we stepped onto the balcony. Fifty feet in front of us, directly outside our grandmother's room flashed what looked like a sheet of brilliant lightening.

"Oh!" we both gasped. I started crying as a shaft of golden light joined the shiny brilliant one outside the hospital room, and then both disappeared.

Gramma, it's you! And Bruce, you came to help Gramma transition. Thank you for waiting for us!

With our matriarch gone, the centerpiece of our clan was surgically dissected and shared; it was the end of an era and our family heritage. Her presence had kept the invading forces at bay, stalling the City of San Diego's complete takeover of our homestead and allowing us to enjoy the land's nurturing refuge.

Soon I was confronting the daily and systematic dismantling of the place I had called home, where the constancy of my grandmother and her loving presence had nurtured my recovery and integration of all that I had experienced. The familiar objects that held her essence intact were shifting and disappearing like props on a stage. Empty space greeted me when I opened a cupboard or drawer. Where furniture had offered familiar support, now there was none.

I remained in her home a few months longer since mine was still not ready. Although the major construction was finished, the skylight and heating/AC ducts were still gaping holes in the ceiling, and the bedrooms and bathrooms were unpainted. I felt quite frantic until Mary, my friend from Montana, came to visit with the mission of helping. Together with friends Linda and Laura, we finished the painting and I retreated to my adobe home, settling into each room as it was finished.

My sister-in-law, aunt, and cousins honored me by sharing portions of their inheritance with me. While I had been living with Solar/Jon, my grandmother had conducted a drawing for her belongings. Absent from the family for years, I did not participate, but at the time, my brother told his wife that when I returned—not *if* but *when*—he was going to share his portion with me. I was overcome with gratitude when my sister-in-law related this, and gifted me some of the furniture they had chosen together. My only regret was in not knowing about it ahead of time so I could have thanked Bruce for his faith in me that I would find my way back.

Settling into the space I had created, I started each day by communing with nature. Sitting in my grandmother's chair, I heralded the sun as it rose above the mountains to the east and cherished my view of the valley and the wildlife that frequented my yard. After twenty-seven years of living in other people's homes or in no home—just a car—at last I had my own to enjoy.

Shepherding the growth of over a hundred trees in the grove and orchard, I searched to balance my needs with those of the coyotes, snakes, and abundant wildlife. I learned that giving the coyotes an ever-present water supply kept them from chewing my irrigation lines, and that I could be awed even by deadly neighbors.

One morning I was pulling weeds from under the canopies of avocado trees with the sprinklers running, thinking that would deter any varmints I might encounter. Reaching a gloved hand into a shower of water, I gathered a handful of weeds, and as I pulled them out, the tail of a rattlesnake cascaded off my hand. Frightened and falling backwards, I sat on my knees as I watched the snake amble its way down the canyon and away from me, with nary a shake or rattle of its tail along the way. I had been protecting the rattlers, prohibiting anyone from killing them while on my property, and even though this meant moving them away from my patio and once from inside my home, I now prayed with gratitude in the cathedral of my grove.

Full-time work and the land competed for my time and energy; I had little room for play. My friend Laura often stopped by or called on her way to Ramona.

"Hey Tarra, want to go riding with me?"

"No, I can't. I'd like to but have too much to do in the grove."

"Okay. I just thought you'd like to go for a ride sometime."

"Yeah, it would be fun. You know, there's something wrong with my life that I'm working so hard with little time for fun. I need to make some changes."

"Well, the invitation is always open."

"Thanks. Maybe someday."

FIFTY-FIVE

After renovating an outside building into an art studio, I began having a social life again. I was dating and had started entertaining in my home. The day before my aunt and uncle were to come for Sunday brunch, I completed planting the flowerbeds around my new patio; having arrived at a resting place with the remodeling. We had planned their much-anticipated visit long ago, and I was glad to share with them the changes I had made.

"Hello and welcome. It's been too long since you've been here. Too bad the east wind is blowing so hard; I've felt discombobulated all morning." I ushered my Aunt Louise and Uncle Bud inside and away from the wind.

We enjoyed our meal, and during the ensuing conversation, decided to check out the neighbor's gate that was now blocking access to their land above me. We headed up the dirt road in my truck and then climbed to the peak on foot to enjoy the view. From our vantage point, we could see two distinct patches of smoke, one to the east and another due south. It was about one-thirty, and unbeknownst to us, we were witnessing the beginning of the Witch Creek and Harris fires, the two largest wildfires in California in 2007.

Before returning to my place, our neighbor met us and shared concerns about the fires. When my aunt and uncle left, I decided to visit the San Pasqual fire station to check on the status of the fire and remind them where I lived.

"Oh yeah, we know where you are. You're the lady with the cross."

"Yes, that's me. I'm glad you've seen my cross."

"Who could miss it? How tall is it anyway?"

"About twenty feet. What about the fire?"

"You should probably stay close; it's burning a thousand acres an hour, but it's going to pass south of you. I wouldn't worry about it."

I wish I didn't have a date tonight. Maybe he won't mind staying here instead of going out. He obliged my worry, but I was not much fun, feeling extremely stressed about the fire. Around six thirty, he decided to leave and I visited the fire station again to inquire about their progress in putting it out.

"We have three units on the fire and still expect it to pass to the south and behind your property."

Although a different firefighter had given me the same story, I was still filled with doubt. "What do you think I should do?"

"I'd pack up a few things for a couple of days, just in case you need to leave."

I called my Montana friends, got a plan together, and called my cousin Donna to ask for her prayer assistance. I hung up to receive a call from my neighbor Patti, who had moved into my grandmother's house. She was in Ramona, helping to evacuate horses threatened by the fire. I relayed the message from the fire department, offered my help and suggested that just in case, she might want to come home to evacuate the horses she boarded.

Stepping outside, I checked the eastern horizon. The sky glowed red and yellow between the crests of the mountains. Black smoke billowed and hovered in the atmosphere, and there was a solid line of cars deadlocked on the highway across the valley. *It looks like all of Ramona is trying to evacuate. I couldn't get out if I wanted to.*

Sand blasted my face, eyes, and the house as the wind hurled it in heavy gusts. It was blowing harder than I had ever experienced, making it difficult to be outside. Loading some clothes and shoes for work in my car, I threw in an overnight bag and then sequestered my cats in carrying cages. They howled in terror with the stench of smoke.

I started leaving messages for help in evacuating some of my things, and my mother got through, bringing a neighbor so they could drive out my truck and ATV. Speech was inaudible outside; the wind was blowing so hard. We put a few things in her car and my truck and then I sent them away, afraid they would not be able to get out. I watched their taillights vanish in front of me, shielded by the smoke-filled darkness and dust filling the air. *I wish Linda and Marty were back from their medical trip in Guatemala.*

Just then, my phone rang: "We're on our way."

"I thought you were still gone."

"We just got home."

Even though they both were sick, they came to help.

"You should take a picture of each room with its contents to document it, just in case," Marty suggested, handing me his digital camera.

"It's not going to burn. I have my firebreak, and the fire station knows where I am. They assured me they'll look out for my place."

"Just in case, Tarra. Do you want to take them, or shall I?" he asked.

"Okay, I guess you're right." I snapped pictures of everything as we toured the interior.

Linda started removing my relics and artwork from the walls.

"You're making me nervous."

"Tarra, what if it burns?"

"Well, it's not going to, but I guess you should take that stuff just in case." And we walked through each room, picking up an antique rocking chair from the early 1800s, my grandfather's hand-carved milking stool and his cowboy boots, and a few other irreplaceable items that were easily transportable.

"We should be going. You're not going to stay here, are you?"

"Well, I'd thought about it, since Bruce and my dad saved the house in 1975 when the last big fire blew through here. They didn't even have firefighting equipment, a firebreak around the house, or fireproofing on the roof like I do. And besides, the fire department is down the hill and air support is right behind me."

"Tarra, you can't stay and fight the fire. Promise me you're going to leave."

"Okay, I promise."

We finished loading their car, and they left. Alone again, I watched the horizon glow through my living room windows. I prayed and paced, and at about 10:00 p.m. I received a reverse-911 call to evacuate immediately.

I called Patti and told her.

"I didn't get a call," she responded.

"Well, I'm leaving now and I hope you do the same."

I packed my cats in the car and left an outside light on and my gate open for the firefighters. Since my aunt and uncle had invited me to stay with them, I robotically drove to Carlsbad. Together we watched the news coverage of the fire until after 2:00 in the morning, when I decided to retire.

About an hour later, my cousin Marci called to check in. She was just leaving the valley. In the middle of our conversation, she witnessed a power line fall into the Guejito Creek bed, igniting it.

"Oh my God, that fire is headed east in the riverbed. It's going toward the Academy."

That's right down the hill from my house.

"Marci!" I said. "Get out of there right now! Please, don't wait another minute."

About two hours later, my cell rang. It was Ray, Marci's husband, his voice breaking. "I'm sorry, Tarra; I'm so sorry. Your home, it's burning."

I threw on some clothes and ran downstairs. My uncle was watching the fire coverage on TV.

"Uncle Bud, Ray called and said my home is burning and the fire department isn't fighting the fire. No one's there trying to save it. I'm going out to the valley. I've got fire hoses and lots of equipment; I'm going to try and put it out."

Racing out the door, I jumped in my car and sped east toward the source of my angst. There were roadblocks everywhere, and when I tried yet another entrance to the valley at Via Rancho Parkway, the police officer apologized repeatedly but kept stating he could not let me go beyond the barrier.

"Is Mary Lane blocked off?" I asked him.

"If you can get through that street, go for it."

Evading the roadblock, I felt triumphant as I cruised down the grade. But as I headed into the valley, I could see that the entire eastern end was engulfed in flames.

"God, Jesus, Gramma, Grandpa, Dad, Bruce, all my ancestors, guides, and guardians, please protect me. I'm going in."

As I descended into what looked like the bowels of hell, I encountered another roadblock at the Cloverdale crossing. Getting out of my car, I ran toward two men at the barrier.

"My home is burning, and I need to get through to put it out!"

One of the men opened his arms and pointed east, shouting back, "Are you going to put out the fire by yourself?"

But he moved the barrier. I ran back to my car and stuck my head out the window as I drove by. "You wouldn't say that if it were your home!"

Entering the flaming darkness, I could see that the upper perimeter of the Wild Animal Park was ablaze, as were all the trees along the road, the riverbed, and the south end of the valley. Everything looked torched and red hot. Fires belched black smoke everywhere, and the wind blasted flying embers, pushing my car with a menacing fierceness. Both north and south sides of the hills had flames or some aspect of fire on them, but I kept driving, praying to avoid the sparks and flying embers all around me.

Orange trees flared, and I passed the burned-down Burkhart house and Country Store. Crossing the bridge, I turned onto Bandy Canyon Road and drove towards the ranch.

"Oh!" I stopped the car. Through the haze I could see my grandmother's home, totally consumed in flames. The roofline and every board, window, and door opening blazed red-hot and transparent. I had a three-dimensional view of the upstairs, my home for fifteen years and inhabited by my family for 112.

I could not watch anymore. Sobbing, I turned the corner and coasted to my driveway, avoiding a fire truck parked on the side of the road—the firefighters watching everything burn. *What are they doing? Don't they have hoses or anything?*

As I approached my driveway I saw a smoldering heap where the J. B. Judson home used to sit. The eucalyptus grove was still burning to the east of it. Gone was the house at the foot of my road where Marci's family once lived. The eucalyptus grove in between was still flaming.

I backed my car up in the driveway next to mine and started walking, then ran past the burning trees to avoid blowing embers. I leapt over burnt logs on my road, but the wind was so strong it blasted me with sand. Shielding my eyes, I looked down at the pavement and labored to climb my driveway. The air was thick with smoke and soot. Several times, I had to move pieces of barbed wire and fence so I could get by—remnants of the fence-post barrier I had erected along my driveway to keep out ever-present trespassers. I finally made it to the steepest part but was choking and struggling to breathe.

Hailed by embers, I dropped down to the road and shielded my head with my hands. *I'm lying on a bed of sand—it's covering my road. Oh, God, my water tank must have burned. All this sand must be from its wake when the water washed down the bank like it did that time it overflowed.*

I started crying. *I don't have any water to fight the fire with.* Desperate, I stood up—frantic to reach my house. Flames were licking at my bedroom patio. I continued climbing. *There's got to be something I can do.*

I inched my way up the driveway. As I rounded the corner, I spied another fire raging ahead of me. *My construction materials are burning at my turn-around. Those trees will be next. I can't go any farther; the road is blocked, and the hills are still burning. It's over!*

The minute I surrendered to reality, something inside me snapped, and the better side of reason started governing my decisions. *Oh, my God, what have I done?* Embers flew all around me. I realized that the Polar Tec shirt I was wearing was a highly flammable synthetic—not one of my best wardrobe decisions.

Awakened to my danger, I turned and, timing the wind gusts to avoid flying embers, ran down my driveway—twisting, turning, brushing my arms over my back to keep the sparks off. I managed to pass through the fallen trees and burning grove again and hopped back into in my car.

While I tried to gather my senses, I was granted, to my horror, an unobstructed view of the ranch and my grandmother's home burning. Memories flashed through my mind as my loss grew. Burning to death was the house my great-grandfather built—where my grandfather and his siblings, and my father and aunt were born; our beloved grandmother's home and ranch. On my left, Frank Judson's dairy was a glow of hot fire, and in front of me, the J. B. Judson home, built by my great-great-grandfather, smoked in its demise.

Shaken back into the present and the danger I still faced, I started my car and pulled onto the road only to be blocked by a fire truck ambling down it. It pulled over to the side just in time, and I jetted past. All the ranch buildings and surrounding trees were consumed in flames. Unable to take in any more, I sped down the road, sailing toward Highway 78. Racing out of the inferno, I climbed the grade out of the valley. *I need to call Uncle Bud.*

"Hello?"

"Hi, Uncle Bud, it's Tarra."

"Are you okay?"

"Yes, but my home is still burning, and Gramma's house is burning along with all the ranch buildings. Everywhere I look, there's fire. The Wild Animal Park is burning at the top, the riverbed is parched, and there are fires over by Fenton's now."

"I'm sorry, Tarra. Are you coming here?"

"I'm on my way back."

"We love you; come home safely."

I hung up. His kindness released a torrent of tears. The entire city of Escondido was shrouded in smoke and soot.

I need a cup of coffee to calm my nerves. I'm shaking all over. Driving to a local shop, I tried to pull myself together as I walked up to the counter and ordered.

The girl behind the counter just stared at me.

"I just lost my home in the fire," I blurted.

She got the coffee and pushed it toward me. "It's on the house."

After returning to my car, I numbly sat there, then noticed that people were staring at me. I pulled down the visor and opened the mirror to see my ash-covered face and matted hair standing straight out. Cascading from my eyes were two distinct lines, the path of my tears, now colored by soot and ash.

If I hadn't been so shocked by my loss, I might have laughed at how frightful I looked. No wonder they were staring.

FIFTY-SIX

My Aunt Margaret and cousin Rease were at my aunt and uncle's home in Carlsbad when I got there. It was comforting to be among family as I described my journey into the valley and helplessness to save my home.

It was a time of extreme stress for many. My mother was also evacuated, then told she could return, only to be ordered to leave again. Later that day, still hoping that some of my home had survived, I returned to the valley. Once again, I convinced the roadblock personnel to let me pass.

Daylight exposed the damage from the fire. Both sides of Highway 78 were burned—where cottonwoods had once obstructed the view across the valley it was now wide open. The vegetation in the riverbed had burned to the ground, and smoldering piles of felled trees lay everywhere.

As I turned onto Bandy Canyon, I could see a faint silhouette of my home, and then came upon the burned-out cavity of my grandmother's house. The ranch buildings—the granary, sheds, workshops, and garage—were all gutted or burned to the ground. All that was left of my grandmother's home were the chimneys and one wall of the annex. Down the road, another chimney towered as a stark reminder of where the J. B. Judson home once stood. There was nothing left of my neighbors' gardens or chickens; it was all gone.

Walking up my driveway, I discovered corrugated pieces of tin strewn along the road, leftovers from the milk and hay barns. The blasting wind had carried the roofing tins a quarter of a mile to my driveway. Ironically, my water tank was still standing—the piles of sand on the road were the top layers of soil from the naked earth. Devoid of all vegetation, the wind had stripped the land raw. Three of the six ranch houses had burned along with the garage of the little house where we had lived before moving up the hill into the adobe. Most of the trees embracing the ranch property had also burned to the ground. *I have never seen the land so barren.*

My grove was still standing—fragile burned-out skeletons of the mature trees they once were. Scorched and dead, my tractor stood in front of the iron frame of what was a wagon. The reservoir of pain inside me grew.

Seeing my destroyed grove was nothing compared to what awaited me once I reached the top of my driveway. The surrounding trees and orchard behind the house had been mercilessly scorched or reduced to piles of charcoal. Landscape plants were dead or gone, and my home was gutted, only the adobe walls standing, framing piles of twisted metal and dusty ashes from the family heirlooms and beloved treasures I had left behind. Perished along with my labor of love and my beloved natural surroundings were the frogs, birds, snakes and wildlife I had enjoyed protecting.

I stared and wept at the starkness before me, and then waded through a foot of sand inside the cavity of my home and art studio. Sand and debris covered the patios, and half-burned beams and roofing were strewn everywhere. All the windows had melted onto the ledges, and the ceramic floor tiles were cracked and splintered. I had yet to uncover a cast iron skillet, branding irons from the ranch, and my tools, melted and twisted by heat.

I couldn't take in more. When I returned to Carlsbad, my friend Laura was visiting—she too had been evacuated. Ironically, everyone enjoyed some lighter moments as we collectively grieved. I shared excerpts from this book with everyone, and as we prepared to retire, my Uncle Bud called to his wife: "Louise, Tarra needs a couple more bars of soap!"

The next day, Patti called. "Tarra, there's a steady stream of people going up your driveway."

"What? Who is it? And how can they get up there? I was out there yesterday, and there were logs and debris blocking the road, not to mention a ton of sand."

"I don't know, but the traffic up your hill hasn't stopped all morning."

"What's wrong with people? Thanks, Patti. I'm on my way to close the gate."

Feeling violated and furious that people were traipsing through my home and burned possessions, I shared the news with my aunt and uncle.

"Do you want us to come? We were planning on going out to see the ranch today."

"Okay. It would be nice to have you with me."

We headed to my property first. Footprints from all the lookie-loos walking through were everywhere in the sand that had blown inside.

"Don't they know how disrespectful it is to come snooping around someone's home they have just lost?"

My aunt and uncle comforted me as we walked around. It was obvious there was nothing to do but leave and close the gate.

"I brought some sandwiches; would you like one before we leave?" my aunt asked.

"Actually, that sounds good. Thank you."

"Bud, do you want a sandwich?"

"Yes, I'll take one, Louise." With a wry look, he added, "I'll go set the table."

Just as we were finishing our sandwiches, more relatives converged and offered their condolences.

My aunt and uncle and I drove down to the ranch and asked Patti's permission to say goodbye to my grandmother's house. We gave my aunt space as she stood in front of the heaps of memories where she was born and grew up.

We toured the other family sites, now historical piles of debris and ashes.

"I'm glad Mom isn't alive to see this," my aunt said.

"Or my dad," I said. "It would have been too crushing for either one of them. Remember when I forced Gramma to stay with you in 2003 when fires were burning on both sides of the valley?"

"She was so mad and just wanted to go home."

"Yeah. She kept telling me that the valley had never burned."

The first couple of days after the fire were the worst. At night, I laid awake shaking. Memories of all the things I had left behind flashed through me, and every time, a voice in my head heckled me for not having taken it, or being better prepared. Each memory piled more guilt onto my regret. Realizing I desperately needed support, I started calling friends until I got through to my childhood friend Linda.

"Why should I go through all this pain?" I asked.

"Because you love life!"

"I'm listening. Say more."

I cried as she listed all the reasons why I should keep on living in spite of the pain and desolation I was feeling. I hung up aware that I would get through this, no matter how painful it was. Even so, my head continued to rattle me with each recollection of another treasured possession left behind.

I must figure out a way to respond to the voices in my head because if I don't, I'm going to continue spiraling downward every time I remember something that burned.

With the next "Why didn't you take...?" thought, I responded, "Because I didn't!" Saying it out loud helped to drown out the voice of guilt. I'd already been so overrun with guilt in my life that I didn't want to bury myself under it again.

Expressing the pain of my loss eventually silenced the guilt-inducing voice, but my internal image and how I identified myself had been built upon a heritage that was now disintegrated. Groping for orientation, I was in shambles again.

With the aim of getting grounded, I coached myself through morning routines, rehearsing the steps I had mindlessly performed when at home reaching for objects, drawers and cupboards that were familiar and supportive in getting me organized for the day. With various items used without effort or thought no longer available, each step of my renewal involved excruciating consciousness. As difficult as it was to deal with my grief, it was equally challenging to accept the outpouring of love, compassion, and support I received. My heart was forced to open and expand to hold it all.

Besides sorrow, my palette of emotions was growing to hold the immense gratitude and absolute humility I felt in response to the tenderness and caring directed at me. Family and friends, colleagues from the Bioenergetics community, and even clients rallied with love and support. An old friend from high school I had reconnected with at our High School 40th reunion helped me sort through the ashes, as did a friend from my Bioenergetics community. My mother spent several days sifting through the debris to salvage what she could.

Everyone's love and support became the foundation upon which I rebuilt myself. I was re-learning that relationships, more worthwhile than all the things I had lost, are what really matter in life.

Once again life was molding my character and priorities, transforming pain into blessings—righting my perspective. My cousin Rease said it eloquently: "I think you built a very beautiful sandcastle, and as with all sandcastles and as with all stuff, it was destined to be swept away. But for some reason your beautiful sandcastle was meant to be swept away by the first wave."

I had been obsessed with fire prevention. Recognizing its potential to steal my heart's creation, I had gone to great lengths to protect my home from burning, and figured that all my measures, including the protective clothing I used for welding, would be sufficient.

I relocated my truck at Linda and Marty's, and got out to speak with Linda. Pointing to the truck and the bed holding the quad I used in my grove, I lamented. "This is all I have left of my country life."

Linda held me as I cried.

"You know I wanted to stay and fight the fire," I said.

"And if you had, I would have jumped up and down on your grave, saying you stupid, stupid woman!"

I decided to return to therapy to help me understand the origins of my silly notions.

"I scare myself with how easily I am willing to risk my life for something that seemed so significant at the time." I related to my therapist.

"I can see how you might be afraid of losing your home," she said. "But you don't seem to recognize your own worth when faced with jumping impulsively into a situation."

"It so reminds me of the quest I pursued with Jon. I believed I had to stay with him because of the information I had been given—thinking it was up to me to inform people we needed to change how we live on the planet, or face dire consequences. I left so many times and kept being pulled back, thinking I had no choice; that I didn't matter."

"And perhaps that same grandiosity led you to believe that you could put out the fire?"

"Totally. How do I stay grounded in reality, and not be hijacked by those notions and fears?"

"I think you forgot how powerful fear can be, driving us to behave irrationally without thinking of consequences. It becomes an automatic reaction that is not based in rational thinking; rather neuronal patterns of behavior."

"But I'm so not in control of myself when that happens."

"You learned to rise above the circumstance or live in your head, thanks to a lack of relational support that would help you recognize the risks that you were taking. This would certainly become a behavioral pattern for you during your years with Jon. I can even see how that started with all the criticism from your mother and sarcasm and rejection from your father. Their rejection of you would generate tremendous fear and shame, forcing you off balance and to disconnect from your feelings because they were so painful. We often lift-up into grandiosity when that happens and lose touch with rational thought processes to avoid feeling the negative emotions inside our bodies.

"Distracting our awareness from emotional pain by focusing on accomplishing some great feat is an ego defense, a way to avoid feeling the pain inside the body. We maintain an illusion of control that way."

"That all makes sense, but I still scare myself."

"I can understand why. Let's work through the feelings so they will not be in control of your choices again. I know that you lived with a great deal of terror in your life, and perhaps this is a time to explore it more."

And so, I continued to peel away unconscious layers of ego defenses I had developed in childhood. I had been terrified of my mother and father as a child. Those fears were reinforced with Jon, and ultimately myself.

Healing from the violence and deprivation I had suffered with Jon gave me enough strength to now face the lifelong terror and unworthiness I felt underneath. My vulnerability lay exposed, as open and raw as the cavity of my home and the stripped landscape surrounding it.

Grieving the loss of my home brought new awareness as I discovered again the powerful healing that love and support provide. I was learning to accept myself with more compassion.

With eyes now wide open, I witnessed the ingredients that made possible awakening into consciousness from the insanity of those twelve years. However, I found it easier to embrace loss from nature's hands than what I had experienced with Solar/Jon. The personal nature of that violation was overwhelmingly offensive to me, as with all human-to-human acts of abuse. It seemed deadlier to my psyche than a random act of destruction wrought by nature. My healing required a personal connection as intimately trustworthy and full of love and integrity as Jon's relationship with me was filled with hate, abuse, and lies.

Returning to Barb, the therapist with whom I had formed a healthy attachment, provided the stage for reorienting back into my life in this next phase.

FIFTY-SEVEN

Learning to honor feelings rather than react to my emotions, I deferred making decisions about what losing my home meant other than the fact that life had brought me a new path to walk and explore. I stayed with my aunt and uncle until I found a house to rent. However, during that time, I had to register my losses. While interviewing at a post-fire recovery agency, I was asked for my home address.

"I have some friends who live on that street," was the interviewer's reaction, "but God was on their side because they didn't lose their home."

"I'm glad for them," I mumbled. Then, awakening to her meaning, I spoke up. "Just because my home burned down doesn't mean that God isn't on my side. I don't believe God works that way." *I don't believe that the fire or whose house was saved or lost had anything to do with God. Shit happens, lady. It took me long enough to learn that.*

I joined a writing class in which our first assignment was to pen a piece in one hundred words or less. Filled with anxiety, I read mine aloud.

The Wicked Witch from the East

Walking through the cadaver of my home, charred adobe walls stood in stark reminder of what was. As my boots pick their way through the melted and morphed debris, I narrate what used to be here and there to the insurance adjustor, now the purser of my estate. The bombsite was from the witch as she flew from the East blazing her way through heart and home, leaving waste in her path. My loss was deep. Gone also were the ancient farmhouses built by great and great-great-grandfathers; homesteads from 100 plus years ago and both now piles of ash, long emptied of the familial lives well-lived, close to heart and land.

Memories swirled through my mind like the smoke I had watched. Relics of the past had melded with mine in a great leveling of my identification of self. The scorched and stripped landscape that once cradled the wildlife I loved now reflected my internal state, also burned, empty of life and will to live.

And yet, the witch with her fiery sweep, gifted freedom— new beginnings and life renewed. The rains came, new growth appeared, birds returned and my life took another turn in the road. Tears washed clean my sorrow and with all the love and support so generously given me, I too am germinating; only different and lighter. I would never have walked this path had I not met with the witch along the way.

No longer distracted by endless work, when I was again invited by my friend Laura to go horseback riding with her, I accepted. The experience was so enjoyable that I leased a horse from the stables where she kept hers.

After a few trail rides, Laura shared an observation. "Tarra, I've noticed your voice has dropped and you seem more relaxed."

"I think riding has been beneficial for me. I feel more settled in my body. Horses have always been therapeutic. Growing up on the ranch, they kept me sane. I love connecting with the backcountry again, but without all the work."

"I think you're healing more each time you ride. I know a free horse who needs a good home. He's a registered quarter horse."

"I don't want to own a horse again. My last one was a Paso, and I had to put her down because she had uterine cancer. That was just too hard. And besides, the last thing I want is to own more things I can lose."

"He's a really good horse. Why don't you just go look at him?"

"Oh, I don't know. Where would I keep him?"

"You could ask Jody if she has room here. Why don't you go see him before you make any decisions?"

Of course, I did, and got a *free* horse named Cash! A delightful rascal, he did not hide his need for love and acceptance. His open heart and playful nature were a gratifying adjunct to all the wonderful love and support I was receiving. Another blessing: Cash was helping me heal and reclaim my aliveness. Since he had been used as a stud early in his life, he did not play well with mares, and had to be kept alone in a paddock. Horses, like people, need community and each other. Without a buddy, Cash was suffering, so I found a five-year-old mustang named Laredo who pulled at my heartstrings. Captured from the range as a yearling, Laredo had spent the past four years of his life locked in a small pen—neglected and untrained.

I enjoyed many hours on the trail with Cash, although sadly, after a few years he developed degenerative bone disease and had to be put down. I had sporadically worked with Laredo, and I discovered first-hand how the brain of a wild animal works, especially when subjected to early traumatization. Being thrown off a horse is very humbling, and I don't bounce like I used to.

On our ranch, horses and children were dominated. I brought that mentality to Laredo until my equine mentor instructed me about the relational and intuitive world of horses. Forcefully removed from his mother and herd, Laredo had been further traumatized when transported to various locations and then abandoned and neglected. Left on his own, he retreated, trusting no one in his unsafe world. Like any neglected or abused human, the softness of Laredo's true nature was inaccessible until we developed a relationship of trust and safety. Then he no longer tried bucking me off when frightened or overwhelmed.

Laredo's fear-based instinctual wildness challenged me to soften and deepen my own inner-self connection and become more compassionate with the broken and neglected parts of both of us. The more love I took in for myself, the more I could love him, and he responded by showing me his heart and the absolute power in tender, loving relationships.

Healing miracles come from loving connections and the powerful influences on behavior that brain-body functions exert. Laredo reminded me that no good comes from attempting to dominate or control—whether a horse, another animal, or a human being.

My four-legged therapists demonstrated my need to further investigate the expanding field of interpersonal neurobiology. Our interactions educated me about the importance of understanding brain/body/mind functions and their respective behavioral responses, shedding much light on how I had been brainwashed and kept submissive all those years.

My Bioenergetics community demonstrated further the power of connection during a group experience at one of our conferences. After a painful and emotional process in my group, they offered their support. I wrote and presented this poem during the conference about that experience I had:

Wild-Woman Wildebeest

Today, the wild-woman wildebeest surfaced and escaped.
Fearing this state called "crazy" no more,
The pounding and mashing I've done inside;
Released—expressed
My PASSION—now outside.

Raging and wailing, thrashing and hitting;
This force begging to be freed

Pacing to and fro, caged and bound by my notions of self
Held motionless in their vice
When suddenly the wildebeest crashes the gate

And tramples its pieces
'Til only splinters remain…

And there it was, the pain I had escaped,
There it was…

As I sink into my despair, a touch, another is there.
Held in the embrace that I am not alone
Eyes I meet reflect compassion and grace…
Touched with the souls of another
I lay basking in my still life—complete

Gentle, soft, delicious and sweet
Caresses and touch, from those near
Their gifts I receive. Oh, so deep.

FIFTY-EIGHT

It had been thirty-three years since I left Colombia with the instructions to share my "mission" with the world—to warn about our imminent destruction if we did not change our ways.

Since our amazing reconnection, Fortune and I had remained in contact. "Tarra," she said, "there's a Peace Corps reunion for all returned volunteers from Colombia. Are you interested in going? Jennifer and I are meeting in Cartagena."

"You're kidding. Cartagena? The reunion's there?"

"Yes. Do you want to go?"

"Yes, I do. I can't believe it. Is that the Jennifer from my group who was stationed in Santa Marta?"

"Yes, she's the one. Jennifer extended her stay, and then her parents joined as well. I was her coordinator when I became Peace Corps staff."

"Incredible! Yes, I would love to join you guys."

Jennifer was the only volunteer I had taken time from work to visit while stationed in Cartagena. Santa Marta, her site, was a short distance along the coast from mine. Fortune, Jennifer, and I decided to room together for our Peace Corps rendezvous.

Incredibly, I was being offered an opportunity to return—a complete circle of my quest that had started with the paranormal experiences dictating my departure from the Peace Corps to share the message given me. Cartagena was where I had felt loved and had found meaningful work. Returning there also meant I would face my unhealed guilt and shame for having abandoned a people and work I passionately loved. Working through the pain of feeling forced to leave seemed like the appropriate next step for me.

In 1981, after guerrillas kidnapped and later released a volunteer, the Peace Corps' existence in Colombia had been terminated. This was the first time since then that Peace Corps volunteers had been officially welcomed back to Colombia. We were 160 in attendance, all previous volunteers in the country. Some were from as long ago as 1961, when JFK had originally formed the Peace Corps. Colombia had been the first country in the world to request volunteers, and the first director, Sargent Shriver, had delivered his introductory speech to some of those present now.

Many hours were spent in conference with Colombia's then-President Álvaro Uribe, the sitting ambassador to the United Nations, the mayor of Cartagena and the U.S. Ambassador, among other dignitaries. ExxonMobil and the Colombian Federation of Coffee Growers (Cafeteros—represented by the ubiquitous "Juan Valdez") wined and dined us. The Cafeteros also sponsored a luncheon and evening cocktails on Colombia's tall ship *El Gloria*—a beautiful sailing vessel from several centuries ago.

In between presentations, we were bussed on tours through the fortress walls and Inquisition weapons of torture and destruction. (I passed on that one.) We were also taken to an emerald store and a ghetto being refurbished by the Colombian government. Native agencies using their own citizens were continuing many projects and programs that Peace Corps volunteers had participated in while serving in the country.

Sweltering in the tropical heat of my former home, I reviewed the gamut of experiences that had transpired since I left—my losses and gains and recent transformation by fire. During this introspection, I realized my work in Colombia had been an honorable venture—contrary to what Solar/Jon had drilled into me. Perhaps I had made a difference here, not personally but collectively, as one of many, in our focused desire to ease suffering and show a way out of the chronic deprivation.

When I left the Peace Corps, my newly formed sense of well-being had been overshadowed by my quest to warn the world of its imminent demise. Until revisiting Cartagena, I had not recognized the depth of my guilt for leaving people and work I had loved so dearly. I was also recognizing that even if I had stayed, I never could have filled their overwhelming need.

For all those years, I believed I had failed—but poverty, filth, and cultural oppression were still abundantly there, although perhaps to a lesser degree.

As I walked the neighborhood tour, tears washed the dust from my perception. Camera in hand, I snapped images of a destiny I had tried in vain to alter. Each step uncovered more of the guilt that had burdened me all this time. No wonder I had not grasped that it was *me* they had accepted. They had loved me for who I was; I had not been required to do anything other than be myself to receive their love.

Bars covering the spaces for windows, dirt floors lying underfoot, and sewage wending its way to the sea were all backdrops to the shacks lining the trail before me. With smiles in abundance and laughter and music ever present, what grandiosity I had entertained to think I could or should shift this tide!

More oppressive than the afternoon heat, my guilt seeped through my pores, leaving empty space in which I pondered. Who was to say we offer a better way? Maybe ours is cleaner, yet we still wrestle between want and need, shame and respect.

I had to wonder: *Am I the one drowning in oppression, having to wade through the overwhelming stimulation of information and the distractions I face in my life?*

When I returned home, this clarity gasped for breath and blurred with my struggle to find myself within the deluge of complexity in our culture, so removed from our roots.

FIFTY-NINE

Returning to my life and work was now much easier after I left my needless guilt in Cartagena. In reality—what I had felt was shame. My expanded clarity showed me that I needed to work through issues I had not been able to address with my father. He had laughed when I related how my dentist, a friend of his, kept putting his arms on my breasts while working on my teeth. My sexual orientation had been a problem for him, and later, so was my profession.

Recognizing my need for a professional male perspective, I consulted a trusted Bioenergetics colleague. I had known Bill White for over twenty years and felt impressed to take advantage of his gifted expertise and my trust of him. Despite all his health issues, my father and I had accomplished much healing, but we never revisited his rejection of me over my intervention with his drinking and my sexual diversity.

Bill complemented my healing arc as we addressed these unresolved wounds and more.

"I'm sure your parents were doing the best they could."

"Yes, but I'm ashamed of how I did my best to show them what a lousy job they did by hooking up with the likes of Jon."

"Well, there again, you were doing the best you could."

"It's been so hard to forgive myself now that I can see what I was doing.

I don't feel very lovable when I revisit all of that."

"Yes, but you're a lovable child of God. I imagine it's difficult to embrace the fact that at the time, you were doing as well as you could."

"That's exactly what Barb said to me over, and over again."

"Let's do some EMDR and then some energy work (Bioenergetics) with that, shall we?"

As I continued to feed my quest for truth and need to understand human behavior, I was led to *A Course in Miracles*. Gaining more insight about my own behaviors, I began wondering whether Jon had *also* behaved in the best manner he could. Even though his tactics had been painful and abusive, this new perspective challenged my long-held hatred for him.

Although I realized it was true, I didn't like having to admit I had no right to hate Jon and make him responsible for hurting me. Author Jack Kornfield once wrote: "When we come into the present, we begin to feel the life around us again, but we also encounter whatever we have been avoiding. We must have the courage to face whatever is present—our pain, our desires, our grief, our loss, our secret hopes, our love—everything that moves us most deeply."

On June 22, 2015, I wrote the following letter to Jon:

> Dear Jon,
>
> I have learned that you recently received a diagnosis of lung cancer. I am truly sorry for you. This information has moved me to write you to say goodbye. You may not have clear memory of our time together, but mine is one of great pain and suffering driven by my need to accomplish my "mission" and sacrifice myself enough to find worth and love for myself and from my family.
>
> When I left you, I discovered a need to understand the dynamics behind such compulsive behaviors, yours and mine. Thus, I became a psychotherapist and specialized in children and

adolescent development, learning how we are wounded from infancy on, when our safety, personal space, and/or emotional needs are violated, neglected, or invalidated. The trauma I experienced with you became very enlightening and most helpful in unraveling and subsequently healing my time with you and my life before that.

I also needed something positive to come from the pain and suffering with you. I wanted to discover what mechanisms operate when people engage in destructive behaviors toward one's self and others.

I am not writing this letter to lecture you on the value of insight gained from introspection and taking personal responsibility for one's actions; rather, I am writing to let you know that I forgive you for all the abuse, lies, coercions, exploitations of my vulnerability, and overall egregious behavior toward my family, my body, my psyche, and me.

However, I do not condone your use of violence or all the dishonest behaviors and actions you so readily engaged in with the others and myself. You may not recall what you did, but there are plenty of witnesses who did, and I encourage you to work on forgiving yourself before you die.

I realize that you and I, plus all the others and our collective families, were behaving the best they could at any given time. I believe that is especially why forgiveness is so important— when we learn better ways of living, we act better toward self and others. Loving relationships, filled with compassion and forgiveness, are key ingredients in that process. I am happy to say that I discovered my family loved me all along, and we have all benefited from forgiving one another with compassion and recognizing the love that was always there, just buried under the emotional wounds and unmet needs of us all.

Hopefully, everyone involved with our saga has learned at least some modicum of wisdom from our experiences. I encourage you to do the same if you have not already.

In closing, I would like to recommend *A Course in Miracles* as dictated to Helen Schucman with the help of William Thetford. It is a course of spiritual transformation given to them by Jesus. From my studies of the materials from the Foundation for Inner Peace, I have learned to forgive you rather than harboring the hatred I nurtured for years against you for all the "wrongdoings" I perceived you had done.

Please rest assured, you owe me nothing; rather, I would like to thank you. From my experiences with you, I truly did discover what God is and what God is not. There is so much richness that came out of my time with you, but not perhaps as you would think. Suffering does temper the ego and teach compassion and give opportunity for forgiveness. Perhaps I would never have discovered that, had I not walked into such darkness with you. I wish you peace of mind and support you in finding love in your heart.

In blessings and forgiveness,

Tarra

AUTHOR'S NOTE

You desire to know the art of living, my friend? It is contained in one
phrase: make use of suffering.

—*Henri Frederic Amiel (1821-1881)*

I offer the following in hopes of shedding light on how I fell under
Solar's spell. When I met him, I was desperate, and driven by core shame
and fear—convinced that my mission in life was to spread the message
given me that night in Medellin, Colombia—to help save the world from
imminent destruction at our own hands. The "pillars of light" and the
other experiences I had in South America unraveled the constructs I had
depended on for making sense of my world. I returned, untethered to my
family, culture, and myself.

Perhaps for years, scientists have felt that humans are facilitating the
destruction of life on earth as we know it, but I had not sought nor wanted
that information. It was difficult to understand, let alone explain in rational
terms for it came to me via a paranormal event. I never objectively embraced
the message and my inability to successfully impart its meaning as I interpreted it, added to my list of failures validating how unlovable I was. Suffering
from core shame resulting from my childhood traumas and the unintended
neglect and emotional abandonment by both parents, the importance I
gave this task became grossly distorted as I unconsciously used it to be
worthy enough to receive my family's love. Becoming "enlightened" and

successfully accomplishing the dissemination of the message became the grandiose "mission" I believed to be mine and the means through which I would be redeemed.

I was born to a mother who endured the suffering and eventual demise of both her parents shortly before and after I came into this world. Depressed and distracted by her grief, she was emotionally unavailable and incapable of reflecting to me the joy and delight I needed to develop an intact sense of self-worth. Infants need a healthy attachment to a parent or caretaker who can provide a positive, safe and emotionally engaged interaction that once internalized, becomes the foundation for their personality development. The failure of such an attuned connection, causes the infant's brain to generate fear and a nervous system reflex experienced as rejection. Repeated enough times, this creates a foundation of shame and the encoded message that one is not accepted within the family due to his/her unworthiness. This core shame contributes to the formation of a fragile self, or what we refer to as low self-esteem, or a low emotional quotient (EQ)—emotional immaturity.

The three miscarriages my mother endured prolonged her grieving process and reinforced these neurological patterns and false beliefs during my development. Although preoccupied with his studies, my father was more emotionally available to me but inconsistent with his attunement to my needs.

When my parents moved us to the family farm, I lost the close connection I had enjoyed with my father, compounding my feelings of rejection and unworthiness.

Being the victim of early-childhood molestation, medical traumas, and the constant volley of criticism aimed at me added to the growing dissonance within me, creating a reservoir of fear, shame, and anger held within both body and brain. Without the soothing of those emotional reactions through receiving sufficient amounts of the love, and validation that I desperately needed and still craved, my brain continued to fester with these unresolved issues. As adults, these neurological patterns drive unconscious and dysfunctional, shame-based behaviors as the brain repeats what is familiar and learned—albeit maladaptive. Because we survive by using these maladaptive behaviors, the brain incorporates them as part of our automatic coping skills.

The hostility between my parents exacerbated my negative emotions and subsequent dysfunctional behaviors. My bisexuality was also a source of invalidation; thinking something was wrong with me because I could not change my attraction to both sexes. Being rejected for this made the resulting shame almost unbearable.

Floundering to spread the message and my equally unsuccessful endeavors to integrate myself back into a culture, family and life to which I could not relate, all served to further upset my emotional stability. From this place of desperation, fraught with unresolved emotions and trauma, I easily committed to Solar's "non-interactive spiritual program," thinking I would arrive at a place of enlightenment and could then successfully spread the message and therefore, be loved and accepted.

Solar deftly exacerbated my vulnerability to his influence when he cut off ties to my personal identity, the awareness of who I was and the personality I had formed from past experiences and relationships. Brainwashing is a process whereby one's ability to think and act for oneself is severely compromised. Losing one's autonomy is an insidious and generally unconscious process as the brainwashing escalates.

The addition of physical and emotional battery for "past" mistakes and ones I made by breaking his impossible rules sealed my fate. My only option was to dissociate, a reaction I had learned in infancy when faced with the impossible task of relating to a depressed mother. Fight or flight—protesting or leaving the offending experience—are natural expressions of the motivating energy our brains generate to get our needs met when that need is frustrated. Fleeing the scene as an infant is not possible, thus freezing or disconnecting from the situation becomes the default defense. This learned neuronal response becomes automatic and a patterned behavior over time and sets the stage for substance abuse and other addictive behaviors. People with a history of trauma, whether from their developmental period or later as an adult are vulnerable if they do not seek support to work through the emotional impact of the trauma.

The course of our lives is unconsciously directed by these early experiences and subsequent false assumptions until they are consciously healed. It takes compassionate, loving and nurturing relationships to replace the negative experiences and self-concepts, and re-orient the person to an awareness of self-worth and lovability.

Solar feigned empathy for my duress to gain my trust. With his encourage-ment to share my narrative, the details of my adult dysfunctional behaviors poured out of me. Motivated by the validation he offered—rare in my life at that point—I deeply committed to his "Program," and when I did, Solar's judgment was swift and vicious. Using my history against me, he defended his betrayal of my confidence by claiming it was necessary to expose my reprehensible experiences that made me "vile and evil." This is a classic torture technique used to psychologically break people who then form a trauma bond with their perpetrator.

With a lack of safety, emotional soothing, and validation, every woman who entered his Program was subjected to this same treatment; facilitating Solar's systematic breaking down of our individually distinct personalities. Allowing him to deny my basic human needs and rights forced me into a dissociated state of non-feeling as he negated me, and my experiences. Through a series of steps well known to Solar with his background in criminal psychology, he systematically planted his seeds of oppression. As my memories were scrubbed free of any self-references—the brainwashing was complete. Twisting and stretching my psyche beyond its boundaries, the meaning of my original experience with the pillars of light became alienated from me, as were most references I had used to orient myself.

It would take years for me to reclaim a body/brain/mind awareness and a grounded connection with myself after leaving Solar/Jon's Program. First and foremost, I needed safety to begin working through the emotions I harbored from all the distortions and mistreatment. Until that time, I would remain lost with the day-to-day struggle to keep his rules and avoid getting hurt. I used survival instincts fueled by the emotionally reactive part of my brain lacking the ability to reality test and utilize critical thinking. Engaged in such an all-encompassing battle, I had no time to objectively process what his Program was doing to me. Only when his abuse caused more pain and discomfort than my dissociation could numb would I risk another escape. However, my flights to freedom repeatedly ended with my return and more abuse, followed by utter despair. Suicide became my only perceived option for escape but when those attempts failed, I was subsequently locked into endless repetitions of trauma; hopeless and helpless to emancipate myself from the entrapment of my mental prison. I had become no different than Pavlov's dog with my automatic, maladaptive reactions.

Leo Tolstoy wrote: "I am always with myself, and it is I who am my tormentor." Filled with trauma, shame, fear and self-hatred, Solar/Jon was my mirror, reflecting-back a troubled psyche doubting her worth and more. Eventually reality shook, rattled, and finally blasted me awake, demanding I attend to the obsessions and adaptations that had blinded and cloaked me from my true self. With gratitude, I have witnessed this exquisite and systematic awakening as my illusions have been whisked away, forcing me from my trance.

I became a therapist to understand how all this could happen to me. I believe in its value as well as what healthy relationships, companion animals, nature, and the underlying force animating it (God) offer. They are energetically interactive and present an unlimited potential for healing and inoculation from being carried away by "trance-like survival mechanisms" or unconscious and malicious behaviors. Human beings who are available for connection or those who are in their "right mind" and possess the capacity for an energetic exchange, or relationship—offer the potential for healing from a trauma and/or preventing emotional shutdown (dissociation). Furthermore, phys- ical movement and expressing one's emotions through art, therapy, dance, yoga, intimate relationships, and so on, are also powerful healing agents in transforming trauma into a learning experience.

My healing journey has also been facilitated by my faith and the power of love and forgiveness so benevolently extended to me, sustaining me through the pain I have shared in these pages. I do not believe myself unique, for I know that there are human beings suffering far greater fates than what I have divulged here. However, it is my hope that you benefit from this journey I have walked and will investigate the beliefs you adhere to and question whether they serve your heart. I encourage you to approach your conflicts with an eye towards resolution and forgiveness—working through your emotions towards releasing them and reclaiming your rightful peace of mind.

Had I paid more attention to my inner self when I first met Solar, I might have spared myself much pain and suffering. However, dropping into my body and out of my head was so painful at the time that living in the ideals of my fantasies had become a convenient and rehearsed substitute for authenticity. Out of my right mind, I was isolated, dissociated, and had become disconnected from my body and separated from the murmurings of my sentient heart. The accumulated negative and traumatic experiences within me had become a composite of unexpressed and unconscious emotions—like sediment piling on top of my essence.

Friedrich Wilhelm Nietzsche claimed, "Our worst enemies are our greatest teachers." I would not ever have thought that inner peace could come from suffering, but my experience teaches me that it is an option, available to us all. The natural motivating energy that arises with offenses to our basic rights and needs can be used quite differently than immediately channeling it through aggression toward another or one's own body-self. Acceptance of "what is" can facilitate a here-and-now connection with the greater, more mature Self within us. Paradoxically, when observing and staying present with both negative and positive feelings, suffering abates.

When subjected to inhumane treatment justified by ideals and beliefs, I feel the most courageous response available to us is to refrain from reciprocating with the same kind of behaviors. Otherwise, we too, risk separating from our true selves as we react with judgments and condemnation, becoming perpetrators as well.

My seemingly noble "quest" eventually did return me to reality and a loving connection with myself; grinding off the layers of unconsciousness obscuring my self-awareness. Truly, I accomplished my goal of experiencing a much closer relationship with God, but I do not recommend the route I took.

I no longer feel driven to warn others about our impending doom. Instead, I am aware that my life choices, thoughts and behaviors are within my realm of responsibility. I am convinced that when I choose acceptance, compassion and forgiveness for myself, or another, rather than self-destructive negative emotions and judgments, I am lessening suffering and the trance of wrong-minded actions that contribute to our world chaos. If the flapping of a butterfly's wings impacts weather two thousand miles away, just imagine what transformation a critical mass of love, compassion, and forgiveness for self and others could cause. With these practices in our repertoire, we could heal ourselves, and the world's chaos; benefiting everything in creation. That is my wish for all of humankind.

ACKNOWLEDGMENTS

Resilience is generated from support. Nature reminds us of this balance when a charred landscape sprouts new growth with the first rain. We humans have that innate capacity but require a little more than water and sunshine to recover from trauma, loss and pain. Loving, nurturing, and accepting relationships offer the nexus for us to heal and bounce back from whatever life, or we, have brought upon ourselves.

This journey would not have been possible without the support of many, some of whom I have previously mentioned within the context of the book. Peggy, Brenda, Lori and Heather all contributed to fleshing out our shared reality. Sadly, I was not able to find Acacia. I hope this book finds her and helps all of those negatively impacted by those events.

Jackie Lair opened my eyes further and facilitated us meeting Marilyn Lily who sheltered us an entire summer. Through Marilyn's connections, we met Sherry Williams who also housed us various times. I wish I knew the names of all the others and hope your generosity was returned to you. There were countless people who helped us alongside the road when we were broken down or stuck somewhere during our travels. I would not be here if not for them and so many who have contributed greatly to my life.

I feel incredibly blessed and the following is an attempt to thank those who have furthered my growth and development. First, I want to thank my mother, father, and brother who were integral to my formation and subsequent transformation. Forgiveness is so important and I am grateful to them for that, for all their love, and for the gift of acceptance.

I never consciously knew my maternal grandparents, but I felt very cared for by my father's parents. The gratitude I have for my paternal grandmother cannot be expressed in words—how do we capture unconditional love in language? I am forever touched and buoyed in my heart for the gift of her presence in my life.

I grew up with the richness of a very large, extended family and am grateful to them all. I would like to especially acknowledge Louise Judson Carroll and her lovely husband William (Bud) Carroll for their generosity and loving support and my great-aunt Margaret Trussell Eller for your caring. My cousin Donna Judson mentored me in so much but most importantly taught me about forgiveness and the power of faith. Her sister, Jeanette Judson Bruner has been a loving and supportive sounding board for me throughout the years. Lynn Judson, my sister-in-law, has my admiration and respect and was instrumental in my growth as well. My brother's widow met the challenge of raising their children alone with tenacious commitment.

My therapist Barbara Thomson was a life preserver in the ocean of my shame, self-loathing, and shattered psyche. Her love, support, wisdom, and nurturing became another cornerstone in my healing. I am forever grateful; thank you for believing in me. Many in the Bioenergetic community walked with me as I shouldered responsibility for my behaviors and experiences. Bev Abbey validated me at my first Bioenergetic Conference as I began to drop down into my body. Jim Elniski, thank you for encouraging my art and showing me how to commit to one's creative expressions. Mac Eaton, Bob Jacques, Pat Mia, and Bob and Virginia Hilton all midwifed my birth into healthier aspects of myself. Jayme Panerai Alves was instrumental in healing a very old wound in my heart and Vin Schroeter mentored me in my supervision and is now a valued friend. In my process, the International and local Bioenergetic communities became another family to me. Bill White, thank you for the depth of your wise and loving guidance you shared with me. My heart is forever warmed and healed from our time together. And of course, I would like to thank Al Lowen posthumously for your wisdom and insistence that the body and brain are connected. Bioenergetic Analysis was only the beginning of what wondrous truths we are discovering about the interconnectedness between brain, body, mind and our human consciousness.

I have many dear friends who have helped me love myself again. I am blessed with the community of support that surrounds me and am grateful to have you all in my life! Some are mentioned in this book, but I would like to single out the following individuals. Linda Oretsky whom I've known since childhood—your love and friendship are a precious gift. Alan and Mary Brutger—you are cherished friends whom I dearly love. I am such a better person for your presence in my life. Laura Partridge, I treasure our friendship and thank you and Mary who have been invaluable muses in the writing of this magnum opus. Marina Peralta, thank you for your book, support, and all your love. Donna Johnson, you inspire me with your courage and I thank you and Laura for your willingness to read version after version of this book.

Fortune Zuckerman, I am blessed to have you in my life and thank you for contributing to the closure I obtained with my Peace Corps experience. And although I never had natural children, I am also grateful to Aaron and Teri for sharing their lives and lovely children with me.

I owe Karen Levine and Monique Martinez my thanks for leading me back to the Foundation for A Course in Miracles and am so very grateful to Ken Wapnick for his inspired wisdom and prolific explanations.

I am humbled with the stories I have heard and continue to learn from the people who have come to me for support as a professional. I appreciate all of you and hope that our time together was beneficial to your lives.

Writing is another endeavor requiring major support. Towards the formal presentation of this book, Ann Marie Welsh helped me in my first foray. I also owe acknowledgment to Marni Freedman who was instrumental in helping me organize this memoir and Jackie Logue and Alyscia McDermott for their corrections. And lastly, thank you Mark Clements for your razor-sharp insight, wise guidance and editing-extraordinaire, as this book entered its final stage of production.

Antoinette Kuritz of Strategies Literary Development has become invaluable in this final process, and I so appreciate all your wisdom, resources, and support. Gwyn Snider, you are a dream-designer. Thank you for your book cover, interior construction and all your creative input.

Finally, I am grateful to all the people I have crossed paths with in my life, and most of all to my Creator who has made this all possible.

Tarra Judson Stariell

CPSIA information can be obtained
at www.ICGtesting.com
Printed in the USA
BVOW08s0316121117
500068BV00003B/223/P